PRAISE FOR
THE GATES OF EUROPE

"[An] exemplary account of Europe's least-known large country . . . one of the joys of reading the *The Gates of Europe* is that what might seem a dense account of distant events involving unfamiliar places and people is leavened by aphorism and anecdote."—*Wall Street Journal*

"Elegantly written."—*New York Review of Books*

"An assured and authoritative survey that spans ancient Greek times to the present day"—*Financial Times*

"[An] admirable new history. . . . Belief in Ukraine's history of tolerance and legality, rooted in European Christian civilization, keeps hope alive. In his elegant and careful exposition of Ukraine's past, Mr. Plokhy has also provided some signposts to the future."—*Economist*

"No one can understand today's sad, tangled confrontation over Ukraine without some knowledge of the complex, crosscutting influences that have shaped Eastern Europe over the millennia. For that history, readers can find no better place to turn than Plokhy's new book. . . . Plokhy navigates the subject with grace and aplomb."—*Foreign Affairs*

"Serhii Plokhy's major distinction from his predecessors is that he has interpreted the history of Ukraine applying the modern concept of national identity, which is still not widely familiar in post-Soviet republics."—*Newsweek*

"A concise, highly readable history of Ukraine. . . . A lively narrative peopled with a colorful cast of Norse and Mongol marauders, free-booting Cossacks, kings, conquerors, and dictators, and conflicted nineteenth-century intellectuals who believed fervently in a Ukrainian cultural identity but were fatally divided as to how that cultural identity could evolve into national entity."
—*Washington Times*

"Buy this book. . . . Give copies to your children and grandchildren. Buy copies for your friends. Make sure they read it."—*Ukrainian Weekly*

"Clear and elegant. . . . An indispensable guide to the tragic history of a great European nation"—*Sunday Telegraph* (UK)

"A fast-moving history, full of prompts and nuggets. . . . A strong rebuttal of the arrogant assumptions of the Putin court that Ukraine, though intrinsically part of the greater Russian nation, is culturally inferior, weaker, and compromised"—*Times* (UK)

"*The Gates of Europe* take us back to the time of Herodotus to tell the tangled story of . . . [Ukraine's] long struggle to win control over its own destiny."—*Sunday Times* (UK)

"A masterly surveyor of Ukrainian history, Plokhy does not belabor the many horrors he describes; he doesn't have to, grim facts speak for themselves."
   —*Independent* (UK)

"Plokhy's careful, engaging history is a series of stories about a spectral nation, one that has appeared and disappeared down the ages. . . . If sense ever prevails, Plokhy's fine book should find its way to Vladimir Putin's desk, if only to show the imperialist that Ukraine itself is far from done, and will not be extinguished"—*Herald Scotland* (UK)

"Plokhy is at his best when describing the Ukrainian Cossacks, free men of what remained of the untamed steppe."—*Spectator* (UK)

"Most comprehensive."—*Literary Review* (UK)

"[A] formidable account of Ukrainian history."—*History Today* (UK)

"*The Gates of Europe* details the enduring conflict for territory and identity between Russia and Ukraine, . . . [and] deconstructs more than 2,000 years of history and how it came to this."—*Toronto Star* (Canada)

"A comprehensive, unbiased history."—*Winnipeg Free Press* (Canada)

"Very readable, providing a compelling story of a country destined as a crossroad for peoples, armies, cultures, and civilizations."—*Russian Review*

"A fascinating and complex story told concisely."—*Russian Life*

"Plokhy's publication is not solely an academic work as it seeks to tackle some of the questions that are currently being raised in the geopolitical debate, including whether Ukraine belongs to the . . . Russian world."
   —*New Eastern Europe* (Poland)

"*The Gates of Europe* is a well-balanced book, one in which the author's voice and opinion do not dissolve in the mire of middle ways between controversial topics and well-known facts."—H-Diplo

"Injecting appropriate nuance and complexity into a single-volume overview of 2,000 years of Ukrainian history is no small task, but Plokhy approaches this charge with dexterity and skill. . . . Plokhy's work serves as a welcome introduction to Ukraine's ethnic and national history."—*Publishers Weekly*

"The timeframe and subjects covered here are extraordinary. . . . Students, academics, and readers with a general knowledge of Ukraine will appreciate. Alternatively, chapters can be read independently, allowing those with a strong interest in the subject to focus on a specific era of Ukraine's history."
   —*Library Journal*

"A sympathetic survey of the history of Ukraine along the East-West divide, from ancient divisions to present turmoil. . . . A straightforward, useful work that looks frankly at Ukraine's ongoing 'price of freedom' against the rapacious, destabilizing force of Russia."—*Kirkus Reviews*

"For a comprehensive, engaging, and up-to-date history of Ukraine one could do no better than Serhii Plokhy's aptly titled *The Gates of Europe*. Plokhy's authoritative study will be of great value to scholars, students, policy-makers, and the informed public alike in making sense of the contemporary Ukrainian imbroglio."—**Norman M. Naimark, Stanford University**

"This is present-minded history at its most urgent. Anyone wanting to understand why Russia and the West confront each other over the future of Ukraine will want to read Serhii Plokhy's reasoned, measured, yet passionate, account of Ukraine's historic role at the gates of Europe."
   —**Michael Ignatieff, Harvard Kennedy School of Government**

"Finally: a compelling and concise history of a country leading the news but which too many know embarrassingly little about. There are no more excuses for ignorance."

—**Peter Pomerantsev, author of** *Nothing Is True and Everything Is Possible*

"Serhii Plokhy has produced a perfect new history of Ukraine for these troubled times—authoritative and innovative, but always clear and accessible, and a delight to read."

—**Andrew Wilson, professor of Ukrainian studies, University College London**

"Serhii Plokhy offers a short yet comprehensive history of Ukraine that contextualizes Mr. Putin's current policies as aggression against the wishes of the Ukrainian people, as well as the order established at the end of the Cold War. A pleasure to read, *The Gates of Europe* will take those familiar with the Moscow narrative on a mind expanding tour of Ukraine's past."

—**John Herbst, former US ambassador to Ukraine**

"Complex and nuanced, refreshingly revisionist, and lucid, this is a compelling and outstanding short history of the blood-soaked land that has so often been the battlefield and breadbasket of Europe. *The Gates of Europe* combines scholarly authority with narrative flair—essential reading for anyone who wants to understand Russia and Ukraine today."

—**Simon Sebag Montefiore, author of** *Stalin: The Court of the Red Tsar*

THE GATES OF EUROPE

THE GATES OF EUROPE

A HISTORY *of* UKRAINE

SERHII PLOKHY

BASIC BOOKS
New York

Basic Books
Hachette Book Group
1290 Avenue of the Americas, New York, NY 10104
www.basicbooks.com

Printed in the United States of America

Second Trade Paperback Edition: May 2021

Published by Basic Books, an imprint of Perseus Books, LLC, a subsidiary of Hachette Book Group, Inc. The Basic Books name and logo is a trademark of the Hachette Book Group.

The Hachette Speakers Bureau provides a wide range of authors for speaking events. To find out more, go to www.hachettespeakersbureau.com or call (866) 376-6591.

The publisher is not responsible for websites (or their content) that are not owned by the publisher.

Print book interior design by Trish Wilkinson

Library of Congress Cataloging-in-Publication Data

Plokhy, Serhii, 1957–
    The gates of Europe : a history of Ukraine / Serhii Plokhy.
        pages cm
    Includes bibliographical references and index.
    ISBN 978-0-465-05091-8 (hardcover) — ISBN 978-0-465-07394-8 (ebook)
1. Ukraine—History. I. Title.
DK508.51.P55 2015
947.7—dc23   2015015256

ISBNs: 978-0-465-05091-8 (hardcover), 978-0-465-07394-8 (hardcover e-book), 978-0-465-09486-8 (paperback), 978-0-465-09346-5 (paperback e-book), 978-1-5416-7564-3 (2021 paperback)

LSC-C

Printing 2, 2022

To the people of Ukraine

CONTENTS

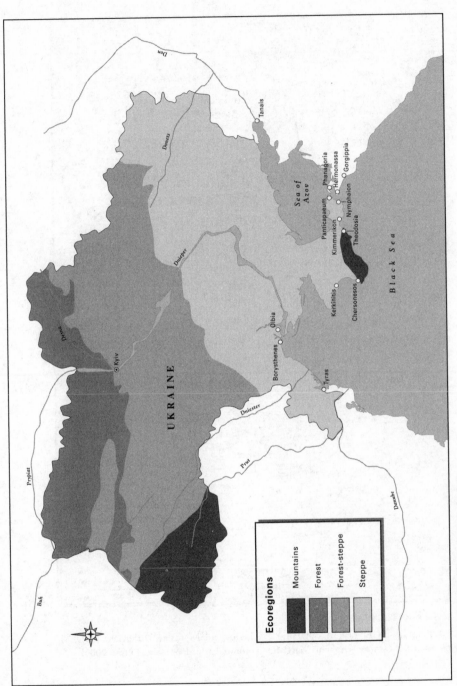

The Greek Settlements, 770 BC–100 BC

Kyivan Rus', 980–1054

Source: Zenon E. Kohut, Bohdan Y. Nebesio, and Myroslav Yurkevich, *Historical Dictionary of Ukraine* (Lanham, Maryland; Toronto; Oxford: Scarecrow Press, 2005).

Rus' Principalities ca. 1100

SOURCE: *The Cambridge Encyclopedia of Russia and the Former Soviet Union* (Cambridge: Cambridge University Press, 1994).

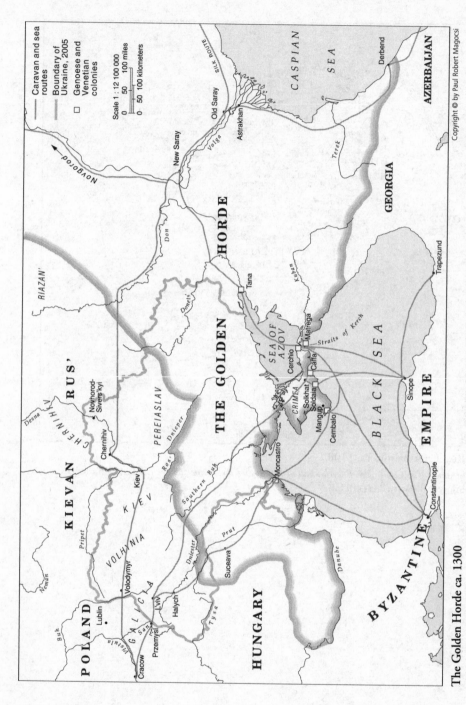

The Golden Horde ca. 1300

SOURCE: Paul Robert Magocsi, *A History of Ukraine: The Land and Its People* (Toronto: University of Toronto Press, 2010), p. 117, map 10.

Copyright © by Paul Robert Magocsi

Boundary of Polish Kingdom, 1454

Boundary of Grand Duchy of Lithuania, 1454

Eastern boundary of Polish Commonwealth, 1634

Boundary of Polish Commonwealth, 1667–1772

Polish Commonwealth, 1582

Livonia

Lithuania

Poland

| 0 | 150 | 300 km |

| 0 | 100 | 200 miles |

Lands of the Polish-Lithuanian Commonwealth in the sixteenth–eighteenth centuries

SOURCE: *Encyclopedia of Ukraine*, ed. Volodymyr Kubijovyč and Danylo Husar Struk, vol. IV (Toronto: University of Toronto Press, 1993).

Cossack Ukraine ca. 1650

SOURCE: Mykhailo Hrushevsky, *History of Ukraine-Rus'*, ed. Frank E. Sysyn et al., vol. IX, bk. 1 (Edmonton and Toronto: Canadian Institute of Ukrainian Studies Press, 2005).

The Hetmanate and surrounding territories in the 1750s

The Hetmanate

Desna River

Dnieper River

RUSSIAN

EMPIRE

Starodub

Chernihiv

POLISH-

Nizhyn

LITHUANIAN

Pryluky

Kyiv

COMMONWEALTH

Pereiaslav

Lubny

Hadiach

Myrhorod

Poltava

COSSACKS OF

Kharkiv

SLOBODA UKRAINE

Izium

SLAVIANO-SERBIA

NOVO-SERBIA

ZAPOROZHIAN COSSACKS

Zaporozhian Sich

TATARS

Sea of Azov

OTTOMAN EMPIRE

Bahçesaray

Black Sea

| 0 | 100 | 200 | 300 km |
| 0 | 50 | 100 | 150 | 200 miles |

The Hetmanate and surrounding territories in the 1750s

SOURCE: Zenon E. Kohut, *Russian Centralism and Ukrainian Autonomy: Imperial Absorption of the Hetmanate, 1760s–1830s* (Cambridge, MA: Harvard University Press, 1988), p. xiv.

The Partitions of Poland

SOURCE: Paul Robert Magocsi, *A History of Ukraine: The Land and Its People* (Toronto: University of Toronto Press, 2010), no. 25, p. 319.

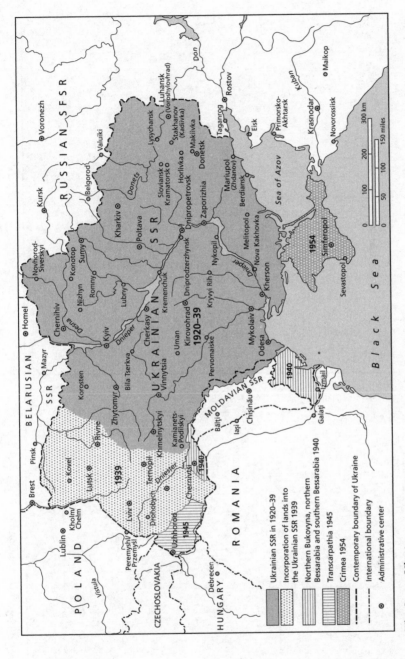

The Soviet Ukraine

SOURCE: Volodymyr Kubijovyc and Danylo Husar Struk, eds. *Encyclopedia of Ukraine*, vol. 5 (Toronto: University of Toronto Press, 1993), p. 441.

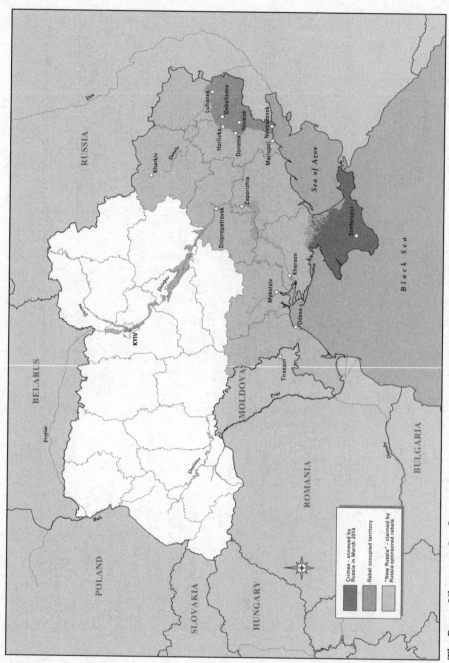

The Russo-Ukrainian Conflict

PREFACE

As AMERICAN PRESIDENTIAL impeachments go, that of Donald John Trump by the House of Representatives of the US Congress in December 2019 was unique. Of the four such impeachments in American history to date, it alone focused on presidential actions pertaining to a foreign country. The country in question was Ukraine.

Many times, over the last few years, I have been asked the same question: "Why has Ukraine gained such prominence in world politics?" I first encountered it in the context of the Maidan protests of 2013 and 2014, followed immediately by Russia's annexation of the Crimea and its aggression against the rest of Ukraine, with the subsequent dramatic worsening of US-Russian and EU-Russian relations. The same question arose concerning Ukraine's role in the impeachment process and then again in the American presidential campaign of 2020.

My answer was and remains the same. The appearance of Ukraine on the center stage of European and then American politics is not a fluke. Ukraine, the largest post-Soviet republic after Russia and now the object of Russian aggression, has become a battleground in the last few years. Unlike its East Slavic neighbors, Russia and Belarus, Ukraine has maintained democratic institutions and politics throughout the tumultuous years of the post-Soviet transition and oriented itself toward the West in its geopolitical aspirations and social and cultural values.

Russia's undeclared hybrid war in Ukraine's Donbas region, which has taken more than 14,000 lives in the past seven years, claims American and Western attention as one of the foremost manifestations of the global struggle between democracy and authoritarianism. The ongoing military conflict in Ukraine is not only a contest of political values. Russia's effort to stem its imperial decline by seizing the Crimea and occupying part of the Donbas presents a major threat to international order, with its bedrock principles of sovereignty and territorial integrity of nation-states, on a level not seen since the end of World War II.

While Ukraine has come to world attention fairly recently, it has a long, dramatic, but also fascinating history, often obscured by the grand narratives of empires that ruled its territory for centuries. Digging out that history, little known in the West until the past few decades, from under the layers of imperial misrepresentation helps to provide a deeper understanding not only of the nation at the center of the world's attention but also of Europe as a whole, both east and west. I have taken the opportunity offered by my publisher to issue an updated edition of the book to add a chapter on Ukraine's most recent history—the years that have passed since the original publication in 2015. It places the story of the country and the region in a new light.

Serhii Plokhy

March 21, 2021

INTRODUCTION

UKRAINIANS PROBABLY HAVE just as much right to brag about their role in changing the world as Scots and other nationalities about which books have been written asserting their claim to have shaped the course of human history. In December 1991, as Ukrainian citizens went to the polls en masse to vote for their independence, they also consigned the mighty Soviet Union to the dustbin of history. The events in Ukraine then had major international repercussions and did indeed change the course of history: the Soviet Union was dissolved one week after the Ukrainian referendum, and President George H. W. Bush declared the final victory of the West in the prolonged and exhausting Cold War.

The world next saw Ukraine on television screens in November 2004, when festive orange-clad crowds filled the squares and streets of Kyiv demanding fair elections and got their way. The Orange Revolution gave a common name to a number of "color revolutions" that shook authoritarian regimes from Serbia to Lebanon and from Georgia to Kyrgyzstan. The color revolutions did not change the post-Soviet world, but they left a lasting legacy and the hope that it would change one day. Ukrainians reappeared on the world's television screens in November and December 2013, when they poured onto the streets of Kyiv once again, this time in support of closer ties with the European Union. At a time when enthusiasm for the European Union was at a low ebb among its member countries, the readiness of the Ukrainians to march and stay on the streets in subzero temperatures for days, weeks, and months surprised and inspired the citizens of western and central Europe.

Events in Ukraine took an unexpected and tragic turn in early 2014, when a confrontation between the protesters and government forces violently disrupted the festive, almost street-party atmosphere of the earlier protests. In full view of television cameras, riot police and government snipers used live ammunition, wounding and killing dozens of pro-European demonstrators in February 2014. The images shocked the world. So did the Russian annexation of the Crimea in March 2014 and, later that spring, Moscow's campaign of hybrid warfare in the Donbas region of eastern Ukraine. In July, the downing by pro-Russian separatists of a Malaysian airliner with almost three hundred people on board turned the Russo-Ukrainian conflict into a truly international one. The developments in Ukraine had a major impact on European and world affairs, causing politicians to speak of a "battle for the future of Europe" and a return of the Cold War in the very part of the world where it had allegedly ended in 1991.

What has caused the Ukraine Crisis? What role does history play in those events? What differentiates Ukrainians from Russians? Who has the right to the Crimea and to eastern Ukraine? Why do Ukrainian actions have major international repercussions? Such questions, asked again and again in recent years, deserve comprehensive answers. To understand the trends underlying current events in Ukraine and their impact on the world, one has to examine their roots. That, in very general terms, is the main task of this book, which I have written in the hope that history can provide insights into the present and thereby influence the future. While it is difficult, if not impossible, to predict the outcome and long-term consequences of the current Ukraine Crisis or the future of Ukraine as a nation, the journey into history can help us make sense of the barrage of daily news reports, allowing us to react thoughtfully to events and thus shape their outcome.

This book presents the *longue durée* history of Ukraine from the times of Herodotus to the fall of the USSR and the current Russo-Ukrainian conflict. But how does one distill more than a millennium of the history of a place the size of France, which has close to 46 million citizens today and has had hundreds of millions over the course of its existence, into a couple of hundred pages? One has to pick and choose, as historians have always done. Their approaches, however, differ. The founder of modern Ukrainian historiography, Mykhailo Hrushevsky (1866–1934), who is a character in this book and the scholar for whom the chair of Ukrainian history at Harvard University is named, regarded his subject as the history of a nation that had existed since time immemorial and known periods of flourishing, decline, and revival, the latter culminating in the creation of Ukrainian statehood in the course and aftermath of World War I.

Hrushevsky established Ukrainian history as a distinct field of research, but many of his critics and successors have questioned his approach. Hrushevsky's students put emphases on the history of Ukrainian statehood; Soviet historians told the history of Ukraine as one of class struggle; some Western writers have emphasized its multiethnic character; today, more and more scholars are turning to a transnational approach. These latter trends in the writing of Ukrainian and other national histories have influenced my own narrative. I have also taken advantage of the recent cultural turn in historical studies and research on the history of identities. The questions I ask are unapologetically presentist, but I do my best not to read modern identities, loyalties, thoughts, motivations, and sensibilities back into the past.

The title of the book, *The Gates of Europe*, is of course a metaphor, but not one to be taken lightly or dismissed as a marketing gimmick. Europe is an important part of the Ukrainian story, as Ukraine is part of the European one. Located at the western edge of the Eurasian steppe, Ukraine has been a gateway to Europe for many centuries. Sometimes, when the "gates" were closed as a result of wars and conflicts, Ukraine helped stop foreign invasions east and west; when they were open, as was the case for most of Ukraine's history, it served as a bridge between Europe and Eurasia, facilitating the interchange of people, goods, and ideas. Through the centuries, Ukraine has also been a meeting place (and a battleground) of various empires, Roman to Ottoman, Habsburg to Romanov. In the eighteenth century, Ukraine was ruled from St. Petersburg and Vienna, Warsaw and Istanbul. In the nineteenth century, only the first two capitals remained. In the second half of the twentieth, only Moscow ruled supreme over most of the Ukrainian lands. Each of the empires claimed land and booty, leaving its imprint on the landscape and the character of the population and helping to form its unique frontier identity and ethos.

Nation is an important—although not dominant—category of analysis and element of the story that, along with the ever changing idea of Europe, defines the nature of this narrative. This book tells the history of Ukraine within the borders defined by the ethnographers and mapmakers of the late nineteenth and early twentieth centuries, which often (but not always) coincided with the borders of the present-day Ukrainian state. It follows the development of the ideas and identities linking those lands together from the times of the medieval Kyivan state, known in historiography as Kyivan Rus', to the rise of modern nationalism and explains the origins of the modern Ukrainian state and political nation. In doing so, the book focuses on Ukrainians as the largest demographic group and, in time, the main force behind the creation of the modern nation and state. It pays attention to Ukraine's minorities, especially Poles, Jews, and Russians, and treats the modern multiethnic and multicultural Ukrainian nation as a work in progress. Ukrainian culture always existed in a space shared with other cultures and early on involved navigating among the "others." The ability of Ukrainian society to cross inner and outer frontiers and negotiate identities created by them constitutes the main characteristic of the history of Ukraine as presented in this book.

Politics, international and domestic, provide a convenient storyline, but in writing this book, I found geography, ecology, and culture most lasting and thus most influential in the long run. Contemporary Ukraine, as seen from the perspective of *longue durée* cultural trends, is a product of the interaction of two moving frontiers, one demarcated by the line between the Eurasian steppes and the eastern European parklands, the other defined by the border between Eastern and Western Christianity. The first frontier was also the one between sedentary and nomadic populations and, eventually, between Christianity and Islam. The second goes back to the division of the Roman Empire between Rome and Constantinople and marks differences in political culture between Europe's east and west that still exist today. The movement of these frontiers over the centuries gave rise to a unique set of cultural features that formed the foundations of present-day Ukrainian identity.

One cannot tell the history of Ukraine without telling the story of its regions. The cultural and social space created by the movement of frontiers has not been homogenous. As state and imperial borders moved across the territory defined by Ukrainian ethnic boundaries, they created distinct cultural spaces that served as foundations of Ukraine's regions—the former Hungarian-ruled Transcarpathia, historically Austrian Galicia, Polish-held Podolia and Volhynia, the Cossack Left Bank of the Dnieper with the lower reaches of that river, Sloboda Ukraine, and finally the Black Sea coast and the Donets basin, colonized in imperial Russian times. Unlike most of my predecessors, I try to avoid treating the history of various regions (such as the Russian- and Austrian-ruled parts of Ukraine) in separate sections of the book but rather look at them together, providing a comparative perspective on their development within a given period.

In conclusion, a few words about terminology. The ancestors of modern Ukrainians lived in dozens of premodern and modern principalities, kingdoms, and empires, and in the course of time they took on various names and identities. The two key terms that they used to define their land were "Rus'" and "Ukraine." (In the Cyrillic alphabet, Rus' is spelled Русь: the last character is a soft sign indicating palatalized pronunciation of the preceding consonant.) The term "Rus'," brought to the region by the Vikings in the ninth and tenth centuries, was adopted by the inhabitants of Kyivan Rus', who took the Viking princes and warriors into their fold and Slavicized them. The ancestors of today's Ukrainians, Russians, and Belarusians adopted the name "Rus'" in forms that varied from the Scandinavian/Slavic "Rus'" to the Hellenized "Rossiia." In the eighteenth century, Muscovy adopted the latter form as the official name of its state and empire.

The Ukrainians had different appellations depending on the period and region in which they lived: Rusyns in Poland, Ruthenians in the Habsburg Empire, and Little Russians in the Russian Empire. In the course of the nineteenth century, Ukrainian nation builders decided to end the confusion by renouncing the name "Rus'" and clearly distinguishing themselves from the rest of the East Slavic world, especially from the Russians, by adopting "Ukraine" and "Ukrainian" to define their land and ethnic group, both in the Russian Empire and in Austria-Hungary. The name "Ukraine" had medieval origins and in the early modern era denoted the Cossack state in Dnieper Ukraine. In the collective mind of the nineteenth-century activists, the Cossacks, most of whom were of local origin, were the quintessential Ukrainians. To link the Rus' past and the Ukrainian future, Mykhailo Hrushevsky called his ten-volume magnum opus *History of Ukraine-Rus'*. Indeed, anyone writing about the Ukrainian past today must use two or even more terms to define the ancestors of modern Ukrainians.

In this book, I use "Rus'" predominantly but not exclusively with reference to the medieval period. "Ruthenians" to denote Ukrainians of the early modern era, and "Ukrainians" when I write about modern times. Since the independent Ukrainian state's creation in 1991, its citizens have all come to be known as "Ukrainians," whatever their ethnic background. This usage reflects the current conventions of academic historiography, and although it makes for some complexity, I hope that it does not lead to confusion.

"Come, and you will see," wrote the anonymous author of *History of the Rus'*, one of the founding texts of modern Ukrainian historiography, at the end of his foreword. I cannot conclude mine with a better invitation.

THE GATES OF EUROPE

I

ON THE
PONTIC FRONTIER

CHAPTER 1

THE EDGE OF THE WORLD

THE FIRST HISTORIAN of Ukraine was Herodotus, the father of history himself. This honor is usually reserved for the histories of countries and peoples belonging to the Mediterranean world. Ukraine—a stretch of steppes, mountains, and forests north of the Black Sea, which was known to the Greeks as the *Pontos euxeinos* (Hospitable Sea, latinized by the Romans as *Pontus euxinus*)—was an important part of that world. Its importance was of a particular nature. The world of Herodotus was centered on the city-states of ancient Greece, extending to Egypt in the south and the Crimea and the Pontic steppes in the north. If Egypt was a land of ancient culture and philosophy to study and emulate, the territory of today's Ukraine was a quintessential frontier where Greek civilization encountered its barbaric alter ego. It was the first frontier of a political and cultural sphere that would come to be known as the Western world. That is where the West began to define itself and its other.

Herodotus, known in Greek as Herodotos, came from Halicarnassus, a Greek city in what is now Turkey. In the fifth century BC, when he lived, wrote, and recited his *Histories*, his birthplace was part of the Persian Empire. Herodotus spent a good part of his life in Athens, lived in southern Italy, and crisscrossed the Mediterranean and Middle Eastern worlds, traveling to Egypt and Babylon among other places. An admirer of Athenian democracy, he wrote in Ionic Greek, but his interests were as global as they could be at the time. His *Histories*, later divided into nine books, dealt with the origins of the Greco-Persian wars that began in 499 and continued until the mid-fifth century BC. Herodotus lived through a good part of that period and researched the subject for thirty years after the end of the wars in 449. He depicted the conflict as an epic struggle between freedom and slavery—the former represented by the Greeks, the latter by the Persians. Although his own political and ideological sympathies were engaged, he wanted to tell both sides of the story. In his own words, he set out "to preserve the memory of the past by putting on record the astonishing achievements of both the Greeks and the Barbarians."

Herodotus's interest in the "barbarian" part of the story turned his attention to the Pontic steppes. In 512 BC, thirteen years before the start of the wars, Darius the Great, by far the most powerful ruler of the Persian Empire, invaded the region to avenge himself on the Scythians, who had played a trick on him. The Scythian kings, nomadic rulers of a vast realm north of the Black Sea, had made Darius march all the way from the Danube to the Don in pursuit of their highly mobile army without giving him a chance to engage it in battle. This was a humiliating defeat for a ruler who would pose a major threat to the Greek world a decade and a half later. In his *Histories*, Herodotus spared no effort in relating whatever he knew or had ever heard about the mysterious Scythians and their land, customs, and society. It would appear that despite his extensive travels, he never visited the region himself and had to rely on stories told by others. But his detailed description of the Scythians and the lands and peoples they ruled made him not only the first historian but also the first geographer and ethnographer of Ukraine.

THE LANDS NORTH of the Black Sea were first settled ca. 45,000 BC by Neanderthal mammoth hunters, as we know from archeological excavations of their dwellings. In the fifth millennium BC, bearers of the so-called Cucuteni-Trypilian culture settled the forest-steppe borderlands between the Danube and the Dnieper, engaged in animal husbandry and agriculture, built large settlements, and produced clay statues and colored ceramics. Some 3,500 years before common era, humans who populated the Pontic steppes domesticated the horse and one thousand years later brought Indo-European languages to Central Europe.

Before Herodotus began to recite parts of his work at public festivals in Athens, most Greeks knew very little about the area north of the Black Sea. They thought of it as a land of savages and a playground of the gods. Some believed that it was there, on an island at the mouth of either the Danube or the Dnieper, that Achilles, the hero of the Trojan War and Homer's *Iliad*, had found his eternal rest. Amazons, the female warriors of Greek mythology who cut off their right breasts to better steady their bows, also lived in that area, supposedly near the Don River. And then there were the ferocious Taurians of the Crimea, a peninsula known to the Greeks as Taurica. Their princess, Iphigenia, showed no mercy to travelers unfortunate enough to seek refuge from Black Sea tempests on the mountainous shores of the Crimea. She sacrificed them to the goddess Artemis, who had saved her from the death sentence pronounced by her father, Agamemnon. Few wanted to travel to lands as dangerous as those bordering the "Hospitable Sea," which was in fact very difficult to navigate and known for severe storms coming out of nowhere.

The Greeks first heard of the lands and peoples north of the Black Sea from a nation of warriors called the Cimmerians, who appeared in Anatolia after the Scythians drove them out of the Pontic steppes in the eighth century BC. The nomadic Cimmerians moved first to the Caucasus and then south toward Asia Minor, encountering Mediterranean cultures with a long tradition of sedentary life and cultural accomplishment. There the nomadic warriors became known as quintessential barbarians, a reputation recorded in the Bible, where Jeremiah describes them as follows: "They are armed with bow and spear; they are cruel and show no mercy. They sound like the roaring sea as they ride on their horses; they come like men in battle formation to attack you." The image of the Cimmerians as savage warriors also made its way into modern popular culture. Arnold Schwarzenegger played Conan the Barbarian—a fictional character invented in 1932 by the writer Robert E. Howard—as the king of Cimmeria in a 1982 Hollywood hit.

The Crimea and the northern shores of the Black Sea became part of the Greek universe in the seventh and sixth centuries BC, after the Cimmerians were forced to leave their homeland. Greek colonies then began to spring up in the region, most of them founded by settlers from Miletus, one of the most powerful Greek states of the era. Sinope, founded by Miletians on the southern shore of the Black Sea, became a mother colony in its own right. Colonies on the northern shore included Panticapaeum near today's city of Kerch, Theodosia on the site of present-day Feodosiia, and Chersonesus near the modern city of Sevastopol, all three in the Crimea. But by far the best-known Miletian colony was Olbia at the mouth of the Southern Buh (Boh) River, where it flows into the estuary of the even larger Dnieper, their combined waters emptying into the Black Sea. The city featured stone walls, an acropolis, and a temple to Apollo Delphinios. According to archeologists, Olbia covered more than 120 acres at its peak. As many as 10,000 people lived in the city, which adopted a democratic form of government and managed relations with its mother city of Miletus by treaty.

Olbia's prosperity, like the well-being of other Greek cities and emporia (trading places) in the region, depended on good relations with the local population of the Pontic steppes. At the time of the city's founding and throughout its most prosperous period, the fifth and fourth centuries BC, the locals happened to be Scythians, a conglomerate of tribes of Iranian origin. The Greeks of Olbia and their neighbors not only lived side by side and engaged in commerce but also intermarried, giving rise to a large population of mixed Greek and "barbarian" blood whose customs combined Greek and local traditions. Olbia's merchants and sailors shipped cereals, dried fish, and slaves to Miletus and other parts of Greece, bringing back wine, olive oil, and Greek artisanal wares, including textiles and metal products, to sell at local markets. There were also luxury items made of gold, as we know from excavations of burial mounds of Scythian kings. The steppes of southern Ukraine are full of such mounds, now largely reduced to small hills and known in Ukrainian as *kurhany*.

BY FAR THE most impressive piece of so-called Scythian gold, a three-tier pectoral, was discovered in southern Ukraine in 1971 and can be seen today at the Ukrainian Museum of Historical Treasures in Kyiv. The pectoral, which probably dates from the fourth century BC and once decorated the chest of a Scythian king, offers a view of the inner workings of Scythian society and economy. At its center is a depiction of two kneeling bearded Scythian men who hold a sheepskin coat. Given the material of which the entire pectoral is made, this reminds one of the golden fleece of the Argonauts—a symbol of authority and kingship. To the right and left of the central scene are images of domesticated animals—horses, cows, sheep, and goats. There are also images of Scythian slaves, one milking a cow, another a ewe. The pectoral leaves little doubt that the Scythians lived in a male-dominated society of steppe warriors whose economy depended on animal husbandry.

If the images of Scythians and domesticated animals take us inside the Scythian world, those of wild animals depicted on the pectoral tell us more about how the Greeks imagined the farthest frontier of their universe than about real life on the Pontic steppes. Lions and panthers pursue boars and deer, while winged griffins—the most powerful animals of Greek mythology, half eagles, half lions—attack horses, the animals most important to the

Scythian way of life. The pectoral is an ideal symbol not only of Greek cultural transfer but also of the interaction of the Greek and Scythian worlds in the Pontic steppes.

That intertwining of cultures allowed Herodotus to collect the kind of information about Scythian life that no archeological dig could provide. The founding myth of the Scythians certainly belongs to that category. "According to the account that the Scythians themselves give, they are the youngest of all nations," stated Herodotus in his *Histories*, allegedly descended from a certain Targitaus, who had three sons. "While they still ruled the land, there fell from the sky four implements, all of gold—a plough, a yoke, a battle axe, and a drinking cup," as Herodotus retold the Scythian founding myth. Two elder brothers tried to take the gifts from the sky, but they burst into flames, and only the youngest brother managed to take and keep them. He was immediately recognized as the supreme ruler of the realm and gave rise to the Scythian tribe known as Royal Scythians, who dominated the Pontic steppes and kept the gold that had fallen from the sky. The Scythians apparently saw themselves as an indigenous population. Otherwise, they would not have claimed that the parents of their founder, Targitaus, were a sky god and a daughter of Borysthenes, known today as the Dnieper, the main river of the realm. The same myth suggests that although ruled by nomads, the Scythians also thought of themselves as agriculturalists. The tools given to them by heaven included not only a yoke but also a plow, a clear sign of sedentary culture.

Indeed, Herodotus described the Scythians as divided into horsemen and agriculturalists, each group occupying its own ecological niche in the northern Black Sea region. On the Right Bank of the Dnieper, as viewed from a ship sailing southward, directly above the Greek colony of Olbia, from whose citizens and visitors Herodotus took most of his knowledge of the region, he identified a tribe called the Callipedae, probably descendants of Greek intermarriage with local Scythians. To the north, along the Dniester and north of the steppes controlled by the Royal Scythians, were the Alazonians, who "in other respects resemble the Scythians in their usages but sow and eat grain, also onions, garlic, lentils, and millet." North of the Alazonians, on the Right Bank of the Dnieper, Herodotus located the Scythian plowmen, who produced corn for sale. On the Left Bank of the river, he placed the Scythian agriculturalists, or Borysthenites. He wrote that these tribes were quite different from the Scythians to the south, who inhabited the Pontic steppes.

Herodotus found the lands along the Dnieper to be among the most productive in the world:

> The Borysthenes, the second-largest of the Scythian rivers, is, in my opinion, the most valuable and productive not only of the rivers in this part of the world but anywhere else, with the sole exception of the River Nile—with which none can be compared. It provides the finest and most abundant pasture, by far the richest supply of the best sorts of fish, and the most excellent water for drinking—clear and bright—whereas that of other rivers in the vicinity is turbid; no better crops grow anywhere than along its banks, and where grain is not sown, the grass is the most luxuriant in the world.

An apt description indeed. The black soil of the Dnieper basin is still considered among the richest in the world, earning modern Ukraine the nickname "breadbasket of Europe."

The lands of the middle Dnieper, settled by agriculturalists, were not yet the end of Herodotus's frontier. There also existed peoples to the north about whom not only the Greeks of the colonies but also Scythians of different walks of life knew little if anything. These peoples inhabited the ultimate frontier. On the Right Bank of the Dnieper, they were called Neuri; on the left, farther to the east and north, they were simply called Cannibals. Herodotus did not know much about them, but the location of the Neuri in the Prypiat marshes on today's Ukrainian-Belarusian border coincides with one of the possible homelands of the ancient Slavs, where a cluster of some of the oldest Ukrainian dialects is to be found.

If one trusts Herodotus and his sources, the Scythian kingdom was a conglomerate of ethnic groups and cultures in which geography and ecology determined the place of each group in the general structure of the polity and its division of labor. Greeks and Hellenized Scythians occupied the coast, serving as intermediaries between the Mediterranean world of Greece and the hinterland in terms of both trade and culture. The main products of trade—cereals and dried fish, as well as slaves—came from the parklands or mixed forest-steppe areas. To reach the Black Sea ports, those products, especially cereals and slaves, had to pass through the steppes inhabited by Royal Scythians, who controlled trade and kept most of the proceeds for themselves, leaving part of their golden treasure in the mounds of the region. The division that Herodotus described between coast, steppe, and forest would become one of the main divisions of Ukrainian history—lasting for centuries, if not millennia.

THE MULTILAYERED SCYTHIAN world depicted in the *Histories* came to an end in the third century BC. The Romans, who took control of the Greek colonies of the northern Black Sea region and extended protection to them in the first century BC, had to deal with different masters of the steppes.

A new wave of nomads from the east, the Sarmatians, defeated, pushed aside, and eventually replaced the Scythian horsemen, who controlled the trade routes between the agricultural regions and the Greek colonies. These newcomers, like the Scythians, were of Iranian stock. Herodotus, who located them east of the Don River, recorded a legend according to which they were descended from the Scythians and Amazon women who escaped Greek captivity. Like the Scythians, the Sarmatians included different tribes and ruled over a variety of peoples, including the Roxolani, Alani, and Iazyges. The Sarmatians ruled the Pontic steppes for half a millennium, until the fourth century AD. At the height of their power, they controlled the whole area from the Volga in the east to the Danube in the west and penetrated central Europe all the way to the Vistula.

The Sarmatians were no less intimidating a power in the region than the Scythians had been, but we know much less about them. This is mainly because the trade between the Greek colonies and the Ukrainian hinterland (and, with it, the flow of information) that had flourished under the Scythians came almost to a halt under the Sarmatians. They drove the Scythians into the Crimea, where the former rulers of the realm created a new kingdom known as Scythia Minor. The Scythians controlled the peninsula and the steppes immediately to its north, including the Greek colonies. The Sarmatians held the rest of the Pontic steppe but had no access to the colonies. The Scythians, for their part, lost control over the steppe and the hinterland. The conflict between the new and old masters of the steppes undermined local trade and prosperity and, in time, the security of the Greek colonies (the Scythians and other nomads demanded money and goods from the colonists, whether trade was flourishing or not). Another equally powerful factor reducing commerce was the appearance of new suppliers of agricultural produce to the Mediterranean markets. Grain was now coming to the Aegean and Ionian shores from Egypt and the Middle East along trade routes secured by the conquests of Alexander the Great and the rise of the Roman Empire.

When the Romans extended their reach to the northern shores of the Black Sea in the first century BC, they revived some of the former commerce by providing the Greek colonies now under their tutelage with a degree of security, but that proved an uphill battle at best. Ovid (Publius Ovidius Naso), who was exiled by Emperor Augustus in 8 AD to a place called Tomis on the Black Sea shore of present-day Romania and died there ten years later, left us a vivid description of the dangers of everyday life in a Greek maritime colony at the turn of the first millennium AD:

> *Innumerable tribes round about threaten fierce war,*
> *and think it's a disgrace to exist without pillage.*
> *Nowhere's safe outside: the hill itself's defended*
> *by fragile walls, and the ingenuity of its siting. . . .*
> *We're scarcely protected by the fortress's shelter: and even*
> *the barbarous crowd inside, mixed with Greeks, inspires fear,*
> *for the barbarians live amongst us, without discrimination,*
> *and also occupy more than half the houses.*

This sorry state of affairs, caused by hostile relations with "barbarian" neighbors and a lack of security, could not but reflect poorly on the state of the once prosperous colonies of the region. Dio Chrysostom, a Greek orator and philosopher who claimed to have visited the city of Olbia (known to the outsiders of his age as Borysthenes) at the end of the first century AD, left a vivid account of a colony in decline:

> The city of Borysthenes, as to its size, does not correspond to its ancient fame because of its ever-repeated seizure and its wars. For since the city has lain in the midst of barbarians now for so long a time—barbarians, too, who are virtually the most warlike of all—it is always in a state of war. . . . For that reason the fortunes of the Greeks in that region reached a very low ebb indeed, some of them being no longer united to form cities, while others enjoyed but a wretched existence as communities, and it was mostly barbarians who flocked to them.

Such was the state of the Greek colonies more than a century after the arrival of the Romans. The region never recovered the prosperity, trade, and links with the hinterland that it had enjoyed in the days of Herodotus. Constantly at war or in fear of war with the local population, the colonists knew little about their neighbors. "The Bosphorus, Don, the Scythian marshes lie beyond it," wrote Ovid, looking north and east from his exile in Tomis, "a handful of names in a region scarcely known. Further there's nothing but uninhabitable cold. Ah, how near I am to the ends of the earth!"

Ovid's contemporary Strabo, author of the acclaimed *Geographies*, knew more about the Pontic steppe than did the famous Roman exile. From Strabo we learn the names of the Sarmatian tribes and the areas under their control. According to him, the Iazyges and Roxolani were "wagon dwellers," or nomads, but the famous geographer gives us literally nothing about the sedentary population of the forest-steppe areas around the Dnieper, not to mention the wooded areas farther to the north. Unlike Ovid, however, he did not live among the peoples of the region; nor were his sources as good as those of Herodotus. They knew nothing about the "northerners," and Strabo complained about the ignorance that prevailed "in regard to the rest of the peoples that come next in order in the north; for I know neither the Bastarnae, nor the Sauromatae, nor, in a word, any of the peoples who dwell above the Pontus, nor how far distant they are from the Atlantic Sea, nor whether their countries border upon it."

Strabo's informants came from one of the colonies, but if Herodotus made numerous references to the Dnieper, Strabo seemed more familiar with the Don. His sources likely came from Tanais, a Greek colony at the mouth of the Don that belonged to the Bosporan Kingdom, the most powerful union of Greek colonies revived with the arrival of the Romans. For Strabo, the Don had a special meaning. It served as the easternmost boundary of Europe, the term used in the Aegean homeland to describe the expanse of the Greek presence in the outer world. Europe lay to the west of the Don, while Asia began to the east of it.

Thus, at the beginning of the first millennium AD, when the Romans came to the Pontic colonies, the Ukrainian territories found themselves once again at the very edge of what would become Western civilization. The northern frontier of the Hellenic world had now become the eastern boundary of Europe. There it would remain for almost two thousand years, until the rise of the Russian Empire in the eighteenth century redrew the map of Europe, moving its eastern boundary all the way to the Urals.

The division of the Pontic steppes into European and Asian parts did not mean much in the time of the Romans. Strabo wrote about the Sarmatians on both the left and right banks of the Don, and Ptolemy, one of his successors, wrote in the second century AD about two Sarmatias, one European, the other Asian—a division that would remain constant in the works of European geographers for another millennium and a half. More important than the imagined eastern boundary of Europe was the real civilizational frontier between the Mediterranean colonies on the northern shore of the Black Sea and the nomads of the Pontic steppes. Unlike the Greek colonies with their surrounding fortifications, that frontier was never set in stone, creating instead a broad zone of interaction between colonists and locals in which languages, religions, and cultures intermixed, producing new cultural and social realities.

The all-important boundary between the steppe nomads and the agriculturalists of the forest-steppe areas that was known to Herodotus became invisible for Strabo. Whether it disappeared altogether or Mediterranean writers simply did not know about it is hard to say. Geography and ecology stayed the same, while the population probably did not. It certainly refused to stay put in the middle of the first millennium AD, when we next encounter references to the region in the writings of learned Greeks.

CHAPTER 2

THE ADVENT OF THE SLAVS

WHEREAS TRADE AND cultural exchange largely defined the relations of the ancient Greeks with the peoples of the Ukrainian steppes in the last centuries BC, the Romans of the first centuries AD had no choice but to mix trade with war. Their relations with the peoples of the steppes became primarily warlike in the fourth century, with the beginning of a period called the "barbarian invasions" in older historiography and now known as the period of migrations. It saw a major movement of peoples and tribes from Eurasia and eastern Europe toward the center and west of Europe that led to the collapse of the Roman Empire under pressure from the "barbarians" in the second half of the fifth century. Although weakened, the eastern part of the empire, known in historiography as Byzantium, managed to survive the onslaught of the steppe nomads and accompanying agriculturalists from the north. It continued to exist until the mid-fifteenth century.

Ukraine played an important role in the drama of the migrations. Some of the key actors in the invasions that led to the fall of the Roman Empire lived in or passed through its territory. Among them were the Goths and Huns, the latter led by their king, Attila "the Hun." In the Pontic steppes, the migrations ended the lengthy era in which the region was controlled by nomadic tribes of Iranian origin, including the Scythians and Sarmatians. The Goths were of German stock, while the Huns, whom most scholars believe to have originated in the steppes of Mongolia, came into the region accompanied by numerous Central Asian tribes. By the mid-sixth century, the Huns were gone, replaced by tribes speaking Turkic dialects.

All the above-mentioned actors in the story of the migrations came to Ukraine, ruled its steppes, stayed for a while, and eventually left. One group, however, once brought to the surface by the upheaval of the migrations, refused to leave the scene. These were the Slavs, a conglomerate of tribes defined in linguistic and cultural terms and represented in various political formations. The Indo-European origins of their languages suggest that they came to Europe from the east sometime between the seventh and third millennia BC and thus settled in eastern Europe long before Herodotus first described the region and its inhabitants. Claiming the forested areas north of the Pontic steppes as their home, they remained invisible to Mediterranean authors throughout most of their early history.

THE SLAVS FIRST came to general attention in the early sixth century AD, when they showed up en masse on the borders of the Byzantine Empire, which had been weakened by the Goths and Huns, and moved into the Balkans. Jordanes, a sixth-century Byzantine author of Gothic descent, distinguished two major groups among the Slavs of his day. "Though their names are now dispersed amid various clans and places," he wrote, "yet they are chiefly called Sclaveni and Antes." He placed the Sclaveni between the Danube and the Dniester, reserving for the Antes the lands between the Dniester and the Dnieper, "in the curve of the sea of Pontus." Linguistic data suggests that the ancestral homeland of the Slavs lay in the forests and forest-steppe zone between the Dnieper and the Vistula, mainly in Volhynia and the Prypiat marshes of today's Ukraine. By the time Jordanes wrote, the Slavs must have moved from their forest recesses into the steppes, creating a serious problem for Emperor Justinian the Great.

Justinian ruled the Byzantine Empire between 527 and 567 and was ambitious enough to attempt a restoration of the Roman Empire in its entirety, both east and west. On the Danube frontier, where the empire faced unceasing attacks from local tribes, Justinian decided to take the offensive. Procopius, a sixth-century Byzantine author who left a detailed account of Justinian's wars, writes that in the early 530s Chilbudius, a commander personally close to the emperor, was sent to wage war north of the Danube. He scored a number of victories over the Antes, which allowed Justinian to add "Anticus" (conqueror of the Antes) to his imperial title. But the success was short-lived. Three years later Chilbudius was killed in battle, and Justinian returned to the old policy of defending the border along the Danube instead of trying to extend it.

Justinian brought back the old Roman tactic of "divide and rule." By the end of the 530s, not without Byzantine encouragement and incentives, the Antes were already fighting the Sclaveni, while Byzantine generals recruited both groups into the imperial army. Even so, the Slavic raids continued. While at war with the Sclaveni, the Antes managed to invade the Byzantine province of Thrace in the eastern Balkans. They pillaged the land and took numerous slaves, whom they brought back to the left bank of the Danube. Having manifested their destructive potential, the Antes offered their services to the empire. Justinian took them under his wing and designated the abandoned Greek city of Turris, north of the Danube, as their headquarters.

Like many other enemies of the empire, the Antes became its defenders in exchange for regular payments from the imperial treasury. They tried to enhance their status by claiming to have captured the emperor's best general, Chilbudius, whom they wanted to recognize as their leader. Since Justinian had granted Chilbudius the title of *magister militum*, or commander of all the imperial troops in the region, such recognition would have made them legitimate citizens of the empire, not merely its gatekeepers. The plot did not succeed. The true Chilbudius was, of course, long dead, his impostor was captured and sent to Justinian, and the Antes had to accept the status of *foederati*—allies rather than citizens of the great empire.

WHO WERE THESE new allies of the Byzantine Empire? What did they look like? How did they fight? What did they believe in? Procopius wrote more than once that the Antes and the Sclaveni shared a common language, religion, and customs. We can thus attribute his rather detailed description of the Slavic way of life to both groups. According to Procopius, the Slavs were seminomadic, living "in pitiful hovels that they set up far apart from one another." They constantly changed their dwelling places. The Slavic warriors were "exceptionally tall and stalwart men." Procopius had the following to say about their looks: "Their bodies and hair are neither very fair nor blond, nor indeed do they incline entirely to the dark type, but they are all slightly ruddy in color." The Slavs lived a "hard life, giving no heed to bodily comforts . . . and . . . [were] continually and at all times covered with filth; however, they [were] in no respect base or evildoers, but they preserve[d] the Hunnic character in all its simplicity."

Although covered with filth, the Slavs entered history under the banner of democracy. "For these nations," wrote Procopius, "the Sclaveni and the Antes, are not ruled by one man, but they have lived from of old under a democracy, and consequently everything that involves their welfare, whether for good or for ill, is referred to the people." They preferred to fight their battles half naked, but, unlike the medieval Scots in Mel Gibson's Hollywood blockbuster *Braveheart*, were more modest when it came to their private parts. "When they enter battle," wrote Procopius, "the majority of them go against their enemy on foot, carrying little shields and javelins in their hands, but they never wear corselets. Indeed, some of them do not wear even a shirt or a cloak, but, gathering their trews [trousers] up as far as their private parts, they enter into battle with their opponents."

Additional information on the Slavic way of making war comes from the Byzantine *Strategikon*, written around the year 600 and attributed to the emperor Mauricius. The author describes in some detail the Slavs who crossed the Danube frontier and settled in the Balkans. He found them hospitable to travelers but freewheeling and reluctant to honor treaties or abide by majority opinion. In their homeland north of the Danube, they built their dwellings in forests along rivers and in marshy areas difficult of access to invaders. Their favorite tactic was the ambush. They preferred not to fight in open fields and did not favor regular military formations. Their weapons were short spears, wooden bows, and short arrows, some of them tipped with poison. They made slaves of their prisoners, but the period of enslavement was limited to a certain term.

Procopius had some interesting things to say also about Slavic religion. The Slavs were anything but monotheists. "They believe that one god, the maker of lightning, is alone lord of all things, and they sacrifice to him cattle and all other victims," he wrote. While honoring one principal god, however, the Slavs by no means renounced their old habits of worshipping nature and offering sacrifices. As Procopius wrote, "They reverence . . . both rivers and nymphs and some other spirits, and they sacrifice to all these also, and they make their divinations in connection with these sacrifices." The Byzantine author found surprising not the Slavs' habit of making sacrifices to their gods, a tradition that they had in common with the pre-Christian Romans, but their failure to accept the Christian religion, as other imperial subjects had done long before. "They neither know it nor do they in any wise admit that it has any power among men," wrote Procopius with some amazement, if not disappointment, "but whenever death stands close before them, either stricken with sickness or beginning a war, they make a promise that, if they escape, they will straightway make a sacrifice to the god in return for their life; and if they escape, they sacrifice just what they have promised, and consider that their safety has been bought with this same sacrifice."

What Procopius and other Byzantine authors tell us about the Slavs finds some corroboration in Ukrainian archeological data. The Antes are usually associated with the Penkivka archeological culture, named after a settlement in Ukraine. The bearers of that culture lived in the sixth, seventh, and early eighth centuries in the Ukrainian forest-steppe zone, between the Dniester and Dnieper Rivers, settling both banks of the Dnieper. That area would include the territories assigned by Jordanes to the Antes. Like the Antes and Sclaveni of Procopius, the Penkivka tribes lived in simple dwellings dug into the ground. They, too, often changed their dwelling places. Settlements were inhabited, deserted, and resettled, suggesting that their inhabitants practiced an itinerant form of agriculture. Archeology also tells us (and Procopius does not) that the Penkivka tribes had fortified towns that served as headquarters of local rulers and centers of administrative and military power.

THE PERIOD IN which the Slavs played an independent role in the region ended in the early seventh century, when the incursion of the Avars, a conglomerate of Turkic-speaking tribes from the northern Caspian steppes, destroyed the Antes' polity.

The Avars left bad memories in the region, some of which lasted into the eleventh and twelfth centuries, when Christian Kyivan monks wrote parts of a historical record that later became known as the Primary Chronicle, or the Tale of Bygone Years. Its initial section was based on local legends combined with Byzantine sources. According to the Primary Chronicle, the Avars "made war upon the Slavs and harassed the Dulebians, who were themselves Slavs"—a reference to a Slavic tribe that lived along the Buh River. "They even did violence to the Dulebian women," wrote the chronicler. "When an Avar made a journey, he did not cause either a horse or a steer to be harnessed but gave command instead that three or four or five women should be yoked to his cart and be made to draw him. Such behavior was punished by divine wrath. "The Avars were large of stature and proud of spirit, and God destroyed them," continues the chronicler. "They all perished, and not one Avar survived. There is to this day a proverb in Rus' that runs, 'They perished like the Avars.'"

The Avars gave way as rulers of the Pontic steppes to the Bulgars and then to the Khazars, who brought the era of migrations to a close and established relative peace in the region by the end of the seventh century. The Khazars left much better memories among the Avars' former subjects in the Ukrainian steppes. "Then the Khazars came upon them as they lived in the hills and forests," wrote a Kyivan chronicler, referring to the Dnieper Slavs, "and demanded tribute from them." According to the chronicler, the locals, previously subject to a Slavic tribe known as the Derevlianians (forest people), paid the tribute with swords—a sign of defiance and a promise of future revenge. Apart from retelling this legend, which exonerated the Kyivans who had agreed to pay tribute to the Khazars, the Kyivan chronicler showed little animosity toward the invaders.

The Khazars had limited control over the forest-steppe borderland; the Dnieper more or less bounded their dominance in the forest zones. The Turkic Khazar elite, interested in peace and trade, was open to foreign influences. The Khazars welcomed a Christian mission to their country and even accepted Judaism, giving rise to a legend about the Khazarian origins of eastern European Jewry. The geographic core of the polity created by the Khazars was in the lower Volga and Don regions, its main centers being Itil on the Volga and Sarkel on the Don. The Khazar elite amassed its wealth by controlling trade routes, of which the Volga route to the Persian Empire and the Arab lands was by far the most important. Initially, it overshadowed the Dnieper route to the Byzantine Empire.

In the 620s the Khazars concluded a treaty with the Byzantine Empire, which by then had reestablished its presence on the northern Black Sea shore. Olbia, taken over by the Goths back in the fourth century, was lost forever, but the Byzantine commanders secured a piece of land on the southern shore of the Crimea, protected from the peninsula's steppes by a range of mountains. There, in Chersonesus, the administrative center of Byzantium's Crimean possessions came into being. The principal towns were garrisoned in the times of Emperor Justinian, and the empire enlisted the Crimean Goths—a splinter group that stayed in the region after their brethren had moved westward, first to central Europe and then all the way to the Iberian Peninsula—to protect the imperial possessions. Imperial engineers helped the Goths fortify their cave towns high in the Crimean mountains. The Khazars became allies of the Byzantines against the Persians and Arabs, trying to maintain the trade routes to the richest market on earth—that of Constantinople.

What do we know about the Slavs living in Ukraine when the Khazars controlled its eastern and central parts? More than about earlier periods, but not much more. Here our main and sometimes only source of information is the narrative of much later Kyivan chroniclers. Archeology tells us that Kyiv, which became the Khazars' westernmost outpost in the Ukrainian forest region, came into existence some time before the turn of the sixth century. But it is the chronicle that provides a sense of why the place was so important and why it was chosen for settlement. A local legend associated the establishment of Kyiv with the river crossing nearby. The inhabitants maintained that the town had been founded by their local ruler, Kyi, whose two brothers gave their names to its hills, while the river flowing through Kyiv into the Dnieper was named after their sister, Lybid. A statue of these four founders of the city stands on the riverbank and is now one of the main landmarks of the Ukrainian capital.

The Kyivan chronicler counted twelve Slavic tribes west of the Carpathians. In the north their settlements extended as far as Lake Ladoga, near present-day St. Petersburg; in the east, to the upper Volga and Oka Rivers; in the south, to the lower reaches of the Dniester and the middle Dnieper region. These Slavs were the predecessors of today's Ukrainians, Russians, and Belarusians. Linguists define them as Eastern Slavs on the basis of dialectal differences that began to develop in the sixth century, setting them apart from the Western Slavs—the predecessors of today's Poles, Czechs, and Slovaks—as well as the South Slavs, who include Serbs, Croats, and other Slavic peoples of the former Yugoslavia.

Seven of the twelve tribes listed by the Kyiv chronicler resided in what is now Ukraine, along the rivers Dnieper, Dniester, Buh, Prypiat, Desna, and Sozh. Only some of those tribes were under Khazar control. While their overlords and politics were different, their customs and mores seem to have been the same as, or fairly similar to, those of their neighbors. This, at least, is the impression conveyed by the Kyivan chronicler, who also happened to be a Christian monk. He considered members of all tribes other than his own to be savages. "They lived in the forest like any wild beast and ate every unclean thing," wrote the chronicler, who looked down on his pagan predecessors and contemporaries.

Archeologists show the Eastern Slavs to have been rather more sedentary. They lived in log houses organized in villages with anywhere between four and thirty houses. The villages were grouped in clusters. In the middle of a cluster, the Slavs built a fortification that served as military headquarters during enemy attack. The Slavs engaged in agriculture and animal husbandry. They had their own chieftains, and one might assume that they practiced military democracy, like the Slavs described by Procopius. Like the

Antes and the Sclaveni, they considered the god of thunder, whom they called Perun, to be their main deity.

Compared to the Slavs of Procopius, those described by the Kyivan chronicler had made some progress with regard to personal hygiene. The chronicler puts the following words into the mouth of St. Andrew, the apostle who allegedly brought Christianity to Kyiv: "I saw the land of the Slavs, and while I was among them, I noticed their wooden bathhouses. They warm them to extreme heat, then undress, and after anointing themselves with an acid liquid, they take young branches and lash their bodies. They actually lash themselves so violently that they barely escape alive."

The Kyivan chronicler, who resided and probably grew up in the vicinity of Kyiv, was not shy about mocking a bathing procedure popular among inhabitants of the northern reaches of present-day Russia and Scandinavia. He was much more scathing about old pre-Christian habits among his countrymen, which he considered barbaric. "The Derevlianians," wrote the chronicler about the former overlords of Kyiv, "existed in bestial fashion and lived like cattle. They killed one another, ate every impure thing, and there was no marriage among them, but instead they seized upon maidens by capture." According to the chronicler, other Slavic tribes were guilty of the same behavior. "There were no marriages among them," he wrote, "but simply festivals among the villages. When the people gathered together for games, for dancing, and for all other devilish amusements, the men on those occasions carried off wives for themselves, and each took any woman with whom he had arrived at an understanding. In fact, they even had two or three wives apiece."

It would be wrong to take the chronicler's account of Slavic marriage practices—or, rather, the lack of them—as a description of a norm rather than a deviation. The Kyivan chronicler, a Christian zealot of a later period, was of course fighting against all deviations from Christian morality and focused his attention on youth festivals that ran counter to the established institution of marriage. Ibrahim ibn Ya'qub, a Moorish Jew from Cordoba who visited the lands of the Western Slavs in the mid-tenth century, found Slavic marriages to be strong and the receipt of dowries to be one of the main ways of accumulating wealth. He noted, however, that both young men and young women were expected to have sexual experience before they married. "Their women, when married, do not commit adultery," wrote Ibn Ya'qub. "But a girl, when she falls in love with some man or other, will go to him and quench her lust. If a husband marries a girl and finds her to be a virgin, he says to her, 'If there were something good in you, men would have desired you, and you would certainly have found someone to take your virginity.' Then he sends her back and frees himself from her."

We know precious little about the Slavs who settled Ukrainian territory prior to the tenth and eleventh centuries. What we do know comes, by and large, either from their Byzantine or Gothic adversaries or from Christian zealots of later centuries, such as the Kyivan chronicler, who saw the Slavs as little more than bearers of pagan superstitions. Both accounts describe them as barbarians fighting either the Christian Empire or Christian dogma and ritual. What was ignored by the chroniclers and remains largely unknown to us is the process of their mostly peaceful colonization of eastern Europe, which took them from their homeland, part of which was in the northwestern regions of present-day Ukraine, deep into the Balkans in the south, beyond the Vistula and toward the Oder in the west, up to the Baltic Sea in the north, and to the Volga and Oka Rivers in the east. The Slavs were agriculturalists who followed in the wake of nomad invasions, as the nomads who "made history" usually did not know what to do with land that was not steppe in which their animals could graze. The waves of Slavic colonization were slow and mostly peaceful, and the results were to prove long-lasting.

CHAPTER 3

VIKINGS ON THE DNIEPER

IN UKRAINE, AS almost everywhere else in Europe, the era of migrations, or "barbarian invasions," gave way to the Viking Age, which lasted from the end of the eighth century to the second half of the eleventh. As one might expect, the end of the "barbarian invasions" was not the terminus of invasions per se. The new attackers came from what are now Sweden, Norway, and Denmark. Those were the Vikings, also known as Norsemen or Normans in western Europe and Varangians in eastern Europe. They plundered, subjugated, and ruled whole countries or parts of them. They also transformed some of the existing polities and created new ones.

When did it all begin? We have an exact date for the start of the Viking Age in Britain: June 8, 793. On that day, Viking pirates who had probably set out from Norway attacked and pillaged a Christian monastery on the island of Lindisfarne off the English coast. They drowned some of the monks in the sea and took others into slavery before disappearing with the monastery's treasures on their longboats. During the same decade, the Vikings/Normans, who would eventually give their name to the province of Normandy, appeared near the shores of France. The Viking Age had begun.

The Byzantine court first came into contact with the Vikings no later than 838, when envoys representing the king of Rus' (Rhos) showed up in Constantinople, offering the empire peace and friendship. They came from the north but were reluctant to return home by the route they had taken for fear of encountering hostile tribes, so the emperor sent them back via Germany. At the court of Louis the Pious, a son of the famous Charlemagne, king of the Franks, they were recognized as Swedes or Norsemen and suspected of espionage. In fact, they were probably anything but spies and had every reason to fear attack—either by Slavic tribes or, more likely, by nomads of the Pontic steppes—on their way back to northern Europe.

The encounter between Byzantium and the Vikings that began so peacefully soon ended in confrontation. In 959, a Viking flotilla made its presence felt in the Mediterranean. In the following year, another group came down the Dnieper, sailed across the Black Sea, entered the Strait of the Bosphorus, and attacked the city of Constantinople. As in the case of the Viking assault on Lindisfarne, we know the exact date—June 8, 860—when the Vikings attacked the capital of the mighty Byzantine Empire. The city and the empire were taken by surprise, as the emperor Michael was fighting at the head of his troops in Asia Minor. His fleet was in the Aegean and the Mediterranean, defending the empire not only from the Arabs but also from the Vikings who had appeared there the previous year. No one expected them to come from the north as well.

The intruders were not equipped for a long siege and could not breach the city's walls, but they attacked the suburbs, pillaging churches and mansions, killing or drowning anyone who offered resistance, and terrifying the citizenry. They then passed through the Bosphorus, entered the Sea of Marmara, and continued plundering on the Prince Islands near the capital. Patriarch Photius, the supreme Christian and imperial official in the city, called for divine protection in his sermons and prayers. In one of his homilies, he described the helplessness of the inhabitants before the invaders: "The boats went past the city showing their crews with swords raised as if threatening the city with death by the sword, and all human hope ebbed away from men, and the city was moored only with recourse to the divine." The intruders were gone by August 4, when Photius attributed the city's miraculous survival to the protection of the Mother of God. This grew into a legend that laid the basis for the later celebration of the Feast of the Protection of the Mother of God, or Pokrova. Ironically, the feast never took hold in Byzantium but became extremely popular in Ukraine, Russia, and Belarus—the lands from which the Vikings had come to attack Constantinople.

THE VIKINGS WHO attacked the Byzantine capital in the summer of 860 were hardly unknown to Photius and his contemporaries. The patriarch called them Rus', like the members of the Rus' embassy of 838. He even stated that they were subjects of Byzantium but left it to subsequent generations of scholars to figure out the details. Who were they? The search for an answer has spanned the last two and a half centuries, if not longer. Most scholars today believe that the word "Rus'" has Scandinavian roots. Byzantine authors, who wrote in Greek, most probably borrowed it from the Slavs, who in turn borrowed it from the Finns, who used the term "Ruotsi" to denote the Swedes—in Swedish, the word meant "men who row." And row they did. First across the Baltic Sea into the Gulf of Finland, then on through Lakes Ladoga, Ilmen, and Beloozero to the upper reaches of the Volga—the river that later became an embodiment of Russia and at the time formed an essential part of the Saracen (Muslim) route to the Caspian Sea and the Arab lands.

The Rus' Vikings, a conglomerate of Norwegian, Swedish, and probably Finnish Norsemen, first came to eastern Europe mainly as traders, not conquerors, as there was little to pillage in the forests of the region. The real treasures lay in the Middle East, beyond the lands through which they needed only the right of passage. But judging by what we know about the Rus' Vikings, they never thought of trade and war—or, rather, trade and violence—as incompatible. After all, they had to defend themselves en route, since the local tribes did not welcome their presence. And the trade in which they engaged involved coercion, for they dealt not only in forest products— furs and honey—but also in slaves. To obtain them, the Vikings had to establish some kind of control over the local tribes and collect as tribute products that they could ship along the Saracen route. They exchanged these in the Caspian markets for Arab silver dirhams, troves of which subsequent archeologists have discovered. They punctuate the Viking trade route from Scandinavia to the Caspian Sea.

The problem was that the Vikings were not the first to invent this business model. They faced competition from the Khazars, whose rulers controlled the Volga and Don trade, collecting tribute from the local tribes. The Khazars also had Byzantium on their side, and some scholars believe that the Rus' attacked Constantinople in retaliation for the Khazars' construction of the fortress of Sarkel with the help of the empire. Located on the left bank of the Don River, Sarkel gave the Khazars complete control of trade on the Sea of Azov. The Khazars also had an outpost in Kyiv, on the Dnieper trade route, but their rule did not extend to the forest areas west of the river, and they would soon lose the control of Kyiv as well.

The Primary Chronicle, the source of most of our knowledge about the period, tells of a struggle for the city that took place in 882 among different groups of Vikings. Two of their chieftains, Askold and Dir (the gravesite of the former can still be visited in Kyiv), were killed by Helgi, known to the chronicler as Oleh. He captured the city, allegedly on behalf of the house of Rorik (called Rurik in the chronicle), which already ruled over Novgorod (Velikii Novgorod) in today's northern Russia. Although one can and should question many details of this story, including its shaky chronology (the chronicler reconstructs much of it on the basis of later Byzantine sources), the legend probably echoes the actual consolidation of power by one group of Vikings in the forested regions of eastern Europe between present-day Velikii Novgorod and Kyiv.

Most of the existing literature refers to this region as lands along the trade route "from the Varangians to the Greeks," but recent research suggests that if such a route really existed, it did not begin to function before the second half of the tenth century, and some parts of it were more active than others. Some scholars prefer instead to speak of a Dnieper–Black Sea route. If the Vikings were not the first to use that shorter route, they certainly revived it when they began to encounter increasing problems along the Volga "Saracen route." In the course of the previous century, internal turmoil in the Khazar realm had rendered the Volga route unsafe. Around the same time, the Arab advance in the Mediterranean disrupted Byzantine trade with southern Europe. The Khazars tried to help their Byzantine allies (and themselves) by serving as intermediaries in Constantinople's trade with the Middle East, now carried on by way of the Black and Azov Seas. The northern trade route took on new importance for the Greeks, probably greater than at any time since the days of Herodotus. By this time, the main products being supplied to the south were no longer cereal crops from the Ukrainian forest-steppe but slaves, honey, wax, and furs obtained from forested areas farther north. The most precious product that the Vikings brought back was silk. The Rus' Vikings secured their trade privileges in Constantinople by concluding treaties with Byzantium, first in 911 and then in 944.

The Byzantine emperor Constantine VII Porphyrogenitus explained in his *De administrando imperio*, written ca. 950, soon after the conclusion of the second treaty, that the merchandise came from Slavic tribes controlled by the Vikings. "When the month of November begins," wrote the emperor, "their chiefs together with all the Rus' at once leave Kyiv and go off on the *poliuddia*, which means 'rounds,' that is, to the Slavic regions of the Vervians and Dragovichians and Krivichians and Severians and the rest of the Slavs who are tributaries of the Rus'." While some tribes obliged, others rebelled. The Derevlianians, who lived on the Right Bank of the Dnieper and had once controlled Kyiv, paid the Vikings a tribute of "one marten skin apiece."

But after the tribute increased from one year to the next, the Derevlianians eventually revolted.

THE PRIMARY CHRONICLE'S description of the Derevlianian revolt and its subsequent suppression gives us an early opportunity to look into the Kyivan world, which Viking princes dominated in the tenth century.

According to the Primary Chronicle, the Derevlianian rebels attacked and killed Helgi's successor, named Ingvar, known as Ihor to the Kyivan chronicler. "The Derevlianians heard that he was . . . approaching, and consulted with Mal, their prince, saying, 'If a wolf come among the sheep, he will take away the whole flock one by one, unless he be killed. If we do not thus kill him now, he will destroy us all,'" wrote the chronicler in explanation of the revolt. The Derevlianians did as they had planned and killed Ingvar. Then they did something even more audacious. The mastermind of the coup, the Derevlianian prince Mal, proposed marriage to Ingvar's widow, Helga, whom, given her importance in Slavic and particularly Ukrainian historical tradition, we shall call by the Ukrainian form of her name, Olha (Russian: Olga). The chronicler explained that Mal made the overture to gain control over Ingvar's young son, Sviatoslav (Scandinavian: Sveinald).

This story indicates that the Viking retinues and the local Slavic elites clashed not only over the issue of tribute but also over the Vikings' control of trade and of the whole realm. Mal clearly wanted to take Ingvar's place as a ruler, not simply as the husband of Olha. But Olha tricked Mal by inviting him and his people to her Kyiv castle, only to burn them alive, allegedly in the boat in which they had arrived. Then she invited another group of matchmakers from among the Derevlianian elite and killed them as well, this time in a bathhouse. She told her guests that she would not see them until they had washed themselves. The Derevlianians evidently had no idea what a Scandinavian steam bath was. It soon became very hot. They were all scalded to death.

The fact that boats and bathhouses were important elements of Norse culture reveals the Scandinavian roots of this legend. The Rus' and Scandinavian burial ritual involved the burning of the deceased in a boat. But the story also hints at the weakness of the Vikings' power in Kyiv. Before burning Mal alive, Olha seems to have made certain that the people of Kyiv would take her side. On her advice, the unsuspecting Derevlianians refused to ride or walk to Olha's castle, demanding instead that the locals take them there in a boat, which upset the Kyivans. According to the chronicle, they lamented,

"Slavery is our lot." In all, before Olha took to the field against the Derevlian-ian army, she used trickery to destroy three groups of their leaders. Still un-able to defeat the rest of the tribal army and take their stronghold, she burned it, resorting once again to subterfuge. That would have been unnecessary if the Vikings had had an overwhelming majority in Kyiv.

PRINCESS OLHA'S SON, Sviatoslav, is the first Kyivan ruler of whom we have a physical description. (The Kyivan chronicler writes that Olha was not only intelligent but also beautiful, but we have no surviving description of her.) Leo the Deacon, a Byzantine chronicler who met Sviatoslav, described the Rus' prince, who took over from his mother in the early 960s. According to Leo, Sviatoslav was a broad-shouldered man of medium height. He shaved his beard but had a bushy moustache. His head was shaved as well, with one lock of hair untouched—a sign of his noble origin. The prince had blue eyes and a short, wide nose. He dressed in simple white clothing. His one golden earring, embellished with a ruby and two pearls, was the only sign of his high status. The meeting took place in July 971, when Leo accompanied his em-peror, John Tzimisces, on a military campaign in Bulgaria.

Sviatoslav's meeting with the Byzantine emperor was a low point rather than a pinnacle of his military career, which began with the war on the Derevlianians waged by his mother, Olha. When she finally brought her troops into open battle with the rebellious tribesmen, the young Sviatoslav was given the honor of starting the fighting. "When both forces were ready for combat," wrote the chronicler, "Sviatoslav cast his spear against the Derevlianians. But the spear barely cleared the horse's ears and struck against his leg, for the prince was but a child. Then Sveinald and Asmund [Viking commanders of Olha's army] said, 'The prince has already begun battle; press on, vassals, after the prince.'" Sviatoslav grew into a warrior, sharing with his retinue the hardships of military life and using his horse's saddle as a pillow while on campaign. Leo the Deacon spotted him rowing a boat with his men, distinguishable from them only by his cleaner clothes.

Sviatoslav's brief reign—he assumed full power in the early 960s and died in battle in 972, probably only thirty years of age—saw a number of success-ful military campaigns. According to some scholars, in the second half of the tenth century the Rus' Vikings switched from trade to war to offset the losses they suffered once the mines of Central Asia, exhausted after decades of ex-ploitation, stopped producing silver and the eastern European trade fueled by the Central Asian silver coins came to an end. In the first of his military campaigns, Sviatoslav took control of the last of the East Slavic tribes still ruled by the Khazars. These were the Viatichians, dwelling in the Oka River basin on lands that include the environs of today's Moscow. After accomplishing that task, Sviatoslav moved against the Khazars themselves. In a series of campaigns, he captured Sarkel, the Khazar fortress in the Don region, and turned it into a Rus' outpost, then pillaged Itil, the capital of the Khazar kaganate, on the Volga, and defeated the Volga Bulgars, who were vassals of the Khazars. The kaganate was no more. The contest between the Khazars and the Vikings for the loyalty of the Slavic tribes was all but over. They all now recognized the supremacy of Kyiv.

But Sviatoslav did not spend much time in his capital. He actually wanted to move it to the Danube. This idea came to him during a Balkan campaign that he launched against Byzantium in the late 960s. The chronicler reports that Sviatoslav wanted to move his capital to the Danube because most of the goods coming from his lands were transported along that river. Rather than a mere landgrab, he probably had in mind the establishment of control over one of the main trade routes of the era. Two of his predecessors on the Kyivan throne, Helgi (Oleh) and Ingvar, had obtained preferential treatment for Rus' merchants trading on the rich Byzantine markets. Legend has it that Helgi even managed to nail his shield to the gates of Constantinople. He did not take the city but allegedly got valuable trade concessions from the emperor.

Sviatoslav became involved in the Balkans on behalf of the Byzantines, who paid him to attack their enemies, the Balkan Bulgars. Sviatoslav destroyed the Bulgar army and occupied a good part of their country. The Byzantines believed that he was supposed to turn that territory over to them, but Sviatoslav disagreed. Thus, they bribed the Pechenegs, a new nomadic tribe on the Pontic steppes, to attack Kyiv. Sviatoslav had to go home to deal with the Pechenegs, but by 969 he was back in Bulgaria. In the following year he besieged the Byzantine city of Adrianople, today's Edirne, less than 150 miles from Constantinople. The court was in a panic, and Emperor John Tzimisces sent one of his best commanders to lift the siege. The emperor soon marched to Bulgaria himself and surrounded whatever remained of Sviatoslav's army. Sviatoslav had to withdraw.

Leo the Deacon witnessed Sviatoslav's first and last meeting with John Tzimisces. In return for a promise not to make war on the empire, to leave Bulgaria, and to renounce any claims to the southern Crimea, the emperor granted Sviatoslav and his people safe passage home. This was Sviatoslav's last military campaign. He died on the way back to Kyiv when he and his troops disembarked from their boats near the Dnieper rapids, a forty-mile stretch of cataracts that is now under water but presented a major obstacle to navigation until the construction of a huge dam in the early 1930s. The travelers had no choice but to portage around some of the biggest rapids. "When the Rus' come with their ships to the barrages of the river and cannot pass through unless they lift their ships off the river and carry them past by portaging them on their shoulders, then the men of this nation of the Pechenegs set upon them, and, as they cannot do two things at once, they are easily routed and cut to pieces," wrote Constantine VII Porphyrogenitus less than a quarter century before Sviatoslav's death.

The need to disembark near the rapids probably gave Pecheneg horsemen their chance to attack and kill Sviatoslav. The Pecheneg chieftain allegedly made a drinking cup out of his skull. Rumor had it that John Tzimisces tipped off the Pechenegs and was behind the attack. But Sviatoslav's death on the steppe bank of the Dnieper indicated a larger problem that neither he nor his predecessors had been able to resolve. Despite all the power they amassed in Kyiv and over the vast forests to the north of the city, they were unable to establish not only full control of the steppelands but even safe passage across them. This made it impossible for the Kyivan rulers to secure the northern shores of the Black Sea and take full advantage of the opportunities, both economic and cultural, offered by the Mediterranean world. Defeating the Khazars was not enough to open the way to the sea.

Historians have referred to Sviatoslav as the "last Viking." Indeed, his military expeditions and his idea of abandoning Kyiv and moving to a new capital to control trade between the Byzantine Empire and the cities of central Europe suggest that he had little interest in administering the realm built by his predecessors and expanded through his own military efforts. Sviatoslav's death marked the end of the Viking Age in Ukraine. While the Varangian retinues would still play an important role in Kyivan history, Sviatoslav's successors would try to reduce their dependence on the foreign warriors. They would focus on ruling the realm they possessed, not on conquering another one somewhere else.

CHAPTER 4

BYZANTIUM NORTH

F ROM THE VERY first reports about the Rus' princes on the Dnieper River, we hear of their attraction to the Byzantine Empire. The same thing that had attracted the Huns and Goths to Rome drew the Viking merchant warriors to the Byzantine capital, Constantinople: earthly riches, along with power and prestige. The Vikings never set out to topple Byzantium, but they tried to get as close to the empire and its capital as possible, launching a number of expeditions to capture Constantinople.

Sviatoslav's death in 972 closed an important period in the history of Rus' and its relations with its powerful southern neighbor. To the next two generations of Kyivan rulers, association with Constantinople was no less desirable than it had been for Sviatoslav. But Sviatoslav's successors were concerned not only with money and commerce but also with the power, prestige, and high culture emanating from Byzantium. Instead of conquering Constantinople on the Bosphorus, as their predecessors had attempted to do, they decided to reproduce it on the Dnieper. This turn in Rus' relations with the Byzantine Greeks and the new expectations of the Kyivan princes came to the fore during the rule of Sviatoslav's son Volodymyr and the latter's son Yaroslav. The two ran the Kyivan realm for more than half a century and are often credited with turning it into a true medieval state—one with a more or less clearly defined territory, system of government, and, last but not least, ideology. Much of the latter came from Byzantium.

As a prince of Kyiv, Sviatoslav's son, Volodymyr, was less bellicose and ambitious than his father but turned out to be more successful in achieving his goals. Fifteen years old when his father died near the Dnieper rapids,

Volodymyr had brothers who wanted the throne for themselves, and a new wave of Scandinavian arrivals eased his path to power. Before wresting the Kyivan throne from one of his brothers, Volodymyr spent more than five years as a refugee in Scandinavia, the ancestral homeland of his clan. He returned to Rus' with a new Viking army. The Kyivan chronicler tells us that after Volodymyr took Kyiv, his soldiers asked for payment. Volodymyr promised to give them tribute from the local tribes but was unable to deliver. Instead, he recruited the Viking commanders as his local administrators in forts that he built on the steppe frontier, allowing the rest of the army to engage in an expedition against Byzantium. He also ordered his people not to let that army into their towns and to prevent them from returning.

Viking troops remained essential to Volodymyr's army after his assumption of the throne, but the account in the Primary Chronicle reflects the serious tension between him and his retinue that characterized his reign. This "second coming" of the Vikings was very different from the first. Now they came not as traders or rulers but as mercenaries in the service of a ruler who was of Viking origin himself but whose prime allegiance was to his princely realm. Volodymyr did not dream of moving his capital to the Danube. He was satisfied with the opportunities available on the Dnieper. Volodymyr would eventually do away not only with the enormous power of the princely retinue but also with the influence of the tribal elites. He countered them by appointing his sons and members of his household to run different parts of his empire, setting the stage for the emergence of future principalities under the auspices of Kyiv.

The Viking Age had indeed come to an end in Rus', the land named after the Vikings. That change found its way into the pages of the Primary Chronicle. Its authors usually described the princely retinue as consisting of Vikings, local Slavs, and Ugro-Finns. The collective name for the first two groups was Rus', but, as time went on, it was applied to members of the prince's retinue in general, then to his subjects in all walks of life, and eventually to the land he ruled. The terms "Rus'" and "Slav" became interchangeable in the course of the tenth and eleventh centuries. One gets that impression not only from the Primary Chronicle but also from Byzantine reports of the era.

VOLODYMYR TOOK THE throne in 980. He spent the first decade of his rule on warfare, ensuring that the realm created by his predecessor stayed together. Following in Sviatoslav's footsteps, he again defeated the Khazars and the

Volga Bulgars, reasserted his power over the Viatichians in the Oka basin, and pushed westward to the Carpathians, taking a number of fortresses from the Poles, including the town of Premyshl (Przemyśl) on today's Polish-Ukrainian border. His main concern, however, was the southern frontier, where the Rus' settlements were under continual attack by the Pechenegs and other nomadic tribes. Volodymyr strengthened border defenses by building fortifications along the local rivers, including the Sula and the Trubizh. He settled those areas with prisoners of war and subjects from other parts of the realm. Rus', born of conquest, now sought stability by defending its borders instead of attacking the frontiers of other states.

Under Volodymyr's rule, Kyiv's relations with Byzantium were also changing. Whereas his predecessor on the Kyivan throne, Helgi, allegedly had sent troops against Byzantium to obtain trade preferences, and Sviatoslav did the same to acquire new territory in the Balkans, Volodymyr invaded the Crimea in the spring of 989 in pursuit of marriage, if not love. He besieged the Byzantine town of Chersonesus, demanding the hand of the sister of Emperor Basil II. A few years earlier, the emperor had asked Volodymyr for military assistance, promising the hand of his sister Anna in return. Volodymyr sent his troops to help up the emperor. But Basil was in no hurry to fulfill his promise. After receiving this slap in the face, Volodymyr refused to turn the other cheek and instead attacked the empire. His tactic worked. Alarmed by news of the fall of Chersonesus, Basil dispatched his sister Anna to the Crimea. She arrived with a retinue that included numerous Christian clerics.

Volodymyr's request for marriage was granted in return for an assurance that the barbarian chieftain (as the ruler of Kyiv was regarded in Constantinople) would accept Christianity. Volodymyr went along. His baptism would start the process of the Christianization of Kyivan Rus' and open a new chapter in the region's history. Once the wedding party had moved back to Kyiv, Volodymyr removed the pantheon of pagan gods, including the most powerful of them—Perun, the god of thunder—from a hill above the Dnieper and put the Christian clergymen to work baptizing the population of Kyiv. The Christianization of Rus' had begun—a long and difficult process that would take centuries to complete.

Our main source on the baptism of Rus', the Kyivan chronicler, writes that Muslim Bulgars, Jewish Khazars, Christian Germans representing the pope, and a Greek scholar who spoke on behalf of Byzantine Christianity, the religion that Volodymyr chose, had all importuned Volodymyr. The story of the choice of faith as told in the Primary Chronicle is of course naïve in many ways. But it reflects certain real alternatives facing the Kyivan ruler, for he indeed did the picking and choosing. Volodymyr chose the religion of the strongest country in the region, in which the emperor was no less important an ecclesiastical figure—more important, in fact—than the patriarch. By choosing Christianity, he gained the prestige of marrying into an imperial family, which promptly elevated the status of his house and realm. Volodymyr's choice of Christian name sheds additional light on his reasons for accepting Christianity. He took the same name as the emperor, Basil, indicating that in Byzantium he had found a political and religious model to emulate at home. A generation later, Kyivan intellectuals such as Metropolitan Ilarion would compare him and his baptism of Rus' to Emperor Constantine and his role in establishing Christianity as the official religion of the Roman Empire.

To be sure, the Byzantine political and ecclesiastical elite helped Volodymyr make the "right choice." They were unhappy with the marriage but not with the conversion. The Byzantines had begun sending missionaries to the region soon after the Rus' Vikings attacked Constantinople in 860. Back then, Patriarch Photius of Constantinople, the same clergyman who left us the description of the Viking attack, had sent one of his best students, Cyril of Thessalonica, to the Crimea and then to the Khazar kaganate. Along with his brother Methodius, Cyril devised the Glagolitic alphabet to transcribe Christian texts into the Slavic languages. The two men subsequently became known as the apostles to the Slavs and gained sainthood. Attempts to convert Kyivan rulers were undertaken long before Volodymyr's conversion, as attested by the story of his grandmother, Olha, who became the first known Christian ruler and the first Christian woman in Kyiv named Helen. Apart from propagating Christianity, the Byzantine elites began to gain influence over the "barbaric" rulers and peoples, who had no fancy genealogies and little in the way of sophisticated culture but a great deal of destructive power.

After Volodymyr's conversion, the patriarch of Constantinople created the Metropolitanate of Rus', one of few ecclesiastical provinces named after its population and not the city where the bishop or metropolitan would reside. The patriarch reserved for himself the right to appoint metropolitans to head the Rus' church—most of them would be Greeks. The metropolitan in turn controlled the appointment of bishops, most of whom would come from the ranks of the local elite. The first monasteries were established, using a Byzantine statute. Church Slavonic, the first literary language of Kyivan Rus', initially functioned predominantly as a translation tool, making Greek texts understandable to local elites. Volodymyr issued regulations defining the rights and privileges of the clergy and gave one-tenth of his income to the church. Christianity in Kyivan Rus' began at the top and moved slowly down the social ladder, spreading from center to periphery along rivers and trade routes. In some remote areas, especially northeastern Rus', pagan priests resisted the new religion for centuries, and Kyivan missionaries who ventured there would end up dead as late as the twelfth century.

Volodymyr's choice would have a profound impact on his realm and on the history of eastern Europe as a whole. Instead of continuing warfare with Byzantium, the new Rus' polity was entering into an alliance with the only surviving part and continuator of the Roman Empire and thereby opening itself to the political and cultural influences of the Mediterranean world. It would prove fateful that Volodymyr not only brought Rus' into the Christian world but also made it part of Eastern Christianity. Many of the consequences are as important today as they were at the turn of the second millennium.

VOLODYMYR BROUGHT CHRISTIANITY to Rus', but it fell to his successors to define what that would mean for the politics, culture, and international relations of the realm and to secure a place for Rus' in the Christian community of nations led by the Byzantine emperor. None of Volodymyr's successors was more important in making those definitions than his son Yaroslav. While Yaroslav's grandfather, Sviatoslav, became known in historiography as "the Brave," and his father, Volodymyr, acquired the designation "the Great," Yaroslav gained renown as "the Wise." He could also have been named "Lawgiver" or "Builder," indicating that the main accomplishments of his rule, which lasted well over a quarter century, from 1019 to 1054, were not won on the battlefield but attained in the realm of peace and culture, state and nation building.

One of Yaroslav's enduring legacies is his large-scale construction. "Yaroslav built the great citadel at Kyiv, near which stands the Golden Gate," wrote the Kyivan chronicler. The Golden Gate was the main entrance in the new ramparts that the prince caused to be built around the area known to archeologists as Yaroslav's town. One can hardly overlook the parallel between Yaroslav's Golden Gate and that of Constantinople, which served as a triumphal arch and official entrance to the imperial capital. Kyiv's Golden Gate was built of stone (as was part of the wall surrounding the castle), and its foundations are still visible. A replica of the old gate was constructed on those foundations in the early 1980s.

The most striking of Yaroslav's construction projects was the Cathedral of St. Sophia, which stood outside the city walls. The cathedral is an impressive building that features five naves, five apses, three galleries, and thirteen cupolas. The walls are built of granite and quartzite, separated by rows of bricks; inside, the walls and ceilings are embellished with mosaics and frescos. Construction was completed no later than the year 1037. There is a consensus among scholars that Yaroslav not only took the name of the cathedral and the main elements of its design from the Hagia Sophia in Constantinople but also brought its architects, engineers, and masons from the Byzantine Empire. He built not just city walls and churches but a capital for his realm modeled on the most beautiful and powerful city that any of the Rus' had ever seen: Constantinople.

The Kyivan chronicler credited Yaroslav with promoting learning and scholarship in addition to building churches and supporting the Christian religion. "He applied himself to books and read them continually, day and night," states the Primary Chronicle. "He assembled many scribes and translated from Greek into Slavic. He wrote and collected many books through which true believers are instructed and enjoy religious education." Yaroslav's rule marked the beginning of literacy in Kyivan Rus', which adopted Church Slavonic, written in the alphabet specifically created by Saints Cyril and Methodius for the Slavs in order to translate texts written in Greek. Teachers, texts, and the language itself came to Rus' from Bulgaria, whose rulers had accepted Christianity earlier than the Kyivan princes.

Under Yaroslav's rule, as the chronicler points out, texts were not only read but also translated in Kyiv. Original writings were soon being produced as well. The "Sermon on Law and Grace," written sometime between 1037 and 1054 by Metropolitan Ilarion, whom Yaroslav appointed, is one of the first examples of such original work. The sermon helped bring the recently Christianized Rus' into the family of Christian nations, comparing Prince Volodymyr to Emperor Constantine, as noted earlier. Another important development was the beginning of historical writing in Kyiv. Most scholars believe that the first Kyivan chronicle was produced in the 1030s, during Yaroslav's reign, probably in St. Sophia Cathedral. Only later did the work of chronicle writing move to the Kyivan Cave Monastery, which, modeled on Byzantine monasteries, traces its origins to the end of Yaroslav's rule.

If Kyiv emulated Constantinople, other cities of the realm emulated Kyiv. That is how the construction of a new Church of St. Sophia began in Polatsk and in Novgorod (where a wooden church of that name had stood before). That is also how the town of Vladimir in northeastern Rus' later acquired its own Golden Gate. More important was the spread of literacy and learning to the regional centers, breaking early Kyiv's monopoly on the study of texts and historical writing. Novgorod literati soon began to write history as well, using the chronicle originally compiled in Kyiv as a basis. It is from a Novgorod chronicler that we learn about Yaroslav the Wise being not only a lover of books and a builder of castles and churches but also a lawgiver.

After coming to power in Kyiv, Yaroslav rewarded Novgorod, where he had served as prince on behalf of his father, Volodymyr, by giving the city freedoms it had not previously enjoyed. This was a token of appreciation for assistance in Yaroslav's struggle for the Kyivan throne. The Novgorod chronicler associated that grant of special rights and privileges with Yaroslav's compilation of a law code known as the Rus' Justice, a codification of common law that had enormous impact on the legal system of Kyivan Rus' and its successor states. We do not know whether the Rus' Justice was indeed compiled under Yaroslav, and chances are that the task was accomplished later, under his successors. But it certainly could not have been done before Yaroslav—there were simply no educated people capable of such an undertaking prior to his rule.

FOLLOWING IN THE footsteps of Constantinople and emulating Byzantine emperors meant achieving a degree of not only legitimacy but also independence that was bound to vex the Greeks of Constantinople. We know of at least two occasions on which Yaroslav did not shy away from showing his independence vis-à-vis the empire. The first was his elevation of a Rus' native, Ilarion, author of the acclaimed "Sermon on Law and Grace," instead of a Greek prelate sent from Constantinople, to the office of Rus' metropolitan. In this case, Yaroslav was emulating the role played by Byzantine emperors in their church, but his decision was also a challenge to the patriarch of Constantinople, who reserved for himself the right to appoint Rus' metropolitans. The elevation of Ilarion was controversial within the Rus' church itself, and Kyiv reverted to the old practice after Yaroslav's death in 1054. Constantinople sent Ilarion's successor to the Rus' capital.

Yaroslav presented another direct challenge to Constantinople in 1043, when a Rus' flotilla headed by one of his sons appeared near Constantinople and demanded money, threatening to attack the city otherwise. The reason for this return to Viking ways of doing business with Byzantium is not clear. Were Yaroslav's efforts to build Constantinople in Kyiv too costly, and was he running out of funds? We can only speculate. It may have been a sign of dissatisfaction with something that the Byzantines had done earlier or a reminder that Rus' was not a power to take lightly. Whatever the reason, the Greeks refused to pay and preferred to fight. The Rus' flotilla defeated the Byzantine fleet but was almost destroyed by a storm and came back to Kyiv empty-handed. Viking practices no longer paid off.

If one treats Byzantine efforts to convert Rus' to Christianity, which began immediately after the first Rus' attack on Constantinople in 860, as a way of ending such attacks and ensuring peaceful relations with the barbaric Rus', then such efforts clearly attained their purpose during the rule of Yaroslav. In general, unlike his predecessors, Yaroslav maintained peaceful and even friendly relations with Byzantium. But religion was hardly the main reason for the Kyivan prince's largely peaceful relations with the empire. Under Yaroslav, expansion was no longer the main goal of the Rus' princes. Keeping and governing what they had was their priority, and Byzantium as an ally and source of knowledge and prestige could offer much more than Byzantium an enemy.

Under Yaroslav's rule, Rus' became a full-fledged member of the Christian community of nations. Later historians would call him the "father-in-law of Europe" because he married his sisters and daughters to European heads of state. His father's acceptance of Christianity from Byzantium and the subsequent importation of cultural influences from Constantinople to Rus' soil were important preconditions for that development. Unlike his father, Yaroslav was not wed to a Byzantine princess, but his son Vsevolod was—to a daughter of the Byzantine emperor Constantine IX Monomachus. Yaroslav himself married a daughter of Olaf Eriksson, the king of Sweden—a reflection of the Viking origins of the dynasty. His daughter Yelyzaveta (Elizabeth) was the consort of Harald Hardrada, the king of Norway. His son Iziaslav married a sister of the Polish king Casimir, who was already married to one of Yaroslav's sisters. Yaroslav's daughter Anastasia became the spouse of Andrew the White of Hungary, and another daughter, Anna, married Henry I of France.

Whatever the political reasons behind these marriages, in purely cultural terms they benefited the European rulers more than they did the princes of Kyiv. Anna's case shows this best. Unlike her husband, Anna knew how to read and sign her name, an indication that the Kyivan chronicler's praise of Yaroslav for his love of books and promotion of learning was hardly excessive.

CHAPTER 5

THE KEYS TO KYIV

THE TERM "KYIVAN RUS'," like "Byzantium," is of later origin—contemporaries of those realms did not use these names. Nineteenth-century scholars came up with the name "Kyivan Rus'." Today the term denotes the polity with its center in Kyiv that existed between the tenth and mid-thirteenth centuries, when it disintegrated under the onslaught of the Mongols.

Who is the legitimate heir to the legacy of Kyivan Rus', and who holds the proverbial keys to Kyiv? These questions have preoccupied much of the historical writing about Rus' for the last 250 years. Initially, the debate focused on the origins of the Rus' princes—were they Scandinavians or Slavs?—and then, from the mid-nineteenth century, it broadened to include the Russo-Ukrainian contest for the legacy of Kyivan Rus'. The twentieth-century battle over the earthly remains of Yaroslav the Wise, whose rule the previous chapter discussed at length, highlights the intensity of that contest.

Yaroslav died on February 28, 1054, and was buried in the Cathedral of St. Sophia, which he had built. His earthly remains were placed in a white marble sarcophagus decorated with carvings of the Christian cross and Mediterranean plants, including palms, which were by no means native to Kyivan Rus'. According to one theory, the sarcophagus—a stone embodiment of Byzantine cultural imperialism—had once been the final resting place of a Byzantine notable but was brought to Kyiv either by marauding Vikings or by enterprising Greeks. The sarcophagus is still preserved in the cathedral, but the remains of Yaroslav the Wise disappeared from Kyiv in 1943, during the German occupation of the city. By some accounts, they ended up in the hands of Ukrainian Orthodox hierarchs in the United States and were spotted in Manhattan after the war. Some suspect that they may now be in the Church of the Holy Trinity in Brooklyn.

What could account for the transfer of Prince Yaroslav's remains all the way to the Western Hemisphere? The answer has nothing to do with American cultural imperialism but is closely associated with the Ukrainian claim to the legacy of Kyivan Rus'. Ukrainian clergymen leaving their homeland removed the relics so as to prevent them from falling into the hands of the advancing Soviet army. Concern that if returned to Kyiv, they might end up in Russia explains enough the continuing refusal of the custodians of the Brooklyn church to discuss the issue of Yaroslav's remains with representatives of the Ukrainian government.

Both Ukrainians and Russians claim Yaroslav the Wise as one of their eminent medieval rulers, and his image appears on the banknotes of both countries. The Ukrainian bill depicts Yaroslav with a Ukrainian-style moustache in the tradition of Prince Sviatoslav and the Ukrainian Cossacks. On the Russian note, we see a monument to him as the legendary founder of the Russian city of Yaroslavl, first mentioned in a chronicle seventeen years after his death. The Russian bill shows Yaroslav with a beard in the tradition of Ivan the Terrible and the Muscovite tsars of his era.

WAS YAROSLAV A Russian or a Ukrainian ruler, or, if neither, then what could his "true" identity and that of his subjects possibly be? It is best to begin the discussion of these questions by focusing on the decades following his death. Yaroslav's demise closed one era in the history of the Kyivan Rus'—that of the consolidation of the realm—and opened another in which it followed in the footsteps of the Carolingian Empire. Less than a century after the death of its founder, Charlemagne (814), that empire disintegrated into a number of smaller states. The reasons for the decline and fall of the two empires were not very different. They included persistent problems of succession to the throne, struggles within the ruling dynasty, the rise of local political and economic centers, and inability to deal effectively with external threats and interventions. The long-term consequence of their collapse was the rise of polities often regarded as precursors of modern nations: France and Germany in the Carolingian case; Ukraine and Russia in that of Kyivan Rus'.

Prince Yaroslav, wise man that he was, foresaw the troubles that would besiege his family after his demise. He probably remembered how long and bloody his own ascent to ultimate power had been. It began in 1015 with the death of his father, Volodymyr, and ended more than twenty years later, in 1036, when his brother Mstyslav, with whom he was forced to divide the realm, met his end. Between those two deaths there were many battles and conflicts, punctuated by the deaths of Yaroslav's numerous brothers. Two of them, Borys and Hlib, were deprived of the Kyivan throne but attained sainthood instead and are celebrated today as martyred princes. Some historians suspect Yaroslav of arranging their murders. One way or another, closer to the end of his life, he apparently wanted to avoid fratricidal struggle among his sons.

According to the Primary Chronicle, Yaroslav left a will in which he divided his realm among his sons, giving each a principality of his own. The throne of Kyiv, which would come not only with Kyivan and Novgorodian lands but also with supreme power over the other princes, was to go to the eldest brother. The others would rule under his patronage and supervision in their separate realms. It was assumed that the Kyivan throne would pass from elder brothers to younger ones until one generation of princes died out. The new generation would start the cycle again, beginning with the eldest son of the eldest brother. Most scholars question the authenticity of Yaroslav's will, but whether it existed or not, the text alleged to constitute such a will reflects the practice prevailing after Yaroslav's death.

Yaroslav had five surviving sons, four of whom are mentioned in the "will." Only three would taste supreme power after their father's demise. The Kyivan throne went to the eldest surviving son, Iziaslav, but he shared power with two of his brothers, who ruled in Chernihiv and Pereiaslav, two cities in close proximity to Kyiv. Together, they made up an informal triumvirate whose decisions were all but binding for the rest of the Rurikid princes—the Kyivan ruling dynasty that traced its roots to the legendary Rurik. The triumvirs dealt with challenges to their power by arresting one of their brothers who ruled over Polatsk (now in Belarus) and imprisoning him in Kyiv. Their capitals became the centers of what the Rus' chronicles call the Rus' Land.

The term was not entirely new. It had appeared in Metropolitan Ilarion's "Sermon on Law and Grace" and can thus be attributed to the times of Yaroslav the Wise. It attained its peak of popularity in the late eleventh and early twelfth centuries, when the triumvirs had already left the scene and their sons and nephews were trying to settle accounts between different branches of the family while fending off aggression from the south. Volodymyr Monomakh, a grandson of Yaroslav the Wise and the Byzantine emperor Constantine IX

Monomachus, made a career of professing and manifesting loyalty to the Rus' Land. A son of one of the triumvirs, he became the prince of Pereiaslav, a huge territory extending from the steppe borderlands in the south to the northeastern forests around Moscow settled by the rebellious tribe of Viatichians.

Monomakh's main concern was not the Viatichians, who resisted Christianization and occasionally killed Kyivan monks sent to enlighten them, but increased nomadic activity on the southern border of the principality. The moment the Rus' princes were able to curtail the Pechenegs (Yaroslav defeated them in 1036), new, more aggressive tribes appeared on the borders of the Kyivan realm. These were the Polovtsians, or Cumans, and by the end of the eleventh century they controlled a good part of the Eurasian steppe, from the Irtysh River in the east to the Danube in the west. The Rus' principalities could not deal with Polovtsian attacks on their own. They needed to join forces, and no one insisted on that more than the prince of Pereiaslav, Volodymyr Monomakh, whom a chronicler credited with organizing a number of successful expeditions against the Polovtsians.

Monomakh, a great promoter of the unity of the Rus' Land, initiated the reform of the system of princely succession. At a congress organized with Monomakh's help in the town of Liubech in 1097, the princes decided to get rid of the cumbersome, conflict-prone lateral (horizontal) system of succession introduced by Yaroslav the Wise. Instead of the sons and grandsons of the triumvirs rotating princely seats, trying eventually to get to Kyiv, each would rule in his own domain. Only descendants of Yaroslav's eldest son, Iziaslav, would succeed to the Kyivan throne. But the system failed to work in practice. Monomakh himself did not abide by it when he claimed the throne of Kyiv in 1113; nor did his successors. In less than forty years, between 1132 and 1169, eighteen rulers succeeded one another in the capital, four more than during the entire previous history of the Kyivan realm.

MOST OF THE new princes appeared in Kyiv as a result of coups or hostile takeovers. Everyone seemed to want Kyiv, and those who had a chance tried their luck. In 1169, however, the pattern was broken. That year, the army of one of the most powerful and ambitious Rus' princes, Andrei Bogoliubsky of the Vladimir-Suzdal principality in what is now Russia, took Kyiv. He did not show up himself, sending his son to fight the battle instead. Once they had captured the city, the victors plundered it for two days in succession. The prince refused to move to Kyiv and establish his capital there.

Bogoliubsky's preference for his own capital of Vladimir on the Kliazma River reflected changes taking place in twelfth-century Rus' politics, economics, and society. The major principalities on the periphery of the Kyivan world were growing richer and stronger at a time when constant internal strife beset Kyiv and the middle Dnieper region. The Halych principality in the foothills of the Carpathian Mountains, in what is now western Ukraine, engaged in trade with the Balkans along the Danube, conducted with the blessing of Constantinople. The princes there did not need the Dnieper route to prosper. In the Vladimir-Suzdal principality, Bogoliubsky successfully challenged the Bulgars' control of the Volga trade. Novgorod in the northwest was enriching itself through Baltic commerce. Kyiv and the Dnieper trade route were still there, and the volume of trade was actually growing despite the hostility of the Polovtsians, but the Dnieper route was no longer the only, or even the main, economic lifeline of the realm.

As the local princes grew richer and more powerful, they sought to assert their autonomy or outright independence from Kyiv. They had every reason to treat the lands inherited from their fathers and grandfathers—not the mythical Rus' Land around Kyiv, Chernihiv, and Pereiaslav—as the main objects of their loyalty. Andrei Bogoliubsky was among the first to do so. While his sack of Kyiv in 1169 left very deep scars in the memory of its inhabitants, he demonstrated other, no less obvious attempts to make himself an independent ruler. It all began with Andrei leaving Vyshhorod near Kyiv against the wishes of his father, Yurii Dolgoruky, and going to the northeast. Yurii, who had founded Moscow in 1147, represented an old way of thinking. A son of Monomakh, he carved the principality of Suzdal out of his patrimony and proceeded to expand and strengthen it. But his ultimate goal was the Kyivan throne, which he obtained by using his powers as prince of Suzdal. He died in office and was buried in a Kyivan church.

Dolgoruky's rebellious son wanted none of that. He moved the capital of his principality from Suzdal to Vladimir and did his best to turn it into Kyiv on the Kliazma. Andrei did not leave Vyshhorod empty-handed. He took with him a local icon of the Mother of God (Theotokos) that later gained fame as the Vladimir Mother of God. The removal of a religious relic from the Kyiv region to Vladimir is a perfect metaphor for Bogoliubsky's transfer of the symbolic power of the Rus' capital from south to north. That Kyiv served as the seat of the metropolitan of all Rus' enhanced its importance. Andrei, who had never considered his realm part of the Rus' Land, wanted a metropolitanate of his own. Around 1162, seven years before the sack of

Kyiv, he sent an embassy to Constantinople asking permission to install his own candidate as a new metropolitan. He was rebuffed—a major disappointment for the ambitious ruler, who had already made all the necessary preparations for the establishment of a metropolitan see. The newly built Golden-Domed Dormition Cathedral, not unlike the Golden-Domed Cathedral of St. Michael in Kyiv, was intended for a metropolitan but eventually housed a bishop.

Andrei Bogoliubsky's other project with unquestionable Kyivan roots was the building of a Golden Gate. Both the cathedral and the Golden Gate are still standing and serve as reminders of the Vladimir prince's ambitions. Like Yaroslav the Wise before him, Andrei emulated the existing imperial capital so as to assert his independence of it. Interestingly enough, Andrei's emulation went further than Yaroslav's: he not only transferred icons, ideas, and names for his architectural projects from Kyiv to Vladimir but also gave Kyivan names to local landmarks. Scholars note the naming of rivers in North-Eastern Rus after their Kyivan prototypes: Lybid, Pochaina, and Irpin.

Yaroslav the Wise and Andrei Bogoliubsky were both Rus' princes and probably shared a similar ethnocultural identity, but their construction projects show that they had different loyalties when it came to the Rus' lands. Yaroslav had a clear loyalty to Kyiv and to his vast realm extending from that city to Novgorod, which set him apart from Sviatoslav, who had no such bond, and Volodymyr Monomakh, whose primary allegiance was to the Rus' Land around Kyiv, Chernihiv, and Pereiaslav. Andrei differed from his predecessors in his attachment to his own patrimony within the larger Rus' realm. We should consider these changing loyalties of the Rus' princes in the context of the development of multiple Rus' identities as they emerge from the pages of the Rus' chronicles and legal texts.

THE AUTHORS OF the Primary Chronicle (the laborious task of recording events and commenting on them passed from one generation of monks to another) had to reconcile three different historical identities in their narrative: the Rus' identity of the Scandinavian rulers of Kyiv, the Slavic identity of the educated elites, and local tribal identity. While the Kyivan rulers and their subjects adopted the name Rus', the Slavic identity associated with that name, not the Scandinavian one, became the basis of their self-identification. Most subjects of the Rurikids, who ruled their realm from the Slavic heartland, were Slavs. More importantly, the dissemination of Slavic identity beyond the Kyiv region was closely associated with the acceptance of Christianity from Byzantium and the introduction of Church Slavonic as the language of the liturgy, sermons, and intellectual discourse of Rus'. Christianity appeared in both the Slavic and non-Slavic parts of the Kyivan realm in the garb of Slavic languages and Slavic culture. The more Rus' became Christian, the more it turned Slavic as well. The Kyivan chroniclers incorporated local history into the broader context of the development of the Balkan Slavs and, more broadly still, into the history of Byzantium and world Christendom.

On the local level, tribal identity gave way slowly but surely to identification with local principalities—the centers of military, political, and economic power associated with Kyiv. Chronicle references to the lands surrounding princely towns replaced references to indigenous tribes. Thus, the chronicler refers to the army that sacked Kyiv in 1169 as consisting of people from Smolensk instead of Radimichians, residents of Suzdal instead of Viatichians or Meria, and natives of Chernihiv instead of Siverians. There was a sense of the unity of all the lands under the rule of the Kyivan rulers, and despite conflicts and wars between Rurikid princes, the inhabitants of those lands were considered "ours," as opposed to foreigners and pagans. The key issue was recognition of the authority of the Rus' princes, and when some of the Turkic steppe nomads accepted that authority, they became referred to as "our pagans."

The political and administrative unification of the diverse tribal territories entailed the standardization of their social structure. At its very top were the princes of the Rurikid dynasty, more specifically the descendants of Yaroslav the Wise. Under them were members of the princely retinue—originally Vikings but also increasing numbers of Slavs who merged with local tribal elites to form the aristocratic stratum called the boyars. They were warriors, but in times of peace they administered the realm. The boyars were the main landholding class, and depending on the principality, they had greater or lesser influence on the actions of the prince. Church hierarchs and their servants were also among the privileged.

The rest of the population paid taxes to the princes. The townspeople, who included merchants and artisans, had some political power that they exercised at town meetings, where they decided matters of local governance. Occasionally, as in Kyiv, or quite regularly, as in Novgorod, such meetings influenced the succession of local princes. The peasants, who accounted for most of the population, had no political power. They were divided into free peasants and semifree serfs. The latter could lose their freedom, usually because of debts, and reclaim it once they had paid their debts off or after a certain period. Then there were the slaves—warriors or peasants captured in the course of military campaigns. The enslavement of warriors could be temporary, but that of peasants was permanent.

The penalties for different crimes set forth in the Rus' Justice, the legal code, best demonstrate the hierarchical structure of Kyivan Rus' society. As the lawgivers sought to abolish or limit blood feuds and fill princely coffers, they introduced monetary penalties to be paid to the princely treasury for killing different categories of people. The penalty for killing a member of the princely retinue or household (boyars) was eighty hryvnias; a freeman in the princely service, forty hryvnias; a tradesman, twelve hryvnias; a serf or a slave, five hryvnias; but it was quite legal to kill a slave if he had hit a free man. While different regions of Kyivan Rus' had diverse customary laws, the introduction of a common legal code helped make the realm more homogeneous, as did the spread of Christianity and Church Slavonic culture emanating from Kyiv. It would appear that this process was gaining ground just as the political fragmentation of the Kyivan realm was becoming all but inevitable: the explosion in the number of Rurikid princes who wanted their own principalities, the vastness of Kyivan realm, and the diverse geostrategic and economic interests of its regions all undermined a polity that managed, for a period, to unite the lands between the Baltic and Black Seas.

The change in the geopolitical aims of the Kyivan princes, from Yaroslav the Wise to Andrei Bogoliubsky, reflects the reduction of their political loyalties from the entire realm of Kyivan Rus' to a number of principalities defined by the term "Rus' Land" and eventually to peripheral principalities that grew strong enough to rival Kyiv in the twelfth and early thirteenth centuries. Historians look to those principality-based identities for the origins of the modern East Slavic nations. The Vladimir-Suzdal principality served as a forerunner of early modern Muscovy and, eventually, of modern Russia. Belarusian historians look to the Polatsk principality for their roots. And Ukrainian historians study the principality of Galicia-Volhynia to uncover the foundations of Ukrainian nation-building projects. But all those identities ultimately lead back to Kyiv, which gives Ukrainians a singular advantage: they can search for their origins without ever leaving their capital.

CHAPTER 6

PAX MONGOLICA

K YIVAN RUS', A polity with no generally recognized date of birth, has a
definite date of death. It occurred on December 7, 1240, when yet
another wave of invaders from the Eurasian steppes, the Mongols, conquered
the city of Kyiv.

In many ways, the Mongol invasion of Rus' marked the return of the
steppe as the dominant force in the region's politics, economy, and, to some
extent, culture. It put an end to the independence of the forest-based polities
and societies united for a time within the boundaries of Kyivan Rus' and
their ability to maintain ties with the Black Sea littoral (primarily the
Crimea) and the larger Mediterranean world. The Mongols turned back the
clock to the times of the Khazars, Huns, Sarmatians, and Scythians, when
steppe polities controlled the hinterland and benefited from trade routes to
the Black Sea ports. But the Mongols were a much more formidable military
force than any of their predecessors, who had managed at best to dominate
the western part of the Eurasian steppe, usually from the Volga basin in the
east to the Danube estuary in the west. The Mongols, at least initially, controlled all of it, from the Amur River and the steppes of Mongolia in the east
to the Danube and the Hungarian plain in the west. They established the
Pax Mongolica, a Mongol-controlled conglomerate of dependencies and
semidependencies of which the Rus' lands became a peripheral but important part.

The arrival of the Mongols ended the illusion of the political unity of the
Kyivan realm and put an end to the very real ecclesiastical unity of the Rus'
lands. The Mongols recognized two main centers of princely rule in Rus': the

principalities of Vladimir-Suzdal in today's Russia and Galicia-Volhynia in central and western Ukraine. Constantinople followed suit, dividing the Rus' metropolitanate into two parts. The political and ecclesiastical unity of the Kyiv-centered Rus' Land had disintegrated. The Galician and Vladimirian princes were now busy building Rus' lands of their own in their home territories. Although they claimed the same name, "Rus'," the two principalities followed very different geopolitical trajectories. Both had inherited their dynasties from Kyiv, which was also their source of Rus' law, literary language, and religious and cultural traditions. Both found themselves under alien Mongol rule. But the nature of their dependence on the Mongols differed.

In the lands of what is now Russia, ruled from Vladimir, the Mongol presence lasted until the end of the fifteenth century and eventually became known as the "Tatar yoke," named after Turkic-speaking tribes that had been part of the Mongol armies and stayed in the region after the not very numerous Mongols left. The view of Mongol rule as extremely long and severely oppressive has been a hallmark of traditional Russian historiography and continues to influence the interpretation of that period of eastern European history as a whole. In the twentieth century, however, proponents of the Eurasian school of Russian historical writing challenged this negative attitude toward Mongol rule. The history of the Mongol presence in Ukrainian territory provides additional correctives to the traditional condemnation of the "Tatar yoke." In Ukraine, ruled by the Galician and Volhynian princes, the Mongols were less intrusive and oppressive than they were in Russia. Their rule was also of shorter duration, effectively over by the mid-fourteenth century. This difference would have a profound impact on the fates of the two lands and the people who settled them.

THE SUDDEN MONGOL rise to world prominence began in the steppes of present-day Mongolia in 1206, when Temujin, a local tribal leader and commander, united a number of tribal confederations and assumed the title of khan of the Mongol hordes. Genghis Khan, as Temujin became known after his death, spent most of his first decade as supreme ruler of the Mongols fighting the Chinese, whose lands were the first he incorporated into his rapidly expanding empire. The next big prize was Central Asia, west of China on the Silk Road. Bukhara, Samarkand, and Kabul were all in Mongol hands by 1220. The Polovtsians and the Volga Bulgars were next, defeated (along with some Rus' princes) by 1223. At this time, the Mongols also invaded the

Crimea and took the fortress of Sudak, one of the key commercial centers on the Silk Road that was then part of the Polovtsian realm.

Before his death in 1227, Genghis Khan divided his realm among his sons and grandsons. The western lands, which then included Central Asia and the steppes east of the Volga, went to two of his grandsons. One of them, Batu Khan, was dissatisfied with his inheritance and pushed the borders of his realm farther west. That push became known as the Mongol invasion of Europe. In 1237 the Mongols besieged and took Riazan on the eastern frontier of the Vladimir-Suzdal principality. Vladimir, the principality's capital, fell in early February 1238. When its defenders took their last stand at the Dormition Cathedral built by Andrei Bogoliubsky, the Mongols set it on fire. Towns that defended themselves with particular determination were massacred wholesale. That was the case in Kozelsk, which fell after a siege of seven weeks. The Rus' princes resisted the Mongol onslaught as best they could, but, divided and disorganized, they were no match for the highly mobile and well-coordinated Mongol cavalry.

As the Mongols approached Kyiv in November 1240, their huge army made a dreadful impression on the defenders. "And nothing could be heard above the squeaking of his carts, the bawling of his [Batu's] innumerable camels, and the neighing of his herds of horses, and the Land of Rus' was full of enemies," wrote the chronicler. When the Kyivans refused to surrender, Batu brought in catapults to destroy the city walls, built of stones and logs in the times of Yaroslav the Wise. The citizens rushed to the Dormition Cathedral, the first stone church built by Volodymyr to celebrate his baptism. But the weight of the people and their belongings proved too heavy for the walls, which collapsed, burying the refugees. St. Sophia Cathedral survived but, like other city churches, was robbed of its precious icons and vessels. The victors pillaged the city; the few survivors remained in terror in the ruins of the once magnificent capital whose rulers had aspired to rival Constantinople. Giovanni da Pian del Carpine, an ambassador of Pope Innocent IV who passed through Kyiv in February 1246 on his way to the Mongol khan, left the following description of the consequences of the Mongol attack on the Kyiv Land: "When we were journeying through that land, we came across countless skulls and bones of dead men lying about on the ground."

Kyiv suffered a deadly blow from the Mongol assault and would not recover its former importance and prosperity for centuries. But the population of the Kyiv and Pereiaslav lands did not abandon the region altogether and did not move to the Volga and Oka basins, as some Russian scholars suggested in the nineteenth century. If the dwellers of the Kyiv Land had to flee the steppe borderlands, they had plenty of opportunity to find safe haven closer to home, in the forests of northern Ukraine along the Prypiat and Desna Rivers. Not incidentally, the oldest Ukrainian dialects were spoken in the Prypiat forests and the foothills of the Carpathians—areas shielded from nomadic attacks by woodlands, marshes, and mountainous terrain.

BY THE TIME Kyiv fell to the Mongols, it no longer reigned over others but was itself ruled by outsiders. The head of the city's defenses, a military commander named Dmytro, owed allegiance to Prince Danylo (Daniel), ruler of Galicia and Volhynia in present-day western Ukraine. Prince Danylo had taken the Rus' capital under his protection the previous year by arrangement with Prince Mykhailo of Kyiv, who fled after originally resisting the Mongols, then losing to them his main stronghold, the city of Chernihiv, and eventually the will to resist.

Danylo of Halych was a rising star of Rus' politics. Like Genghis Khan, he had been orphaned in childhood. He was four years old in 1205 when his father, Roman, whom the chronicler calls "the autocrat of Rus'," fell in battle with the Poles. In the previous few years, Roman, whose patrimony had originally included the principality of Volhynia, had managed to take control of the neighboring principality of Galicia, becoming the ruler of all Rus' lands west of Kyiv. Danylo and his younger brother, Vasylko, inherited the title but not the possessions of their father. Those were contested by rival Rus' princes, as well as by rebellious Galician boyars, and then by the Poles and Hungarians. Not until 1238, the year of the Mongol attack on northeastern Rus', did Danylo finally reestablish control over both Volhynia and Galicia and install his own *voevoda*, or military commander, in Kyiv.

The Mongol invasion put Danylo's skills as a ruler and military commander to the test. More importantly, it revealed his talent as a diplomat. When the Mongol military commander demanded that Danylo turn over his capital city of Halych to the Mongols, he went to see Batu Khan in his capital, Sarai, on the Volga. It was the kind of visit other Rus' princes had paid the khan earlier, the purpose being to pledge allegiance to the Mongols and receive the khan's *yarlyk*, or conditional right to rule their principalities. "Do you drink black milk, our drink, mare's *kumis*?" the khan asked Danylo, according to the Rus' chronicler. "I have not drunk it so far. But if you so ordain, I shall drink it," answered Danylo, showing the khan respect and obedience. In this way the chronicler metaphorically described Danylo's submission and his initiation into the Mongol elite.

The chronicler, critical of the very idea of Christian Rus' princes swearing allegiance to pagan Mongol khans, described three models of their behavior vis-à-vis the Mongols. Prince Mykhailo of Chernihiv exemplified the first, which met with the chronicler's utmost approval. Since he allegedly refused Batu's demand to kowtow before a bush and compromise his Christian religion, he was killed on orders of the khan. Prince Yaroslav of Vladimir-Suzdal represented the second model: apostasy. He allegedly agreed to bow to the bush and thereby earned the chronicler's condemnation. Danylo followed a third model, which involved neither complete rejection of, nor full submission to, Mongol rule. According to the chronicler, who was sympathetic to Danylo, the prince did not kneel before the bush and besmirch his Christian faith, but he drank *kumis*, indicating acceptance of the khan's secular authority.

In actual fact, the Mongols never asked the Rus' princes to abandon their faith and showed maximum tolerance of the Orthodox Church in general. But the chronicler's differentiation of three models of behavior reflected very real gradations in the Rus' princes' collaboration with and resistance to Mongol authority. Prince Mykhailo, who was indeed killed on Batu's orders, refused to capitulate to the Mongols in 1239 and even killed the envoys sent by the khan to receive his surrender. Yaroslav of Vladimir, by contrast, was the first of the Rus' princes to pledge allegiance to the Mongols, which gained him the title of grand prince of Rus' and the right to install his *voevoda* in Kyiv. He remained loyal to the Mongols until his death in 1246, as did his son and successor, Aleksandr Nevsky, whom the Russian Orthodox Church later recognized as a saint for his role in defending the Rus' lands from western aggressors, the Swedes and the Teutonic Knights. Danylo took a different course: while he swore allegiance to Batu Khan, he did not abide by his oath very long.

Danylo received Batu's *yarlyk* for Galicia and Volhynia in exchange for his promise to pay tribute and take part in Mongol military campaigns in the region. Mongol suzerainty shielded him from claims on his territory not only by rival Rus' princes but also by aggressive western and northern neighbors. Danylo took advantage of the new atmosphere of political stability to initiate the economic revival of his realm. It was less devastated than other parts of Ukraine and served as a destination of choice for refugees from lands close to the steppe, where the Mongols had their outposts and exercised direct control. If one trusts the Rus' chroniclers, economic opportunities in the

Volhynian and Galician towns under the protection of Prince Danylo attracted many refugees from the Kyiv region.

Danylo moved his capital farther from the steppe to the newly established town of Kholm (present-day Chełm in Poland). He was eager to turn it into a major economic center. "When Prince Danylo saw that God favored that place, he began to summon settlers—Germans and Rus', members of other tribes, and Liakhs [Poles]," wrote the chronicler. "They came day in and day out. Both youths and masters of all kinds fled [here] from the Tatars—saddlers, bowmen and fletchers, and smiths of iron, copper, and silver. And activity began, and they filled the fields and villages around the town with dwellings." Kholm was not the sole object of Danylo's attention. He established new cities—such as Lviv, the future capital of the region, first mentioned in the chronicle in 1256 and named after Danylo's son Lev—and fortified old ones.

Under the rule of Danylo and his successors, the Galician-Volhynian principality gathered within its boundaries most of the Ukrainian lands settled at that time. Its rise to prominence was due to political, economic, and cultural processes that weakened the power of Kyiv and favored the emergence of borderland principalities. The Mongol invasion facilitated this rise. Some historians have argued that accommodating the Mongols was the best policy for the Rus' princes to follow if they cared about their subjects' well-being. Mongol rule—so goes the argument—brought stability and trade to the region. True, Kyiv was devastated and would take centuries to recover. But this long-term impact had more to do with the shifting of trade routes from the Dnieper to the Don and Volga in the east and the Dniester in the west than with the scope of the destruction.

Also far from devastating was the Mongol takeover of the Crimea. Contrary to popular belief based on early historiography, the Mongols did not bring the Crimean Tatars to the peninsula. They simply facilitated the Turkic (Kipchak) takeover, which began long before the Mongol invasion. The Sudak fortress, taken by the Mongols in the 1220s, in time gave way to Feodosiia, or Caffa, first under Venetian and then Genoan rule as a major trading center. The Crimea remained a commercial hub of the region, linking the Eurasian steppes with the Mediterranean world during the period of Mongol rule.

THE MONGOLS WERE a powerful but often absent force in the Ukrainian lands during the second half of the thirteenth century, and the rulers of

Galicia-Volhynia were eager to take advantage of that circumstance. They sought to become independent of the Horde by building local alliances.

Danylo focused his foreign policy on rebuilding relations with his western neighbors and forging alliances to assist in a future revolt against the Mongols. In 1246, on his way back from visiting Batu, Danylo encountered papal envoy Giovanni del Carpine, whose account of the Mongol destruction of Kyiv we cited earlier. They discussed the establishment of relations between Danylo and the pope. Upon his return to Galicia, Danylo sent an Orthodox cleric to Lyon, where the papacy was located at the time, to establish direct contact. Pope Innocent IV wanted the Rus' princes to recognize him as their supreme religious leader. Danylo, for his part, wanted the pope on his side to consolidate support from the Catholic rulers of central Europe against the Mongols.

This contact between the Galician prince and the pope, established with the help of del Carpine, eventually led Innocent IV to issue a bull in 1253 urging the Christian rulers of central Europe and the Balkans to take part in a crusade against the Mongols. He also sent his legate to Danylo and bestowed on him the crown of a Christian king. Prince Danylo became King Daniel, *rex ruthenorum* (king of the Rus'). Apart from getting the pope's backing, Danylo finally concluded an alliance with the king of Hungary, who agreed to marry his daughter to Danylo's son. His other son married the daughter of an Austrian duke. In 1253, emboldened by promises of support from central Europe, Danylo began military action against the Mongols. He soon took control of parts of Podolia and Volhynia that had been under Mongol rule. He could not have better timed his offensive, since Batu Khan of the Golden Horde died in 1255, and each of his two successors ruled for less than a year.

It took the Mongols five years to return to Galicia and Volhynia with a new army, seeking to restore their possession of those lands. Western support was crucial at that point, but it never materialized. The central European rulers ignored the papal bull calling for an anti-Mongol crusade. Matrimonial ties also turned out to be of little help, as Hungary was recovering from a recent defeat by the Czechs. Danylo had to face the new Mongol army alone. The Mongol military commander, Burundai, who arrived in Galicia-Volhynia at the head of a large army, demanded Danylo's participation in campaigns against the Lithuanians and the Poles, destroying alliances he had built in the region. Burundai also required Danylo to destroy the fortifications he had built around his towns, rendering the principality vulnerable to potential attacks from the steppe. Danylo obliged. He once again declared himself a vassal of the Mongols.

Danylo's alliance with the pope in the 1250s came at a price with regard to not only the anti-Mongol crusade but also his relations with the Orthodox clergy, both in Constantinople and at home in Rus'. After the sack of Constantinople in 1204 by participants in the Fourth Crusade, the divisions between Eastern and Western Christendom became more than a matter of theological and jurisdictional nuances. They grew into open hostility, exacerbated in Rus' by metropolitans sent from Constantinople. Danylo eventually managed to silence opposition to his alliance with Rome from the local clergy but not from Constantinople. When in 1251 Danylo's protégé as metropolitan of all Rus', the former bishop of Kholm, Cyril, came to Byzantium for a blessing, he was confirmed as metropolitan on condition that he not reside in Galicia, whose prince was known to be conspiring with the pope. Cyril, a native of Galicia, moved to the Vladimir-Suzdal principality.

The transfer of the see became official in 1299, during the tenure of Cyril's successor, a Greek metropolitan named Maximus. In 1325 the metropolitan see was moved to Moscow by another Galician appointee, Metropolitan Petro. This would become a major factor in the rise of the Moscow princes as leaders of northeastern Rus'—the core of modern Russia. Mongol rule over much of what is now Russia was much stricter and lasted longer than their rule over other parts of Rus'. The areas around Moscow were simply closer to the heart of the lands possessed by the khans of the Golden Horde. The Mongols created the office of grand prince of Rus' to help administer their realm and collect tribute. It first went to the princes of Vladimir-Suzdal but was later contested by the two leading principalities of the region, Moscow and Tver. In the long run, the princes of Moscow, the "owners" of the metropolitan see, emerged victorious in the struggle for the office and, more importantly, for mastery of the Mongol part of Rus'.

The see moved from Kyiv to Vladimir and Moscow retained the name Metropolitanate of All Rus'. As compensation, Constantinople allowed the Galicians to create their own metropolitanate in 1303. This new see, established in the town of Halych, the capital of the principality of Halychyna, or Galicia in Latin, was called the Metropolitanate of Little Rus'. It included six of the fifteen eparchies, or dioceses, that had been under the jurisdiction of Kyiv at some point. Among them were not only the eparchies on the territory of present-day Ukraine but also the eparchy of Turaŭ in today's Belarus. The notion of Little Rus', which some scholars believe the Greeks to have understood as "inner" or "closer" Rus', was born. Much later, the term would become a bone of contention in battles over Ukrainian national identity, with the appellation "Little Russians" attached in the twentieth century to proponents of all-Russian or pro-Russian self-identification among Ukrainians.

The Mongols' invasion and their prolonged presence in the Pontic steppes confronted the Rus' elites for the first time with the dilemma of choosing between the East, represented by both the nomads of the steppe and the Christian tradition of Byzantium, and the West, embodied by central European rulers who recognized the ecclesiastical authority of the pope. Finding themselves for the first time on Europe's major political and cultural fault line, the post-Kyivan elites of the territories of modern Ukraine began a balancing act that prolonged their de facto independence of both East and West for at least another century.

HISTORIANS OFTEN CONSIDER the Galician-Volhynian principality the last independent state in the Ukrainian lands until the rise of the Cossack Hetmanate in the mid-seventeenth century. This judgment requires some qualification. While often in disagreement and occasionally at war with the khans of the Golden Horde, Galicia-Volhynia remained a tribute-paying vassal until the very end of its existence in the 1340s. In exchange for tribute, the khans allowed the Galician-Volhynian rulers complete independence in their internal affairs. In the international arena, Galicia-Volhynia benefited from the Pax Mongolica to the end. The weakening and eventual breakdown of that international order in eastern Europe facilitated the fall of Galicia-Volhynia as a unified state.

The disintegration of Galicia-Volhynia began with an event that would seem trivial today but held extreme importance for medieval and early modern polities: the extinction of a ruling house, in this case the Galician-Volhynian princely dynasty. In 1323 the two great-grandsons of Prince Danylo died: some historians believe that they met their end in combat with the Mongols—the wrong battle to fight at the time. As Danylo had no other male descendants, Prince Bolesław of Mazovia in Poland, a maternal nephew of the deceased princes, took over the principality. A Catholic by birth, Bolesław accepted Orthodoxy and changed his name to Yurii—to him, the political prize was clearly worth a liturgy. That was not enough for the local Rus' aristocracy, the boyars, who despised their new ruler for neglecting their interests and relying on the advice of people he had brought from Poland. In 1340 the boyars poisoned Yurii-Bolesław, the last ruler to style himself *dux*

totius Russiae Minoris (duke of all Little Rus'), leading to a period of prolonged struggle over Galicia-Volhynia and the eventual demise of the principality. In the second half of the fourteenth century, the former mighty
principality was split in two, with Galicia and western Podolia going to Poland and Volhynia to the Grand Duchy of Lithuania.

King Casimir III of Poland was the main actor in the drama of the Polish
takeover of Galicia. He first attempted to take Lviv, the Galician capital from
the 1270s, in 1340. The local elites, led by the Galician boyar Dmytro
Dedko, turned for help to the Mongols and repelled the Polish onslaught
with their assistance. But Casimir came back in 1344 and this time managed
to seize part of the principality. In 1349, after Dedko's death, Polish troops
occupied Lviv and the rest of the Galician-Volhynian principality. The Lithuanian and local troops expelled them from Volhynia in the following year,
but they kept their holdings in Galicia. In the mid-fourteenth century, hundreds of Polish nobles from other parts of the kingdom moved to Galicia in
search of land offered in exchange for military services. From Casimir's point
of view, conditional land ownership was a means of ensuring that the nobility would not neglect its duty to defend the new province.

The Kingdom of Poland fully incorporated the Rus' lands of Galicia and
western Podolia only in the 1430s, as the palatinates of Rus' (Ruthenia) and
Podolia. Also around that time, in response to the demands of the local nobility (both Polish and Ukrainian), the right to unconditional landholding
was extended to noble residents. By far the most important political development associated with the incorporation of Galicia and parts of Podolia into
the Kingdom of Poland was the extension to the local nobility of the political rights enjoyed by their Polish counterparts. Those included the right to
participate in dietines, or local noble assemblies that discussed not only local
affairs but also matters of state and foreign-policy issues. The nobles also received the right to elect representatives to the Diets of the entire kingdom,
and as the defense of the Galician-Podolian borderland from incursions of
steppe tribesmen took on greater importance between the fourteenth and
sixteenth centuries, they used it to the full to lobby their interests at the
courts.

The integration of Galicia and western Podolia into the Kingdom of
Poland—which opened the region to the influence of the Polish model
of noble democracy, the German model of urban self-rule, and the benefits
of Italian Renaissance education—came at a price that some historians of
Ukraine consider too high. The region lost its semi-independent status, and

the boyar aristocracy, its princely power and dominance in local politics. Cultural Polonization affected not only the aristocracy but also the local nobility; Rus' artisans were squeezed out of the towns at an accelerating rate, and Orthodoxy faced powerful competition from the Roman Catholic Church.

The Grand Duchy of Lithuania offered another model of incorporation of Ukrainian lands into a foreign polity. The grand duchy had taken over Volhynia in a fierce competition with its Polish rivals; it also gained control of the Kyiv Land, which, unlike Galicia-Volhynia, had been under more or less direct Mongol rule until the fourteenth century. The Lithuanian model was more conducive to the preservation of the local elites' political influence, social status, and cultural traditions than the Polish one.

The grand duchy became an actor on the Ukrainian scene in the first half of the fourteenth century under its most famous ruler, Grand Duke Gediminas, an effective empire builder and the founder of the Lithuanian ruling dynasty. By some accounts, Gediminas managed to install a prince of his own in Kyiv in the early fourteenth century. That does not appear to have had any immediate effect on the status of the principality, but change would come as the Lithuanian princes, supported by local retinues, began to push the Tatars farther into the steppes. The decisive battle took place in 1362. That year, Lithuanian and Rus' troops led by Gediminas's son Algirdas defeated the forces of the Noghay Tatars—the leading tribe of the Golden Horde in the Pontic steppes—in battle on the Syni Vody, a river in today's central Ukraine. As a result, the border of the Grand Duchy of Lithuania shifted south to the Dniester estuary on the Black Sea coast. The Grand Duchy of Lithuania became not just a powerful successor to Kyivan Rus' but also the holder of most of the Ukrainian lands.

The Lithuanians brought representatives of their own Gediminian dynasty to Rus', but Gediminas' descendants went native more quickly than their Rurikid predecessors of the tenth century. The Lithuanian rulers married into local Rus' families, gladly accepting Orthodoxy and Slavic Christian names. Overwhelming Rus' dominance in the cultural sphere facilitated Lithuanian acculturation. The authority of Byzantine Orthodoxy now swayed the Lithuanian elite, which had remained pagan into the fifteenth century. The Rus' chancery language, based on the Church Slavonic brought to Kyiv at the end of the tenth century by Christian missionaries, served as the language of administration throughout the grand duchy; its law code, which became known as the Lithuanian Statute in the sixteenth century, was a version of the Rus' Justice. The grand duchy effectively became an heir to Kyivan Rus' in every respect but dynastic continuity. Some historians used to refer to it not as a Lithuanian state but as a Lithuanian-Rus' or even a Rus'-Lithuanian polity.

As the Kingdom of Poland and the Grand Duchy of Lithuania took over most of the Ukrainian lands, they brought about political, social, and cultural change. The two states had very different policies with regard to the accommodation and assimilation of Rus' elites and society. But in both cases we see the emergence and strengthening of similar tendencies that led to the decline of the Rus' principalities' rights of autonomy. By the end of the fifteenth century, they would be wiped off the political map of the region, ending the princely era that had begun in Kyivan Rus' back in the tenth century.

II

EAST MEETS WEST

CHAPTER 7

THE MAKING OF UKRAINE

W ITH THE UKRAINIAN territories integrated by the end of the fourteenth century into the Kingdom of Poland and the Grand Duchy of
Lithuania, the policies of these two states, as well as relations between them,
began to determine the political, economic, and cultural life of Ukraine. Especially important for the future of the Ukrainian lands were a series of
agreements between the two states concluded between the fourteenth and
sixteenth centuries.

In 1385, in the town of Kreva (now in Belarus), the thirty-three-year-old
grand duke of Lithuania, Jogaila, who called himself by God's grace "Grand
Duke of the Lithuanians and Lord of Rus'," signed a decree that was, in all
but name, a prenuptial agreement with representatives of the twelve-year-old
queen of Poland, Jadwiga. In exchange for the Polish throne, he agreed to
accept Catholicism for himself and his realm and brought about a union of
the lands of the Kingdom of Poland and the Grand Duchy of Lithuania. A
year later, Jogaila was crowned king of Poland. Another year passed, and in
1387 the combined Polish and Lithuanian forces helped to attach Galicia
once again to the Polish kingdom.

A number of other unions would follow the one negotiated in Kreva,
strengthening ties between the two polities and culminating in the Union of
Lublin (1569), which created the Polish-Lithuanian Commonwealth. The
borders between the kingdom and the duchy were realigned within the commonwealth, transferring most of the Ukrainian territories to the kingdom
and leaving the Belarusian ones within the boundaries of the duchy. The
union of Poland and Lithuania thus meant the separation of Ukraine and

Belarus, and in that regard we can hardly overestimate the importance of the Union of Lublin. It would initiate the formation of the territory of modern Ukraine and its intellectual appropriation by the local elites.

FROM THE VIEWPOINT of the Rus' elites of the Grand Duchy of Lithuania, the unions with the Kingdom of Poland had caused nothing but trouble. The immediate outcome of the Union of Kreva was the loss of Rus' influence on the grand prince, who not only moved out of the duchy but also became a Catholic, setting a precedent for his brothers, some of whom were Orthodox. The Orthodox hierarchs' hope of establishing Byzantine rather than Latin Christianity in the last pagan realm in Europe were dashed.

But the real challenge to Rus' political status came in 1413, when the Union of Horodło, which historiography treats as a dynastic union, enhanced the Union of Kreva, a personal union between the Kingdom of Poland and the Grand Duchy of Lithuania. Concluded between Jogaila, now king of Poland, and his cousin Vytautas, the grand duke of Lithuania, the new agreement extended many of the rights and privileges of the Polish nobility, including the right to unconditional ownership of land, to the Lithuanian nobility. Close to fifty Polish noble families offered to share their coats of arms with the same number of families from the grand duchy. But there was a catch: only Lithuanian Catholic families were invited to the party. The new rights and privileges were not accorded to the Orthodox elite. This was the first instance of discrimination against the Rus' elites at the state level. Denied the new privileges, the Orthodox aristocrats were thus barred from holding high office in the central administration of the grand duchy. To add insult to injury, the Union of Horodło came on the heels of the curbing of Rus' autonomy by one of the authors of the new union, Grand Duke Vytautas, who replaced the prince of Volhynia and rulers of some other lands with his own appointees.

An opportunity for the Rus' elites to express their unhappiness with this encroachment on their status came soon after Vytautas's death in 1430. In the succession struggle for the Lithuanian throne, which deteriorated into a civil war, the Rus' nobles, led by the Volhynian boyars, supported their own candidate, Prince Švitrigaila. His rival, Prince Žygimantas, responded in 1434 by extending the rights and privileges guaranteed by the Union of Horodło to the Orthodox elites of the grand duchy, turning the tide of war in his favor. Although the Rus' princes and nobles of Volhynia and the Kyiv Land remained suspicious of the intentions of Žygimantas, their support for

Švitrigaila declined, allowing the grand duchy to return to a state of relative peace. With religion eliminated as a source of grievance among the Rus' elites, the Lithuanian court had more room to maneuver in its continuing efforts to restrict the autonomy of the Rus' lands and principalities.

In 1470, the grand duke and king of Poland, Casimir IV, abolished the last vestige of the princely era: the principality of Kyiv itself. Ten years later, the Kyivan princes conspired to kill Casimir and install one of their candidates, but their plot failed, leading to the arrest of the ringleaders and forcing the other conspirators to flee the grand duchy. With their departure came an end to the last hopes of restoring the way of life associated with the princely traditions of Kyivan Rus'. By the turn of the sixteenth century, not only Ukraine's political map but also its institutional, social, and cultural landscape showed few traces of the period two centuries earlier when Galicia-Volhynia had striven to throw off Mongol suzerainty and become a fully independent actor in the region. While Rus' law and language remained well established, they began to lose their previous dominance. These essentials of Rus' culture could no longer compete with latinizing influences and the Polish language, which took pride of place in the grand duchy after the Union of Kreva.

ALL OVER EUROPE, the sixteenth century was marked by the strengthening of royal authority, centralization of the state, and regularization of political and social practices. The other side of the coin was increasing aristocratic opposition to the growth of royal power, which in the Polish-Lithuanian case came from the aristocratic houses of the grand duchy, many of them deeply rooted in the princely tradition of Kyivan Rus' and Galicia-Volhynia. But in the mid-sixteenth century, elite opposition to increasing royal power diminished in response to the growing external threat to the grand duchy, which it could meet only with the help of Poland. The threat came from the east, where in the course of the fifteenth century a major new power had been rising: the Grand Duchy of Muscovy.

In 1476 Grand Prince Ivan III, the first Muscovite ruler to call himself tsar, declared the independence of his realm from the Horde and refused to pay tribute to the khans. He also launched a campaign of "gathering the Rus' lands," taking Novgorod, Tver, and Viatka and laying claim to other Rus' lands outside the former Mongol realm, including those of today's Ukraine. In the last decades of the fifteenth century, the newly created Tsardom of Muscovy and the Grand Duchy of Lithuania entered into a prolonged conflict over the heritage of Kyivan Rus'. Muscovy was on the offensive, and by the early sixteenth century the grand dukes had to recognize the tsar's rule over two of their former territories, Smolensk and Chernihiv. It was the first time that Muscovy had established its rule over part of what is now Ukraine.

The westward advance of Muscovy, stopped by the grand dukes at the beginning of the sixteenth century, resumed in the second half. In 1558, Ivan the Terrible, the decisive and charismatic but also erratic, brutal, and ultimately self-destructive tsar of Muscovy, attacked Livonia, a polity bordering on the grand duchy that included parts of what are now Latvia and Estonia, starting the Livonian War (1558–1583), which would last for a quarter century and involve Sweden, Denmark, Lithuania, and eventually Poland. In 1563, Muscovite troops crossed the borders of the grand duchy, taking the city of Polatsk and raiding Vitsebsk (Vitebsk), Shkloŭ (Shklov), and Orsha (all in present-day Belarus). This defeat mobilized support for the grand duchy's union with Poland among the lesser Lithuanian nobility.

In December 1568 Sigismund Augustus, who was both king of Poland and grand duke of Lithuania, convened two Diets in the city of Lublin—one for the kingdom, the other for the grand duchy—in the hope that their representatives would hammer out conditions for the new union. The negotiations began on a positive note, as the two sides agreed to the joint election of the king, a common Diet, or parliament, and broad autonomy for the grand duchy, but the magnates would not return the royal lands in their possession— the principal demand of the Polish nobility. The Lithuanian delegates packed their bags, assembled their retinues of noble clients, and left. This move backfired. Unexpectedly for the departing Lithuanians, the Diet of the Kingdom of Poland began to issue decrees, with the king's blessing, transferring one province of the grand duchy after another to the jurisdiction of the Kingdom of Poland.

The Lithuanian magnates who had feared losing their provinces to Muscovy were now losing them to Poland instead. To stop a hostile takeover by their powerful Polish partner, the Lithuanians returned to Lublin to sign an agreement dictated by the Polish delegates. They were too late. In March 1569, the Podlachia palatinate on the Ukrainian-Belarusian-Polish ethnic border went to Poland. Volhynia followed in May, and on June 6, one day before the resumption of the Polish-Lithuanian talks, the Kyivan and Podolian lands were transferred to Poland as well. The Lithuanian aristocrats could only accept the new reality—they stood to lose even more if they continued to resist the union. In his magisterial depiction of the Lublin Diet,

Jan Matejko, a famous nineteenth-century Polish artist, portrayed the chief opponent of the union, Mikalojus Radvilas, on his knees but with his sword drawn in front of the king.

The Union of Lublin created a new Polish-Lithuanian state with a single ruler, to be elected by the nobility of the whole realm, and a single Diet. It extended the freedoms of the Polish nobility to their counterparts in the Grand Duchy of Lithuania, which maintained its own offices, treasury, judicial system, and army. The new state, called the Commonwealth of Both Nations—Polish and Lithuanian—was a quasi-federal polity dominated by the geographically expanded and politically strengthened Kingdom of Poland. The kingdom incorporated the Ukrainian palatinates not as a group but one by one, with no guarantees but those pertaining to the use of the Ruthenian (Middle Ukrainian) language in the courts and administration and the protection of the rights of the Orthodox Church.

AT THE LUBLIN Diet, the local aristocracy—princes and boyars, the same stratum that had opposed the union in Lithuania—represented the Ukrainian lands. But unlike their Lithuanian counterparts, the Ukrainian delegates opted for joining the kingdom, while asking for guarantees for their law, language, and religion. Why did the Ukrainian elites, the princely families in particular, agree to such a deal? This question takes on particular importance, given that the new boundary between Poland and Lithuania would later become the basis of administrative divisions determining the modern border between Ukraine and Belarus.

Did the Ukrainian provinces of the grand duchy join the Kingdom of Poland because their identity and way of life differed from those of Belarus, or did the Lublin border serve to differentiate these two East Slavic peoples? There is no indication that in the mid-sixteenth century the Ukrainians and Belarusians spoke two separate languages. Today, in Ukrainian-Belarusian borderlands people speak transitional Ukrainian-Belarusian dialects, as they probably did in the sixteenth century, making it all but impossible to draw a clear dividing line based exclusively on linguistic criteria. It appears, however, that the Lublin border, based on the boundaries of historical Rus' lands, reinforced differences long in the making. Historically, the Kyiv Land and Galicia-Volhynia differed significantly from the Belarusian lands to the north. From the tenth to the fourteenth centuries, they were core areas of independent or semi-independent principalities. In the fifteenth and sixteenth

centuries, the location of the Ukrainian lands on the periphery of the Grand
Duchy of Lithuania and the challenges they faced on the open steppe frontier
also set them apart from the rest of the Lithuanian world.

Unlike the Lithuanian aristocracy, the Ukrainian elites saw little benefit
in maintaining the de facto independence of the grand duchy, which was ill
equipped to resist increasing pressure from the Crimean and Noghay Tatars.
The Kingdom of Poland could help the grand duchy fight the war with
Muscovy, but it was unlikely to assist the Ukrainians in their low-intensity
war with the Tatars. Incorporation of the frontier provinces into the kingdom might engender a different attitude. One way or another, the Ukrainian
princes approved the incorporation of their lands into Poland. We have no
indication that they ever regretted the move. The Volhynian princely families not only held onto their possessions but dramatically increased them
under Polish tutelage.

Kostiantyn Ostrozky, by far the most influential of the local princes, decided the fate of the union by throwing his support behind the king. He kept
his old posts as captain of the town of Volodymyr and palatine of Kyiv. He
also extended his landholdings. At the end of the sixteenth century, Ostrozky
presided over a huge personal empire that included 40 castles, 1,000 towns,
and 13,000 villages, all owned by the prince. By the early seventeenth century, his son Janusz would have in his private treasury enough gold, silver,
and coins to cover two annual budgets of the entire commonwealth. Ostrozky alone could muster an army of 20,000 soldiers and cavalrymen—ten
times the size of the king's army in the borderlands. At various times in his
career, Ostrozky was a contender for both the Polish and the Muscovite
thrones. The lesser nobles were in no position to defy this powerful magnate,
on whom they depended economically and politically. Thus, Ostrozky continued to preside over an extensive network of noble clients who did his
bidding in the local and Commonwealth Diets. Not only the local nobility
but even the king and the Diet did not dare to challenge the authority of this
uncrowned king of Rus'. The Diet prohibited the princes from fielding their
own armies in wartime, but because of the constant danger of Tatar attacks
on the steppe frontier, the commonwealth's standing army could not do
without the military muscle of the princes.

The Ostrozkys were the richest of the Ukrainian princes who maintained
and increased their wealth and influence after the Union of Lublin, but they
were not the only ones. Another highly influential Volhynian princely family
was the Vyshnevetskys. Prince Mykhailo Vyshnevetsky branched out of his

Volhynian possessions, which were quite insignificant in comparison to Ostrozky's, into the lands east of the Dnieper. Those lands were either uncolonized or had been abandoned by settlers in the times of Mongol rule and were now open to attack by the Noghay and Crimean Tatars. The Vyshnevetsky family expanded into the steppelands, creating new settlements, establishing towns, and funding monasteries. The possessions of the Vyshnevetskys in Left-Bank (eastern) Ukraine soon began to rival those of the Ostrozkys in Volhynia. These two princely families were the largest landowners in Ukraine.

Changes introduced in the region in the aftermath of the Union of Lublin assisted the Volhynian princes, the prime movers behind the colonization of the steppe borderlands, in their efforts. The Polish Crown's creation of a small but mobile standing army, funded from the profits of the royal domains, helped repel Tatar raids and promote the continuing population of the steppe. Another major incentive for the colonization of the steppe borderlands came from their inclusion in the Baltic trade. With increasing demand for grain on the European markets, Ukraine began to earn its future reputation as the breadbasket of Europe. This was the first time that Ukrainian grain had appeared on foreign markets since the days of Herodotus. Peasants moved into the area en masse, fleeing serfdom in lands closer to government centers. They simply migrated to the steppe borderlands of Ukraine, where princes and nobles were establishing duty-free settlements that allowed the new arrivals not to perform corvée (statute) labor or pay duties for a substantial period. In exchange, they had to settle and develop the land.

Eastward migration created new economic and cultural opportunities for Ukrainian Jewry. According to conservative estimates, the number of Jews in Ukraine increased more than tenfold from the mid-sixteenth to the mid-seventeenth century, rising from approximately 4,000 to more than 50,000. They formed new communities, built synagogues, and opened schools. But the new opportunities came at a price, placing the Jews of Ukraine between two groups with opposing interests: peasants and landowners. Originally, both groups were Orthodox. By the mid-seventeenth century, however, with many princes converting to Catholicism and Polish nobles pouring into the area, the Jews found themselves caught between resentful Orthodox serfs and money-hungry Catholic masters. This was a ticking time bomb.

CONTRARY TO THE expectations of King Sigismund Augustus, the Union of Lublin did not rein in the oppositionist aristocracy. If anything, it gave greater prominence to Ostrozky and other Ukrainian princes. But their story is not only one of building wealth and appropriating land. For the first time since the fall of the Galician-Volhynian principality, the princes began to involve themselves in cultural and educational projects. This cultural awakening took place on both sides of the new Polish-Lithuanian border, fueled by the political aspirations of the princes and directly linked to the religious conflicts of the time.

In the Grand Duchy of Lithuania, the Radvilas family set an example of linking politics, religion, and culture. The main opponent of the Union of Lublin, Mikalojus Radvilas the Red was also the leader of Polish and Lithuanian Calvinism and founder of a school for Calvinist youth. His cousin, Mikalojus Radvilas the Black, funded the printing of the first complete Polish translation of the Bible, issued in the town of Brest on the Ukrainian-Belarusian ethnic border. In the 1570s, Kostiantyn Ostrozky began his own publishing project in the Volhynian town of Ostrih. There Ostrozky assembled a team of scholars who compared Greek and Church Slavonic texts of the Bible, amended the Church Slavonic translations, and published the most authoritative text of scripture ever produced by Orthodox scholars. The project was truly international in scope, involving participants from not only Lithuania and Poland but also Greece, while the copies of the Bible on which they worked originated in places as diverse as Rome and Moscow. The Ostrih Bible was issued in 1581 in a print run estimated at 1,500 copies. Some four hundred copies have survived, and visitors can see one of them today in the Houghton Library at Harvard University.

The publication of a Church Slavonic translation of the Bible in Ostrih before such a text appeared in Constantinople or Moscow indicated the new prominence of Ukraine in the Orthodox world. Ostrozky did not stop with the publication of the Bible. Not only did he continue his publishing program, both in Church Slavonic and in Ruthenian, which was much more accessible to the public, but the establishment of a school for Orthodox youth, not unlike the one founded by Radvilas for the Calvinists, expanded the activities of the prince's academic circle. Nor was that the limit of Ostrozky's ambitions. There are clear indications that he was exploring the notion of moving the patriarchal throne of Constantinople to Ostrih. The idea never materialized, but in the late sixteenth century Ostrih became perhaps the most important center of Orthodox learning.

Ostrozky, the uncrowned king of Rus', sought historical and religious justification of the role that he actually played in the region. The introductory texts to the Ostrih Bible and the works of the authors assembled by the prince portray him as a continuator of the religious and educational work begun in Rus' by Princes Volodymyr the Great and Yaroslav the Wise. "For Volodymyr enlightened the nation by baptism / While Kostiantyn [Ostrozky] brought them light with the writings of holy wisdom," wrote one of the editors of the Bible. He continued, "Yaroslav embellished Kyiv and Chernihiv with church buildings / While Kostiantyn raised up the one universal church with writings." Herasym Smotrytsky, a renowned theologian and the most likely author of the verses quoted above, came from "Polish Rus'," that is, Galicia and western Podolia. There, Ruthenian (Ukrainian and Belarusian) nobles and burghers benefited from the fruits of Polish Renaissance education much earlier than their counterparts in the Grand Duchy of Lithuania.

The team of intellectuals assembled or supported by Ostrozky was international, and some of its most prominent members had Polish backgrounds. Ostrozky's panegyrists, who came from the ranks of the Polish nobility, had little interest in his contribution to the Orthodox cause but did their best to build up his credentials as a semi-independent ruler. If Orthodox intellectuals linked Ostrozky to Volodymyr and Yaroslav, the Polish panegyrists "established" his historical ties with Danylo of Halych, the most famous ruler of Ostrozky's native Volhynia. The Poles who served the Ostrozkys, as well as the princes Zaslavskys, who were associated with the Ostrozkys by marriage, carved out for their patrons a new historical and political space not defined by the existing boundaries of the Orthodox Church or the Ruthenian (Ukrainian and Belarusian) lands of the Grand Duchy of Lithuania. That space was "Polish Rus'"—the Orthodox lands of the Kingdom of Poland. By imposing on the old map of Orthodox Rus' the boundaries established by the Union of Lublin, the panegyrists created a historical and political reality that would later provide a geographical blueprint for the formation of the modern Ukrainian nation.

Beyond the realm of arts and letters, imposition of the Lublin boundaries on the old map also included actual mapmaking. A map produced in the 1590s by Tomasz Makowski showed the new border between Polish and Lithuanian Rus', or, in modern terms, Ukraine and Belarus. Titled "The Grand Duchy of Lithuania and Adjoining Territories," it included the Ukrainian lands and an inset of the Dnieper River. Scholars believe that Kostiantyn Ostrozky supplied the material for the Ukrainian part of the map. The local term "Ukraine" probably made its way onto the Makowski map thanks to the prince or his servitors. The word denoted part of the lands south of the new border, referring to the territory on the Right Bank of the Dnieper extending from Kyiv in the north to Kaniv in the south. Beyond Kaniv, if one trusted the cartographer, there were wild steppes, marked *campi deserti citra Boristenem* (desert plains on this side of the Borysthenes). "Ukraine" thus covered a good part of the region's steppe frontier. It seems to have been a booming area, dotted with numerous castles and settlements that had not appeared on earlier maps. The alternative name of the region used on the same map was *Volynia ulterior* (Outer Volhynia), a designation that stressed the close link between the new "Ukraine" and the old Volhynia, the homeland of the Ostrozkys.

The Union of Lublin created a new political space for mastering and exploitation first and foremost by the Orthodox princely elite, which, instead of losing its prestige and power as a result of the union, in fact enhanced them. As the princes' intellectual retainers began to fill that space with content related to the political ambitions of their masters, they looked to history for parallels and precedents, such as the activities of Volodymyr the Great, Yaroslav the Wise, and Danylo of Halych. For all their attention to the past, they were actually creating something new. Their invention would eventually become "Ukraine," a term that appeared in the region for the first time during this sixteenth-century revival of princely power. It would take time for the name and the new space created by the Union of Lublin to become coterminous.

CHAPTER 8

THE COSSACKS

IN THE COURSE of the fifteenth and sixteenth centuries, the Ukrainian steppes underwent a major political, economic, and cultural transformation. For the first time since the days of Kyivan Rus', the line of frontier settlement stopped retreating toward the Prypiat marshes and the Carpathian Mountains and began advancing toward the east and south. Linguistic research indicates that two major groups of Ukrainian dialects, Polisian and Carpatho-Volhynian, began to converge from the north and west, respectively, shifting east and south to create a third group of steppe dialects that now cover Ukrainian territory from Zhytomyr and Kyiv in the northwest to Zaporizhia, Luhansk, and Donetsk in the east and extending as far to the southeast as Krasnodar and Stavropol in today's Russia. This mixing of dialects reflected the movement of population at large.

The origins of that profound change were in the steppe itself. The struggle that began in the mid-fourteenth century within the Golden Horde, also known as the Kipchak Khanate, led to its disintegration by the mid-fifteenth century. The Crimean, Kazan, and Astrakhan khanates became successors to the Horde, none of them capable of uniting it and some even losing their independence. The Crimea became independent of the Golden Horde in 1449 under the leadership of a descendant of Genghis Khan, Haji Devlet Giray. The Giray dynasty, established by Haji Devlet, would last into the eighteenth century, but his realm would not remain independent. By 1478, the khanate had become a vassal state of the Ottoman Empire—the huge Turkic-dominated Muslim polity that replaced Byzantium as the major power in the western Mediterranean and Black Sea regions in the course of the fourteenth and fifteenth centuries. The Ottomans, who made Istanbul, the former Constantinople, their capital in 1453, took direct control over the southern shores of the Crimea, establishing their main center in the port city of Kaffa, today's Feodosiia. The Girays controlled the steppelands of the Crimea north of the mountains, as well as the nomadic tribes of southern Ukraine, with the Noghay Horde becoming the most powerful of those tribes in the sixteenth century.

Security concerns and commercial interests attracted the Ottomans to the region. In particular they were interested in slaves. The slave trade had always been important in the region's economy, but it now became dominant. The Ottoman Empire, whose Islamic laws allowed the enslavement only of non-Muslims and encouraged the emancipation of slaves, was always in need of free labor. The Noghays and the Crimean Tatars responded to the demand, expanding their slave-seeking expeditions to the lands north of the Pontic steppes and often going much deeper into Ukraine and southern Muscovy than the frontier areas. The slave trade supplemented the earnings that the Noghays obtained from animal husbandry and the Crimeans from both husbandry and settled forms of agriculture. Bad harvests generally translated into more raids to the north and more slaves shipped back to the Crimea.

All five routes that the Tatars followed to the settled areas on their slave-seeking raids went through Ukraine. Two of them east of the Dniester led to western Podolia and then to Galicia; two on the other side of the Southern Buh River led to western Podolia and Volhynia, then again to Galicia; the last passed through what would become the Sloboda Ukraine region around Kharkiv to southern Muscovy. If the demand for cereals led to the incorporation of the Ukrainian lands of the sixteenth century into the Baltic trade, their connection to the Mediterranean trade was due largely to Tatar raiding for slaves. Ukrainians, who constituted an absolute majority of the population of the steppe borderlands north of the Black Sea and moved into the steppes in search of grain, became the main targets and victims of the Ottoman Empire's slave-dependent economy. Ethnic Russians northeast of the Crimea were a close second.

Michalon (Michael) the Lithuanian, a mid-sixteenth-century author who visited the Crimea, described the scope of the slave trade by quoting from his conversation with a local Jew who, "seeing that our people were constantly being shipped there as captives in numbers too large to count, asked us whether our lands also teemed with people, and whence such innumerable mortals had come." Estimates of the numbers of Ukrainians and Russians brought to the Crimean slave markets in the sixteenth and seventeenth centuries vary from 1.5 million to 3 million. Children and adolescents brought the highest prices. The fates of the slaves differed. Most of the male slaves ended up on Ottoman galleys or working in the fields, while many women worked as domestics. Some got lucky, but only in a matter of speaking. Talented young men made careers in the Ottoman administration, but most of them were eunuchs. Some women were taken into the harems of the sultans and high Ottoman officials.

One Ukrainian girl known in history as Roxolana became the wife of the most powerful of the Ottoman sultans, Suleiman the Magnificent, who ruled from 1520 to 1566. Her son became a sultan under the name Selim II. Under the name Hürrem Sultan, Roxolana sponsored Muslim charities and funded the construction of some of the best examples of Ottoman architecture. Among these is the Haseki Hürrem Sultan Hamamı, a public bathhouse not far from Hagia Sophia in Istanbul, constructed by the best-known Ottoman architect, Mimar Sinan. In the course of the last two hundred years, Roxolana has figured as the heroine of novels and a number of television dramas in Ukraine and Turkey. To be sure, her life and career were the exception, not the rule.

The Tatar attacks and the slave trade left deep scars in Ukrainian memory. The fate of the slaves was the subject of numerous *dumas*—Ukrainian epic songs that lamented the fate of the captives, described their attempts to escape from Crimean slavery, and glorified the men who saved and freed slaves. Those folk heroes were known as Cossacks. They fought the Tatars, undertook seagoing expeditions against the Ottomans, and, indeed, freed slaves from time to time.

WHO WERE THE Cossacks? The answer depends on the period one has in mind. We know for certain that the first Cossacks were nomads. The word itself is of Turkic origin and, depending on context, could refer to a guard, a freeman, or a freebooter. The first Cossacks were all of the above. They formed small bands and lived in the steppes outside the settlements and campsites of their hordes. Living off the steppe, they turned to fishing, trapping, and banditry. Many trade routes crisscrossed the steppe, and the early Cossacks preyed on merchants who ventured there without sufficient guards. We first hear of the existence of Cossacks in the steppe, coming not from the east or south but from the north, the settled area of the Grand Duchy of Lithuania, in connection with one such attack on merchants.

In 1492, the year Christopher Columbus landed on the Caribbean island he named San Salvador and King Ferdinand and Queen Isabella signed a decree expelling the Jews from Spain, the Cossacks made their first appearance in the international arena. According to a complaint sent that year to Grand Duke Alexander of Lithuania by the Crimean khan, subjects of the duke from the cities of Kyiv and Cherkasy had captured and pillaged a Tatar ship in what seems to have been the lower reaches of the Dniester. The duke never questioned that these might be his people or that they might have engaged in steppe-style highway robbery. He ordered his borderland (the term he used was "Ukrainian") officials to investigate the Cossacks who might have been involved in the raid. He also ordered that the perpetrators be executed and that their belongings, which apparently had to include the stolen merchandise, be given to a representative of the khan.

If Alexander's orders were carried out, they had no lasting effect. In the following year, the Crimean khan accused Cossacks from Cherkasy of attacking a Muscovite ambassador. In 1499, Cossacks were spotted at the Dnieper estuary ravaging the environs of the Tatar fortress at Ochakiv. To stop Cossack expeditions going down the Dnieper to the Black Sea, the khan considered blocking the Dnieper near Ochakiv with chains. It does not appear that the plan was ever implemented or had any impact on Cossack activities. The khan's complaints to the grand duke were also of little avail.

The Lithuanian borderland officials were trying to stop Cossack raids with one hand while using the Cossacks to defend the frontier from the Tatars with the other. In 1553 the grand duke sent the captain of Cherkasy and Kaniv, Prince Dmytro Vyshnevetsky, beyond the Dnieper rapids to build a small fortress in order to stop Cossack expeditions from proceeding farther down the river. Vyshnevetsky used his Cossack servants to accomplish the task. Not surprisingly, the Crimean khan saw the Cossack fortress as an encroachment on his realm, and four years later he sent an army to expel Vyshnevetsky from his redoubt. In folk tradition, Prince Vyshnevetsky became a popular hero as the first Cossack hetman—the title that the Polish army reserved for its supreme commanders—and a fearless fighter against the Tatars and Ottomans.

By the mid-sixteenth century, the lands south of Kyiv were full of new settlements. "And the Kyiv region, fortunate and thriving, is also rich in population, for on the Borysthenes and other rivers that flow into it there are plenty of populous towns and many villages," wrote Michalon the Lithuanian. He also explained the origins of the settlers: "Some are hiding from paternal authority, or from slavery, or from service, or from [punishment for] crimes, or from debts, or from something else; others are attracted to [the region], especially in spring, by richer game and more plentiful places. And, having tried their luck in its fortresses, they never come back from there." Judging by Michael's description, the Cossacks supplemented their gains from hunting and fishing with robbery. He wrote that some poor and dirty Cossack huts were "full of expensive silks, precious stones, sables and other furs, and spices." There, he found "silk cheaper than linen, and pepper cheaper than salt." Merchants had been transporting these delicacies and luxury items from the Ottoman Empire to Muscovy or the Kingdom of Poland.

While the original Cossacks were town dwellers along the Prypiat and Dnieper rivers, by the end of the sixteenth century local peasants had swelled their ranks. This influx ended the uncertainty about the Cossacks' political, ethnic, and religious identity—whether they were Crimean and Noghay Tatars, Ukrainian subjects of dukes and kings, or a mixture of all peoples and religions. The absolute majority of Cossacks were Ukrainians who came from the huge manorial estates, or latifundia, of the magnates and nobility to avoid what historians call the "second serfdom." As discussed in chapter 7, the magnates and gentry tried to attract new settlers to their newly acquired estates in the Ukrainian borderlands, which were dangerous to live in because of the continuing threat of Tatar raids, by promising tax-free periods. As these periods expired, many peasants moved farther into the hazardous steppe territories to avoid taxation. Quite a few of them joined the Cossacks and radicalized their social agenda.

The settlement of Ukraine—the steppe borderland along the middle Dnieper depicted on Tomasz Makowski's map, as described in the previous chapter—was a common project of the Volhynian princes and the Dnieper Cossacks. In 1559, Kostiantyn Ostrozky became palatine of Kyiv—the viceroy of the vast territories of Dnieper Ukraine. His jurisdiction expanded to Kaniv and Cherkasy, and his responsibilities included the Cossacks, who both enabled and hindered the continuing settlement of the steppelands with their freebooting expeditions against the Tatars and Ottomans. Ostrozky initiated the first efforts to recruit the Cossacks into military service, not so much to use them as a fighting force as to remove them from the lands beyond the rapids and establish some form of control over that unruly crowd. The Livonian War increased the demand for fighting men on the Lithuanian border with Muscovy, and a number of Cossack units were formed in the 1570s, one of them numbering as many as five hundred men.

The reorganization of the Cossacks from militias in the service of local border officials into military units under the command of army officers inaugurated a new era in the history of Cossackdom. For the first time, the term "registered Cossack" came into use. Cossacks taken into military service and thus included in the "register" were exempted from paying taxes and not subject to the jurisdiction of local officials. They also received a salary. There was, of course, no shortage of those wanting to be registered, but the Polish Crown recruited only limited numbers, and salaries were paid and privileges recognized only during active service. But those not included in the register to begin with or excluded from it at the end of a particular war or military campaign refused to give up their status, giving rise to endless disputes between Cossacks and border officials. The creation of the register solved one problem for the government, only to breed another.

IN 1590, THE Commonwealth Diet decreed the creation of a force of 1,000 registered Cossacks to protect the Ukrainian borderlands from the Tatars and the Tatars from the unregistered Cossacks. Although the king issued the requisite ordinance, little came of it. By 1591, the first Cossack uprising had engulfed Ukraine. The Cossacks, who until then had been harassing Ottoman possessions—the Crimean Khanate, the principality of Moldavia (an Ottoman dependency), and the Black Sea coast—now turned their energies inward. They rebelled not against the state but against their own "godfathers"— the Volhynian princes, in particular Prince Janusz Ostrozky (Polish: Ostrogski) and his father, Kostiantyn. Janusz was the captain of Bila Tserkva, a castle and Cossack stronghold south of Kyiv, while Kostiantyn, the palatine of Kyiv, "supervised" his son's activities. The Ostrozkys, father and son, had full control of the region. No one from the local nobility dared defy the powerful princes, who were busy extending their possessions by taking over the lands of the petty nobility.

One of the Ostrozkys' noble victims, Kryshtof Kosynsky, turned out to be a Cossack chieftain as well. When Janusz seized Kosynsky's land, which he held on the basis of a royal grant, Kosynsky did not waste time on a futile complaint to the king but gathered his Cossacks and attacked the Bila Tserkva castle, the younger Ostrozky's headquarters. A private army assembled by the Ostrozkys and another scion of Volhynia, Prince Oleksandr Vyshnevetsky, eventually defeated him. The princes managed to put down the revolt without asking for help from the royal authorities. Ironically, the godfathers of the Cossacks punished their unruly children with the help of other Cossacks in their private service. By far the best known of Ostrozky's Cossack chieftains was Severyn Nalyvaiko. He led the Ostrozky Cossacks into battle against Kosynsky's army and then gathered dispersed Cossacks in the steppes of Podolia to lead them as far away as possible from the Ostrozkys' possessions.

There was, however, a limit to how much the Ostrozkys could control or manipulate the Cossack rebellion. The Cossacks elected their own commander, whom they followed in battle, but once the expedition was over, they were free to remove or even execute him if he acted against their interests. Then there were major divisions among the Cossacks themselves, which were not limited to registered versus unregistered men. The registered Cossacks were recruited from the landowning Cossack class, whose members resided in towns and settlements between Kyiv and Cherkasy. They had a chance to obtain special rights associated with royal service. But there was also another group, the Zaporozhian Cossacks, many of them former peasants, who had a fortified settlement called the Sich (after the wooden palisade that protected it) on the islands beyond the rapids. They were beyond the reach of royal officials, caused most of the trouble with the Crimean Tatars, and, in turbulent times, served as a magnet for the dissatisfied townsmen and peasants who fled to the steppes.

Nalyvaiko, charged by Ostrozky with managing the Cossack riffraff—largely runaway peasants—soon found himself in an uneasy alliance with the unruly Zaporozhians. By 1596 he was no longer doing Ostrozky's bidding but acting on his own, leading a revolt greater than the one initiated by Kosynsky. The early 1590s saw a number of years of bad harvest, which caused famine. Starvation drove more peasants out of the noble estates and into Cossack ranks. This time the princely retinues were insufficient to suppress the uprising: the royal army was called in, headed by the commander of the Polish armed forces. In May 1596, the Polish army surrounded the Cossack encampment on the Left Bank of the Dnieper. The "old," or town, Cossacks turned against the "new" ones and surrendered Nalyvaiko to the Poles in exchange for an amnesty. Executed in Warsaw, the princely servant turned Cossack rebel became a martyr for the Cossack and Orthodox causes in the eyes of the Cossack chroniclers and poets of the romantic era, including the Russian poet Kondratii Ryleev, who was executed in 1826 for his own revolt against the authorities.

AT THE END of the sixteenth century, the Cossacks entered into the foreign-policy calculations not only of the commonwealth and the Ottoman Empire but also of central and western European powers. In 1594 Erich von Lassota, an emissary of the Holy Roman Emperor, Rudolf II, visited the Zaporozhian Cossacks with a proposal to join his master's war against the Ottomans. Three years later, a papal representative, Alessandro Comuleo, arrived on a similar mission. Little came of those missions, apart from Comuleo's letters and Lassota's diary, which described the democratic order that prevailed in the Zaporozhian Sich and have enriched our knowledge about the early history of the Cossacks. But the Cossacks, now known in Vienna and Rome, would soon gain notice as far afield as Paris and London, and present a major threat to Moscow.

The Ukrainian Cossacks, who had begun their international career in the 1550s by serving the tsar of Muscovy, Ivan the Terrible, paid an unsolicited visit to Moscow during the first decade of the seventeenth century. Muscovy was then in turmoil because of an economic, dynastic, and political crisis known as the Time of Troubles. It began at the turn of the seventeenth century with a number of devastating famines caused in part by what we today call the Little Ice Age—a period of low temperatures that lasted half a millennium, from about 1350 to 1850, peaking around the beginning of the seventeenth century. The crisis afflicted Muscovy at a most inopportune time, when its Rurikid dynasty had died out and a number of aristocratic clans contested the legitimacy of the new rulers. The dynastic crisis came to an end in 1613 with the election to the Muscovite throne of the first Romanov tsar. But before the crisis was resolved, a number of candidates for the throne, some of them "pretenders" claiming to be surviving relatives of Ivan the Terrible, tried their political luck, opening the door to foreign intervention.

During the lengthy interregnum, the Cossacks supported the two pretenders seeking the Muscovite throne, False Dmitrii I and False Dmitrii II. Up to 10,000 Cossacks joined the army of Field Crown Hetman Stanisław Żółkiewski of Poland when he marched on Moscow in 1610. The election to the Muscovite throne three years later of Tsar Mikhail Romanov, founder of the dynasty that lasted until the Revolution of 1917, did not end Cossack involvement in Muscovite affairs. In 1618, a Ukrainian Cossack army of 20,000 joined Polish troops in their march on Moscow and took part in the siege of the capital. The Cossacks helped end the war on conditions favorable to the Kingdom of Poland. One of them was the transfer to Poland of the Chernihiv land, which the Grand Duchy of Lithuania had lost in the early sixteenth century. By the mid-seventeenth century, Chernihiv would become an important part of the Cossack world. As always, however, the Cossacks both helped and hindered the Polish kings in advancing their foreign-policy agenda. In its war with Muscovy, the Polish-Lithuanian Commonwealth never got the support it hoped for from the Ottoman Empire, partly because of continuing Cossack seagoing expeditions and attacks on the Ottoman littoral.

In 1606, descending the Dnieper and entering the Black Sea on their longboats, called "seagulls" (*chaiky*), the Cossacks stormed Varna, one of the strongest Ottoman fortresses on the western Black Sea shore. In 1614 they pillaged Trabzon on the southeastern shore, and in the following year they entered the Istanbul harbor of the Golden Horn and pillaged the suburbs, much as the Vikings had done some 750 years earlier. But whereas the Vikings had also traded with Constantinople, the Cossack expeditions were akin to pirate attacks on seashores from the Mediterranean to the Caribbean. They came to rob, take revenge, and, as Ukrainian folk songs related, liberate long-suffering slaves. In 1616, they attacked Kaffa, the main slave-trading center on the Crimean coast, and liberated all the captives.

The sultan, his court, and the foreign ambassadors who witnessed one Cossack attack after another on the mighty Ottoman Empire were stunned. The Christian rulers could now take the raiders seriously as potential allies in a war against the Ottomans. The French ambassador in Istanbul, Count Philippe de Harlay of Césy, wrote to King Louis XIII in August 1620, "Every time the Cossacks are near here on the Black Sea, they seize incredible booty despite their weak forces and have such a reputation that strokes of the cudgel are required to force the Turkish soldiers to do battle against them on several galleys that the grand seigneur [the sultan] sends there with great difficulty."

While Count Philippe was informing his king about the inability of the Ottomans to curb the Cossack seagoing expeditions, advisers to sixteen-year-old Sultan Osman II were considering how to wage war on two fronts: against the Polish army on land and the Cossacks at sea. In the summer of 1620, the Ottoman army marched toward the Prut River in today's Moldova against the commonwealth, whose troops included private Cossack armies of Polish and Ukrainian magnates. The campaign aimed ostensibly to punish the commonwealth for not curbing Cossack attacks on the Ottomans. In reality, the agenda was much broader. The Ottomans were trying to protect their vassals in the region from the growing influence of the commonwealth. The Polish army, numbering some 10,000 soldiers, and the Ottoman force, twice as large according to some estimates, clashed in September 1620 near the town of Ţuţora on today's Moldovan-Romanian border. The battle went on for twenty days, ending with a crushing defeat for the commonwealth.

Since the commonwealth had no standing army, the court and the entire country panicked. Everyone expected the Ottomans to continue their march on Poland. Indeed they did. In the following year, a much larger Ottoman army, estimated at 120,000 soldiers and led by the sultan himself, passed through Moldavia on its way to the commonwealth. The Ottomans met a commonwealth force approximately 40,000 strong, half of it made up of Ukrainian Cossacks, led by Petro Konashevych-Sahaidachny, hero of the Cossacks' raid of 1616 on Kaffa and commander of their march on Moscow two years later. The battle lasted a whole month, waged on the banks of the Dniester River near the fortress of Khotyn, which the Ottomans besieged.

The Battle of Khotyn ended with no clear victory for either side, but that uncertain outcome was regarded in Warsaw as a triumph for the Kingdom of Poland. The Poles had stopped the huge Ottoman army at their borders and signed a peace treaty that involved no territorial losses. Everyone understood that this result would have been all but impossible without the Cossacks. For the first time—and a short time at that—the Cossacks became the darlings of the entire commonwealth. Books that appeared soon after the battle would lionize Petro Konashevych-Sahaidachny, whose monument stands today in the Podil district of Kyiv at the head of the street named after him, as one of the greatest Polish warriors.

THE COSSACKS' MILITARY achievement at Khotyn allowed them to reassert their political and social agenda in the commonwealth. Their main demand was noble status for the Cossack officers, if not for the whole army. In 1622, when Petro Konashevych-Sahaidachny died in Kyiv from the wounds he had sustained at Khotyn, Kasiian Sakovych, a professor at the Kyiv brotherhood school, wrote verses on the death of the Cossack hetman that the Kyivan Cave Monastery press soon published. There he lauded the Cossacks as heirs to the Kyivan princes, who had stormed Constantinople back in the times of Kyivan Rus'. According to Sakovych, the Cossacks had fought for and deserved "Golden Liberty"—a code word for the same rights and liberties as enjoyed by the commonwealth nobility. "All strive ardently to attain it," wrote Sakovych. "Yet it cannot be given to everyone, only to those who defend the fatherland and the lord. Knights win it by their valor in wars: not with money but with blood do they purchase it." Recognition of the Cossacks as knights would take them only one step away from nobility.

The Cossacks did not achieve their social agenda. Their attempt to take part in the Diet to elect the new king (restricted to nobles alone) was rebuffed in 1632. This humiliation came on the heels of a number of military defeats. The authorities crushed the Cossack uprisings of 1625 and 1630. At Khotyn they had had 20,000 warriors, but now the register was limited first to 6,000 and then to 8,000 Cossacks. The Cossacks rose once more in 1637 and 1638, only to suffer defeat by the royal army yet again. They claimed to be fighting not only for Cossack liberties but also for the Orthodox faith. Although this won them support initially, the government's efforts to accommodate the Orthodox Church made it increasingly difficult to maintain the bond between the church and the Cossacks. Whereas in 1630 part of the Kyivan clergy had supported the Cossacks, in 1637 and 1638 their appeals fell on deaf ears, and they felt betrayed. The panegyrics issued by the Cave Monastery print shop no longer eulogized Cossack hetmans: instead, they lauded Orthodox nobles who had fought against them.

The suppression of the Cossack uprisings of 1637 and 1638 led the authorities to attempt a long-term settlement. The model was relatively simple—a grant of legal status for the warriors on condition of their integration into the commonwealth's legal and social structure under a new leadership imposed by the king and trusted by the government. The Cossack ordinance of 1638 went far in accommodating the demands of the Cossack officer elite. It recognized the Cossacks as a separate estate with its own rights and privileges not limited to periods of military service, including the right to pass on such status and landed property to their descendants. The government took measures to control the newly recognized estate by limiting access to it on the part of other strata of the population, especially the townsfolk, with whom the Cossacks lived side by side in the towns of the steppe borderland.

Furthermore, the Polish authorities reduced the number of registered Cossacks to 6,000 (the quota of 1625) and placed them under the jurisdiction of the Crown grand hetman—the commander in chief of the Polish army. The Cossack commissioner and six Cossack colonels were all Polish nobles. The highest rank that a Cossack could attain in the Cossack army was that of captain. The six regiments had to take turns in serving as garrison troops at the Zaporozhian Sich, the rebel stronghold of the Cossacks beyond the rapids. To stop Cossack seagoing expeditions and improve relations with the Ottomans, the authorities rebuilt the fortress of Kodak at the head of the Dnieper rapids, originally built in 1635 but subsequently burned down by the Cossacks. The architect sent to supervise the reconstruction was a French engineer, Guillaume Levasseur de Beauplan, who in 1639 produced the first map of Ukraine—the steppe borderlands of the commonwealth, including the palatinates of Podolia, Bratslav, and Kyiv. Beauplan's numerous maps of the region made Ukraine a household word among European cartographers of the second half of the seventeenth century.

With the Cossacks pacified and accommodated to some degree, the Dnieper closed as an avenue to Black Sea expeditions, and the Zaporozhian Sich under control, the commonwealth entered a decade that became known as the Golden Peace. It brought continuing colonization of the steppe borderlands and expansion of noble holdings and latifundia. The population grew as new magnates, new peasants, and Jewish settlers acting as new middlemen moved in to take advantage of burgeoning economic opportunities. As things turned out, this was the calm before the storm. A new and much larger Cossack revolt was in the making.

The Cossacks had come a long way—from small bands of fishermen and trappers foraging in the steppes south of Kyiv to settlers of new lands along the steppe frontier; from private militiamen in the employ of princes to fighters in an independent force that foreigners treated with respect; and, finally, from refugees and adventurers to members of a cohesive military brotherhood that regarded itself as a distinct social order and demanded from the government not only money but also recognition of its warrior status. The Polish state could benefit from the military might and economic potential of the Cossacks only if it managed to accommodate their social demands. As subsequent developments would show repeatedly, that was no easy task.

CHAPTER 9

EASTERN REFORMATIONS

ONE OF THE many stereotypes of contemporary Ukraine is its image as a cleft country, divided between the Orthodox east and the Catholic west. Samuel Huntington's best-selling book *The Clash of Civilizations* includes a map that shows the line between Eastern and Western Christian civilization passing right through Ukraine. It leaves the western regions of the country, including Galicia and Volhynia, on the Catholic side of the divide, and the rest of Ukraine on the Orthodox side. Problems with the map begin as soon as one tries to follow it and finds very little Roman Catholicism in the allegedly Catholic part of the country. Volhynia is a predominantly Orthodox land, and in Galicia, Catholics constitute a plurality but not the majority of Christian believers: even so, one has a hard time distinguishing their churches and liturgies from those of the Orthodox, as most Ukrainian Catholics share the Orthodox rite.

One should not be too harsh on the mapmakers. It is difficult, if not impossible, to draw a straight line in a country such as Ukraine. This is true for all cultural frontiers, but the existence of a hybrid church that combines elements of Eastern and Western Christianity further complicates the Ukrainian situation. That church was originally called Uniate, reflecting its purpose of uniting those elements. It is known today as the Ukrainian Greek Catholic Church, with "Greek" referring to the Byzantine rite, or simply as the Ukrainian Catholic Church—by far the most successful institutional attempt to bridge one of the most ancient schisms of the Christian world. The church came into existence in the late sixteenth century, an era that saw the eastward advance of Western political and religious models and their adaptation to traditionally Orthodox lands. But resistance and growing self-assertiveness on the part of indigenous societies often accompanied that process. Both accommodation and resistance to Western trends found their embodiment in Ukrainian Orthodoxy, which underwent considerable transformation in the first half of the seventeenth century in response to challenges from the West.

THE PRO-WESTERN MOVEMENT began within the Rus' Orthodox Church in the early 1590s in response to a crisis that engulfed the Kyiv metropolitanate. The church possessed large landholdings, and the nobility considered church offices excellent career choices for their sons. Such candidates often had little interest in religion but a strong attraction to ecclesiastical wealth. Thus bishops and archimandrites of leading monasteries often received appointment from the king with the help of secular benefactors of the church and without even taking monastic vows. Priests had just an elementary education, and so, often, did bishops. Even if they wanted more knowledge, there was no place to obtain it. Meanwhile, Calvinist and Catholic schools and colleges began opening their doors to the sons of Orthodox nobles. That was especially true of Jesuit schools. One of them, soon to become an academy, was established in Vilnius, near the Belarusian border, and another was founded in the town of Jarosław in Galicia.

The situation in the Kyiv metropolitanate did not differ much from the situation that had prevailed before the Reformation and the start of Catholic reform in other parts of Europe. In many ways, it was business as usual, but parts of the Orthodox elite began to perceive it as a crisis. The Catholic Church in the commonwealth was busy reinventing itself with the help of Jesuit schools and colleges, posing an implicit challenge to unreformed Orthodoxy. The publishing and educational activities of the circle around Prince Kostiantyn Ostrozky were an initial response to that challenge. No less concerned about the state of church affairs were the members of Orthodox brotherhoods—organizations of Rus' merchants and tradesmen in major Ukrainian cities. The members of the Lviv brotherhood, the richest and most influential of them all, challenged the authority of the local Orthodox bishop, whom they believed to be corrupt and thus a liability in their dealings with the dominant Catholics. In 1586 the Lviv burghers succeeded in establishing their independence of the bishop, and in 1591 they opened their own school without waiting for him to do so.

The Orthodox hierarchs found themselves in an impossible position. Their status in the Catholic-ruled commonwealth was secondary to that of the Catholic bishops, who were members of the senate and had direct access to the king. (Ostrozky and other princes and nobles felt that they were the true masters of the church.) The brotherhoods were in open revolt, undermining the bishop's monopoly on teaching church dogma, and the patriarch of Constantinople, instead of helping the bishops, took the rebels under his protection (they knew how to appeal to the cash-strapped hierarch). A solution to this conundrum suddenly presented itself in the idea of union with Rome. The vision of church union shared by the Orthodox hierarchs rested on a model proposed by the joint Catholic-Orthodox Council of Florence in 1439. In the twilight years of the Byzantine Empire, both the emperor and the patriarch grew desperate to save it from Ottoman attacks. A promise of assistance came from Rome, at the price of uniting the two churches under papal authority. The Byzantine leaders agreed to that condition, which subordinated their church to Rome and replaced Orthodox dogmas with Catholic ones. In particular, they agreed with the Catholics on the all-important issue of the *filioque*, admission that the Holy Spirit proceeded not only from God the Father but also from God the Son, Jesus Christ. They managed, however, to maintain the institution of the married priesthood, the Greek language, and the Byzantine liturgy.

In the summer of 1595, two Orthodox bishops set off on the long journey to Rome, bringing along a letter from their fellow Orthodox hierarchs asking the pope to accept them into the Catholic Church on conditions close to those of the Union of Florence. In Rome, Pope Clement VIII received the travelers and welcomed the "return" of the bishops and their church at a ceremony in the Hall of Constantine in the Vatican. The bishops, armed with a papal bull and numerous breves to the king and other commonwealth officials, returned home to convene a church council that would declare the conclusion of the union and announce the transfer of the Kyiv metropolitanate to the jurisdiction of Rome. The king gladly arranged the time and location of the council: it was to take place in October 1596 in the town of Brest on the Polish-Ukrainian-Belarusian border.

It seemed for a while that it was a done deal—the pope, the king, and the bishops all wanted the union. The problem was with the faithful or, more precisely, with the major stakeholders in the church. These included Prince Ostrozky and his fellow Orthodox magnates, members of the brotherhoods, and the monastic and a good part of the parish clergy. The magnates did not want to lose control of the church—in the age of the Reformation, it was a valuable political and religious asset not to be taken lightly; the brotherhoods wanted reform from below, not greater power for the bishops; some of the archimandrites, who ran the monasteries without taking monastic vows, wanted to continue managing church landholdings; and some of the monks, clergy, and rank-and-file faithful could not imagine betraying the holy Orthodox Church by abandoning the patriarch of Constantinople. It was a haphazard but powerful coalition of reformers and conservatives, true believers and opportunists that placed the plans of Rome, Warsaw, and the Orthodox hierarchs in jeopardy.

Prince Kostiantyn Ostrozky, arguably the most powerful man in Ukraine, was determined to prevent the church union. In the form suggested by the bishops, it threatened to wrest the church from his control and limit his ability to use Orthodoxy as a weapon in the struggle with royal power to keep a special place for the Ruthenian princes in commonwealth society. He must also have felt personally betrayed. One of the two bishops who had gone to Rome asking for the union was his old friend Ipatii Potii, whom Ostrozky had persuaded to abandon a political career in order to become a bishop, with the goal of reforming the church. Ostrozky told Potii that he was for the union but only with the consent of the patriarch of Constantinople. Potii, who knew that such consent was not forthcoming, opted for union without Constantinople. Potii's fellow traveler on the road to Rome was Bishop Kyryl Terletsky, who was not only the exarch, or personal representative, of the patriarch of Constantinople, charged with defending patriarchal interests in the region, but also the bishop of the Volhynia eparchy—Ostrozky's stronghold.

Appalled, the old prince had dispatched armed servants to intercept the two bishops on their way to Rome, but they escaped unharmed. Now Ostrozky headed for Brest to take part in the church council with a small army of supporters consisting of Orthodox nobles and servants. He also had support from his Protestant allies—the Lithuanian aristocrats. One of them offered his own home as the venue for the church council, as the king had ordered the town's Orthodox churches closed. The king's representatives arrived in Brest with their own armed retinues. In this charged atmosphere, the pending union of churches might well descend into not just disunion but bloody battle.

THE SINGLE EVENT known in historiography as the Council of Brest never actually took place, for it split into two gatherings, Catholic and Orthodox.

The Catholic council, which featured among its participants the Orthodox metropolitan and most of the bishops, proclaimed the union. The Orthodox council, with a representative of the patriarch of Constantinople presiding, included among its participants two Orthodox bishops as well as scores of archimandrites and representatives of the parish clergy. It refused to join the union and swore continuing allegiance to the patriarch of Constantinople. The Kyiv metropolitanate was now divided, with part of it declaring loyalty to Rome. The schism within the metropolitanate had a clear geographic dimension: Galicia, with Lviv and Peremyshl, remained Orthodox, while Volhynia and the Belarusian eparchies supported the new Uniate Church. The situation on the ground was in fact much more complex than this general description suggests, with religious loyalties sometimes splitting families, while individual parishes and monasteries switched allegiance more than once.

Despite strong opposition to the Union of Brest, the king held fast to it. He recognized only one council of Brest—the one that had proclaimed the union—and, henceforth, acknowledged the Uniate Church as the sole legitimate Eastern Christian church in his country. Two bishops, scores of monasteries, thousands of churches, and hundreds of thousands, if not millions, of Orthodox faithful were now considered lawbreakers. The Orthodox nobility took the fight to the local and Commonwealth Diets, claiming that the royal authorities were mounting an assault on the freedom of religion guaranteed to the nobility. Indeed they were. Back in the 1570s, immediately after the death of Sigismund Augustus, the Protestant nobles had made freedom of religion a central tenet of the "articles" to which every elected king of Poland had to swear allegiance.

Now the Protestant nobles backed their Orthodox counterparts, helping to turn the Diets into religious battlegrounds and raising the need for the "accommodation of the Rus' nation of the Greek rite" at every Commonwealth Diet. But no substantial change took place before the death of King Sigismund III in 1632. For more than thirty years, the Orthodox Church existed without official status or recognition. As new bishops could not be appointed without royal assent, the Uniates hoped to leave the Orthodox Church without bishops after those who refused to accept the union died out. The Orthodox Church survived only by disobeying the king and the royal authorities. Instead of strengthening royal power, the Union of Brest undermined it. Like the Union of Lublin before it, the church union produced results contrary to the expectations of its authors.

Not limited to the Diets, the struggle for and against the union spilled into a much broader public arena through publications. In Ukraine and Belarus, there was an explosion of treatises, protestations, attacks, and counterattacks known today under the general rubric of "polemical literature." Initially, both sides were ill equipped to conduct serious religious polemics and were served by their Polish supporters. Piotr Skarga, a Jesuit who had attended the council of Brest, was among those who used his pen in support of the union. Ostrozky employed the talents of one of his Protestant clients to fight back. From then on, Protestants would write under pen names, usually Greek ones, so as to stress their Orthodox credentials and the authority of their texts. Consequently, they wrote most of the earlier tracts in Polish, which they continued to use even in the later period, when local authors began to write in Ruthenian.

As time passed, both Uniates and Orthodox began to employ authors from their own milieu who could engage the other side on issues of religious policy, church history, and theology. Among the Orthodox, an author who gained special prominence was Meletii Smotrytsky, the son of one of the editors of the Ostrih Bible, Herasym Smotrytsky. A man of many talents, Meletii was also author of the first grammar of Church Slavonic, which became a standard reference on the subject for the next two centuries. Judging by the number of publications, the Orthodox were more active than the Uniates, perhaps because they lacked other channels for defending their cause as well as the support of the courts.

THE UNION OF Brest and the rise of Cossackdom led to a southward and eastward shift of Ukraine's two main cultural frontiers, Christian-Muslim and East-West Christian. That shift brought about a number of major changes in the economic, social, and cultural life of Ukraine. One of the most emblematic of them was the return of the city of Kyiv to the center of Ukrainian history for the first time since the Mongol invasion of the mid-thirteenth century. In the first half of the seventeenth century, that ancient city would become the center of the Orthodox Reformation—an effort on the part of Orthodox churches from Constantinople to Moscow to catch up with the Reformation and Counter-Reformation in Europe and reform themselves in the process.

The revival of Kyiv as a religious and cultural center began in the early seventeenth century as the old city became a safe haven for Orthodox intellectuals from Galicia. They found conditions there more favorable for their religious and educational work than in western Ukraine, where Warsaw put increasing pressure on the Orthodox to join the union with Rome. The key to turning Kyiv into an Orthodox center was continuing Orthodox control (despite the Union of Brest) over the Kyivan Cave Monastery—by far the richest monastic institution in Ukraine and Belarus. In 1615 the archimandrite of the monastery, Yelisei Pletenetsky, moved the printing press once managed by the Orthodox bishop of Lviv to Kyiv. From Lviv and Galicia came not only the press but also writers, proofreaders, and printers who created a new intellectual center under Pletenetsky's guidance and protection. In the same year, an Orthodox brotherhood was founded in Kyiv and opened a school of its own, as the Lviv brotherhood had done. The school would later develop into a Western-style college, while the printing house would publish eleven books before Pletenetsky's death in 1624. By that time, Kyiv had replaced Ostrih and Vilnius as the headquarters of Orthodox publishing activity.

Since the late sixteenth century, the region south of Kyiv had become a Cossack freehold in all but name, a fact that assisted the rise of Kyiv as the focus of religious, educational, and cultural activities opposed to Polish Catholic authority. The Cossacks contributed to the Kyivan renaissance in two major ways. First, their presence minimized the Tatar threat, making the city much more secure as a place for religious dissidents to live and work, as well as for the monks and peasants who tilled the Cave Monastery's lands to produce the revenue needed to fund publishing and education. Second, when the Kyivan monks found themselves under growing pressure from the Polish government in Warsaw, the Cossacks provided the Orthodox refugees from Galicia with the protection they needed. In 1610, their hetman promised in writing to kill a representative of the Uniate metropolitan sent to Kyiv to convert the local Orthodox. Eight years later, the Cossacks acted on his threat and drowned the man in the Dnieper. "What other nations strive to win by means of words and discourses, the Cossacks accomplish with actions themselves," wrote the Orthodox intellectual Iov Boretsky, who was for some time an apologist for the Cossacks.

The Cossacks played a crucial role in consecrating a new Orthodox hierarchy—an all-important act that saved the church from extinction. Left without bishops because of the king's refusal to allow any new consecrations, the church was thus bound to disappear. In the fall of 1620, Petro Konashevych-Sahaidachny, by far the best-known and most respected Cossack leader of the time, convinced Patriarch Theophanes of Jerusalem, who was then traveling through Ukraine, to consecrate a new hierarchy. The consecration not only gave new life to the Orthodox metropolitanate but also reestablished Kyiv as an ecclesiastical capital. It happened almost by default. The king did not recognize the new metropolitan, Yov Boretsky, and issued an order for his arrest and the detention of the rest of the new hierarchy. That made it impossible for Boretsky to live in Navahrudak, a town near Vilnius that had served as the residence of the Orthodox metropolitans since the fourteenth century. He had no choice but to reside in Kyiv, the hub of the Cossack-controlled Dnieper region. The Orthodox Church now had its own army in the Cossacks, while the Cossacks gained Orthodox ideologues and a printing press to promote their social and political agenda.

The Cossack-Orthodox alliance became especially worrisome for Warsaw in the fall of 1632, when the Muscovite army crossed the commonwealth border in an attempt to recapture Smolensk and other territory lost during the Time of Troubles. The commonwealth was caught unprepared, with few troops to defend its borders, almost as in 1621, when Sahaidachny had saved the country at the Battle of Khotyn. To make things worse, the commonwealth was preoccupied with the lengthy election of a new king, as Sigismund III had died in the spring of that year. The death of the king who had helped engineer the Union of Brest presented the commonwealth elites with both a problem and an opportunity to find new ways of dealing with the religious crisis. Instead of assuaging religious differences, the union had divided Rus' society and turned a good part of it against the government.

THE MADE-IN-WARSAW SOLUTION to the problem was called the Accommodation of the Ruthenian Nation of Greek Worship. The Orthodox Church would receive recognition as a legal entity with rights and privileges equal to those of the Uniate Church. The deal, negotiated at the Commonwealth Diet with representatives of the Orthodox nobility and backed by the future king, Władysław IV, achieved certain political goals. In the short run, it bought Orthodox loyalty to the commonwealth and ensured Cossack participation in the Smolensk War on the side of the commonwealth forces. Recognition of the church by the royal authorities also drove a wedge between the Orthodox hierarchy and the Cossacks. The church no longer needed Cossack protection to survive and henceforth oriented itself toward Warsaw.

As the sponsors of the deal saw it, the rapprochement of the Orthodox Church with the royal authorities called for new ecclesiastical leadership. To strengthen the hand of the "peace with Warsaw" party, the Orthodox participants in the Diet elected a new metropolitan, Peter Mohyla. On entering

Kyiv, Mohyla arrested his predecessor, putting him in a cellar at the Kyivan Cave Monastery. A former officer of the Polish army and archimandrite of the Cave Monastery, the new Orthodox leader knew what he was doing. As one who had been close to Smotrytsky and Boretsky, Mohyla had little use for the Cossacks or their protégés in the church. He also had the full support of the royal authorities—he was, after all, the scion of a ruling family.

Peter Mohyla was not of royal blood, but as a son of the Orthodox ruler (*hospodar*) of the principality of Moldavia, he was certainly a member of the commonwealth aristocracy. Mohyla's panegyrists celebrated him as the new leader of Rus'. He took the place of princes such as Ostrozky and of Cossacks such as Sahaidachny, whom Orthodox intellectuals had glorified as heirs and continuators of the Kyivan princes Volodymyr the Great and Yaroslav the Wise. "Do you recall how famous Rus' was before, how many patrons it had," wrote one of the panegyrists, speaking "on behalf" of the St. Sophia Cathedral, the architectural legacy of Prince Yaroslav, now reconstructed by Mohyla. "Now there are few of them; Rus' wants to have you."

Mohyla took the task of restoring Rus'-era churches with utmost seriousness, rebuilding quite a few of them. "Restoration" in the mid-seventeenth century, however, meant something quite different than it does today. As the exterior of the St. Sophia Cathedral shows even now, Mohyla and his architects never tried to go back to the original Byzantine models. The new style in which they "restored" their churches came from the West and was influenced by the European baroque. The St. Sophia Cathedral as we know it today is a perfect example of the mixture of cultural styles and trends that defined the essence of Mohyla's activities as metropolitan. Although Byzantine frescos embellish its interior, the cathedral has the exterior of a baroque church.

The westernization of the Byzantine heritage and the adaptation of the Orthodox Church to the challenges of the Reformation and Counter-Reformation were the driving forces of Mohyla's ecclesiastical and educational innovations. As in the case of architecture, it was not merely that models were coming from the West but that they were also Catholic. The Uniates and the Orthodox were in competition, trying to emulate Catholic reform without giving away too much of their Byzantine heritage. While the Uniates could send their students to Rome and to Jesuit colleges in central and western Europe, the Orthodox did not have that luxury. Mohyla addressed the challenge by establishing the first Orthodox college in Kyiv to adapt the Jesuit college curriculum to its needs. The college, created in 1632 through a merger of the Kyiv brotherhood school with the school at the Cave Monastery, later became known as the Kyiv Mohyla Academy and is now one of the leading universities in Ukraine. As it was in the seventeenth century, the academy is the most Western-oriented university in the country.

Mohyla secured Kyiv's role as the leading publishing center in the Orthodox lands of the commonwealth and elsewhere. The books published in Kyiv in the 1640s found readers far beyond the borders of Ukraine. One of them, the *Liturgicon*, was the first book to systematize Orthodox liturgical practices. Another, titled *Confession of the Orthodox Faith*, presented the first thorough discussion of the basics of the Orthodox faith, offering answers to 260 questions in catechism style. It was written around 1640, approved by a council of Eastern patriarchs in 1643, and published in Kyiv in 1645. Heavily influenced by Catholic models, the *Confession* became a response to the Protestant-oriented catechism of 1633 issued by Patriarch Cyril Lucaris of Constantinople. The Eastern patriarchs' stamp of approval made it a standard work for the whole Orthodox world, including Muscovy.

The educational and publishing projects initiated by Mohyla had as their primary goal the reform of Kyivan Orthodoxy. An educated clergy, a clearly defined confession of faith, and standardized liturgical practices went hand in hand with the metropolitan's efforts to increase the power of bishops in the church, strengthen ecclesiastical discipline, and improve relations with the royal authorities. All these measures responded to the challenges of the Reformation and the Counter-Reformation—hallmarks of the confessionalization of religious life all over Europe. "Confessionalization" meant a number of things. In the course of the sixteenth century, all churches along the Catholic-Protestant divide were busy formulating professions of faith, educating their clergies, strengthening discipline, and standardizing liturgical practices in cooperation with the secular authorities. By the mid-seventeenth century, under the leadership of Peter Mohyla, the Orthodox had joined this general European trend.

Remarkably, Kyiv, a city scarcely noted on the map of the Orthodox world since the Mongol invasion of 1240, played the leading role in the Orthodox Reformation, not Moscow or Constantinople. A number of reasons underlay that development in addition to those outlined above. After the Time of Troubles, the patriarchs of Moscow were isolated not only from the Western but also from the Eastern Christian world, believing that there was no true religion outside the Tsardom of Muscovy. Constantinople, under the control of the Ottomans, tried to conduct reform on the Protestant model but did not get very far. In 1638, Patriarch Cyril Lucaris, who nine years earlier had published a Latin-language Orthodox profession of faith (*Confessio*) heavily influenced by Protestant doctrine, was strangled on orders of the sultan for allegedly instigating a Cossack attack on the Ottoman Empire. In the same year a church council in Constantinople anathematized him for his theological views. In the contest between Mohyla and Lucaris and between Catholic and Protestant models for the reform of Orthodoxy, Mohyla's model emerged victorious. His reforms would have a profound impact on the Orthodox world for another century and a half.

THE UNION OF Brest left the Ruthenian (Ukrainian and Belarusian) society of the commonwealth in general, and the Ukrainian elites in particular, split between two churches—a division that endures in today's Ukraine. But the struggles over the fate of the union also left that society much more conscious of its commonalities, including history, culture, and religious tradition. For all its verbal ferocity and occasional physical violence, that struggle helped form a new pluralistic political and religious culture that allowed discussion and disagreement. Ukraine's location on the religious boundary between Western and Eastern Christianity produced not one "frontier" church that combined elements of the two Christian traditions (a distinction often ascribed to the Uniates alone) but two. The Orthodox, too, embraced new religious and cultural trends from the West as they sought to reform themselves and adjust to conditions in the decades following the Union of Brest. In the early seventeenth century, it was even more difficult to draw a clear line between Christian East and Christian West in Ukraine than it is now.

The polemics over the Union of Brest helped awaken Rus' society on both sides of the religious divide from a long intellectual sleep. The issues discussed by the polemicists included the baptism of Rus', the history of the Kyiv metropolitanate, the rights of the church and of the Rus' lands under the Lithuanian dukes and of the Orthodox under the Union of Lublin, and the royal decrees and Diet resolutions of the subsequent era. For those who could read and took part in the political, social, and religious developments of the day, the polemicists created a sense of self-identity that had not previously existed. If they were at odds on issues of religion, the polemicists all showed the highest regard for the entity that they called the Ruthenian nation (*naród Ruski*), in whose interest they allegedly conducted their struggles.

CHAPTER 10

THE GREAT REVOLT

THE COSSACK UPRISING that began in the spring of 1648, known in history as the Great Revolt, was the seventh major Cossack insurrection since the end of the sixteenth century. The commonwealth had crushed the previous six, but this one became too big to suppress. It transformed the political map of the entire region and gave birth to a Cossack state that many regard as the foundation of modern Ukraine. It also launched a long era of Russian involvement in Ukraine and is widely regarded as a starting point in the history of relations between Russia and Ukraine as separate nations.

The Great Revolt began in exactly the same manner as the first Cossack uprising, led by Kryshtof Kosynsky in 1591—with a dispute over a land grant between a magnate and Bohdan Khmelnytsky, a petty noble who also happened to be a Cossack officer. Aged fifty-three at the time, he was an unlikely leader of a Cossack rebellion, having served the king loyally in numerous battles and become chancellor of the Cossack Host following the uprising of 1638. After the servant of a prominent commonwealth official took his estate of Subotiv from him, Khmelnytsky turned to the courts, but to no avail. More than that, his powerful opponents put him in prison. He escaped and went directly to the Zaporozhian Sich, where the rebellious Cossacks welcomed him as one of their own and elected him their hetman. It was March 1648. The Golden Peace was over; the Great Revolt had begun.

Up to that point, developments resembled those of previous Cossack uprisings, but Khmelnytsky changed the familiar pattern. Before marching northward, capturing towns, and confronting the commonwealth army, he went south in search of allies. In a dramatic reversal of established steppe politics, he offered the Crimean khan his friendship and an opportunity. The cautious khan allowed his vassals, the Noghay Horde north of the Crimea, to join the Cossacks. For Khmelnytsky and the Cossack rebels, this was a major coup. While the popular image of the Cossack nowadays is a man on horseback, in the mid-seventeenth century most Cossacks were in fact infantrymen. They lacked a cavalry of their own because maintaining one was too expensive: only nobles could afford to keep a battle-ready horse, often more than one. Khmelnytsky's new alliance with the Tatars, who fought on horseback, solved the cavalry problem. From then on, the Cossacks could not only take poorly fortified borderland towns or defend themselves in fortified camps but also confront the Polish army in the field.

It did not take long for the alliance to prove its worth. In May 1648, Cossack and Tatar forces defeated two Polish armies, one near the Zhovti Vody (Yellow Water) River near the northern approaches to the Zaporozhian Sich, the other near the town of Korsun in the middle Dnieper region. A key to Cossack success, apart from the participation of Noghay cavalry (close to 4,000 horsemen) in both battles, was the decision of some 6,000 registered Cossacks to switch sides, abandon their Polish masters and join the Khmelnytsky revolt. The Polish standing army was completely wiped out. Its two chief commanders, the Crown grand hetman and the Crown field hetman, as well as hundreds of officers, ended up in Tatar captivity.

While the Cossacks' sudden success shocked the commonwealth, Khmelnytsky and his closest supporters could not believe their luck. The hetman did not know what move to make next. In June 1648, with the Polish armies gone and the commonwealth in disarray, Bohdan Khmelnytsky took something of a summer hiatus and retired to his native Chyhyryn to consider what to do. But the rebels refused to take any breaks. With the old registered Cossacks gathered near Bila Tserkva, a town south of Kyiv, the popular uprising began in earnest in the rest of Ukraine. Inspired by the news of Cossack victories, the peasants and the townspeople took matters into their own hands, attacking the estates of large landowners, harassing their retreating private armies, settling scores with nobles, and hunting down Catholic priests. But those who suffered most from the peasant revolt in the summer of 1648 were the Jews of Ukraine.

The first letters that Khmelnytsky sent to the authorities as the revolt began already mentioned Jewish leaseholders. The Cossack hetman complained of the "intolerable injustices" that the Cossacks were suffering at the hands of the royal officials, the colonels—Polish commanders of the registered Cossacks—and "even" the Jews. Khmelnytsky mentioned the Jews in passing, placing them in the third or even fourth echelon of Cossack enemies, but the rebels in Right-Bank Ukraine, where Jews began to suffer attack en masse in June 1648, had their own priorities. They assaulted and often killed Jews (especially men), leading to the destruction of entire communities, which they all but wiped from the map in the course of three summer months of 1648. We do not know the number of victims, as we do not know the number of Jews living in the region before the revolt, but most scholars estimate Jewish losses at 14,000 to 20,000 victims—a very high number, given the time and place. For all its rapid economic development, seventeenth-century Ukraine was relatively sparsely settled.

Twentieth-century Jewish and Ukrainian historians have placed considerable emphasis on the underlying social causes of anti-Jewish antagonism in Dnieper Ukraine of that period. Rivalry between Jewish and Christian merchants and artisans in the cities and towns, as well as the Jewish leaseholders' role as middlemen between nobles and peasants, did indeed contribute to the violence unleashed by the Cossack revolt. But one should not lose sight of religious motives in the attacks on Ukrainian Jewry. Religion was essential to social identity on both sides of the Christian-Jewish divide. It was not for nothing that the best-known Jewish chronicler of the massacres, Nathan Hannover, called the attackers "Greeks," referring to their Orthodox religion, not their nationality. Some rebels felt that they were on a religious mission to convert those Jews who had escaped the massacre. Forced conversion to Christianity saved the lives of many Jewish men. Some of them joined the Cossack ranks, while others returned to Judaism once the threat of annihilation was over.

By the time Khmelnytsky and his armies began moving west of the Dnieper in the fall of 1648, they had annihilated Jews, Polish nobles, and Catholic priests throughout the region as far as the Polish strongholds of Kamianets in Podolia and Lviv in Galicia. The Uniates were gone as well, either retreating westward or converting to Orthodoxy. The latter was easy to do, as the two Eastern Christian churches differed in jurisdiction only. Few people understood or cared about dogmas. The newly assembled Polish army tried to stop the joint Cossack-Tatar march westward but suffered another major defeat at Pyliavtsi in Podolia. By the end of the year, Cossack and Tatar units were besieging Lviv and the town of Zamość on the Polish-Ukrainian

ethnic border. But they did not proceed much farther. Political considerations dictated the end of the offensive, not military ones, as there were no
troops between the Cossack armies and Warsaw.

BOHDAN KHMELNYTSKY'S NEW agenda was no longer the mere defense of
Cossack rights and privileges, as in the first months of the revolt, but neither
was it the destruction of the commonwealth. The Cossack hetman spelled
out his new program during negotiations with the Polish emissaries who visited him in January and February 1649 in the town of Pereiaslav southeast of
Kyiv. Khmelnytsky declared that he was now the sole master of Rus' and
threatened to drive the Poles beyond the Vistula River. Khmelnytsky must
have been thinking about himself as an heir to the princes of Kyivan Rus'.

Such was the mind-set that had led him to arrange a triumphant entrance
into Kyiv for himself in January 1648. There the metropolitan of Kyiv
greeted the hetman, as did the patriarch of Jerusalem, who addressed Khmelnytsky as a prince and gave him his blessing for war with the Poles. The
professors and students of the Kyivan College established by Mohyla were
eager to welcome the new leader of Rus'. They called him Moses for delivering the Rus' nation from Polish enslavement—a distinction they never dared
to give their previous patron, Metropolitan Mohyla, who had died two years
earlier, in December 1647. The Cossack hetman was taking on the leadership of the whole nation, no longer fighting for the rights of the Cossacks
alone. The way to secure the rights of the Rus' nation was to create a "principality," or a state. This was a revolutionary development. The Cossacks, who
had come into existence on the margins of society, in opposition to an established polity, were now thinking about creating a state of their own.

The borders of the new state would be drawn in battle, and the battle
most crucial to that process was fought in the summer of 1649 near the town
of Zboriv in Podolia. There Khmelnytsky's forces, assisted by the Crimean
Tatars under Khan Islam III Giray, attacked the army of the new Polish king,
John II Casimir. The battle ended in victory for the Cossacks, who, with the
help of their Crimean allies, forced the Polish officials to sign an agreement
giving royal recognition to the officially autonomous but actually independent Cossack state within the commonwealth. The king agreed to increase
the Cossack register to 40,000. (In reality, the Cossack army at Zboriv attained a strength of 100,000 Cossacks and armed peasants and townsmen.)
The Cossacks received the right to reside in—effectively, to rule over—the

three eastern palatinates of the commonwealth. Those were the palatinates of Kyiv, Bratslav, and Chernihiv, which constituted the territory of the new Cossack state, known in history as the Hetmanate. A good part of the Hetmanate happened to be in the steppelands that Polish and French cartographers of earlier decades had called "Ukraine." The Hetmanate would soon come to be known by that name.

The head of the new state, as well as its military commander, was the hetman. He ruled the Cossack realm with the help of his general staff, which included a chancellor, an artillery commander, a general judge, and other officials. The military democracy of early Cossack times, which had also been vital in the first months of the revolt, was receding into the past. General councils in which every Cossack had the right to take part gave way to councils of colonels and members of the general staff, who decided the most important matters. Since the revolt against the latifundia system had destroyed the old economy and killed or driven away its major actors, including the Jews, while the peasants now declared themselves Cossacks and refused to work the fields of the nobility, the new state filled its treasury with the help of war booty, customs duties, and the mill tax for grinding grain.

The old commonwealth administrative system was theoretically left in place, with the post of palatine of Kyiv going to an Orthodox noble loyal to the king, but the Cossack hetman actually ruled, without even informing the king about his actions. In the areas under their control, the Cossacks introduced an administrative system based on their borderland experience and military type of social organization and influenced by military/administrative models from the Ottoman Empire. They divided the territory of the Hetmanate into "regiments," placing a colonel in charge of each regiment's administrative, judicial, and fiscal bodies but, first and foremost, its military organization. Each of the twenty regiments, named after its principal town, was obliged to produce a battle-ready Cossack military regiment. The same combination of military, administrative, and judicial powers in one office was introduced on the level of smaller towns and villages. Cossack captains ran these, tasked mainly with mustering a company (a "hundred") in time of war.

The alliance with the Crimean Tatars made the Cossack victories of the first two years of the revolt possible. This alliance drew Khmelnytsky into the geopolitical web of the Ottoman Empire, which had a number of dependencies in the northern Black Sea region. These included the Crimea, Moldavia, and Wallachia (part of today's Romania), and their relations with Istanbul provided Khmelnytsky with a model for establishing his independence vis-à-vis the king without giving up the hard-won Cossack statehood. Cossack Ukraine was prepared to join other Ottoman dependencies as a protectorate of the sultans—that was the essence of the negotiations that Khmelnytsky conducted with Istanbul in the spring and summer of 1651. Preparing for another major confrontation with the commonwealth, he even signed a document recognizing the suzerainty of the sultan.

In exchange Khmelnytsky wanted immediate protection—Ottoman troops on the ground, attacking the Polish army, as they had done at Ţuţora in 1620 and at Khotyn in 1621. But the Ottomans were fully engaged in sea battles with the Venetians. Instead of sending their own troops, the advisers of the nine-year-old Sultan Mehmed IV ordered the Crimean khan to provide military support for Khmelnytsky. This was not what the hetman desired: the Crimeans were playing their own game, trying to sustain conflict in the area as long as possible so as to prevent the Cossacks from achieving a decisive victory over the commonwealth. That had been the case at Zboriv in 1649, where the khan negotiated a peace with the king instead of helping Khmelnytsky defeat the Polish army. The same situation could easily recur.

In fact, it did, and in the worst possible circumstances. In the summer of 1651, in a battle near the town of Berestechko in Volhynia, the Crimean Tatars deserted the battlefield in the midst of the fray, leading to the encirclement and annihilation of the core of the Cossack army. Khmelnytsky, who retreated together with the khan, became a hostage of his ally until his release to reorganize his defenses and prevent a complete demise of Cossack statehood. His reliance on the Crimean Tatars had ended in disaster. In the fall of 1651, Khmelnytsky negotiated a new agreement with the commonwealth: his Cossack register was cut in half to 20,000 men, while Cossack territory was reduced to the Kyiv palatinate—those of Bratslav and Chernihiv were supposed to return to direct commonwealth jurisdiction. Since that condition was not fulfilled, another war was clearly in the offing.

The Cossack state needed new allies. Khmelnytsky focused particularly on the principality of Moldavia, which, while officially a vassal state of the Ottomans, had traditionally carried on a balancing act between Istanbul and Warsaw. In 1650, the Cossack hetman forced Moldavia into a formal alliance by sending a Cossack army there and prevailing upon the Moldavian ruler, Vasile Lupu, to engage his daughter Roxanda to Khmelnytsky's son Tymish. After the Cossack defeat at Berestechko, Lupu tried unsuccessfully to extricate himself from the arrangement. In 1652, Khmelnytsky once again sent thousands of Cossack "matchmakers" to Moldavia. On their way they defeated a large Polish army in battle at Batih and then celebrated the wedding of Tymish and Roxanda at the court of Vasile Lupu. By this expedient, Khmelnytsky joined the club of internationally recognized rulers.

But there were limits to how much Khmelnytsky could achieve by allying himself with the Ottomans and their dependencies. This became painfully obvious in the fall of 1653, when the Cossacks fought another battle against the royal army near the town of Zhvanets in Podolia. Once again, the Crimean Tatars were on the Cossack side and prevented the Cossacks from winning the battle. It ended exactly how the Crimean khan wished, with no decisive outcome. The Kingdom of Poland and the Cossack Hetmanate returned to the deal they had made at Zboriv: a Cossack register of 40,000, and three palatinates under Cossack control. Everyone knew it was another ceasefire, not a meaningful compromise or a lasting peace. The Cossacks wanted all of Ukraine and parts of Belarus, while the king, and especially the Diet, resisted acknowledging Cossack rule even over the three eastern principalities that they actually controlled.

Khmelnytsky and the Cossack state had to look for different allies. Reaching a compromise with the commonwealth authorities was turning out to be impossible, and the Cossacks could not survive in conflict with such a powerful enemy on their own. The Crimeans allowed them to stand up to but not to defeat the Poles. The Ottomans were not prepared to commit their troops, and the Moldavian alliance ended in a personal tragedy for Khmelnytsky. In September 1653 his eldest son, the twenty-one-year-old Tymish, was killed defending the fortress of Suceava (in present-day Romania) against the united forces of Wallachia and Transylvania, whose leaders were unhappy with the Khmelnytsky-Lupu alliance. In late December 1653, Khmelnytsky buried his son at his estate of Subotiv near Chyhyryn. A legend claims that the burial took place in the Church of St. Elias, an example of baroque architecture on the Cossack steppes that still survives and is depicted on Ukrainian banknotes. With the burial of Tymish, the aging hetman's plans to integrate his country into the Ottoman political network also expired.

THE TURNING POINT in the internationalization of the Khmelnytsky Revolt took place on January 8, 1654, in the town of Pereiaslav. On that day, Bohdan Khmelnytsky and a hastily gathered group of Cossack officers swore allegiance to the new sovereign of Ukraine, Tsar Aleksei Romanov of Muscovy. The long and complex history of Russo-Ukrainian relations had begun. In 1954, the Soviet Union lavishly celebrated the tricentennial of the "reunification" of Ukraine and Russia. The implication was that all of Ukraine had chosen at Pereiaslav to rejoin Russia and accepted the sovereignty of the tsar. What actually happened at Pereiaslav in 1654 was neither the reunification of Ukraine with Muscovy (which would be renamed "Russia" by Peter I) nor the reunion of two "fraternal peoples," as suggested by Soviet historians. No one in Pereiaslav or Moscow was thinking or speaking in ethnic terms in 1654.

Bohdan Khmelnytsky's speech at the council of Cossack officers, recorded in the materials of the Muscovite embassy, gives some idea of how the Ukrainian hetman presented and explained his actions:

> We have convened a council open to the whole people so that you, together with us, might choose a sovereign for yourselves out of four, whomever you wish: the first is the Turkish tsar [sultan], who has often appealed to us through his envoys to come under his rule; the second is the Crimean khan; the third is the Polish king, who, if we wish, may still take us into his former favor; the fourth is the Orthodox sovereign of Great Rus', the tsar, Grand Prince Aleksei Mikhailovich, the eastern sovereign of all Rus', whom we have now been entreating for ourselves for six years with incessant pleadings. Now choose the one you wish!

No doubt, Khmelnytsky was playing games. The choice had already been made: he and the Cossack officers had decided in favor of the sovereign of Muscovy. According to the ambassadorial report, the hetman made his argument by appealing to the Orthodox solidarity of his listeners. Those taking part in the council shouted their desire for the "Eastern" Orthodox tsar as their ruler.

It sounded like one of the many religion-based alliances of the Reformation and Counter-Reformation: the Thirty Years' War, in which the countries of Europe lined up largely on the basis of their religious identities, had ended only five years earlier. There is no need to blame either the Muscovite elites or their Ukrainian counterparts for not considering each other brothers and members of the same Rus' nation. The two sides needed interpreters to understand each other, and Khmelnytsky's letters to the tsar survived in the Russian archives largely in translations prepared by such official interpreters. The tradition of Kyivan Rus' as represented by historical memory and religious belief still existed, but it was embodied only in a few handwritten chronicles.

Four centuries of existence in different political conditions, under the rule of different states, had strengthened long-standing linguistic and cultural differences that divided the future Belarus and Ukraine from the future Russia. Those differences came to the fore when Khmelnytsky and the colonels wanted to discuss conditions of the agreement with the Russian envoy, Vasilii Buturlin; he told them that the tsar would treat them better than the king had but refused to negotiate. Khmelnytsky objected, saying that they had been accustomed to negotiating with the king and his officials, but Buturlin responded that the Polish king, being an elective monarch, was not the equal of the hereditary Russian tsar. He also refused to take an oath with regard to the broad promises he had made to the Cossacks: the tsar, said Buturlin, swears no oath to his subjects. Khmelnytsky, who wanted Muscovite troops in battle as soon as possible, agreed to swear allegiance to the tsar with no reciprocal oath.

The Cossacks thought of the Pereiaslav agreement as a contract with binding obligations on both sides. As far as Khmelnytsky was concerned, he and his polity were entering into a protectorate under the tsar's authority. They promised loyalty and military service in exchange for the protection offered by Muscovy. The tsar, however, perceived the Cossacks as new subjects toward whom he would have no obligations after granting them certain rights and privileges. As for his right to the new territory, he thought in dynastic terms. As far as he and his chancellery were concerned, the tsar was taking over his patrimony: the cities of Kyiv, Chernihiv, and Pereiaslav.

WHATEVER THE LEGAL and ideological underpinnings of the Pereiaslav agreement, the tsar honored Buturlin's promise and gave the Cossacks what the Polish king had never agreed to: recognition of Cossack statehood, a Cossack register of 60,000, and privileged status for the Cossack estate. He also recognized the liberties enjoyed by other social strata under the Polish kings.

First and foremost, however, the agreement laid the foundations for a military alliance. It established no western boundary for the Cossacks' territory—they could go as far as their sabers would take them. The Muscovite and Cossack armies entered the war against the commonwealth on their separate fronts: the Cossacks, assisted by a Muscovite corps, led the offensive in Ukraine, within the boundaries of the Kingdom of Poland; the Muscovite troops launched an offensive near Smolensk and moved west through Belarus and then into Lithuania, north of the Lublin border between the grand duchy and the kingdom. The joint offensive of Muscovite and Cossack troops brought unexpected results. Whereas in 1654 the Polish and Lithuanian troops, assisted by the Crimean khan, had managed to resist the offensive from the east, in the summer and fall of 1655 the Polish-Lithuanian counteroffensive collapsed: the Cossacks once again besieged Lviv, and Muscovite troops entered Vilnius, the capital of the grand duchy.

This was the beginning of the era known in Polish history as the Deluge. Not only did the Muscovite and Cossack armies move deep into the commonwealth, but in July 1655 the Swedes launched an offensive of their own across the Baltic Sea. By October, both Warsaw and the ancient Polish capital of Cracow were in Swedish hands. Alarmed by the prospect of a complete Polish collapse and a dramatic expansion of Sweden, which now claimed the parts of the Grand Duchy of Lithuania conquered by Muscovite troops, in the fall of 1656 Muscovite diplomats concluded an agreement with the commonwealth in Vilnius that put an end to Polish-Muscovite hostilities. Khmelnytsky and the Cossack officials were enraged at being denied access to the negotiations. The separate peace with Poland was leaving the Cossacks one on one with their traditional enemy. As far as they were concerned, the tsar was reneging on his main obligation under the Pereiaslav agreement—the military protection of his subjects.

Bohdan Khmelnytsky ignored the Muscovite-Polish deal and sent his army to help an ally of Sweden, the Protestant ruler of Transylvania, fight the Poles. Now, even the military alliance between the tsar and the Cossacks came into question. Khmelnytsky had been looking for new allies since Sweden's entry into the war with Poland. The Swedes seemed determined to destroy the commonwealth, which Khmelnytsky also wanted. Negotiations to conclude a Ukrainian-Swedish agreement that would put an end to the commonwealth and guarantee the inclusion not only of Ukraine but also parts of what is now Belarus in the Cossack state gained new impetus from what the hetman regarded as the tsar's betrayal of Ukraine.

Khmelnytsky, however, did not live to see the conclusion of this new international alliance. He died in August 1657, leaving the state he had created and the Cossacks he had led at a crossroads. Although Khmelnytsky believed that his alliance with the tsar had already run its course, he formally abided by the deal he had made in Pereiaslav. Events there became an important part of the old hetman's large and contradictory legacy. Cossack chroniclers of the eighteenth century celebrated him very much in the same vein as the professors and students of the Kyivan College had done on his entrance into Kyiv in December 1648. They extolled him as the father of the nation, the liberator of his people from the Polish yoke, and the hetman who had negotiated the best possible arrangement with the tsar: they considered the Articles of Bohdan Khmelnytsky, approved by the tsar after Pereiaslav, a Magna Carta of Ukrainian liberties in the Russian Empire.

CHAPTER 11

THE PARTITIONS

THE KHMELNYTSKY UPRISING unleashed a long period of wars that led many historians to refer to the decades following the revolt as the Ruin. While the destruction and depopulation of the Ukrainian lands, especially on the Right Bank of the Dnieper River, indeed dealt a huge blow to the economic, political, and cultural life of the region, the main long-term consequence of the wars was the division of Ukraine along the Dnieper between Muscovy and Poland. The Dnieper boundary became a major factor in early modern Ukrainian history, and some consider it relevant even today, influencing the cultural and at times political preferences of Ukrainians on both sides of the former Polish border.

Bohdan Khmelnytsky's vision for the Cossack state was one of territorial expansion, not fragmentation. But the fissures within the Cossack officer class that eventually led to the division of the Hetmanate became apparent soon after the old hetman's death in August 1657. The trigger was the contested succession to the highest office in the land—a problem that plagued more than one medieval and early modern polity. Khmelnytsky was thinking of creating his own dynasty, and shortly before his death, he engineered the election to the Cossack hetmancy of his son Yurii, a rather sickly sixteen-year-old youth who suffered from occasional bouts of epilepsy. What happened next will come as no surprise to anyone who has read Aleksandr Pushkin's *Boris Godunov*. An experienced courtier, appointed to serve as the youth's regent, removed him—in the Ukrainian case, without spilling any blood—and engineered his own election to the leadership.

The drama that would lead to the partitions had begun. If Khmelnytsky had expected succession to the hetmancy to work as it did in Poland, with election to the throne of members of the same dynasty one after another, the system that came into existence was more like the one in the principality of Moldavia, where new leaders were elected and disposed of at the wish or with the approval of the Ottomans. Unlike in the case of Moldavia, three major powers would contest Ukraine—the Muscovites, Poles, and Ottomans. No matter which of these three powers won, the Cossacks would invariably lose. Their succession system was thoroughly dysfunctional, serving to destabilize the whole region.

THE MAN WHO assumed the hetman's mace after pushing Yurii Khmelnytsky aside in the fall of 1657 was Ivan Vyhovsky. His life trajectory and career differed greatly from those of Bohdan Khmelnytsky. Born into a well-established Orthodox noble family, Vyhovsky had no problem with recognition of his noble status. His election as hetman was a victory for the nobles within the Cossack elite as opposed to the officers, who were veterans of the pre-1648 Cossack register. Very telling in this regard was his choice of a new general chancellor. The post went not to a veteran Cossack officer but to a Ukrainian magnate whose latifundia rivaled those of the Vyshnevetsky princes. His name was Yurii Nemyrych.

Exceptionally well educated by the standards of the time, Nemyrych belonged to the radical wing of the Polish Reformation, the group known as Antitrinitarians. (A founder of the Unitarian Church, Joseph Priestley, would bring their brand of religion to the United States in the late eighteenth century.) Nemyrych studied in an Antitrinitarian school in Poland and then moved to western Europe, where he took courses at the universities of Leiden, Basel and, by some accounts, Oxford and Cambridge. At the time of the Deluge in Poland, he sided with a fellow Protestant, King Charles X of Sweden. Soon disillusioned with the Swedes, however, he converted to Orthodoxy, made friends with Bohdan Khmelnytsky, and moved to Cossack Ukraine, close to his possessions, which the hetman returned to him.

Many in the Cossack ranks were unhappy with the rise to power of the noble faction led by Ivan Vyhovsky. The Cossacks beyond the Dnieper rapids expressed open disapproval. They had elected Khmelnytsky hetman in the spring of 1648. Since then, the new Cossack state that had arisen north of the steppelands, in the settled area of the middle Dnieper, had taken away not only their exclusive right to elect the hetman but also their very name—

the Hetmanate was officially known as the Zaporozhian Host. The Zaporozhians, now marginalized, claimed that election of a new hetman should
take place beyond the rapids. They questioned the legitimacy of Vyhovsky's
election, and some Cossack colonels were prepared to listen to them and offer support. No less importantly, Moscow was encouraging opposition to
Vyhovsky by recognizing the right of the Zaporozhian Cossacks to communicate directly with the tsar's officials. The Muscovite authorities sought to
exploit the division in Cossack ranks to weaken the hetman and make him
less independent than his predecessor, Bohdan Khmelnytsky.

Vyhovsky would have none of it. In June 1658 his army, backed by the
Crimean Tatars, confronted the Zaporozhians and their allies among the Hetmanate's Cossacks near the city of Poltava in Left-Bank Ukraine. Vyhovsky
emerged victorious, but the death toll was enormous. According to some estimates, close to 15,000 people died. It was the first time since 1648 that Cossacks had fought Cossacks, establishing a precedent that would ruin their
state. Vyhovsky had no doubt that Moscow was behind the rebels. But how
was he to protect himself?

The hetman believed that, like Khmelnytsky, he had entered into a conditional agreement with the tsar (he called it "voluntary subordination") and
could renounce it if the tsar did not keep his part of the bargain. The tsar, for
his part, believed in no conditionality: the only conditions he recognized were
those that he could impose on his subjects. While Khmelnytsky, dissatisfied
with his arrangement with the tsar of Muscovy, had nowhere to turn but the
Swedes and the Ottomans, his successors discovered another option—a new
deal with Poland. They were part and parcel of the Polish political system,
knew its strengths and weaknesses, and believed that an agreement reincorporating their country into the commonwealth while maintaining broad autonomy was not only desirable but possible.

In September 1658, Vyhovsky summoned a Cossack council in the Left-
Bank town of Hadiach that approved conditions for the Hetmanate's return
to the jurisdiction of the Polish kings. The resulting Polish-Cossack treaty,
called the Union of Hadiach, was the brainchild of Vyhovsky's right-hand
man, Yurii Nemyrych. The treaty was nothing if not a realization of the
dreams nurtured by the Ukrainian nobility of the first half of the seventeenth
century. In the struggles over the Union of Brest, the Orthodox nobles had
developed an anachronistic interpretation of the Union of Lublin as an arrangement that recognized not only the Grand Duchy of Lithuania but also

the Rus' lands of Poland-Lithuania as an equal partner in the commonwealth. Now Nemyrych decided to turn that vision into reality by refashioning the Hetmanate as the principality of Rus', which would join the commonwealth as a coequal third partner along with Poland and Lithuania.

The Great Revolt had made some members of the Polish elite more open to the idea of a Rus' principality than ever before, but the rise of Cossackdom had also made it difficult to reincorporate a realm that had developed its own distinct form of political and social organization. Thus, responding to the pre-1648 demands of the Cossack elite, the Union of Hadiach offered noble status to 1,000 Cossack families immediately and, after that, to a hundred Cossack families per annum in each of the Cossack regiments. Apart from satisfying Cossack social demands, the union also addressed Cossack and noble concerns about religion. Only the Orthodox would have the right to hold administrative positions in the new principality. Curiously enough, the treaty also contained a clause dealing with the Kyivan College founded by Peter Mohyla, recognizing it as an academy. The nobles negotiating the deal from the Cossack side were clearly interested in something more than Cossack rights.

News of the signing of the union with Poland prompted the tsar to issue an appeal calling on the Cossacks to rebel against the "traitor" Vyhovsky. Muscovite troops and Cossack enemies of Vyhovsky, including Zaporozhians, took control of southern parts of the Hetmanate. In the spring of 1659, Vyhovsky issued his own appeal, explaining that the tsar was violating his agreement with the Cossacks and encroaching on Cossack rights and freedoms. He summoned his Crimean allies and attacked the advancing Muscovite army. The Battle of Konotop, fought near the present-day Russo-Ukrainian border in June 1659, ended in a spectacular victory for Vyhovsky. The Muscovite army, approximately 70,000 strong, was defeated, up to 15,000 soldiers were killed, and the flower of the Muscovite cavalry was annihilated. The Tatars moved on, pillaging the southern borderlands of Muscovy. Rumors filled Moscow that the tsar was about to leave the capital.

Vyhovsky never moved on Moscow. Despite his victory at Konotop, Muscovite garrisons in Ukraine held on, and the revolt against Vyhovsky among the Cossacks gathered strength. News about the Polish Diet's ratification of the Union of Hadiach gave it further impetus. The version of the treaty approved by the Diet failed to deliver on a number of promises made to Vyhovsky by the Polish negotiators. It limited the lands of the new principality to the Kyiv, Bratslav, and Chernihiv palatinates, even though the hetman also wanted what is now western Ukraine, including Volhynia and Podolia. It also limited the Cossack register to 30,000, along with 10,000 mercenaries, for a total of 40,000, or 20,000 fewer than Khmelnytsky had negotiated with the tsar immediately after Pereiaslav. Yurii Nemyrych went to Warsaw in person to plead the case for the union before the Diet. "We were born in liberty, brought up in liberty and, as free men, we are returning to it," he told the deputies. They approved the union but not in the form that Nemyrych and Vyhovsky wanted. When Vyhovsky received the revised text, he told the courier that he was bringing him death.

Most of the Cossack elite now saw Vyhovsky as a traitor. Nemyrych was killed in a skirmish with Vyhovsky's opponents. The other Cossack delegates to the Polish Diet were executed at a Cossack council summoned by the hetman's enemies. Vyhovsky himself had to flee. He had won every battle he fought, either against his opponents, as was the case at Poltava, or against the Muscovite forces at Konotop, but he had lost the debate within his own ranks over the issue of relations with Poland. Stepping down as hetman, he left for western Ukraine, where he became the captain of Bar in Podolia while maintaining his title of palatine of Kyiv and the seat in the Polish senate that came with it. This was the only provision of the Union of Hadiach that was actually implemented.

Vyhovsky's hetmancy opened a new page in the history of Cossack Ukraine—a page marked by internal strife and fratricidal war. Since Cossack forces were insufficient to defend the Hetmanate, whoever held the office of hetman had to keep Cossack ranks united while constantly maneuvering among the major powers in the region. It was a task that few could accomplish. Khmelnytsky had managed to keep the Cossack officers in line with such disciplinary measures as chaining troublemakers to a cannon, as he did with the firebrand of the 1648 massacres, Colonel Maksym Kryvonis, or even ordering the execution of Cossack rebels. Vyhovsky had failed to maintain the unity of the Cossack realm. The task passed once again to Bohdan Khmelnytsky's son Yurii, who was reelected to the hetmancy after the ouster of Vyhovsky. The dynasty was back, but Ukraine's problems were no closer to solution.

YURII KHMELNYTSKY CAME to power in the fall of 1659 with the support of Cossack officers who believed that they could reach an agreement with the tsar on conditions no worse than those negotiated by the old Khmelnytsky. They miscalculated. When Yurii Khmelnytsky and his supporters began negotiations with the Muscovites, they found themselves in a trap. A new Cossack council, called at the initiative of a Muscovite military governor (*voevoda*) and surrounded by a Muscovite army of 40,000, confirmed the election of the young Khmelnytsky but on conditions that reduced the rights and privileges given to his father. From now on, the hetman's election required the express permission of the tsar, and he had no right to conduct foreign relations or appoint colonels without the consent of Moscow. Muscovite military garrisons were to be stationed in all major towns of the Hetmanate.

Vyhovsky's defection to the Poles had resulted not in new concessions from the Muscovite side, as his opponents had hoped, but in the curtailment of the Hetmanate's previous rights. The tsar's officials wanted his subjects to realize that they would not tolerate breaches of the union with Muscovy under any circumstances. In January 1660, the Muscovite *voevodas* sent Khmelnytsky a message making that particular point. The corpse of Danylo Vyhovsky, a brother of the former hetman and a cousin of Yurii Khmelnytsky, who had fallen into Muscovite hands during a failed attack on the Muscovite garrison in Kyiv, was delivered to the young hetman's residence on his ancestral estate of Subotiv. Danylo's captors had tortured him to death. What the hetman saw in the coffin caused him to break down in tears. "His whole body was torn to pieces by whips, his eyes plucked out and the sockets filled with silver, his ears turned inside out with a drill and filled with silver," wrote a Polish diplomat who happened to be there at the time. "His fingers had been sliced. His legs had been butchered along the veins. In a word, it was unheard-of savagery."

If the tsar and his officials wanted to intimidate the young hetman and his entourage, they did not achieve their purpose. According to the same source, the arrival of the Cossack officer's massacred remains not only made the young Khmelnytsky weep but also aroused outrage at his court. Danylo Vyhovsky's young widow cursed her husband's killers. Revenge came later that year. In the fall of 1660, during a battle between a Muscovite army and Polish detachments backed by Crimean Tatars, the young Khmelnytsky and his troops switched sides and swore allegiance to the Polish king. The Muscovite army was defeated. Its commander spent twenty years in Crimean captivity.

While this Polish victory gratified the Cossacks, it did nothing to secure the Hetmanate. The Cossacks returned to the king's jurisdiction on conditions even less favorable than those offered by the version of the Union of

Hadiach approved by the Polish Diet. The new treaty expunged the very name of the Rus' principality, so important to the Cossack authors of the Hadiach union. Every time the Cossacks switched sides in the ongoing Muscovite-Polish war for control of Ukraine, they lost additional elements of their sovereignty. The pressure exerted on the Cossack polity by its much more powerful adversaries, the Tsardom of Muscovy and the Kingdom of Poland, soon became too strong for the Hetmanate to bear, and it split into two parts along the Dnieper River.

In 1660, as Yurii Khmelnytsky established his headquarters on the Right Bank of the Dnieper, the regiments on the Left Bank, with Muscovite support, elected their own acting hetman. Khmelnytsky organized a number of expeditions to subdue the rebellious regiments but failed to achieve his goal. The region was close to the Muscovite border, and the tsardom's military governors solidified their hold on it. In early 1663, in utter despair, the twenty-two-year-old hetman resigned and entered a monastery. This was the official end of the united Hetmanate. That year, the Right-Bank Cossacks elected a hetman subordinate to Poland, while those on the Left Bank elected a hetman who recognized the sovereignty of Muscovy. Four years later, in 1667, Muscovite and Polish diplomats signed the Truce of Andrusovo, which divided Cossack Ukraine, with the Left Bank going to Muscovy and the Right Bank to Poland.

THE OLD HETMANATE did not go down without a fight. Colonel Petro Doroshenko, a scion of one of the best-known Cossack families, led those opposed to the division of the state, which they considered their true fatherland, into battle. Doroshenko's grandfather had been a Cossack hetman in the 1620s, his father a colonel under Bohdan Khmelnytsky. A native of Chyhyryn, Petro began his service at the hetman's court. After his promotion to the rank of colonel, he took part in a number of diplomatic missions, including negotiations with the Swedes, Poles, and Muscovites. He even led one of the Cossack embassies to Moscow. A supporter of Yurii Khmelnytsky, he ended up in Right-Bank Ukraine, and in 1665 the local Cossacks elected him hetman.

News of the impending partition of Cossack Ukraine had shocked and galvanized the Cossack elite, and Doroshenko won election with an agenda of raising another revolt against Poland and uniting Ukraine on both sides of the Dnieper. Like Bohdan Khmelnytsky before him, Doroshenko counted on the support of the Crimean Tatars. Together they attacked the Polish armies in the fall of 1667, forcing the king to grant autonomy to the Right-Bank Hetmanate. Doroshenko then crossed the Dnieper and took control of Left-Bank Ukraine, which was already in revolt against Moscow. The tsar's officials had aroused discontent by trying to conduct a census for tax purposes. News of the partition of Ukraine at Andrusovo had turned it into open revolt.

Doroshenko, already hetman of the Right Bank, was now elected on the Left Bank as well. The Cossack Hetmanate once again became united, despite the two partitioning powers. But the unity did not last long. Soon Doroshenko had to leave Left-Bank Ukraine to deal with a new Polish offensive and a new hetman sponsored by the Poles. Meanwhile, Muscovite troops occupied the Left Bank. The Ottomans were now Doroshenko's only hope. In July 1669, Sultan Mehmed IV sent him new insignia of office, including a hetman's mace and banner. The sultan took Doroshenko and his Cossacks under his protection on the same condition as the rulers of Moldavia and Wallachia: that they mobilize troops at his first summons. The lands claimed by Istanbul included not only Cossack Ukraine on both sides of the Dnieper but also the Rus' lands all the way to the Vistula in the west and the Nieman in the north.

It was an ambitious agenda, but conditions seemed to favor Cossack efforts to realize Khmelnytsky's dreams of twenty years earlier and bring all the Rus' lands of the commonwealth under their control. This time, the Ottomans not only offered the hetman's insignia but also put troops on the ground. In 1672, a 100,000-strong Ottoman army crossed the Danube and, with the support of its Crimean, Wallachian, Moldavian, and now Cossack vassals, moved against the Polish forces. They went much farther than Khotyn, the site of the crucial battle of more than half a century earlier, and besieged the fortress of Kamianets in Podolia. Located on a high cliff and surrounded by a deep ravine, it was considered impregnable but fell to the Ottomans after a siege of only ten days. Soon the sultan's army was besieging Lviv. The Poles sued for peace and renounced their claim to Podolia and the middle Dnieper region. Doroshenko and his supporters were in a celebratory mood.

But Doroshenko's hopes were not realized. The Ottomans took the fortress of Kamianets and the adjacent Podolia region under their direct control, while the Cossacks got their old possessions on the middle Dnieper in lieu of an independent state. There were no plans to extend the offensive to the Left Bank or northward to Volhynia and Belarus. But that was only the beginning of Doroshenko's troubles. The Ottomans aroused indignation by turning some Christian churches into mosques and allowing the Crimean Tatars to conduct their slave-hunting raids in the region. Support for Doroshenko was dwindling as quickly as the population of the Right Bank under his nominal control. It was turning into a desert as inhabitants fled both east and west. Many crossed the Dnieper to the Left Bank, where the Muscovites crushed the opposition of the Cossack elites, installed a loyal hetman, and promoted an economic revival. The Right Bank became a ruin, giving that name to an entire period of Ukrainian history.

It was only a matter of time before Doroshenko left the Ukrainian political scene. Instead of uniting Ukraine under a loose Ottoman protectorate, he brought one more partitioning power into the region—one that turned out to be more destructive than any of its predecessors. In 1676, when Muscovite troops supported by their Left-Bank Cossack allies crossed the Dnieper and approached Doroshenko's capital of Chyhyryn, the Cossack hetman resigned his office and swore allegiance to the tsar. His life was spared, and, as one who had "seen the light," he received the title of *voevoda* and went to serve the tsar in Viatka (present-day Kirov), almost nine hundred kilometers east of Moscow. He was allowed to retire to the village of Yaropolets in today's Moscow oblast. Married to a Russian noblewoman (one of their descendants was Aleksandr Pushkin's wife, Natalia), he died there in 1698. Ironically, a society of natives of Ukrainian Podolia, the region that suffered most from the Ottoman rule that Doroshenko helped bring to Ukraine, rebuilt the small chapel over his grave in 1999.

Direct Ottoman rule over parts of Ukraine did not last long—the Ottomans gave low priority to that part of their frontier, and they needed resources elsewhere, especially in the Mediterranean. The year Doroshenko died, Podolia reverted to Polish control. The Ottomans were out of the picture, and the Muscovite-Polish border on the Dnieper, against which Doroshenko had rebelled in 1666, was now fully reestablished. The Cossack state did not disappear altogether, but its territory and autonomy, not to speak of its independence, were severely curtailed—it survived only in Left-Bank Ukraine. The Cossack land, which had been booming in the first half of the seventeenth century, could muster enough human, economic, and military resources to challenge the major powers in the region but not to defend the accomplishments of the Cossack revolution. When it came to foreign alliances, the Cossacks tried everything, starting with the Crimea and the Ottomans and ending with Muscovy, the Swedes, and Poland. Nothing worked—the unity not only of Cossack Ukraine but of the Ukrainian lands in general was lost. Until the end of the eighteenth century, most of Ukraine formerly controlled by Poland would remain divided between Poland and Russia. The division would have profound effects on Ukrainian identity and culture.

CHAPTER 12

THE VERDICT OF POLTAVA

THE COSSACK HETMANATE, which survived under the suzerainty of the Muscovite tsars only on the Left Bank of the Dnieper, served as a construction site for a number of nation-building projects. One of them, closely associated with the name "Ukraine" and a view of the Hetmanate as a distinct Cossack polity and fatherland, became the foundation for the development of modern Ukrainian identity. Another, associated with the official Russian name of the Hetmanate, "Little Russia," laid the basis for what would later become known as "Little Russianism," the tradition of treating Ukraine as "Lesser Russia" and the Ukrainians as part of a larger Russian nation.

Both intellectual traditions coexisted in the Hetmanate before the last major Cossack revolt, led by Hetman Ivan Mazepa in 1708. Mazepa's revolt targeted Muscovy and the official founder of the Russian Empire, Tsar Peter I. It ended in defeat as the Russians overcame the Swedish army, which Charles XII led into Ukraine. The Battle of Poltava in 1709 profoundly changed the fate of the Cossack Hetmanate and Ukraine as a whole. The loss for Charles was a double loss for Mazepa and his vision of Ukraine as an entity separate from Russia. In subsequent years, the Little Russian interpretation of Ukrainian history and culture as closely linked to Russia would become dominant in the official discourse of the Hetmanate. The idea of Ukraine as a separate polity, fatherland, and indeed nation did not disappear entirely but shifted out of the center of Ukrainian discourse for more than a century.

IN THE LAST decades of the seventeenth century, the Muscovites kept Left-Bank Ukraine under their control thanks not only to their superior military force but also because they turned out to be much more flexible than their competitors. While the tsars used the election of every new hetman to whittle away at the rights and privileges given to the Hetmanate under Bohdan Khmelnytsky, they also knew when to relent. In 1669, in the midst of the revolt led by Petro Doroshenko, Moscow agreed to return to conditions close to those granted to Khmelnytsky. It did so at a time when the Poles were reducing the much less substantial body of Cossack privileges in effect on their side of the river. The result was not hard to predict. The Left Bank attracted new settlers from the Cossack lands under Polish rule and kept growing economically, while the Right Bank turned into a virtual desert. The tsars allowed their Cossacks more rights, but they also got to keep them as subjects.

In relatively short order, the Left-Bank economic expansion led to the economic and cultural revival of Kyiv. Classes resumed at the Kyivan College. The professors who had fled the city in the 1650s now welcomed a new generation of students. New subjects were taught, new poetry written, and new plays performed. Ukrainian baroque literature, initiated in the early seventeenth century by Meletii Smotrytsky, reached its peak in the writings of poets such as Ivan Velychkovsky and in the prose of Lazar Baranovych, a former professor at the college who became archbishop of Chernihiv. His student Simeon Polotsky brought the Kyiv baroque literary style to Moscow, where he helped lay the foundations for the emergence of Russian secular literature. The introduction of Kyivan texts, practices, and ideas into Muscovy in the second half of the seventeenth century would cause a split in that country's Orthodox Church. While the tsar and the patriarch backed Peter Mohyla–style reforms, conservatives rebelled and united around the leaders of the Old Belief. It was no accident that the name applied to them by the official church, *raskol'niki*, or schismatics, came from Ukraine.

But cultural influence flowed in both directions. While Kyivan clerics brought Western cultural models from Ukraine to Muscovy, they also borrowed from the arsenal of Muscovite political ideology. Key to that ideology was the notion of the Orthodox tsar as the linchpin of a new political and religious universe. The Orthodox intellectuals of the commonwealth, long without a king of their own, embraced the opportunity to enter an idealized Orthodox world inspired by the Byzantine vision of symphony between an autocratic ruler and the one true church. In the end, however, practical considerations outweighed idealism. As early as the 1620s, the newly consecrated Orthodox bishops, hard pressed by Warsaw, had turned to Muscovy as a source of support and a possible place of exile. The desire for the tsar's protection only increased after the Pereiaslav agreement (1654) and reached its peak after the Truce of Andrusovo (1667), which divided Cossack Ukraine in half.

According to the conditions of the truce, Kyiv, located on the Right Bank of the Dnieper, was supposed to become a Polish possession after a two-year grace period. But the prospect of submitting once again to the rule of a Catholic king terrified the Kyivan clergy. They summoned all the powers of persuasive rhetoric they had acquired at the Kyivan College and the Jesuit schools of Europe to convince the tsar that the city of Kyiv should stay under his control. They succeeded only too well. Inokentii Gizel, the archimandrite of the Kyivan Cave Monastery and one of the leading figures in the campaign to "persuade the tsar," wanted to keep Kyiv under tsarist rule while maintaining the independence of the Kyiv metropolitanate. Things worked out otherwise. In the 1670s, the tsar retained his control over the city, but in the next decade Muscovite officials and their supporters in Ukraine succeeded in transferring the Kyiv metropolitanate from the jurisdiction of Constantinople to that of Moscow. The transfer took place in 1685, and so the Kyivan clergy received the tsar's protection at the cost of their independence.

The battles over the fate of Kyiv gave birth to one of the most influential texts of the premodern Russian Empire, the first printed "textbook" of Rus' history, published at the Cave Monastery under Gizel's supervision. The book had a long, baroque title: *Synopsis, or a Brief Compendium of Various Chronicles About the Origin of the Slavo-Rossian Nation and the First Princes of the Divinely Protected City of Kyiv and the Life of the Holy, Pious Grand Prince of Kyiv and All Rus', the First Autocrat, Volodymyr.* It appeared in 1674, when Kyiv was preparing for an Ottoman attack and the Poles were demanding it back from Muscovy. In the *Synopsis,* Kyiv figured as the first capital of the Muscovite tsars and the birthplace of Muscovite Orthodoxy—a city that simply could not be abandoned to infidels or Catholics. References to the Slavo-Rossian nation, which, according to the authors of the *Synopsis,* united Muscovy and the Cossack Hetmanate in one political body, further supported this argument. This was the foundation of the myth still accepted by most Russians today about the Kyivan origins of their nation. In the seventeenth century, however, the Muscovite elites were not yet thinking in terms of national affinity. Russian empire builders would fully appreciate the innovation of the Kyivan monks, who treated the inhabitants of Muscovy and Ukraine as one nation, only in the nineteenth century.

The crisis caused by the partition of Ukraine between Muscovy and Poland forced not only the Kyivan clergy but also the Cossack officer stratum to come up with a new model of identity. The Cossack elite no longer had to defer to the clergy in that regard: the Kyivan College listed among its alumni not only priests and bishops but also Cossack officers, including a number of hetmans. If the clergy could not envision their homeland without an Orthodox tsar, the Cossack officers needed no tsar at all. They pledged their allegiance to a common Cossack "fatherland" embracing both sides of the Dnieper.

Until 1663, when the first de facto partition of Ukraine took place, the Cossack officers used the term "fatherland" to refer either to the entire commonwealth or to the Kingdom of Poland. At the time of the Union of Hadiach (1658), they were lured back to the suzerainty of the Polish king by appeals to return to their Polish fatherland. But things changed after the partition. First one hetman and then another began to argue in their circular letters or universals for the unity of their Ukrainian fatherland—the Hetmanate on both sides of the river. After the Truce of Andrusovo all of them, including Petro Doroshenko and Yurii Khmelnytsky, referred to the interests of the Ukrainian fatherland as their supreme object of loyalty, superseding any other allegiances or commitments. The Cossack fatherland was more than the Zaporozhian Host—a much more traditional object of Cossack loyalty. It included not just the Cossack Host but also the territory and inhabitants of the Hetmanate. They called that fatherland Ukraine. After 1667, the Cossacks began to refer to it as Ukraine on both sides of the Dnieper.

THE LAST COSSACK hetman who tried to unite the Left and Right Banks under his rule was Ivan Mazepa (1639–1709). The banknotes of independent Ukraine depict only two of all the Ukrainian hetmans. The first is Bohdan Khmelnytsky, whose image appears on the five-hryvnia note, and the second is Ivan Mazepa, depicted on the ten-hryvnia bill. Mazepa is arguably better known outside Ukraine, especially in the West, than Khmelnytsky: Voltaire, Lord Byron, Aleksandr Pushkin, and Victor Hugo all wrote about Mazepa's life and exploits. He came to figure in European operas and North American theatrical shows, gaining literary and cultural fame as both a ruler and a lover under the French spelling of his name—Mazeppa. During Mazepa's hetmancy the notions of fatherland, Ukraine, and Little Russia became contested once again. The outcome of Mazepa's rule was the formation of a new type of Little Russian identity.

Mazepa ruled the Hetmanate longer than any of his predecessors, for more than two decades (1687–1709), and died a natural death. That was an achievement in its own right. Two of his predecessors had been either killed or executed. The two hetmans who ruled immediately before Mazepa were accused of "treason," arrested by Muscovite *voevodas*, and sent to Siberia. Members of their families were also persecuted. To lose the hetman's office, personal freedom, or life itself, one did not have to conspire against the tsar or try to join the Poles, Ottomans, or Swedes. It was enough to fall out of favor with the Moscow courtiers.

Mazepa's life trajectory reflected the general fate of Cossackdom in the last decades of the seventeenth century. A native of Left-Bank Ukraine, the future hetman came from a noble Orthodox family. Educated at the Kyiv Mohyla College and a Jesuit school in Warsaw, he studied the craft of artillery in western Europe. After coming back, the young Mazepa began his diplomatic and military career at the court of the Polish king. He later joined Hetman Petro Doroshenko, but the Zaporozhian Cossacks allied with Muscovy captured him. According to the story first related to western European readers by Voltaire and then repeated by others, Mazepa ended up with the Zaporozhians as a result of an affair that turned catastrophic. He allegedly became the lover of the young wife of a prominent Polish official who, upon learning of this, ordered that Mazepa be stripped naked and bound to a horse that was released into the wild steppes. According to that story, Zaporozhian Cossacks found Mazepa half dead and nursed him back to health. Whatever the truth of the story, the Zaporozhians certainly gave a boost to Mazepa's career with the Cossacks. They sent their catch to Hetman Ivan Samoilovych, who enlisted the highly educated and well-traveled officer into his service.

Mazepa was part of a large group of Cossack notables, rank-and-file Cossacks, townsfolk, and peasants who migrated from the Right Bank to the Russian-controlled Left Bank of Ukraine in the last decades of the seventeenth century. The political stability of the region, coupled with the relatively broad autonomy granted to the Hetmanate by the tsars, helped revive the economy and cultural life, which, as in the times of Peter Mohyla, centered on Kyiv, the metropolitan see, the Cave Monastery, and the Kyivan College. After assuming the hetmancy, Mazepa did his best to promote the continuing economic revival of the Hetmanate and the flourishing of its religious and cultural life.

Hetman Mazepa commissioned the restoration of churches that had fallen into disrepair during the long Cossack wars. Among them was the

St. Sophia Cathedral, first restored by Mohyla, as well as the Dormition Cathedral and the Holy Trinity Church in the Cave Monastery—all parts of
the architectural legacy of the Kyivan Rus' era. He also commissioned the
construction of new churches, including the Church of the Nativity of the
Mother of God in the Cave Monastery and numerous churches in Kyiv and
in his capital, the town of Baturyn in the northeastern corner of the Hetmanate, close to the Muscovite border. Most of the churches outside the
Cave Monastery did not survive the 1930s: demolition crews destroyed them
one after another as the Bolsheviks tried to turn Kyiv into a truly socialist
capital. But those within the monastery built by Mazepa, as well as part of its
walls, still stand and attest not only to the generosity but also to the wealth
of the hetman. It was the first commissioning of new buildings in Kyiv since
Mohyla. The style of the architectural monuments of that era became known
as Cossack or Mazepa baroque.

Unlike any previous hetman, Mazepa was able to concentrate in his
hands both economic and political power. This was due to the unprecedented support he was getting from the very top of the imperial pyramid.
Tsar Peter I considered Mazepa his loyal servant. During Peter's contest for
power with his half-sister, Princess Sofia, Mazepa took the side of the future
ruler. Subsequently, Peter made him the first recipient of the Order of
St. Andrew, a prestigious award created by the tsar himself. When the
Cossack officers complained to the tsar about their hetman and customarily
accused him of treason, Peter sent the denunciations back to Mazepa, contrary to the well-established tradition of Muscovite rulers using such denunciations to undermine the Cossack hetmans. Peter showed even more trust
in Mazepa by allowing him to execute his accusers among the ranks of the
Cossack elite.

The Peter-Mazepa alliance came to a sudden end in the autumn of 1708,
at the height of the Great Northern War (1700–1721) fought by Muscovy
and Sweden, assisted by their respective allies, in the Baltics. At the start of
the war, Sweden appeared to have the upper hand. After defeating Muscovy's
ally Augustus the Strong of Poland and forcing him to step down, the young
and ambitious king of Sweden, Charles XII, began his march on Moscow.
Peter was in retreat, using scorched-earth tactics to slow his enemy's advance.

Such destructive measures exacerbated the old grievances of the Cossack
elites, pushing them away from Peter and toward Charles. The Cossack colonels had complained for years to Mazepa about Peter's use of Cossack

regiments outside the Hetmanate, especially to dig canals in and around St. Petersburg, the future capital of the Russian Empire, which the tsar had founded in 1702. There the Cossacks died like flies from cold and disease. Moreover, Peter's introduction of new taxes and administrative reforms threatened to turn the Hetmanate into a regular province of the Muscovite state, not its privileged enclave. All that, argued the colonels, violated the protectorate agreement concluded by Bohdan Khmelnytsky with Muscovy.

Mazepa corresponded with the Polish allies of Charles XII and explored his foreign-policy options but refused to act. Only when the Swedish king decided to make a detour to Ukraine on his way to Moscow, and the tsar refused to help with any troops—Mazepa was supposed to defend the 'Hetmanate on his own and burn the towns and villages in Charles's path—did the hetman yield to the demands of the colonels and switch sides. Muscovy was not performing its primary function—the defense of the Hetmanate—under the numerous agreements with the Cossack hetmans. It was time to think of another option even in Left-Bank Ukraine. The Cossack officers began to study the conditions of the fifty-year-old Union of Hadiach. In November 1708, with a group of trusted courtiers and a small detachment of Cossacks, Mazepa left his capital of Baturyn and joined the advancing army of Charles XII.

For the sake of secrecy, Mazepa conducted no anti-Peter agitation in the Hetmanate before his sudden departure from Baturyn. That was a prudent decision with regard to Mazepa's personal security, but it was a major problem for the revolt. Upon learning of Mazepa's defection, Peter sent a corps to Ukraine under the command of his right-hand man, Aleksandr Menshikov, but no Cossack forces had been mobilized to stop him. The Muscovite troops were able to take the hetman's capital of Baturyn by surprise, seizing military supplies and provisions that Mazepa had prepared for his own army and the Swedes. Even more damaging was the effect of the capture of Baturyn on Ukrainian society in general. Menshikov not only took the town but also ordered the massacre of its population. More than 10,000 defenders and citizens of Baturyn, including women and children, died at the hands of their captors. Archaeologists working there today (Baturyn is a major tourist attraction as well as an excavation site) keep finding skeletons of those who perished. Menshikov's message was loud and clear: the tsar would not tolerate defections.

The battle for the loyalty of the Cossacks and the inhabitants of the Hetmanate had begun. It was carried on mainly through proclamations issued by Peter, to which Mazepa responded in kind. The so-called war of manifestos lasted from the fall of 1708 to the spring of 1709. The tsar accused Mazepa of treason, calling him a Judas and even ordering that a mock order of St. Judas be prepared for awarding to Mazepa once he was captured. Mazepa rejected the accusations. Like Vyhovsky before him, he regarded relations between the tsar and the hetman as contractual. As far as he was concerned, the tsar had violated the Cossack rights and freedoms guaranteed to Bohdan Khmelnytsky and his successors. His loyalty, argued the hetman, was not to the sovereign but to the Cossack Host and the Ukrainian fatherland. Mazepa also pledged his loyalty to his nation. "Moscow, that is, the Great Russian nation, has always been hateful to our Little Russian nation; in its malicious intentions it has long resolved to drive our nation to perdition," wrote Mazepa in December 1708.

The war of manifestos, along with the decisive actions of the Muscovite troops and the election of a new hetman on Peter's orders, caused another split in Mazepa's ranks. Terrified by the prospect of retributions, the Cossack colonels who had earlier pressured Mazepa to rebel failed to bring their troops to him. Many joined the Muscovite side. There was little support for Mazepa on the part of rank-and-file Cossacks, townspeople, and peasants. The populace preferred the Orthodox tsar over the Catholic, Muslim, or, in this case, Protestant ruler. When the time came for a showdown between Charles and Peter, there were more Cossacks on the Muscovite side than on the Swedish one.

In early July 1709, a Swedish corps of 25,000 faced a Muscovite army twice as large in the fields near the city of Poltava. Cossacks fought on both sides as auxiliaries—a reflection not only of the fact that their loyalty was suspect but also that they were no match for regular European armies: the once formidable Cossack fighting force was a thing of the past. Between 3,000 and 7,000 Cossacks backed Mazepa and the Swedes; at least three times as many flocked to the Muscovite side. The enemy's numerical superiority was never an issue for Charles XII, who had defeated much more numerous Russian and Polish forces in the past. But this battle was different. A winter spent in hostile territory had weakened his army. Charles XII, who usually led his troops into battle in person, had been wounded a few days earlier and delegated his duties not to one commander but to a number of officers, creating confusion in the Swedish ranks at the time of the battle.

The outcome was a decisive victory for Muscovite arms. Charles XII and Mazepa had to flee Ukraine and seek refuge in Ottoman Moldavia. Ivan Mazepa died in exile in the Moldavian town of Bender in the fall of 1709. It took Charles five years to get back to his kingdom. Historians often consider the Battle of Poltava a turning point in the Great Northern War. By a strange turn of fate, the military conflict for control of the Baltics was decided on a Ukrainian battleground, undermining Sweden's hegemony in northern Europe and launching Russia on its career as a great European power. But the consequences of Poltava were nowhere as dramatic as in the lands where the battle was fought.

THE MUSCOVITE VICTORY opened a new stage in relations between the Kyivan clergy and the tsarist authorities. In the fall of 1708, the tsar had forced the metropolitan of Kyiv to condemn Mazepa as a traitor and declare an anathema against him. After the battle, the rector of the Kyivan College, Teofan Prokopovych, who had earlier compared Mazepa to Prince Volodymyr, delivered a long sermon before the tsar condemning his former benefactor. What Mazepa would have considered treason was a declaration of loyalty in Peter's eyes. Prokopovych would later become the chief ideologue of Peter's reforms. He would support the tsar's drive for absolute power and develop an argument for his right to pass on his throne outside the normal line of succession from father to son: Peter tried his son Alexei for treason and caused his death in imprisonment. Prokopovych was the primary author of the *Spiritual Regulation*, which replaced patriarchal rule in the Orthodox Church with the rule of the Holy Synod, chaired by a secular official. He was also behind the idea of calling Peter the "father of the fatherland," a new designation brought to Muscovy by Prokopovych and other Kyivan clerics. They had earlier used it to glorify Mazepa.

The spectacular imperial career of Teofan Prokopovych reflected a larger phenomenon—the recruitment into the imperial service of westernized alumni of the Kyivan College, whom Peter needed to reform Muscovite church culture and society along Western lines. Dozens and later hundreds of alumni of the Kyivan College moved to Muscovy and made their careers there. They assumed positions ranging from acting head of the Orthodox Church to bishop and military chaplain. One of the Kyivans, Metropolitan Dymytrii Tuptalo of Rostov, was even raised to sainthood for his struggle against the Old Belief. They helped Peter not only to westernize Muscovy but also to turn it into a modern polity by promoting the idea of a new Russian fatherland and, indeed, a new Russian nation, of which Ukrainians or Little Russians were considered an integral part.

If Peter's policies intended to strengthen his authoritarian rule and centralize state institutions offered new and exciting opportunities to ecclesiastical leaders, they were nothing short of a disaster for the Cossack officers. Mazepa's defection added urgency to the tsar's desire to integrate the Hetmanate into the institutional and administrative structures of the empire. A Russian resident now supervised the new hetman, Ivan Skoropadsky. His capital was moved closer to the Muscovite border, from the destroyed Baturyn to the town of Hlukhiv. Muscovite troops were stationed in the Hetmanate on a permanent basis. Family members of Cossack officers who had followed Mazepa into exile were arrested and their properties confiscated. More followed once the Northern War ended with a Muscovite victory in 1721. Tsar Peter changed the name of the Tsardom of Muscovy to the Russian Empire and had himself proclaimed its first emperor. In the following year, the tsar used the death of Skoropadsky to liquidate the office of hetman altogether. He placed the Hetmanate under the jurisdiction of the so-called Little Russian College, led by an imperial officer appointed by Peter. The Cossacks protested and sent a delegation to St. Petersburg to fight for their rights—to no avail. The tsar ordered the arrest of the leader of the Cossack opposition, Colonel Pavlo Polubotok, who would die in a cell of the St. Peter and Paul Fortress in St. Petersburg.

Mazepa had gambled and lost. So did the state he tried to protect. We do not know what the fate of the Hetmanate might have been if Charles XII had not been wounded before the battle and the Cossacks had supported Mazepa in larger numbers. We can say, however, what kind of country Mazepa's successors wanted to build and live in. Our knowledge comes from a document called *Pacta et conditiones* presented to Pylyp Orlyk, the hetman elected by the Cossack exiles in Moldavia after Mazepa's death. Needless to say, they did not recognize Skoropadsky, elected on Peter's orders, as their legitimate leader. The *Pacta*, known in Ukraine today as the Constitution of Pylyp Orlyk, is often regarded as the country's first constitution, adopted, many say with pride, even before the American one. In reality, the closest parallel to the *Pacta* would be the conditions on which the Polish Diets elected their kings. The document tried to limit the hetman's powers by guaranteeing the rights of the Cossack officers and the rank-and-file Cossacks, especially the Zaporozhians, many of whom had followed Mazepa into exile.

The *Pacta* presented a unique vision of the Hetmanate's past, present, and future. The Cossack officers gathered around Orlyk, who had been Mazepa's general chancellor, traced their origins not to Kyiv and Prince Volodymyr—a foundational myth already claimed by Kyivan supporters of the tsar—but to the Khazars, who were among the nomadic predecessors of Kyivan Rus'. The argument was linguistic rather than historical, and, while laughable today, it was quite solid by the standards of early modern philology: "Cossack" and "Khazar" sounded quite similar, if not identical, in Ukrainian. At stake was a claim to the existence of a Cossack nation separate and independent from that of Moscow. Orlyk and his officers described it as Cossack, Ruthenian, or Little Russian, depending on circumstances. Most of Orlyk's ideas remained unknown or unclaimed by his compatriots. At home, in Ukraine, the Cossacks were fighting hard to preserve whatever was left of their autonomy.

THE COSSACKS IN the Hetmanate regarded the death of Peter I in February 1725, a few weeks after the demise of the imprisoned Cossack colonel Polubotok, as divine punishment for the tsar's mistreatment of them. They also viewed it as an opportunity to recover some of the privileges usurped by the tsar. The restoration of the office of hetman topped the Cossack agenda. In 1727 the Cossack officers achieved their goal by electing one of Peter's early opponents, Colonel Danylo Apostol, to the newly reinstated hetmancy. They celebrated this restoration of one of the privileges given to Bohdan Khmelnytsky by rediscovering a portrait of the old hetman and reviving his cult not only as the liberator of Ukraine from Polish oppression but also as a guarantor of Cossack rights and freedoms. In his new incarnation, Khmelnytsky became the symbol of the Hetmanate elite's Little Russian identity, which entailed the preservation of special status and particular rights in return for political loyalty.

What exactly was that new identity? It was a rough-and-ready amalgam of the pro-Russian rhetoric of the clergy and the autonomist aspirations of the Cossack officer class. The main distinguishing feature of the Little Russian idea was loyalty to the Russian tsars. At the same time, Little Russian identity stressed the rights and privileges of the Cossack nation within the empire. The Little Russia of the Cossack elite remained limited to Left-Bank Ukraine, distinct in political, social, and cultural terms from the Belarusian territories to the north and the Ukrainian lands west of the Dnieper. The DNA of the new polity and identity bore clear markers of earlier nation-building projects. The Cossack texts of the period (the early eighteenth

century saw the appearance of a new literary phenomenon, Cossack historical writing) used such terms as Rus'/Ruthenia, Little Russia, and Ukraine
interchangeably. There was logic in such usage, as the terms reflected closely
interconnected political entities and related identities.

In defining the relationship between these terms and the phenomena they
represented, the best analogy is a nesting doll. The biggest doll would be the
Little Russian identity of the post-Poltava era; within it would be the doll of
the Cossack Ukrainian fatherland on both banks of the Dnieper; and inside
that would be the doll of the Rus' or Ruthenian identity of the Polish-
Lithuanian Commonwealth. At its core, Little Russian identity preserved the
memory of the old commonwealth Rus' and the more recent Cossack
Ukraine. No one could know, in the aftermath of the Battle of Poltava, that
it was only a matter of time before the Ukrainian core emerged from the
shell of the Little Russian doll and reclaimed the territories once owned or
coveted by the Cossacks of the past.

III

BETWEEN THE EMPIRES

CHAPTER 13

THE NEW FRONTIERS

THE LAST QUARTER of the eighteenth century saw a dramatic change in the geopolitics of eastern and central Europe. Its major feature and cause was the rise of the military might and geopolitical influence of the Russian Empire, which the 1709 Battle of Poltava had launched on its career as a European superpower. Oleksandr Bezborodko, a descendant of a prominent Cossack officer family in the Hetmanate and grand chancellor of the Russian Empire at the end of the century, once told a younger interlocutor, "In our times, not a single cannon in Europe could fire without our consent." The borders of the Russian Empire advanced rapidly west and south, causing the retreat of the Ottomans from the northern Black Sea region and the partition of the Polish-Lithuanian Commonwealth, which disappeared from the map of Europe.

These striking changes took place with the active involvement of many Ukrainians. Bezborodko, who played a key role in the formulation of Russian foreign policy in the 1780s and early 1790s, was one of them. The changes Bezborodko helped to introduce affected his compatriots at home. Ukraine found itself at the center of this major geopolitical shift, at once its victim and its beneficiary. At this point the Hetmanate vanished from the map of Europe and the Russian Empire. The two main cultural frontiers of Ukraine—one between Eastern and Western Christianity, the other between Christianity and Islam—also began to shift. The change in imperial Russia's borders altered cultural spaces as well. In the west, the Russian authorities halted the advance of the Catholic and Uniate churches at the Dnieper and pushed it back; in the south, the "closing" of the steppe frontier gave new impetus to the further Ukrainian advance toward the Black Sea and the Sea of Azov.

HISTORIANS OF POLITICS, ideas, and culture know the eighteenth century first and foremost as the Age of Enlightenment, an era extending from the mid-seventeenth to the late eighteenth century and defined by the rise, in both philosophy and politics, of the ideas of individualism, skepticism, and reason—hence another term for the period, the Age of Reason. Reason, however, was understood in more than one way. The ideas of liberty and the protection of individual rights took center stage in the writings of the period, but so did the notions of rational governance and monarchical absolutism. The modern republic and the modern monarchy both have deep roots in the ideas of the French philosophes. Both the founding fathers of the United States and the absolute rulers of eighteenth-century Europe were disciples of the Enlightenment. Three of the latter—Catherine II of Russia, Frederick II of Prussia, and Joseph II of Austria—became known in history as "enlightened despots." In addition to being their countries' second monarchs to bear their names, as well as their belief in rational administration, absolute monarchy, and their right to rule, another commonality united them: they all took part in the partitions of Poland (1772–1795), which ultimately crushed the commonwealth's Enlightenment-inspired efforts to reform itself. The first partition was welcomed by none other than Voltaire, who considered it a victory for the cause of liberalism, toleration, and, yes, reason. He wrote to Catherine, suggesting that the Russian government could finally bring order to that part of Europe.

The ruler's absolute power, good government, and the application of universal norms to all parts of the empire and all its subjects: these principles informed the thinking and reforms of Catherine II, who ruled the Russian Empire for more than thirty years, from 1762 to 1796. None of these principles boded well for the Hetmanate, an autonomous enclave whose very existence rested on the idea of special status within the empire. The abolition of internal borders and the full incorporation of the Cossack state into the empire became one of the empress's first priorities in the region. "Little Russia, Livonia, and Finland are provinces governed by confirmed privileges," wrote Catherine in 1764. "These provinces, as well as Smolensk, should be Russified in the easiest way possible so that they cease looking like wolves to the forest. The approach is easy if wise men are chosen as governors of the provinces. When the hetmans are gone from Little Russia, every effort should be

made to eradicate from memory the period and the hetmans, let alone promote anyone to that office."

The first Russian ruler to eliminate the office of hetman was Peter I. He
did so after the death of Ivan Skoropadsky in 1722. The revival of the
Hetmanate's autonomy after his death in 1725, with the election of a new
hetman two years later, did not last very long. It came to an end in the mid-
1730s, when the imperial government barred the election of a new Cossack
leader after the death of Hetman Danylo Apostol. The Hetmanate again came
under the control of a government body called the Little Russian College.
With the hetmancy's short-lived restoration in 1750, the mace went not to a
Cossack colonel or a member of the general staff but to the president of the
Russian Imperial Academy of Sciences. This man of many worlds and talents
was the twenty-two-year-old Kyrylo Rozumovsky.

A native of the Hetmanate educated at the University of Göttingen, Rozumovsky was, more than anything, an imperial courtier. The secret of his
early and spectacular career lay in his family ties. His elder brother Oleksii, a
Cossack youth from the town of Kozelets between Kyiv and Chernihiv, was
a talented singer and ended up in the court chorus in St. Petersburg, where
he sang, played the bandura, and met a granddaughter of Peter I named Elizabeth, a future empress of Russia. They became lovers and, by some accounts, were secretly married. One way or another, the Cossack Oleksii
Rozum became the Russian count Aleksei Razumovsky (Ukrainian: Rozumovsky). And on the advice of the "Emperor of Night," as some courtiers
called Rozumovsky, Empress Elizabeth restored the office of hetman, which
went to his younger brother.

If the elder Rozumovsky was instrumental in bringing Elizabeth to the
throne (he was running the court at the time of her accession in 1741), the
younger one played an important role in the succession of Catherine II.
She became empress as the result of a coup backed by the imperial guards,
which saw her husband and the lawful ruler of the realm, Peter III, assassinated. The killing of her husband aside, Catherine, born Sophie Friederike
Auguste von Anhalt-Zerbst-Dornburg, had no more than a shaky claim to
the Russian throne. Those who brought her to power believed that she owed
them a debt. "Every guardsman when he looks at me can say: 'I made that
woman,'" wrote Catherine to Voltaire. Among those who thought that way
was Hetman Kyrylo Rozumovsky of Ukraine. In return for his services he
wanted a hereditary hetmancy. His subjects in the Hetmanate also wanted
broader autonomy and a local legislature.

Some of the Cossack patriots regarded the Hetmanate, which they, too, now called Little Russia, as a polity equal to the imperial core, which they called Great Russia. "I did not submit to you but to your sovereign," wrote Semen Divovych in his poem "A Conversation Between Great and Little Russia." With these words, written soon after Catherine's accession to the throne, a personified Little Russia addresses Great Russia. Divovych continued, "Do not think that you yourself are my master, / But your sovereign and mine is our common ruler." This vision of a dynastic union of Little and Great Russia harked back to the ideas of the Union of Hadiach. The sovereign in question, Catherine II, had no intention of presiding over a confederation of polities that claimed special rights and privileges. She envisioned a centralized empire divided rationally into administrative units, not enclaves like the Hetmanate.

Catherine's recall of the hetman to St. Petersburg and abolition of the hetmancy altogether in the fall of 1764 dashed not just Rozumovsky's hopes but also those of many Ukrainian patriots in the Hetmanate. The new ruler of the Hetmanate, or whatever was left of it, was General Petr Rumiantsev. An ethnic Russian, he assumed the newly created office of governor-general of Little Russia and took command of the Russian army in the region. His rule lasted more than twenty years and witnessed the introduction of serfdom in the Hetmanate, as well as imperial tax and postal systems. In the early 1780s, he presided over the liquidation of the territorial autonomy of the Hetmanate and the abolition of the administrative and military system based on Cossack regiments. The regular army incorporated the military detachments, and Cossack administrative units were merged to create three imperial provinces according to the new administrative system introduced by Catherine throughout the empire.

When it came to realizing her vision of a well-ordered imperial state, Catherine clearly took her time. The whole process of assimilating the Hetmanate, from the abolition of the hetman's office to the administrative integration of the Hetmanate into the empire, took almost twenty years. The transition happened gradually, without new revolts or the creation of new martyrs for the cause of Ukrainian autonomy. It took place with the support of numerous natives of the Hetmanate who believed that imperial incorporation was a godsend. Many of the Hetmanate's institutions and practices seemed out of date, incapable of responding to the challenges of the Age of Reason. Imperial integration turned auxiliary Cossack detachments into disciplined army units and introduced such public services as a school system and regular mail delivery. It also brought serfdom, but few Cossack officers protested, as they stood to benefit from serf labor.

The Cossack elite ruled in the Hetmanate and Sloboda Ukraine—a region around Kharkiv and Sumy that had remained under direct Russian administration since the seventeenth century—but peasants accounted for most of the population of those two areas. In the course of the eighteenth century, they found themselves increasingly losing not only their land but also their freedom—the great achievement of the Khmelnytsky Uprising. In the second half of the century, close to 90 percent of peasants in the Hetmanate and more than half of those in Sloboda Ukraine lived on estates owned by Cossack officers, now members of the gentry, and by the Orthodox Church. A decree issued by Catherine in May 1783 prohibited close to 300,000 peasants living on gentry estates from leaving their locations and obliged them to perform free labor for the landowners. This was a third onset of serfdom.

Some have argued that at least one voice advocated against enserfment in the Hetmanate. That voice belonged to Vasyl Kapnist, a descendant of a Cossack officer family from the Poltava region, who wrote one of the best-known oppositional texts of the Catherinian era, the "Ode on Slavery" (1783). According to some scholars, Kapnist protested the enserfment of the peasantry; others see him as arguing against the liquidation of the Hetmanate's institutions. In fact, he may have opposed both developments, which coincided closely in time and were enacted by decrees of the same ruler. Kapnist did not hide his disappointment with the consequences of Catherine's rule for his homeland. With regard to the empress's treatment of her people, he wrote, "And you burden them: You place chains on the hands that bless you!"

Kapnist was one of many members of the Ukrainian elite who made a good part of their careers in St. Petersburg and contributed to the development not only of Ukrainian but also of Russian literature and culture—his "Ode" became a canonical text of Russian literature. Whereas in Peter's time Ukrainian clerics moved to Russia and joined the imperial church, the age of Catherine saw the migration to St. Petersburg of the sons of Cossack officers and alumni of the Kyivan Academy who opted for secular professions. Between 1754 and 1768 alone, more than three hundred alumni of the academy chose the imperial service or moved to Russia. Their educations prepared them well to continue their studies abroad and then return to serve the empire. There were twice as many Ukrainian as Russian doctors in the empire, and in the last two decades of the century, more than one-third of the students at the St. Petersburg teachers' college came from the lands of the Hetmanate. Catherine stopped the recruitment of Ukrainian clergymen for the Russian church (when she took office, most of Russia's bishops were migrants from Ukraine), but the influx of Ukrainians into the civil service and the military continued apace.

THE CAREER OF Oleksandr Bezborodko offers a good example of how the new generation of Cossack officers combined loyalty to the Hetmanate with service to the empire. Born in 1747 to the family of the general chancellor of the Hetmanate, Bezborodko received his education at the Kyivan Academy. A few decades earlier, such a background would have been a perfect starting point for a spectacular career in the Hetmanate. But times were changing. Bezborodko attained the rank of colonel by serving not the hetman but the imperial governor of Little Russia, Petr Rumiantsev. The young Bezborodko took part in a war with the Ottomans, showed his bravery in a number of battles, and served with distinction as the head of Rumiantsev's chancellery. Promoted to colonel in 1774, by the following year he was in St. Petersburg, serving at the pleasure of the empress herself.

The 1768–1774 Russo-Turkish War, which propelled Bezborodko's career and moved him from the former Hetmanate to the imperial capital, had a major impact not only on the Hetmanate but also on the Ukrainian lands in general. A revolt that began in Right-Bank Ukraine in the spring of 1768 triggered the conflict.

In fact, two revolts happened at the same time. The first was an uprising or, in the language of that time and place, a "confederation" of the Catholic (Polish and Polonized) nobility against the decisions of the Diet of the Polish-Lithuanian Commonwealth that gave religious dissidents, especially the Orthodox, equal rights with Catholics. Catherine forced the decision of the Diet on its Catholic deputies through her envoy, who threatened to use the Russian troops at his disposal to achieve his goal. For Catherine, this was a way of demonstrating her Russian and Orthodox credentials. The rebels refused to obey the Diet resolution, which they interpreted as a Russian ploy to undermine not only their religion but also the sovereignty of their state. This noble uprising became known as the Confederation of Bar after the name of the Podolian town where it broke out.

As the members of the confederation went after the remaining Orthodox believers in Right-Bank Ukraine, their actions provoked a different kind of revolt. This one involved the Orthodox Cossacks, townspeople, and peasants who, encouraged by Russian government and church officials, rebelled against the Catholic nobles, prompting fears of a massacre on the scale of 1648—the first year of the Khmelnytsky Revolt. Once again, the Zaporozhian Cossacks joined forces with those Cossacks who served the authorities. The first group was led by Maksym Zalizniak, the second by Ivan Gonta—two future heroes of Ukrainian populist and later Soviet historical narratives. As in 1648, the victims were Polish nobles, Catholic and Uniate priests, and Jews. The Jews had returned to the region in the eighteenth century and reestablished their economic, religious, and cultural life in Right-Bank Ukraine. Many of them were the followers of Rabbi Israel Baal Shem Tov, who in the 1740s began teaching Hassidism in the Podolian city of Madzhybizh. The Catholic rebels wanted a Catholic state without Russian interference, while the Orthodox wanted a Cossack state under the jurisdiction of Russia. The Jews wanted to be left alone. None of the groups got what it wanted.

In the summer of 1768, the Russian army crossed the Dnieper border with the commonwealth, attacking both the Catholic confederates and the Orthodox Cossacks and peasants. This took the latter in particular by surprise, since they regarded the tsarist troops as their liberators. The empire, however, had its own logic. Both revolts threatened stability in the region, and both were crushed—but not before a detachment of Ukrainian Cossacks claiming to be in the Russian service crossed the Polish border at the town of Balta and entered the territory of the Ottoman Empire, apparently in pursuit of members of the Confederation of Bar. The Ottomans, concerned, along with the French, about growing Russian influence in the region, exploited the incident to declare war on the Russian Empire. Russia accepted the challenge.

Governor-General Petr Rumiantsev led one of the imperial armies, along with a Cossack detachment, into Moldavia and Wallachia. After a number of successful battles (Bezborodko distinguished himself in those fought at Larga and Kagul), the Russians took control of those two principalities, including their capitals, Jassy and Bucharest. Also captured were the Ottoman fortresses of Izmail and Kiliia on the Danube, which are now in Ukraine. Russian forces also took the Crimea, and most of southern Ukraine came under Russian control. The Ottomans were on the run. In the Mediterranean, the Russian fleet destroyed the Ottoman navy with the help of British advisers.

The Treaty of Kuchuk Kainarjae, signed in 1774, looked like a setback for Russian aspirations in the Black Sea region. Imperial troops had to leave the Danube principalities of Moldavia and Wallachia. St. Petersburg also had to remove its troops from the Crimea. The reason was simple: a number of European powers were unhappy with the sudden growth of Russian influence in the region. But the treaty benefited the Russian Empire in other ways. It effectively expelled the Ottomans from the northern Black Sea region and the Crimea. Russia established its outposts on the Azov and Black Seas. The Crimean Khanate was now declared an independent state. That was a one-sided description: while the peninsula became independent of Istanbul, it now depended on St. Petersburg.

The formal annexation of the Crimea to the Russian Empire took place in 1783, with the Russian army entering the peninsula and sending the last Crimean khan into exile in central Russia. Bezborodko, by then a leading architect of Russian foreign policy, played an important role in this development. He was also an author of the so-called Greek Project, a plan to destroy the Ottoman Empire and establish a new Byzantium under Russian control, as well as to create Dacia, a new country on the Danube consisting of Moldavia and Wallachia. The project never came to fruition, but its echoes still resonate in the Greek names given by the imperial authorities to the Crimean towns, including Simferopol, Yevpatoria, and the most famous of them, Sevastopol—the Russian naval base established on the peninsula two years after its annexation.

Alarmed by Catherine's trip to the Crimea in 1787 and rumors of the Greek Project, the Ottomans began a new war for control of the northern Black Sea coast. They lost once again, this time to allied Russian and Austrian troops. According to the peace treaty signed at Jassy in 1792 by Oleksandr Bezborodko, the Russian Empire extended its control to all of southern Ukraine. The Ottomans now recognized both the Crimea and the Kuban region across the Strait of Kerch as Russian territories. With a stroke of Bezborodko's pen, the Russian Empire had closed the Ukrainian steppe frontier. The cultural frontier, however, remained in place, simply becoming an internal one.

THE MILITARY CLOSURE of the steppe frontier opened it for colonization, encouraged and directed by the imperial government. The Cossacks were no longer needed in the area. In fact, the imperial authorities wanted them out, considering them liable to cause revolts, skirmishes, and conflicts with neighboring powers. The government got one more confirmation of that in the participation of the Russian Cossacks in the 1773–1774 Pugachev Uprising. The following year, Russian imperial troops returning from the Moldavian front surrounded the Zaporozhian Host and dispersed the Cossacks. Some of them were recruited into new Cossack formations, including the Black Sea Cossacks, who were eventually shipped to the Kuban Peninsula, bordering on the turbulent North Caucasus. Others stayed, but no longer as an organized force. Grigorii Potemkin, the favorite of Catherine II, showed their settlements to the empress during her trip to the Crimea in 1787. The presentation that gave birth to the expression "Potemkin village" was false in the sense not that the villages did not exist but that they were hardly the result of Potemkin's efforts: they had been there before.

The mass colonization of the steppes of southern Ukraine began while they were still under Cossack control. The Zaporozhians themselves invited peasant refugees to the region, and the government subsequently established new settlements of its own on the lands taken from the Cossacks. Serbian refugees from Ottoman rule settled north of Yelysavethrad (present-day Kropyvnytsky) and Bakhmut (till recently Artemivsk in Donetsk oblast) in districts called, respectively, New Serbia and Slavo-Serbia. As the line of Russian fortresses moved south and the empire absorbed new lands as a result of the Russo-Turkish wars and the annexation of the Crimea, all Zaporozhian lands became part of an imperial province called New Russia. (Its borders changed over time, including or excluding the Donets River region and the Crimea, but it never included the Kharkiv region of Sloboda Ukraine, as claimed by the Russian idealogues of the partition of Ukraine in 2014.) Centered on the former lands of the Zaporozhian Cossacks, New Russia became the primary destination of domestic and foreign migration in the last decades of the eighteenth century.

From 1789 to 1790, the first Mennonites moved into the region from Prussia in an attempt to avoid obligatory military service and settled on the Cossack island of Khortytsia immediately beyond the Dnieper rapids. More coreligionists from their old homeland, as well as German Protestant and Catholic colonists from central Europe, would soon join them. Most of the "foreigners," however, came from the Ottoman Empire: Greeks, Bulgarians, and Moldavians. The imperial authorities, seeking farmers and artisans with a proven record, encouraged their immigration and provided the settlers with land, tax breaks, and benefits that Russian subjects could only dream of.

The imperial elites celebrated the settlers' multiethnic composition, which they saw as proof of the greatness of the empire and its ruler. "The Moldavian, the Armenian, the Indian, and the Hellene or the black Ethiopian—whatever the sky beneath which he came into the world, Catherine is the mother of all," wrote late-eighteenth-century poet V. P. Petrov. By the end of the century, "foreigners" constituted up to 20 percent of the region's overall male population of approximately half a million. The rest were Eastern Slavs. Some of the latter were Russian religious dissenters exiled to the borderlands, but most of them were Ukrainian Cossacks and peasants from the Hetmanate and Right-Bank Ukraine. Despite its imperial origins and multiethnic bent, the province of New Russia was largely Ukrainian in ethnic composition.

Whereas New Russia was largely Ukrainian, the province of Taurida, which included the Crimean Peninsula, was predominantly Crimean Tatar. St. Petersburg did its best to smooth the incorporation of the peninsula into the empire, offering Crimean nobles Russian noble status along with the lands that had once belonged to the khans. The other social arrangements of the khanate, as well as the dominant role of Islam, remained intact. The empire was taking its time. As with the Hetmanate, the incorporation of the Crimean Khanate would take more than a generation. Caution was necessary for several reasons. One was outmigration: before the end of the eighteenth century, close to 100,000 former subjects of the Crimean khan had left the peninsula and the Black Sea steppes to its north for the Ottoman Empire. The desire to live under an Islamic ruler was one explanation for this migration; the decline of economic opportunity with the closing of the steppe frontier—the slave trade and war booty had completely dried up—was another.

In 1793, a year after Bezborodko signed the Jassy agreement, which legalized Russian possession of the Crimea and southern Ukraine under international law, another dramatic event took place on the western borders of the former Hetmanate. The long-established Russo-Polish border along the Dnieper, which had divided Ukraine for more than 120 years, suddenly ceased to exist. Russian troops, some of them led by former Cossack officers who now held high rank in the imperial Russian army, crossed the Dnieper and began to advance westward. They occupied Eastern Podolia, including the fortress of Kamianets-Podilskyi, and part of Volhynia, including the town of Zhytomyr. In the north, the Russian army occupied the Belarusian towns of Minsk and Slutsk.

The development that put an end to the existence of the Dnieper boundary and realized the age-old Ukrainian Cossack dream of uniting Right- and Left-Bank Ukraine was the second partition of Poland. The first partition had taken place in 1772, when three great European powers—Russia, Austria, and Prussia—took over parts of the Polish-Lithuanian Commonwealth. Prussia's share included the area of Gdańsk, connecting its core possessions with East Prussia; Russia took eastern Belarus; and Austria claimed Galicia. For the Russian Empire, which had controlled the entire commonwealth for most of the eighteenth century through its Diets, which were vulnerable to military and political pressure, and more recently through a loyal king, the partition was more of a loss than a gain. In fact, it was a way of avoiding military conflict, for which St. Petersburg was unprepared. Alarmed by Russian victories in the 1768–1774 Russo-Turkish War, Austria had sided with the Ottomans, threatening to attack Russia. By agreeing to the first partition, Russia was in fact bribing Austria to stay out of the Ottoman--Russian conflict.

The Austrians took the bait. They wanted Silesia, a province centered on present-day Wrocław (Breslau), but were offered Galicia. The Austrian (Habsburg) empress Maria Theresa detested the term "partition," which in her opinion implied the unlawful character of the whole enterprise, and sought historical justification for the new acquisition. She found it in the historical claims of the Hungarian kings to the medieval Galician-Volhynian principality, and so the new territory became known as the Kingdom of Galicia and Lodomeria. The Austrians took their invented Galician-Volhynian connection very seriously. In 1774, claiming the right of the Galician princes to Bukovyna, the Habsburgs annexed that territory from Moldavia. As the entire province of Transcarpathia (the westernmost region of today's Ukraine) had been under Vienna's control since 1699, the Habsburgs united under their scepter three future Ukrainian provinces—a development with major implications for modern Ukraine and eastern Europe in general.

The first partition added no Ukrainian lands to the Russian Empire—all its territorial gains were in Belarus and Latvia. But the situation changed in 1793, during the second partition of Poland, triggered by events in Warsaw. In May 1791, the delegates to the Polish Diet had adopted a new constitution that promised to put the commonwealth back on its feet. A product of the Enlightenment and the ideas of the French Revolution, the new constitution promoted centralization, good governance, and education; it also made progress in the realm of religious toleration. More importantly from the perspective of the partitioning powers, it promised to make the Polish government workable again by strengthening the authority of the king and removing the requirement to pass all Diet resolutions by unanimous vote—the famous, or rather infamous, *liberum veto*.

It appeared that despite (or because of) the shock of the first partition, the commonwealth would lift itself out of the chaos of infighting between aristocratic clans and reemerge as a strong state in the center of Europe. To prevent this, Prussia and Austria annexed even more Polish territory. Russia did likewise under the pretext of protecting the old Polish rights and liberties, including the *liberum veto*. The Dnieper frontier in Ukraine had to go; the new one was established in Volhynia and Podolia. It made the Habsburgs and the Romanovs neighbors, as the Russians had moved the imperial border all the way to the eastern boundary of Austrian Galicia. Like Empress Maria Theresa, Catherine cared about legitimacy. After the second partition, Russian imperial authorities issued a medal with a map showing the new boundaries and bearing the inscription "I have restored what was torn away"—a reference to the lands that had once belonged to Kyivan Rus'.

The Russian borders soon moved even farther west. This had nothing to do with a reexamination of maps of Kyivan Rus' but stemmed from an uprising in the commonwealth caused by the second partition. It was led by Tadeusz Kościuszko, a native of Belarus, supporter of the Confederation of Bar, and participant in the American War of Independence, during which he constructed fortifications at West Point and was promoted to the rank of brigadier general by the Continental Congress. In 1784 he returned to the commonwealth, where he served as a major general in the Polish army. In 1794 he began the uprising in Cracow, assuming command of all the commonwealth armed forces. All three partitioning powers—Russia, Prussia, and Austria—sent their troops across the Polish borders to crush the revolt. The outcome was the complete destruction of the Polish state.

The enlightened despots now divided up whatever remained of the commonwealth after the second partition. Austria competed with Russia for the acquisition of Volhynia ("Lodomeria") but lost the claim and took part of Poland with Cracow instead. To make the acquisition look legitimate, Austria treated the territory as part of Galicia. Prussia extended its possessions south of the Baltic Sea, reaching Warsaw. But the greatest beneficiary was Russia, whose share of the loot included the Baltic provinces, Lithuania, western Belarus, and, in Ukraine, Volhynia with the towns of Rivne and Lutsk.

Some regard the partitions of Poland as reunifications of Ukraine—that was certainly the line taken by Soviet historiography. In fact, they resulted in the reunification of some of the Ukrainian lands and the division or partitioning of others. If before the partitions the Polish-Lithuanian Commonwealth and the Russian Empire divided up most of the Ukrainian lands, now the division was between the Russian and Habsburg empires. When it comes to the Ukrainian lands, Russia turned from a minority into a majority "stakeholder," controlling most of Ukrainian ethnic territory. As a result of the partitions, the share of ethnic Ukrainians in the Russian Empire increased from 13 to 22 percent, while the share of ethnic Russians decreased from 70 to 50 percent. More than 10 percent of the population of the newly acquired Ukrainian territories was Jewish, while roughly 5 percent consisted of Poles and Polonized Catholics. It was an ethnic mosaic on a par with or even greater than the one the empire promoted and celebrated in southern Ukraine. But the loyalty to the empire of its new Polish, Jewish, or even Ukrainian (in the parlance of the time, Little Russian) subjects was anything but a given. The multiethnic inhabitants were not newcomers to the area; the state that claimed them was. It embraced some of its new subjects but not the others. As early as 1791, the imperial government introduced the Pale of Settlement, limiting the areas open to the Jewish settlement to the former provinces of the commonwealth and later adding to them newly acquired territories in the south. Most of Ukraine became part of the Pale.

The key figure in the negotiations that led to the major shift of Ukrainian frontiers in the second half of the eighteenth century was none other than the "Cossack prince" Oleksandr Bezborodko. We know that in St. Petersburg he remained a loyal patriot of his Cossack homeland, which he called his fatherland. He helped publish a Cossack chronicle and himself wrote the history of the Hetmanate from the death of Hetman Danylo Apostol in 1734 to the start of the Russo-Turkish War of 1768. The chronicle was filled with descriptions of Cossack wars and battles with the Ottomans, Crimean Tatars, and Poles. We do not know, however, whether in his proposals to annex the Crimea, in his negotiations in Jassy over the fate of the northern Black Sea region, or, finally, in his talks with the Austrians and Prussians over the partitions of the commonwealth, Bezborodko ever felt the influence of his "Little Russian" upbringing and identity. By the time he helped erase the Crimea and the commonwealth from the map of Europe, his own fatherland had ceased to exist on that map as well. The eighteenth century was not only an age of enlightenment and reason. More than anything else, it was an age of empire.

CHAPTER 14

THE BOOKS OF THE GENESIS

T HE UKRAINIAN NATIONAL anthem begins with the words "Ukraine has not yet perished," hardly an optimistic beginning for any kind of song. But this is not the only anthem whose words do not inspire optimism. The Polish national anthem starts with the familiar line "Poland has not yet perished." The words of the Polish anthem were written in 1797 and those of the Ukrainian one were penned in 1862, so it is quite clear who influenced whom. But why such pessimism? In both cases, Polish and Ukrainian, the idea of the death of the nation stemmed from the experience of the late eighteenth century—the partitions of Poland and the liquidation of the Hetmanate.

Like many other anthems, the Polish one was originally a marching song written for the Polish legions fighting under the command of the future emperor of France, Napoleon Bonaparte, in his Italian campaigns. The song was originally known as the "Dąbrowski mazurka," named for a commander of the Polish troops, Jan Henryk Dąbrowski. Many of the Polish legionnaires, including the commander himself, had taken part in the Kościuszko Uprising, and the lyrics were meant to lift their spirits after the destruction of their state by the partitioning powers. The song's second line asserts that Poland will not perish "as long as we are alive." By associating the nation not with the state but with those who considered themselves its members, the Polish anthem gave hope not just to the Poles but also to representatives of other stateless nations. A new generation of patriots in Poland and Ukraine refused to accept the disasters of the previous century as the final verdict on their nations. Both Polish and Ukrainian activists promoted a new understanding of a nation as a democratic polity made up of citizen patriots rather than a territorial state.

IN THE FIRST decade of the nineteenth century, Napoleon and his soldiers brought the ideas of nation and popular sovereignty to the rest of Europe in their songs and at the points of their bayonets. In 1807, the dream of the Polish legionnaires came a step closer to realization when, after defeating Prussia, the French emperor created the Duchy of Warsaw out of territories annexed by that country during the partitions of Poland. To the Poles, this offered the exciting prospect of the restoration of their homeland. In 1812, after Napoleon's invasion of the Russian Empire, Poles under Russian rule rose in support of the French invader, whom they considered a liberator. Adam Mickiewicz, the foremost Polish poet of the era, reflected the Polish nobility's excitement at the advance of the French army into today's Belarus in his epic poem *Sir Thaddeus*, which is still required reading in today's Polish (but not Belarusian) schools. "Glory is ours already," says one of the poem's Polish characters, "and so we shall soon have our Republic again."

In 1815, when entering the University of Vilnius, the sixteen-year-old Mickiewicz gave his name as Adam Napoleon Mickiewicz. By that time, Polish hopes of having "our Republic again" had been crushed. Napoleon, Dąbrowski, and their French and Polish troops had retreated from the Russian Empire in defeat. Slightly more than a year later, Russian troops took Paris, while Napoleon went into exile on the island of Elba. But not all was in vain. The Congress of Vienna (1814–1815), which decided the fate of post-Napoleonic Europe, restored Poland to the map of the continent. On the ruins of the Duchy of Warsaw created by Napoleon, with the addition of some territory previously annexed by Austria, the congress established the Kingdom of Poland. It was to have the same ruler as its mighty neighbor, the Russian Empire, and in Russian it was called a tsardom, not a kingdom. Tsar Alexander I granted it rights of autonomy and privileges that no other part of the empire could have dreamed of.

Catherine's Age of Reason, entailing imperial unification and the standardization of administrative and legal practices, was over; the era of special arrangements was back. Those who had lost their privileges regarded the Poles with envy. Among them were the elites of the former Hetmanate. But whereas modern Polish nationalism grew under Napoleon's wing, its Ukrainian counterpart made its first steps under the anti-Bonaparte banner. During the Napoleonic Wars, Russian imperial journals began to publish the first patriotic poems written not in Russian but in Ukrainian. One of the first appeared in 1807 under the title "Aha! Have You Grabbed Enough, You Vicious Bastard Bonaparte?" One way or another, Napoleon was awakening local patriotism and national feelings. While the Poles, Germans, and Russians expressed those feelings in their native tongues, some Ukrainians decided that they could do so in their language as well. In Ukraine, as in the rest of Europe, language, folklore, literature, and, last but not least, history became building blocks of a modern national identity.

AMONG THE UKRAINIANS prepared to fight Napoleon with arms in hand was the founder of modern Ukrainian literature, Ivan Kotliarevsky. A native of the Poltava region in the former Hetmanate, he formed a Cossack detachment to join the struggle. The son of a minor official, Kotliarevsky studied in a theological seminary, worked as a tutor of children of the nobility, and served in the Russian imperial army, taking part in the 1806–1812 Russo-Turkish War. In 1798, while on military service, the first part of his poem *Eneïda* appeared in print, a travesty based on Virgil's *Aeneid*, whose main characters were not Greeks but Zaporozhian Cossacks. As one would expect of true Zaporozhians, they spoke vernacular Ukrainian. But the choice of language for the poem seems logical only in retrospect. In late eighteenth century Ukraine, Kotliarevsky was a pioneer—the first to write a major poetical work in the vernacular.

Why did he do so? We have no indication that he was trying to make a political statement of any kind. In fact, his choice of the genre of travesty indicates that he was playing with the language and subject rather than attempting to produce a work of high seriousness. Kotliarevsky clearly had literary talent and an impeccable sense of zeitgeist. In the late eighteenth century, intellectuals all over Europe were busy imagining the nation not only as a polity with sovereignty invested in its people but also as a cultural entity, a sleeping beauty to be awakened by a national renaissance. In Germany, Johann Gottfried Herder based his new understanding of the nation on language and culture. In other countries of western and central Europe as well, enthusiasts who would later be called folklorists were collecting tales and songs of the people or inventing them when no "good" samples were to be found. In Britain, James Macpherson, the "discoverer" of the ancient bard Ossian, successfully turned Irish folklore into Scottish national myth.

Kotliarevsky wrote the first part of *Eneïda* when the shell of Church Slavonic, which had dominated Russian imperial literature of the previous era, was crumbling and falling apart, allowing literatures based in one way or another on the vernacular to make their way into the public sphere. Russia found its first truly great poet in Alexander Pushkin; Ukraine got its own in the person of Kotliarevsky. Whatever his original motives for using Ukrainian, Kotliarevsky never regretted his choice. There would be five more parts of *Eneïda*. He would also author the first plays written in Ukrainian, among them *Natalka-Poltavka* (*Natalka from Poltava*), a love story set in a Ukrainian village. The language of Kotliarevsky's homeland, the Poltava region of the former Hetmanate, would become the basis of standard Ukrainian for speakers of numerous Ukrainian dialects from the Dnieper to the Don in the east and to the Carpathians in the west. With Kotliarevsky, a new literature was born. The language received its first grammar in 1818 with the publication of the *Grammar of the Little Russian Dialect* by Oleksii Pavlovsky. A year later, the first collection of Ukrainian folk songs by Mykola (Nikolai) Tsertelev appeared in print.

Kotliarevsky and his writings might have remained a footnote to literary history, a mere curiosity, if not for the work of dozens and then hundreds of talented authors. Not all of them wrote in Ukrainian, but most of them were romantics, sharing the early nineteenth-century fascination with folklore and tradition and its emphasis on emotion rather than the rationalism of the Enlightenment. The birthplace of Ukrainian romanticism was the city of Kharkiv, where the imperial government opened a university in 1805, inviting professors from all over the empire to fill vacant positions. Being a professor at that time often meant taking an interest in local history and folklore, and Kharkiv had a rich tradition. It served as the administrative and cultural center of Sloboda Ukraine, settled by Ukrainian Cossacks and runaway peasants in the times of Bohdan Khmelnytsky. In the late eighteenth and early nineteenth centuries, this land was often referred to as "Ukraine." Not surprisingly, the first literary almanac that began to appear there in 1816 was titled the *Ukrainian Herald*. Though published in Russian, it also accepted texts in Ukrainian, and many of its authors discussed themes in Ukrainian history and culture.

The centrality of the Cossack past to romantic literary interests, already manifested by Kotliarevsky's *Eneïda*, was further evidenced by the Kharkiv romantics' readiness to embrace and popularize by far the most influential Ukrainian historical text of the period, *Istoriia rusov* (*The History of the Rus'*). Authorship of this history of the Ukrainian Cossacks was attributed to eighteenth-century Orthodox archbishop Heorhii Konysky, but the real author (or authors) came from the ranks of descendants of Cossack officers in the Starodub region of the former Hetmanate. Whoever wrote the *History* was concerned about the inequality among the Cossack officers and the

Russian nobility and argued more broadly for the equality of Little and Great Russia—an old theme sounded in Cossack writings of the eighteenth century but now presented in a way that fitted the sensibilities of the romantic age.

The *History* portrayed the Cossacks as a distinct nation and glorified its past with descriptions of the heroic deeds of the Ukrainian hetmans, their battles, and their deaths at the hands of their enemies. Those enemies, and the villains of the narrative, were generally representatives of other nationalities—Poles, Jews, and Russians. The *History of the Rus'* ignited the imagination of romantic writers and poets all over the empire. In St. Petersburg, these included Kondratii Ryleev, Alexander Pushkin, and Nikolai Gogol; in Kharkiv, the main promoter of the mysterious text was a professor at the local university, Izmail Sreznevsky. Like Macpherson before him, he was not above creating his own folklore. But whereas Macpherson used Irish myths for that purpose, Sreznevsky found inspiration in the *History of the Rus'*. The work, which became extremely popular in the former Hetmanate in the 1830s and 1840s, made an all-important step toward the creation of a modern Ukrainian nation, turning a history of the Cossack social order into an account of a rising national community.

The former Hetmanate provided a key historical myth, a cultural tradition, and a language as building blocks of the modern Ukrainian nation. It supplied the architects as well. Ivan Kotliarevsky, author of *Eneïda*, Mykola Tsertelev, publisher of the first collection of Ukrainian folk songs, and Oleksii Pavlovsky, author of the first grammar of Ukrainian, all came from the Hetmanate. The reason for such prominence or even dominance of Hetmanate elites in the early stages of Ukrainian nation building was quite simple: the territory of the former Cossack state was the only region of nineteenth-century Ukraine where the landowning elites shared the culture of the local population. Catholic Poles or Polonized Ukrainian nobles dominated the political and cultural scene in Austrian Galicia and Russian Volhynia, Podolia, and Right-Bank Ukraine. In the southern steppes, colonized during the era of Catherine II, the ruling elite was either ethnically or culturally Russian. The scions of the old Cossack nation of the Hetmanate ended up in the forefront of battles for the new nation almost by default. Not surprisingly, the Cossack lands gave that nation not only its language but also its name, Ukraine.

WHILE THE BEGINNINGS of modern Ukrainian nation building—some scholars call it the heritage-gathering stage—came during and immediately after the Napoleonic Wars, the Polish uprising of 1830 influenced the next stage, which led to the formulation of the political program of the nascent national movement.

The uprising was long in the making. According to the resolutions of the 1814–1815 Congress of Vienna, Alexander I, the liberal ruler of Russia who had now added to his title of emperor of Russia that of tsar of Poland, provided his new possession with one of the most liberal constitutions in Europe. But the tsar soon proved that he was an emperor not only in name. Alexander's liberalism ran its course soon after the European powers recognized his sovereignty over the kingdom. His representatives often ignored the Polish parliament, curtailed freedom of the press, and disregarded other civic liberties the tsar had originally granted. When dissatisfied young Poles formed clandestine organizations, the police began hunting them down.

The situation only worsened after the Decembrist Uprising of 1825, which saw Russian military officers, some of them descendants of prominent Cossack families, lead their troops in revolt, demanding the adoption of a constitution. The revolt was crushed, inaugurating thirty years of conservative rule by Emperor Nicholas I. In November 1830, a mutiny of young Polish officers in Warsaw soon turned into an uprising that engulfed the rest of the kingdom as well as former Polish territories in today's Lithuania, Belarus, and Ukraine. A Polish military corps was sent to Volhynia, and Polish nobles rebelled in Volhynia, Podolia, and Right-Bank Ukraine. They called on the Ukrainian peasants to join them, sometimes promising emancipation from serfdom. The empire used its military superiority to put down the uprising. Many of its leaders, participants, and supporters, including Adam Mickiewicz, fled Poland, most of them to France. Less fortunate ones ended up in Russian prisons or in exile.

The November Uprising not only mobilized Polish patriotism and nationalism but also prompted a strong nationalist reaction from the Russian side. Russian imperial patriotism, which had developed clear anti-French overtones during the Napoleonic Wars, now became fiercely anti-Polish. People of the caliber of Alexander Pushkin led the ideological assault on the Polish rebels and their French backers. One of his poems, "To the Maligners of Russia," called on the French defenders of the Polish cause to leave the solution of the Russo-Polish conflict to the Slavs themselves. In the Polish insurrection, Pushkin saw a threat to Russian possessions far beyond the Kingdom of Poland. In his view, it was a contest for Ukraine as well. In a poem on the Russian takeover of rebellious Warsaw, Pushkin wrote,

Where shall we shift the line of forts?
Beyond the Buh, to the Vorskla, to the [Dnieper] Estuary?
Whose will Volhynia be?
And Bohdan [Khmelnytsky's] legacy?
Right of rebellion recognized,
Will Lithuania spurn our rule?
And Kiev, decrepit, golden-domed,
This ancestor of Russian towns—
Will it conjoin its sainted graves
With reckless Warsaw?

During the November Uprising, Pushkin even contemplated writing a history of "Little Russia."

The defense of Ukraine and other former Polish possessions against Western and, in particular, Polish influence became the leitmotif of Russian policy in the region in the decades following the uprising. The empire of the Romanovs was now ready to "go native" and employ Russian patriotism and nascent nationalism to defend its territorial acquisitions. At that point the imperial minister of education, Count Sergei Uvarov, formulated the foundations of the new Russian imperial identity: autocracy, Orthodoxy, and nationality. If the first two elements of Uvarov's triad were traditional markers of imperial Russian ideology, the third was a concession to the new era of rising nationalism. Uvarov's "nationality" was not general but specifically Russian. He wrote that his three principles formed "the distinctive character of Russia, and belong only to Russia." They "gather into one whole the sacred remnants of Russian nationality." That nationality included Russians, Ukrainians, and Belarusians.

While historians still argue about the exact meaning of Uvarov's triad, its clear and simple structure provides a good framework for the discussion of imperial policies in the Western borderlands from the 1830s on. The ideal subject of the Romanovs had to be not only loyal to the empire (that had sufficed during the Age of Reason) but also Russian and Orthodox. The Polish November Uprising had called into question the Ukrainian peasantry's loyalty to the empire. In the eyes of the imperial authorities, the peasants were definitely Russian but often not Orthodox—most in the newly acquired territories remained Uniate. Thus, to ensure loyalty to the empire and create an ideal subject of the tsars, they had to convert the Uniates to Orthodoxy to break the religious solidarity between Catholic nobles and Uniate peasants. The tactic used to achieve that goal essentially reversed the method of the Union of Brest. Instead of proselytizing among Uniates on an individual basis, the government and its supporters among the Uniate clergy would turn the entire church over to the Orthodox, more or less as the Polish authorities had done for the Uniate Church in the late sixteenth century and then again in the early eighteenth.

In 1839, a Uniate church council, convened with the support of the government, declared the "reunification" of the Uniates with the Russian Orthodox Church and asked for the tsar's blessing. The emperor approved the request and moved the army into the region to ensure that the union in reverse would not meet with a new revolt. More than 1,600 parishes and, by some estimates, over 1.5 million parishioners in Ukraine and Belarus were "returned" to Orthodoxy overnight. In Belarus, Volhynia, Podolia, and a good part of the Right Bank, Orthodoxy and nationality were brought together in the service of autocracy. It was the beginning of a long process of "Orthodoxization" of former Uniates, accompanied by their cultural Russification. Since Orthodox seminaries used Russian as their language of instruction, the intellectual elite of the church was being converted not only from Uniate Catholicism to Orthodoxy but also from Ukrainian or Ruthenian to Russian nationality.

Much more complex and difficult was the battle for the "hearts and minds" of the secular elites in territories threatened by the Polish uprising. At first the empire adopted its usual tactic: integration of the Polish nobility into the empire with no detriment to its legal status or landowning rights. Emperor Alexander made use of Polish aristocrats and intellectuals to promote his liberal reforms. Especially useful were Polish contributions in the realm of education, where Poland had made significant progress before being crushed by its neighbors in 1795.

The scion of a Polish aristocratic family, Prince Adam Jerzy Czartoryski, played a key role in creating a new educational system in the Ukrainian provinces of the empire. During the first decade of the nineteenth century, he served as an advisor to Alexander and, for a few years, was the de facto head of Russian foreign policy. Alexander also put Czartoryski in charge of the Vilnius educational district, centered on Vilnius University, which had jurisdiction over a good part of western Ukraine. Another Polish aristocrat, Seweryn Potocki, head of the Kharkiv educational district, with its center in Kharkiv University, supervised the rest of Ukraine. The founding of both universities and the development of a public school system throughout the region were among the main achievements of the reform, which the first minister of education of imperial Russia, Kyiv Mohyla Academy alumnus Petro Zavadovsky, supervised.

If there was any nationality policy in St. Petersburg in the early nineteenth century, it rested on the idea of the Slavic unity of the Russians (understood as including Ukrainians) and the Poles. That changed with the November Uprising. Adam Czartoryski, who remained in charge of the Vilnius educational district until 1823, became the leader of the Polish revolutionary government in December 1830. Later, from his suite in the Hotel Lambert in Paris, he led the activities of the "Great Emigration," the term for the members of the uprising who fled west. The alliance between the Russian autocracy and the Polish Catholic nobility came to an end. So did the advancement of education, which relied on Polish participation and loyalty. The imperial government picked up the gauntlet of cultural war thrown down by the leaders of the November Uprising, instituting measures to Russify Ukraine and the other former Polish territories of the empire. Count Uvarov was eager to develop Russian-language education and culture as counterweights to the dominant Polish culture of the borderlands.

Vilnius University, which rivaled the University of Oxford in enrollment for some time, was closed in 1832. The government had no more patience with a school it considered a hotbed of Polish nationalism. Other Polish-run educational institutions in the region also shut their doors, among them a lyceum in the town of Kremianets in Volhynia. The government transferred the lyceum's rich library, collection of sculptures, and trees and shrubs from the botanical garden to Kyiv, where it created a new imperial center of learning to replace Vilnius University in 1834. The Polish language was banned there; Russian was the only language of instruction. The new university was named after Prince Volodymyr (Vladimir) the Great—the first Orthodox autocrat and a Russian to boot, as far as official historiography was concerned.

The imperial authorities set about turning Kyiv, a city of only 35,000 inhabitants that Pushkin called "decrepit" in comparison with Warsaw, into a bastion of empire and Russianness on the European cultural frontier. They restored Orthodox churches according to the imperial taste of the time and banned Jews from the city. They built new boulevards and streets, and new names appeared on the map of the ancient city. One of them was Gendarme Way, reflecting the symbolic and practical importance of police for the regime and its stability in the borderlands. In 1833, the new governor of Kyiv, Podolia, and Volhynia, sent to Kyiv with instructions to "merge" the Right

Bank with the rest of the empire, suggested building a monument to Prince Volodymyr. Tsar Nicholas I personally examined the proposal. He loved the idea. It took twenty years to realize the project, but in 1853 the city got its statue. It stands today not near the university, as originally planned, but on the bank of the Dnieper, its ideological meaning and historical legacy open to a range of interpretations, from symbolizing Russo-Ukrainian religious and ethnic unity to memorializing the founder of the first Ukrainian state. Few people realize today that the statue was originally meant to assert an imperial claim to former Polish possessions on the Right Bank of the Dnieper.

The founding of the new university in Kyiv (the third one in the Ukrainian lands after the universities in Lviv and Kharkiv) was an important turning point in the history of the region. The university's main goal was to educate local cadres to serve as agents of Russian influence and promoters of Russian identity. The government also created a historical commission with the task of collecting and publishing manuscripts and documents to establish that Right-Bank Ukraine, Podolia, and Volhynia were historically Russian lands. It all began as planned. The local talent, mostly descendants of Cossack officer families and sons of priests and junior officials from the former Hetmanate, came to Kyiv to join the new institutions and engage in intellectual combat with the traditional Polish enemies of the Cossacks. But by the end of the 1840s, the imperial authorities found themselves in a precarious situation: the university and the historical commission, envisioned as bastions of struggle for Russian identity against the Polish challenge, had become hotbeds of a new identity and a new nationalism.

IN FEBRUARY 1847, a student of law at Kyiv University named Aleksei Petrov turned up in the office of the Kyiv educational district to denounce a secret society that aimed to turn the Russian Empire into a republic. The investigation launched into Petrov's allegations uncovered the clandestine Brotherhood of Saints Cyril and Methodius, named for the Christian missionaries who had enlightened the Slavs not only with a new religion but also with a new language and alphabet. Its members included a professor of history at Kyiv University, Mykola (Nikolai) Kostomarov—he would later become the founder of modern Ukrainian historiography—and a newly appointed drawing instructor, Taras Shevchenko. Born to the family of a Russian noble in Voronezh province on the border with Sloboda Ukraine, Mykola Kostomarov often stressed that his mother was a Ukrainian peasant woman. Whether that was true or not, mid-nineteenth-century Kyiv intellectuals prized peasant origins—they all wanted to work for the people and be as close to them as possible.

No member of the brotherhood had better populist credentials than Kostomarov's coconspirator Taras Shevchenko. Born in 1814 into a family of serfs in Right-Bank Ukraine, the young Shevchenko joined the household of a rich Polish landlord and first went to Vilnius and then to St. Petersburg as a member of his court. There Shevchenko showed his talent as an artist. A Ukrainian painter in St. Petersburg discovered him while he was drawing in the city's famous Summer Garden. Shevchenko was introduced to some of the leading figures of the Russian cultural scene of the time, including Russia's best-known poet before Pushkin, Vasilii Zhukovsky, and a founder of Russian romantic art, Karl Briullov. Shevchenko's work, personality, and life story made such an impression on the artistic community of St. Petersburg that its members decided to free the young serf no matter what. They bought his freedom with 2,500 rubles, an astounding sum by the standards of the time; the funds were the proceeds of the auction of a portrait of Zhukovsky, painted specifically for that purpose, by Briullov.

Shevchenko became a free man at the age of twenty-four. He turned out to be not only a talented artist but also an outstanding poet. In 1840, two years after acquiring his freedom, Shevchenko published his first collection of poems, titled *Kobzar* (*Minstrel*). This would become his second name for generations to come. Though published in St. Petersburg, the collection's language was Ukrainian. Why did Shevchenko, who left Ukraine as a teenager and matured as an individual, artist, and poet in St. Petersburg, decide to write in Ukrainian and not Russian, the language of St. Petersburg's streets and artistic salons?

The immediate reasons included the influence on Shevchenko of his Ukrainian acquaintances in St. Petersburg who helped set him free. One of them, a native of Poltava named Yevhen Hrebinka, was completing a Ukrainian translation of Alexander Pushkin's poem about the Battle of Poltava (1709) when he met Shevchenko. Hrebinka clearly believed that Ukrainians should have a literature, including works in translation, in their own language. In 1847 Shevchenko explained his reasons for writing in Ukrainian in a preface to a new edition of *Kobzar*:

A great sorrow has enveloped my soul. I hear and sometimes I read: the Poles are printing, and the Czechs and the Serbs and the Bulgarians and the Montenegrins and the Russians—all are printing. But from us not a peep, as if we were all dumb. Why is this so, my brethren? Perhaps you are frightened by an invasion of foreign journalists? Do not be afraid; pay no attention to them. . . . Do not pay attention to the Russians. Let them write as they like, and let us write as we like. They are a people with a language, and so are we. Let the people judge which is better.

Shevchenko specifically took issue with Nikolai Gogol, a native of the former Hetmanate who became a founder of modern Russian prose with his books on Ukrainian themes, including *Taras Bulba*. "They give us the example of Gogol, who wrote not in his own language but in Russian, or Walter Scott, who did not write in his own language," wrote Shevchenko. He was not convinced by these examples. "Why have not V. S. Karadžić, Šafárik and others become German—it would have been so convenient for them—but instead remained Slavs, true sons of their mothers, and gained good fame?" he wrote about the major figures of the Serbian and Slovak cultural movements. "Woe to us! But do not despair, my brethren, and work wisely for the sake of Ukraine, our ill-fated mother."

Shevchenko wrote these words after he had left St. Petersburg and moved to Ukraine, where his friends included the members of the Brotherhood of Saints Cyril and Methodius. If we do not know why Ivan Kotliarevsky, the founder of modern Ukrainian literature, wrote in Ukrainian, in his preface to *Kobzar*, Shevchenko left no doubt about his own motives and those of his friends and coconspirators. They came out of the pan-Slavic movement of the early nineteenth century, which took shape in response to the pan-Germanic movement of the era. They believed that Ukraine was lagging behind in the development of its own language, literature, and culture, but they also assumed that it had much to offer the rest of the Slavic world, if only her sons such as Gogol would turn their talents to serve their country. They envisioned Ukraine as a free republic in a broader Slavic union.

Mykola Kostomarov wrote the brotherhood's programmatic document, titled *The Books of the Genesis of the Ukrainian People*. One inspiration for Kostomarov's work came from the *Books of the Polish People and the Polish Pilgrimage*, in which Adam Mickiewicz presented Polish history as a story of the messianic suffering of the Polish nation. According to Mickiewicz, the Polish nation would rise from the grave and save all enslaved nations. Kostomarov reserved that role for Ukraine, whose Cossack origins had made it democratic and egalitarian: unlike the Russians, the Ukrainians had no tsars, and unlike the Poles, they had no nobility. The members of the Brotherhood of Saints Cyril and Methodius cherished the Ukrainian Cossack past, aspired to the abolition of serfdom, and advocated the transformation of the empire into a federation of equal republics, one of which would be Ukraine.

The society had a small membership and did not last much longer than a year. Its members were soon arrested—Kostomarov a few days before his wedding and Shevchenko on his arrival in Kyiv, where he had come to take part in his friend's marriage. Some imperial bureaucrats discerned the beginnings of a new and potentially dangerous trend in the brotherhood's activities. They described the suspects' ideas as "separatist," and the emperor himself called them the result of Paris (meaning exile Polish) propaganda. But others believed that the members of the brotherhood were loyal subjects of the empire, true defenders of Rus' against Polish influence, who had pushed their local Little Russian patriotism too far and should not be punished too harshly. Ultimately, government officials decided to impose relatively mild sentences so as not to attract too much attention to the brotherhood and drive the Ukrainophiles—the term came into existence in government circles in the mid-nineteenth century—into an alliance with the Polish national movement.

The Russian authorities described the brotherhood's aspirations as the unification of the Slavs under the scepter of the tsar. They kept its true program a secret even from the highest officials of the empire. Kostomarov was sentenced to a year in prison. Other members of the brotherhood received prison sentences of six months to three years or were sent into internal exile, usually working at bureaucratic jobs in the more distant provinces. Emperor Nicholas I gave the harshest sentence to Shevchenko, sending him to serve as a private in the imperial army for ten long years without the right to draw, paint, or write. The emperor was appalled by the personal attacks on himself and his wife in Shevchenko's poems and drawings. Shevchenko held the autocracy responsible for the plight of his people and his land, which was not Russia but Ukraine. His work thus attacked two of the three elements of Uvarov's "official nationality": autocracy and nationality. Nor was his Orthodoxy of an imperial kind.

Through their writings and activities, Kostomarov, Shevchenko, and other members of the Brotherhood of Saints Cyril and Methodius had initiated what we would now call a Ukrainian national project. For the first time, they used the findings of antiquarians, folklorists, linguists, and writers to formulate a political program that would lead to the creation of a national community. In the course of the next century, the ideas advocated by the members of the brotherhood and presented to a broad audience in Shevchenko's impassioned poetry would profoundly transform Ukraine and the entire region. The most obvious sign of that change today is the Shevchenko monument in front of the main building of Kyiv University. It replaced a statue to the university's founder, Emperor Nicholas I.

CHAPTER 15

THE POROUS BORDER

IN 1848, ONE year after the Russian imperial authorities cracked down on the Brotherhood of Saints Cyril and Methodius, the Ukrainians of the Habsburg Empire created their first political organization in Lviv, the Supreme Ruthenian Council. The Galician Ukrainians referred to themselves as Ruthenians or Rusyns and were generally known by those names in the empire. The council was a very different type of organization from the one that had existed in Kyiv in 1846 and 1847. Whereas the brotherhood acted in secrecy, had few members, and was destroyed by the Russian imperial authorities, the council got started with the help and encouragement of the Austrian governor of Galicia and enjoyed a large membership and broad public support.

Despite all the differences between the two organizations, the coincidence in the timing of their creation points to a very important feature in the development of Ukrainian culture, national identity, and political activism. That development had two tracks, and when movement on one slowed down or stopped, progress on the other could proceed or even gain speed. Separated by the imperial Russo-Austrian border, the Ukrainian activists were united by a myriad of links in the process of nation building. Such links extended across a political border that also became religious in the course of the nineteenth century, dividing Ukrainian Catholics (Uniates) from Ukrainian Orthodox. More often than not, contacts between the two groups of Ukrainian activists continued despite the wishes of the two competing imperial powers and developed along multiple channels, which helped the two branches of the movement to engender a common vision of Ukraine's future.

HELPING THE UKRAINIAN activists, divided by political borders but united in spirit and national ideology, to overcome their limitations was the simple fact that the two imperial governments followed very different policies toward their Ukrainian minorities. Nowhere were those differences more pronounced than in the treatment of the Uniate Church, which the two states had inherited from the Polish-Lithuanian Commonwealth. Unlike the Russian authorities, the Austrian ones had never persecuted the Uniates or tried to "reunify" them with the dominant (in their case, Catholic) "mother church." In fact, they treated the Uniates with respect, as indicated in their new official name, Greek (that is, Byzantine-rite) Catholics. Their Polish Catholic brethren were called Roman Catholics. The government also created a seminary to educate the Greek Catholic clergy, first in Vienna and then in Lviv. In the early nineteenth century, the church acquired its independence of the remaining Uniate bishoprics in the Russian Empire by raising the Lviv bishopric to the status of metropolitanate. With most of the secular elite embracing Catholicism and Polish culture, the Greek Catholic clergy were the only leaders of Ruthenian society, and in time they formed the backbone of the modern Ukrainian national movement.

Why did the Habsburgs act as they did? Paradoxically, for the same reason as the Romanovs. The two empires shared the same concern—rising Polish nationalism—but chose different strategies to fight it. The Russian imperial government liquidated the Uniate Church and arrested the development of the Ukrainian movement in an effort to protect the imperial Russian nation against Polish "propaganda," whereas the Austrian authorities tried to counteract that propaganda by building up the Ruthenian movement in their realm. They never sought to turn the Ruthenians into Germans and had no problem with their development as a distinct nation. In fact, they encouraged that process as a counterweight to the well-developed and organized Polish movement.

Such was the policy first put into effect by the Austrian authorities in the revolutionary year of 1848. From Palermo to Paris to Vienna, liberal nationalism was on the rise in Europe, challenging the Congress of Vienna's borders and the governments that ruled within them. In March 1848, inspired by the revolutionary events in Paris, the Hungarians demanded independence from the Habsburg Empire. They would fight for their freedom with arms in hand. The Poles followed them, rising in Cracow and then in Lviv with demands for civic freedom and autonomy. Many of these demands sat well with neither the government in Vienna nor with at least half the Galician population. The Ukrainians made up about half of the 4.5 million residents of the province. The Poles accounted for about 40 percent and Jews close to 7 percent. Ukrainians constituted an absolute majority in so-called Eastern (original) Galicia, while Poles were in the majority in Little Poland, now called Western Galicia, which included the city of Cracow. Jews lived throughout the enlarged imperial province, with approximately 60 percent of Eastern Galician Jewry residing in cities and small towns.

The province was agricultural and less economically developed than most of the Habsburg possessions. After the partitions, Emperor Joseph II removed the traditional Polish elite from the business of running the government and brought in imperial bureaucrats—mostly Germanized Czechs from Bohemia—to create a new administrative system; he also raised the educational and cultural level of the population and protected the peasants from the abuses of their masters. While he removed the Polish elite from power, Joseph originally ignored the Jews, allowing them to keep their autonomy in exchange for paying a so-called toleration tax. Then in 1789 he issued an Edict of Toleration, which was a major step toward the emancipation of Austrian Jewry, but it also disbanded traditional Jewish institutions, prohibited the use of Yiddish and Hebrew in official documents, established German-language schools, and introduced military service for Jews. When the revolution came to Lviv in March 1848, many Jews were happy to join forces with Polish opposition to the empire. Yet, as the Austrian army crushed the Hungarian Revolution with the help of Russian troops, Polish hopes for the restoration of the commonwealth and Jewish hopes for equality were also dashed.

THE GALICIANS WHO benefited most from the revolution were the Ukrainians—arguably the most loyal to the empire and originally the most reluctant participants in the events. They were not eager to join the Polish revolt, as the original Polish appeals made no mention of the Ukrainian population of the region or its needs. In April 1848, the leaders of the Ukrainian community, all of whom happened to be clerics of the Uniate Church, issued their own appeal to the emperor, declaring their loyalty and requesting protection against Polish domination and rights for the Ruthenian language. With the blessing and support of the Austrian governor of Galicia, Count Franz Stadion, the Greek Catholic clergy created their Supreme Ruthenian

Council. The chief of the Lviv police, Leopold von Sacher-Masoch (father of the future writer), approved the founding of the first Ukrainian newspaper, the *Galician Star*. Stadion saw the new council as "a means of paralyzing Polish influence and getting backing for Austrian rule in Galicia."

Under its ecclesiastical leadership, the Supreme Ruthenian Council turned out to be an effective counterweight to the Polish National Council, which spearheaded the Polish national revolution. The supreme council differed in its demands from the Polish National Council on almost every major issue. If the Poles were radical, the Ukrainians were highly conservative. On the future of Galicia, while the Poles wanted autonomy for the entire province, the Ukrainian leaders wanted it divided, with the restoration of the former, smaller Galicia, where Ukrainians formed a 70 percent majority. Two hundred thousand people signed a petition to partition the province. It did not happen: Galicia remained intact. But the Ukrainians emerged from the revolution with a political organization and a newspaper of their own, mobilized as never before.

By far the most revolutionary development was the abolition of serfdom and the beginning of active peasant participation in electoral politics. Both came about in Galicia in response to Polish revolutionary demands but were introduced by the Austrian authorities and benefited the Ukrainians, who made up most of the province's peasantry. In Galicia, sixteen of twenty-five Ukrainian members of the Austrian parliament were peasants; in Bukovyna, all five elected Ukrainians were of peasant stock. The election of Ukrainian deputies to parliament had a major impact on the community, as it introduced the Habsburg Ukrainians to the world of electoral politics and taught them self-organization for purposes not of revolt (there were peasant revolts as well) but political action.

The end of the revolution spelled the demise of the Supreme Ruthenian Council—the government abolished it in 1851—but not of the Ukrainian movement born of the events of 1848. Throughout the 1850s and a good part of the 1860s, people of the same ecclesiastical stock led it. They became known as the St. George Circle, named for the principal Greek Catholic cathedral in the city of Lviv. Their ethnonational orientation gave them a second appellation: Old Ruthenians. Loyal to the empire and conservative in their political and social views, the Greek Catholic bishops and clergymen leading the Ruthenian movement thought of themselves and their people in the Habsburg Empire as members of a distinct Ruthenian nation. Their main enemies were the Poles and their main ally was Vienna, while their fellow Ukrainians, or Little Russians, across the Russo-Austrian border seemed hardly to register in their consciousness.

While the Revolution of 1848 promoted the formation of a new Ukrainian nation, it left open the question of what kind of nation it was. The "Ruthenian" option represented by the leaders of the Supreme Ruthenian Council included a number of alternatives best represented by the identity choices made by the Ruthenian Triad, a group of romantic writers and poets who appeared on the literary stage in the 1830s. The three leading members of the group, Yakiv Holovatsky, Markian Shashkevych, and Ivan Vahylevych, were students at the Greek Catholic branch of the theological seminary in Lviv. Like national awakeners throughout Europe, they collected folklore and were fascinated with history. They were inspired by the cultural activities of other Habsburg Slavs, and their ideas were rooted in the works of Ukrainian awakeners in the Dnieper region: Ivan Kotliarevsky's *Eneïda*, collections of Ukrainian folk songs published in the Russian Empire, and the works of the Kharkiv romantics. They published their first and last almanac, *Rusalka dnistrovaia* (*The Nymph of the Dniester*), in Buda in 1836.

At the time of publication, all three leaders of the group considered the Habsburg Ukrainians to be part of a larger Ukrainian nation. In time, that belief would be shaken and contested. Only one of the three, Markian Shashkevych, is celebrated today as the founder of Ukrainian literature in Galicia. He died in 1843, well before the Revolution of 1848 and the political and intellectual turmoil that it brought about. His colleague Ivan Vahylevych joined the pro-Polish Ruthenian Congress in 1848, and the leaders of the Ukrainian movement subsequently considered him a traitor. In the 1850s the third member of the triad, Yakiv Holovatsky, became a leader of the Galician Russophiles, who regarded the Galician Ukrainians as part of a larger Russian nation. Thus, to use later historiographic terms, the members of the triad became coterminous with the Ukrainian orientation (Shashkevych), the pro-Polish orientation (Vahylevych), and the Russophile orientation (Holovatsky) of the Ukrainian movement in Galicia.

The choice of orientation was closely associated with the choice of alphabet for writing Ukrainian texts. The "alphabet wars" that rocked Ukrainian society in the 1830s and then again in the 1850s contested three options: the traditional Cyrillic used in Church Slavonic texts; the civic Cyrillic, not unlike that used in the Russian Empire; and, finally, the Latin alphabet. The Austrian authorities and Polish elites preferred that later, as it brought the emerging Ukrainian literature closer to the imperial standard and made it more susceptible to cultural Polonization. But when the government attempted in 1859 to introduce the Latin alphabet for use in Ukrainian texts, the Ukrainians united in opposition. It soon became clear that the new nation taking shape in Galicia would use no script other than the Cyrillic. Whether that nation would be a separate entity or part of a larger Russian or Ukrainian nation remained an open question.

THE GALICIAN ALPHABET war of 1859 had a strong echo on the other side of the imperial border. That year the Russian authorities prohibited the publication or import from abroad of Ukrainian and Belarusian texts in the Latin alphabet. The measure was regarded as anti-Polish. Its initiator, a Kyiv censor named Novytsky, wrote in a memo that in Galicia the authorities were trying to turn "Russians" into Poles by means of the Latin alphabet. He believed that the use of the Latin script in the Russian Empire could have the same effect. "The peasants of the western gubernias, encountering books here that are written in the Little Russian language, but in Polish letters, will naturally have a greater preference to learn the Polish alphabet than the Russian one," wrote Novytsky. That in turn could lead them to read Polish books and expose them to Polish influences, alienating them from the "spirit and tendency of Russian literature." The ban was implemented almost immediately.

The censor's primary concern was with the peasants, who were about to be emancipated. Serfdom was indeed abolished in the Russian Empire in 1861, twelve and a half years after the emancipation of the serfs in Galicia and Bukovyna. It happened without a revolution but not without a Polish uprising, which took place in the Russian Empire in 1863. Like the peasants of Habsburg Ukraine, their Russian-ruled counterparts received personal freedom but very little land, making them economically dependent on the nobility. But unlike the Habsburg Ukrainians, the Ukrainian peasants of the Romanov realm received neither the right to participate in electoral politics nor institutions of their own. They would have no university chairs or books in their native language. Moreover, the imperial government forbade the publication of religious and educational texts in the "Little Russian dialect."

The prohibition of virtually all Ukrainian publications in the Russian Empire came in the summer of 1863, in the middle of the Polish uprising that had begun in January of that year. At stake once again was the loyalty of the Ukrainian peasantry. The government decided that when it came to the Ukrainian language, its main concern was the consolidation of the imperial Russian nation, which required shielding the peasantry from unwanted advances on the part of the Ukrainophiles. "Previous works in the Little Russian language were aimed only at the educated classes of southern Russia, but now the proponents of Little Russian ethnicity have turned their attention to the uneducated masses, and those who seek to realize their political ambitions have taken, under the pretense of spreading literacy and education, to publishing reading primers, alphabet books, grammar and geography textbooks, etc.," wrote the minister of interior, Petr Valuev, in the directive prohibiting Ukrainian-language publications, now not only in the Latin but also in the Cyrillic alphabet. The Valuev directive did not extend to works of fiction, of which there were very few in the early 1860s. In the five years between 1863 and 1868, when Valuev resigned his office, the number of Ukrainian-language publications fell from thirty-three to one.

At first considered a temporary measure, the prohibition became permanent in May 1876. That month, Emperor Alexander II issued a decree known as the Ems Ukase (he was relaxing at a spa in the German town of Ems). The new decree went further than the Valuev directive, prohibiting all publications in Ukrainian, as well as the import of Ukrainian-language books from abroad. It also banned Ukrainian-language theater productions and public performances of Ukrainian songs. Like the Valuev directive, the Ems Ukase was kept secret from the general public. The restrictions were loosened in the 1880s, with the removal of plays and songs from the list, but the publication or import of any Ukrainian-language text remained prohibited for another quarter century. The government held to the formula ascribed to Petr Valuev, who claimed that "there was not, is not, and cannot be any special Little Russian language." The Ukrainian language, culture, and identity came to be seen as a threat no less serious to the unity of the empire than Polish nationalism: the very unity of the Russian nation seemed to be at stake.

While Alexander II signed the Ems Ukase in faraway Germany, its main initiator and promoter lived in Kyiv. Mikhail Yuzefovich, an ethnic Ukrainian from the Poltava region in the former Hetmanate, had studied at the noble pension (lyceum) at Moscow University. Also a poet who had been on friendly terms with Alexander Pushkin in his youth, Yuzefovich had fought as an army officer and been wounded in the Caucasus. He became an important figure in the Kyiv educational and cultural scene in the 1840s, when he assumed a leading position in the Kyiv educational district and took an active part in the work of the Archaeographic Commission, tasked with documenting that Right-Bank Ukraine had always been Russian. In his political and cultural views, Yuzefovich was a "Little Russian" par excellence. He was a local patriot who saw himself as working for the benefit of Little Russia on both banks of the Dnieper; a moderate populist who believed in the need to protect the Little Russian peasantry from the Polish nobility, Jewish leaseholders, and Catholic (and Uniate) clergymen; and a believer in the unity of all the "tribes" of the Russian nation. He was a loyal subject of the empire, in which he saw an ally and protector of his brand of Little Russian patriotism.

Depending on time and circumstance, Yuzefovich was both an ally and an adversary of the group of intellectuals known to officials as Ukrainophiles since the times of the Brotherhood of Saints Cyril and Methodius. He was a key participant in the arrest of members of the brotherhood, but turned out to be on their side rather than that of the authorities. Yuzefovich refused to accept a written denunciation from the student who came to him to inform on the brotherhood's subversive activities. He later warned Mykola Kostomarov about an impending police search and helped him destroy incriminating documents. Yuzefovich did not believe that the activities of Kostomarov and his friends were harmful to the state. He saw them as allies in the struggle against Polish cultural domination of Right-Bank Ukraine and Volhynia. The monument to Bohdan Khmelnytsky erected in downtown Kyiv with Yuzefovich's active participation embodies his beliefs and loyalties. The original inscription on the monument was "Russia, one and indivisible, to Bohdan Khmelnytsky."

By the time of the monument's unveiling in 1888, Yuzefovich no longer believed that the Ukrainophiles were a harmless bunch. In 1875 he had written a memo to the imperial authorities titled "On the So-Called Ukrainophile Movement," accusing his opponents from the Ukrainophile camp of trying to tear Ukraine away from Russia. The Valuev directive had not worked, argued Yuzefovich, as it had served only to strengthen ties between Ukrainophiles in the Russian Empire and Austrian Galicia, where the latter acted as agents of the Poles. More drastic measures were therefore needed to stop the destructive activities of the Ukrainophiles. While local officials, including the governor-general of Kyiv, considered Yuzefovich's accusations exaggerated, the authorities in St. Petersburg, concerned about the unity of the empire and possible intrigues on the part not only of the Poles but also of the Habsburgs, embraced his arguments and logic. The emperor signed a decree that not only prohibited Ukrainian-language publications and their import into the Russian Empire but also provided a subsidy for a Galician newspaper that was supposed to fight Ukrainophilism in the Habsburg realm.

Who were the Ukrainophiles whom Yuzefovich considered so dangerous to the Russian Empire? One was Pavlo Chubynsky, the author of the lyrics to the anthem "Ukraine Has Not Yet Perished." Another was a professor of ancient history at Kyiv University, Mykhailo Drahomanov. Both were members of the Kyiv Hromada (Community), an organization of Ukrainian intelligentsia concerned almost exclusively with cultural work. None of them argued that Ukraine should secede from the Russian Empire or held pro-Polish sympathies. They were critical, however, of the older generation of Little Russian leaders of the Ukrainian movement who had failed to lift the prohibitions introduced by the Valuev directive. More importantly for the origins of the 1876 Ems Ukase, Drahomanov and his supporters removed Yuzefovich from the leadership of the Kyiv Geographic Society—the hub of academic activities in the city. Yuzefovich fought back, with a result that no one could have predicted at the beginning of the conflict.

The generational tension between the Ukrainophiles and the proponents of the Little Russian idea developed into an ideological one as the Ems Ukase radicalized the Ukrainophiles. This applied particularly to Mykhailo Drahomanov, who, dismissed from his university professorship, left the empire for Switzerland. Drahomanov settled in Geneva, where he created a body of written work that made him the most influential Ukrainian political thinker of the nineteenth century. He was also the first to embrace socialist ideas. In the 1880s, he argued for the distinctness of the Ukrainian nation and promoted the idea of a European federation that would include Ukraine, going back to the ideas expressed by Kostomarov in his *Books of the Genesis of the Ukrainian People*. Drahomanov's federation, however, was not to be Slavic but all-European. Through Drahomanov's writings, the Ukrainian movement reemerged from the shock created by the destruction of the Brotherhood of Saints Cyril and Methodius and began to think again about the political goals and implications of its cultural activities.

Drahomanov was also the first political thinker whose ideas made a strong impact on developments in Austrian Ukraine. While most of Yuzefovich's accusations against the Ukrainophiles were false, his claims that they had established close contacts with Galicia and that the Valuev circular had only strengthened those contacts were true. With no possibility of publishing their works in Ukrainian in the Russian Empire, the Ukrainophiles took advantage of the opportunities existing in Galicia. The Ems Ukase, inspired by Yuzefovich's denunciations, made Galicia even more attractive for that purpose. With literary publications prohibited in Russian-ruled Ukraine, Ukraine's best-known literary figures, including the writer Ivan Nechui-Levytsky and the playwright Mykhailo Starytsky, published their works in Galicia. The Ems Ukase did not stop the development of Ukrainian literature, but it created a situation in which most of the prominent authors resided in the Russian Empire, while their readers were across the border in Austria. The writers had no direct access to their readers, and vice versa. Ironically, this situation helped promote the development of a common literary language and culture on both sides of the imperial border.

BY THE TIME eastern Ukrainians discovered Galicia as a place for the free expression of their thoughts and a publishing market, the Galician Ukrainians had effectively split into two competing groups, Russophiles and Ukrainophiles. The split became fully apparent in the wake of the constitutional reform of 1867 in the Habsburg Empire. After losing wars to Italy and Prussia, two rising nation-states, the Austrian government decided to prolong the existence of the empire by making major concessions to its most belligerent constituents—the Hungarians. The Austro-Hungarian Compromise created a dual monarchy known as Austria-Hungary. The Kingdom of Hungary acquired its own parliament and broad autonomy, linked to the rest of the empire through the person of the emperor and a common foreign and military policy. But the Hungarians were not the only Habsburg nationality to benefit from the deal: the Poles and Croats also obtained autonomy. To the horror of the Ukrainians, Polish autonomy came at their expense: Vienna turned the province of Galicia over to rule by its traditional Polish elite.

The leaders of the Ukrainian movement felt betrayed: the Hapsburgs had punished their loyalty while rewarding the rebel nationalities. The compromise of 1867 sounded a death knell for the dominance of the church hierarchy and the Old Ruthenians. It strengthened the Russophile movement, whose leaders, including the Greek Catholic priest Ivan Naumovych, argued that the Ruthenians had gotten nothing for their loyalty and had to change their attitude to the government if they wanted to resist Polonization. He also attacked efforts to establish a separate Ruthenian nation. Indeed, there was no chance of its withstanding the Polish political and cultural onslaught.

According to Naumovych, the Austrian Ruthenians were part of a larger Russian nation. His supporters considered themselves Little Russians, arguing that the literary Russian language was in fact a rendition of Little Russian and that a "Little Russian" could master it in an hour. The task turned out to be much more difficult: attempting to master Russian, the leaders of the movement created a mixture of Russian and Church Slavonic in which they tried to communicate with one another and write their works.

In the late 1860s, the Russophiles took control of most Ukrainian organizations in Galicia and Bukovyna. In Transcarpathia, the newly empowered Hungarian masters of the land arrested any local cultural development by introducing a policy of aggressive Magyarization. The Russian government supported Russophile activities with stipends and scholarships, predictably arousing suspicion in Vienna. In 1882, the Austrian authorities arrested Naumovych and charged him with treason. He had authored a peasant petition to establish an Orthodox parish in a traditionally Greek Catholic village, which was regarded as an attempt at pro-Russian propaganda. Along with Naumovych, the authorities put on trial a number of other leaders of the Russophile movement from Galicia and Transcarpathia. They were convicted of various crimes against the state and sent to prison. Later, many of the accused, including Naumovych himself, emigrated to the Russian Empire.

Other prosecutions of Russophile activists followed the trial of 1882. While the Russian imperial authorities went after those who questioned that Ukrainians were part of the Great Russian nation, the Austrians persecuted those who promoted the idea. The official crackdown on Russophile activities impaired the movement and helped propel another group of activists to center stage on the Galician political scene. Known as populists or Ukrainophiles, their roots are usually traced back to the Ruthenian Triad and the group's main ideologist, Markian Shashkevych, but their immediate origins lay in the Prosvita (Enlightenment) Society established in 1868, a year after the Austro-Hungarian compromise. Like the Russophiles, the Ukrainophiles believed that the old policy of orienting the Ruthenian movement toward the imperial government had run its course, as had the model of nation building promoted by the Old Ruthenians. But the way forward proposed by the Ukrainophiles differed quite a bit from that of their opponents. They suggested that the Habsburg Ruthenians were indeed part of a larger nation—not the Russian imperial nation but the Ukrainian one immediately across the border. The Ukrainophiles were at odds with the clerical elite that had traditionally led the Ruthenian movement and presented themselves as defenders of the people's interests; hence the name "populists," which stuck to them.

Galician populists and their publications became natural allies of the Ukrainophiles in the Russian Empire. In 1873, with the help of a gift from a relative of the Cossack hetman Ivan Skoropadsky, Yelyzaveta Myloradovych, the Galician populists established their own scholarly society. To stress its links with Russian-ruled Ukraine and its all-Ukrainian focus and aspirations, it was appropriately named after Taras Shevchenko. The Kyiv Ukrainophiles helped their Galician counterparts establish Ukrainian-language newspapers and journals that served both communities, east and west. With help from the east, the Galician Ukrainophiles were slowly but steadily winning the battle with the Russophiles. In the mid-1880s, the Ukrainophiles took control of Ruthenian organizations in Bukovyna. Intellectual support from Russian-ruled Ukraine turned out to be a crucial factor in the rise of the Ukrainophiles in both Austrian provinces, Galicia and Bukovyna. The two branches of the Ukrainian movement needed each other and benefited, each in its own way, from their cooperation. The Galician Ukrainians radicalized the thinking of the Kyiv Ukrainophiles, helping them imagine their nation outside the embrace of the pan-Russian imperial project.

UKRAINE ENTERED THE last decade of the nineteenth century divided by the Austro-Russian border, as it had been a century earlier, during the partitions of Poland. But now it was also united in unprecedented ways. The new unity did not come from the church: the division between Orthodox and Uniates remained, now coinciding with the imperial border after the "reunification" of the Uniates under Russian rule. It came from the new idea of nationality. The concept of a distinct Greek Catholic Ruthenian nationality under Habsburg rule, although strengthened by the revolutionary events of 1848, lasted a mere twenty years and did not survive the transformation of the Habsburg Empire into the Dual Monarchy. Since the late 1860s, the national movement in the Habsburg Empire had shed its ecclesiastical exclusivity. Both Russophiles and Ukrainophiles were building bridges with their Orthodox brethren across the border. In both camps, there was no doubt that Habsburgs' Ruthenians and the Romanovs' Little Russians were part of the same nation. The question was which one—pan-Russian or pan-Ukrainian?

Ukrainian activists on the Russian side of the border, also divided between proponents of pan-Russian and pan-Ukrainian projects, tried to answer the same question as their counterparts in Austria-Hungary. A response would come, both in Austria-Hungary and in the Russian Empire, from the generation of national activists that appeared on the political scene in the last decades of the nineteenth century. Theirs would be an era of rapid industrial development, urbanization, spread of literacy, and mass politics.

CHAPTER 16

ON THE MOVE

I N 1870, John James Hughes, a Welsh entrepreneur, sailed from Britain at the head of eight ships. The load consisted of metallurgical equipment, while the passengers included close to a hundred skilled miners and metalworkers. Most of them, like Hughes himself, came from Wales. Their destination was the steppe on the Donets River in southern Ukraine, north of the Sea of Azov. The expedition aimed to construct a full-cycle metallurgical plant. "When I commenced these works, I set my mind upon training of the Russian workmen who would be attached to the place," wrote Hughes later. The project took several years. With the help of unskilled Ukrainian and Russian labor, Hughes and his crew soon built not only iron-smelting and rail works but also a small town around them. These were the beginnings of Yuzivka, today's Donetsk, till recently a city of more than a million people and the main center of the Donbas—the Donets River industrial basin.

Hughes' arrival signaled the beginning of a new era in Ukrainian history. The late nineteenth and early twentieth centuries saw major shifts in the region's economy, social structure, and population dynamics. These changes stemmed from rapid industrialization, as eastern and southern Ukraine became a major beneficiary of economic expansion and urbanization, and the influx of Russian peasants, who provided manual labor in the cities and become the backbone of the industrial proletariat. The same processes were taking place in Galicia, where the oil industry began its European career in the mid-nineteenth century. Rapid industrialization and urbanization were common features of European history in that period, and Ukraine was an important participant. Those processes changed its economic, social, and political landscape for generations to come.

IN RUSSIAN-RULED UKRAINE, first changes began in September 1854 with the landing of British and French expeditionary forces in the Crimea. The invasion was the latest act in the Crimean War, which had started a year earlier with conflict between France and Russia over control of Christian holy places in Palestine. At stake was the future of the declining Ottoman Empire and the great powers' influence over its vast possessions. The British and French besieged Sevastopol, the base of the imperial Russian navy, which the allies saw as a threat to their interests in the Mediterranean. After a lengthy siege and military operations that resulted in heavy losses on both sides (the disastrous charge of the Light Brigade in the Battle of Balaklava stunned the British public), Sevastopol fell to the invading forces in September 1855. This became an indelible moment of sorrow and humiliation in Russian historical memory. The Paris Peace Treaty, which formally ended the war, precluded the Russian Empire from having naval bases either in Sevastopol or anywhere else on the Black Sea coast.

Russia's loss of the Crimean War provoked extensive soul-searching in the imperial government and society. How could the Russian army, which had conquered Paris in 1814, suffer defeat forty years later on territory it considered its own? The death of Emperor Nicholas I, who, weakened by the stress of war, died in March 1855 after thirty years on the throne, made a change of government policy almost inevitable. The new emperor, Alexander II, launched an ambitious reform program to catch up with the West and modernize Russian society, economy, and military. During the war, Russia had nothing but sailing ships to confront the steamboats of the British and French. It sank the ships of its Black Sea Fleet in order to prevent enemy ships from entering Sevastopol's harbor. Now Russia needed a new navy no matter what. It also needed railroads, lack of which had made it difficult to move troops, ammunition, and provisions to places as remote from the center of the empire as the Crimea. Embarrassingly for St. Petersburg, the British, not the Russians, built the first railroad in the Crimea to connect Balaklava with Sevastopol during the siege of the city.

If Russia wanted to keep the Crimea, it needed a railroad connection to the peninsula and its naval base. The government decided to sell Alaska—another remote part of the empire that was difficult to defend and, as officials believed, vulnerable to seizure by the British—to the United States. But Russia would keep the Crimea. The Crimean Tatars were migrating to the Ottoman Empire, and the Russian fleet and fortifications were gone, but Sevastopol became a site of popular veneration—a new holy place of the Russian Empire. The government approved a plan to connect Moscow and Sevastopol by rail via Kursk and Kharkiv. The problem was lack of money. The treasury did not have it, and the Russian crackdown on the Polish rebels in 1863 produced a reaction that would resemble international sanctions of a later era. The French government convinced James Mayer de Rothschild, a major financier of railroad construction in France, to stop lending money to Russia, while British companies that were prepared to build the railroad could not raise enough capital in the City. The construction of the Moscow-Sevastopol line was postponed until the 1870s, but the idea of building railroads in southern Ukraine firmly established itself in the minds of Russian government, military, and business elites.

The first railroad built there was much more modest than the line that would link Moscow and Sevastopol. It connected Odesa (Odessa) on the Black Sea coast, northwest of the Crimea, with the town of Balta in Podolia. The new railroad was constructed in 1865, four years after a railway line linking Lviv with Peremyshl (Przemyśl), Cracow, and Vienna. Unlike the Lviv line, the one beginning in Odesa had nothing to do with politics, strategy, or administration. Its raison d'être began and ended with economics. In the mid-nineteenth century, Ukraine accounted for 75 percent of all exports of the Russian Empire. The times of Siberian furs as a major imperial export were gone, while those of Siberian oil and gas had not yet arrived. Thus Ukrainian grain filled the gap in the imperial budget. Podolia was one of the main grain-producing areas in the empire, and Odesa, a city established in 1794 on the site of a former Noghay settlement, became the empire's main gateway to the markets of Europe.

The cash-strapped empire wanted to increase its exports, which required a railroad, which in turn required money for construction. The governor of Odesa broke that vicious circle with the suggestion of using punitive battalions of the Russian army. Forced labor did the trick—neither for the first nor last time in the empire's long history. Envisioned as the first section of a railroad linking Odesa with Moscow, the Odesa-Balta line was supposed to go through Kyiv, connecting the Right Bank, with its rebellious Polish nobility, with the imperial heartland and thereby reducing the influence of

Warsaw. But the plan made little economic sense. There was little to export from the Kyiv region and the forest zone north of the city; hence imperial strategists dreaming of the political integration of the empire eventually lost the battle to the business lobby. The line from Balta went not to Kyiv but to Poltava and Kharkiv, where it would later connect to the Moscow-Sevastopol line. The latter was built in 1875 after long delays.

The Moscow-Sevastopol line played an important role in the building of a new Russian navy in Sevastopol: in 1871, after the French defeat in the Franco-Prussian War, the Russian Empire regained its right to a navy on the Black Sea. But the main significance of the line was economic and cultural. On the economic side, it contributed to regional trade and the development of eastern and southern Ukraine; in cultural terms, it linked the distant Crimea to the center of the empire in ways previously unimaginable, promoting Russian cultural colonization of the peninsula. By the end of the nineteenth century, Yalta, originally a small fishing village on the Black Sea coast, had become the summer capital of the empire. The emperor and his family built spectacular mansions on the Crimean coast and supported the construction of Orthodox churches and monasteries there. In addition to the tsar and the imperial family, numerous courtiers, senior and middle-rank officials, and, last but not least, writers and artists spent the summer months in the Crimea. Anton Chekhov, who had a modest house in Yalta, described the experiences of Russian visitors to that Crimean resort in his story "Lady with a Lapdog." The Russian elite made the Crimea part of its expansive imperial home.

In 1894, when Tsar Alexander III died in his Livadia mansion near Yalta, his body was taken by carriage to Yalta, then by boat to Sevastopol, and from there by railroad to St. Petersburg. By the time of his death, railways crisscrossed Ukraine, linking Odesa with Poltava, Kharkiv, and Kyiv, as well as Moscow and St. Petersburg. From Odesa one could also take a train to Lviv, and Kyiv was linked to Lviv and Warsaw. The first Odesa-Balta line was a mere 137 miles long; by 1914, the overall length of railroads in Ukraine exceeded 10,000 miles. The railways promoted economic development, increased mobility, and broke down old political, economic, and cultural boundaries. Nowhere was that change more profound than in the empire's newest possessions—the steppe regions of Ukraine.

The steppelands formerly claimed by the nomads had come under the control of the nobility and acquired the reputation of the breadbasket of Europe. The region seemed only to have a short supply of people able to cultivate the virgin land. Chichikov, the main character of Nikolai Gogol's classic *Dead Souls*, tries to solve the problem by selling the souls of deceased peasants to the government and "moving" them to the region. But in practice, fewer "souls" and more land meant a better-off peasantry, and nowhere else in the empire were peasants doing as well as in southern Ukraine. At the turn of the twentieth century, the average peasant landholding in Tavrida gubernia, which included the Crimea and steppelands to the north of the peninsula, was forty acres per household, as compared to nine acres in Podolia and Volhynia.

The centuries-old difference between the settled forest-steppe regions and the nomadic south, highlighted by the Christian-Muslim divide and the Ottoman-Polish-Russian border, was slowly receding into the past. Railroads linked grain-producing areas to the north with Black Sea ports in the south, thereby connecting the Ukrainian hinterland to the Mediterranean Sea and rich European markets. The Dnieper, Dniester, and Don trade routes, threatened by nomadic attacks for most of Ukrainian history, were now safe and contributed to the economic revival of the region. The Dnieper–Black Sea trade route around which the Vikings had built the Kyivan state was now delivering on its promise, with the Dnieper rapids as the only remaining logistical impediment.

RAILROAD CONSTRUCTION CONTRIBUTED to the rapid rate of urbanization, which once again benefited the south. The growth of cities was a general phenomenon in Ukraine: by the turn of the twentieth century, Kyiv was the Russian Empire's seventh-largest city, its population having grown from 25,000 in the early 1830s to 250,000 in 1900. But even that spectacular growth paled in comparison to what was going on in the south. The population of Odesa grew from 25,000 inhabitants in 1814 to 450,000 in 1900. Much of the urban growth resulted from rapid industrialization, and there the south also led the way. The city of Yuzivka—whose population increased more than five times in the decade leading up to 1897, when it reached close to 30,000 inhabitants, and more than doubled in the next twenty years, attaining 70,000 by the revolutionary year 1917—highlights the close link between industrialization and urbanization in southeastern Ukraine.

The story of Yuzivka began in London in 1868. That year, the successful fifty-three-year-old businessman, inventor, and manager of the Millwall Iron Works Company, John James Hughes, whose departure from Britain begins this chapter, decided to take a sharp turn in life. After the shock of the Crimean

War, the Russian government was busy fortifying approaches to the empire on land and sea. During the war, the British and French fleet had bombarded Kronstadt, the island fortress protecting St. Petersburg from the Baltic Sea. To reinforce its fortifications against possible British attack, the Russian government turned, ironically enough, to the Millwall Iron Works. None other than General Eduard Totleben, a hero of the Russian defense of Sevastopol, conducted the negotiations. Hughes went to St. Petersburg to arrange the project. There the Russians offered him a concession to establish metal works in their empire. Hughes accepted the challenge.

Upon arriving in the Azov steppes, the Welshman and his party established themselves in the homestead of Ovechii, a small settlement founded by Zaporozhian Cossacks back in the seventeenth century. But Hughes was hardly interested in the Cossack past of the region. He had bought the land and come to Ovechii for one simple reason—four years earlier, Russian engineers had designated that area as an ideal site for a future metal works, with iron ore, coal, and water all in close proximity. The government had tried to build a plant in that area but failed, lacking expertise in constructing and running metal works. Hughes provided proficiency in both. In January 1872, his newly built iron works produced its first pig iron. In the course of the 1870s, he added more blast furnaces. The works employed close to 1,800 people, becoming the largest metal producer in the empire. The place where the workers lived became known as Yuzivka after the founder's surname ("Hughesivka"). The steel and mining town would be renamed Staline in 1924 and Donetsk in 1961.

Hughes was one of a very few Western entrepreneurs who actually moved to Ukraine himself, but hundreds of skilled laborers came to the Ukrainian steppes from Britain, France, and Belgium. They were chasing millions of francs and pounds transferred to that region from their home countries. Mainly French, British, and Belgian bankers provided the financial capital that transformed the Ukrainian south. In the early decades of the twentieth century, foreign companies produced more than 50 percent of all Ukrainian steel, over 60 percent of its pig iron, 70 percent of its coal, and 100 percent of its machinery. Russian companies had limited capital and know-how, which they devoted mostly to developing the industrial potential of Moscow and St. Petersburg.

The empire could supply one resource in almost unlimited quantities: unskilled labor. Improved sanitary conditions and technological advances meant that more infants survived, and those who survived lived longer. More people in a village meant smaller plots of land per household. Relative over-population became a major issue in the villages of Ukraine and Russia in the decades following the emancipation of the serfs. The Industrial Revolution, which arrived in the empire after a significant delay, meant that "surplus" population could now funnel into the growing cities. Since the 1870s, the booming company towns of southern Ukraine had become magnets for hundreds of thousands of peasants leaving their impoverished villages. Most came to the region from the southern provinces of Russia, where the soil was much less productive than in Ukraine and land hunger more pronounced.

Among the Russian peasants attracted by the jobs available in Yuzivka, which were dangerous but well paid by the standards of the time, was the young Nikita Khrushchev. He was fourteen years old in 1908, when he moved from the Russian village of Kalinovka, approximately forty miles northeast of the Cossack capital of Hlukhiv, to Yuzivka to join his family. His father, Sergei, a seasonal worker on a railroad in the Yuzivka region before he moved his family there and became a full-time miner, never abandoned his dream of saving enough money to buy a horse and move back to Kalinovka. His son, who had no such dream, embraced city life and became a mining mechanic before joining the Bolshevik Party in the midst of the Revolution of 1917 and embarking on a stunning political career. He would be the leader of the Soviet Union during the launch of Sputnik in 1957 and the Cuban Missile Crisis of 1962.

Nikita Khrushchev was not the only future Soviet leader whose family left a village in Russia to benefit from the industrial boom in southern Ukraine. A few years earlier than the Khrushchevs, Ilia Brezhnev, the father of Leonid Brezhnev, Khrushchev's onetime protégé and successor at the helm of the Soviet Union, moved to the Ukrainian industrial town of Kamenske (till recently Dniprodzerzhynsk). Leonid was born in that steel town in 1906. The Khrushchevs and the Brezhnevs took part in a major Russian peasant migration into southern Ukraine that contributed to the underrepresentation of ethnic Ukrainians in the cities. In 1897, the year of the first and only imperial Russian census, approximately 17 million Ukrainians and 3 million Russians resided in the Ukrainian gubernias of the empire—a ratio of almost six to one. But in the cities, they were on a par, with slightly more than 1 million Russians and slightly fewer than 1 million Ukrainians. In the major cities and industrial centers, Russians constituted a majority. They accounted for more than 60 percent of the population of Kharkiv, more than 50 percent in Kyiv, and almost 50 percent in Odesa.

Few ethnic Ukrainians joined the entrepreneurial class, and those who did so lived mainly in central Ukraine, where in the second half of the nineteenth century development of the sugar industry, dependent on local beet production, made the fortunes of a number of Ukrainian entrepreneurs, most notably the Symyrenko family. One of its members, Platon Symyrenko, supported Taras Shevchenko after his return from exile and sponsored an edition of his *Kobzar*. (Today, the family is known mainly for the Renet Semerenko apple, named in honor of Platon by his son Lev, who developed the fruit.) The Symyrenkos were more the exception than the rule. Russian, Polish, and Jewish entrepreneurs outnumbered Ukrainians by significant margins.

With the start of rapid industrialization and urbanization, the same ethnic ratio applied to the industrial working class, which was largely Russian. Jewish artisans dominated the trades as they moved from the small towns of formerly Polish-ruled Ukraine to the large centers in the east and south. Kharkiv, in the east, was beyond the Pale of Settlement—the area where Jews were allowed to settle—but the rest of Ukraine, including the cities of Odesa and Katerynoslav (today Dnipropetrovsk), was open to Jewish settlement. Jews constituted between 12 and 14 percent of the overall population of Volhynia, Podolia, and southern Ukraine but comprised the majority in the small towns and made up significant minorities in the cities. They accounted for 37 percent of the citizens of Odesa and were the second-largest ethnic group in Katerynoslav.

Why were most Ukrainians uninvolved in the processes of industrialization and urbanization, although they made up the country's ethnic majority? Here again, the stories of the Khrushchevs and Brezhnevs are useful for understanding the situation. Both families came to southeastern Ukraine from the Russian gubernia of Kursk, where in the second half of the nineteenth century the size of an average peasant landholding did not exceed seven acres. They came to the Katerynoslav gubernia, where that figure was twenty-five acres, and the land, the so-called black earth, was much more fertile than in the Kursk region. As noted earlier, the local peasants were doing better than their counterparts anywhere else in the Russian Empire. They preferred and often could afford to stay home. If pressed, many preferred to resettle as farmers in the distant steppes of the imperial east than to move to a nearby steel or mining town and work in the grinding conditions of early-twentieth-century industry.

This applied particularly to peasants from the central and northern provinces of Ukraine, such as the Chernihiv gubernia, where the average household landholding did not exceed seventeen acres of rather poor land. The family story of another Soviet leader, Mikhail Gorbachev, offers a glimpse into that part of the history of Ukrainian migrations. In the early twentieth century, Gorbachev's maternal grandfather, Panteleimon Hopkalo, moved from the Chernihiv gubernia to the steppes of the Stavropol region, where Gorbachev was born in 1931. Conditions in Stavropol and the North Caucasus were as close to those in Ukraine as one could imagine under the circumstances. Many Ukrainian peasants unwilling to move to the city and searching for free land migrated much farther, all the way to the Russian Far East. In the two decades before the start of World War I, more than 1.5 million Ukrainians settled on the southern and eastern frontiers of the Russian Empire, where land was available.

THE PEASANT MIGRATION driven by land hunger was truly an all-Ukrainian story, even more significant in Austrian Galicia, Bukovyna, and Transcarpathia than in the Russian Empire. The average size of a landholding in eastern Galicia in the early twentieth century was six acres—three acres less than in the most overpopulated Ukrainian province of Volhynia on the Russian side of the border. Besides, land in the Carpathian Mountains was usually much less productive than in Volhynia and Podolia. Peasants were leaving the region en masse. "This land cannot hold so many people and endure so much poverty," says a character in Galician Ukrainian writer Vasyl Stefanyk's short story "The Stone Cross," written in 1899 and inspired by the mass exodus of Galician peasants to North America. In Stefanyk's native village alone, five hundred peasants left their homes in search of a better life.

Approximately 600,000 Ukrainians bade farewell to Austria-Hungary before 1914. They made their way to Pennsylvania and New Jersey in the United States, where Ukrainian migrants worked in the mines and mills, and to the provinces of Manitoba, Saskatchewan, and Alberta in Canada, where peasants received land and settled the prairies. Ukrainians were not the only group seeking a better life in North America. Jews from the small towns of Galicia and Bukovyna often preceded them. Approximately 350,000 Jews left Galicia for the United States in the decades leading up to World War I.

The reason was simple: like peasants, impoverished townsfolk had little economic future in the eastern provinces of Austria-Hungary. Emigrants of all ethnicities and religious affiliations contributed handsomely to the economies and cultures of their new homelands. Among the Galician émigrés to the United States were ancestors of many Hollywood stars and entertainment celebrities, including the Ukrainian parents of Jack Palance (Palahniuk) and the Jewish grandparents of Barbara Streisand. The parents of Ramon (Roman) Hnatyshyn, the governor-general of Canada from 1990 to 1995, came from Bukovyna; those of Andy Warhol, from the Lemko region.

Galicia was the poorest province of the empire—a situation decried by Polish businessman and member of the imperial and provincial parliaments Stanisław Szczepanowski in his book *Galician Misery* (1888). Comparing labor productivity and consumption with the rest of Europe, he wrote, "Every resident of Galicia does one-quarter of a man's work and eats one-half of a man's food." Industrialization did not bypass Galicia entirely, but it did not markedly improve the economic fortunes of the region or the well-being of its population. The petroleum that bubbled to the surface around the towns of Drohobych and Boryslav had caused nothing but trouble for local residents since time immemorial, and only in the mid-nineteenth century was the malodorous black substance first put to use by local pharmacists, who learned how to extract kerosene. Among the first beneficiaries of the new discovery were the doctors and patients of the Lviv General Hospital. In 1853, it became the first public building in the world to use only petroleum lamps for lightning.

Szczepanowski was one of the first entrepreneurs to make a fortune out of Galician oil by introducing steam drills. An idealist and a Polish nation builder by persuasion, he provided health care for his workers, many of whom were Polish migrants to the region, and tried to improve their plight but eventually went bankrupt. Business and nation building did not necessarily go hand in hand in Austrian Galicia. In the last decades of the nineteenth century, British, Belgian, and German companies moved into the region, employing deep-drilling methods first introduced by Canadian engineer and entrepreneur William Henry McGarvey. New management replaced small entrepreneurs, many of them Jewish. Nor was the unskilled labor of Ukrainian and Polish peasants (the former constituted up to half the workforce, the latter about a third) in demand any longer. By 1910, oil production had increased to 2 million tons, accounting for about 4 percent of world output, the greatest producers at the time being the United States and the Russian Empire.

Oil brought more money and educational opportunities to the region. A mining school opened in Boryslav. A number of city buildings constructed in that era still stand, reminding visitors of the "good old days." But overall, the oil boom had a limited impact on the economic situation in the region. The population of Boryslav, the town at the center of the action, tripled in the course of the second half of the nineteenth century and reached 12,500 inhabitants. So did the population of the entire oilfield district, which grew to 42,000 in the last decade of the century. But that was a drop in the bucket if one takes Galicia as a whole. The population of the capital city of Lviv increased from roughly 50,000 to more than 200,000 between 1870 and 1910. This looks impressive, but only if one does not compare it with the impact of economic development in the same period in the cities of Dnieper Ukraine. The population of Katerynoslav, at the center of the metallurgical boom, increased eleven times in slightly more than fifty years, reaching 220,000 by 1914. The largest city in Ukraine was Odesa, with 670,000 citizens, closely followed by Kyiv, with its 630,000 inhabitants. That represented almost a tenfold increase of Kyiv's population since the mid-nineteenth century.

DESPITE DIFFERENCES IN levels of industrialization and urbanization in the Russian and Austro-Hungarian provinces of Ukraine, both parts of the country underwent major economic and social transformation in the late nineteenth and early twentieth centuries. The increasingly rapid movement of capital, goods, and people, as well as ideas and information, marked the birth of modern society. The new division of labor changed the relative importance of traditional social groups and helped create new ones, especially the industrial working class, leading to the economic rise of some regions and the decline of others. Among the beneficiaries of the change was the Ukrainian south, with its burgeoning international trade channeled through the Black Sea ports and its rapidly growing industrial base.

A new economic and cultural boundary replaced the old one that had distinguished Ukraine's agricultural north and center from its nomadic south. The south now became the country's industrial and agricultural powerhouse. Its rural population remembered the times of the Zaporozhian Cossacks, had hardly experienced serfdom, and was better-off than the rest of the country. The discovery of iron ore and coal deposits turned the region into an industrial boom area. Coming of age under the control of the Russian imperial administration, with a population more ethnically and religiously diverse than in the areas further north and with the highest urbanization rate in Ukraine, this region would lead the country into the political, social, and cultural turmoil of the twentieth century.

CHAPTER 17

THE UNFINISHED REVOLUTION

O N THE COLD winter morning of Sunday, January 9, 1905, close to 20,000 workers and members of their families began to proceed from the outskirts of St. Petersburg toward its center. Father Georgy Gapon, a thirty-five-year-old native of Poltava gubernia and alumnus of the St. Petersburg Theological Academy, led the demonstration. The people in the first rank carried a portrait of Emperor Nicholas II along with church banners and icons, and the crowd sang religious songs that included prayers for the tsar. The workers wanted to present the tsar with a petition drafted by Father Gapon calling on the sovereign to protect them against abuses perpetrated by their bosses.

Major St. Petersburg factories were on strike, but the factory owners refused to satisfy the workers' demands, which included introduction of an eight-hour workday. The Industrial Revolution had produced a new social phenomenon, the working class, and it was appealing to the tsar for recognition of its basic rights. "We did not ask for much; we wanted only that without which there is no life, only hard labor and constant suffering," wrote Father Gapon. But the petition also included a number of political demands, chief among them the election of a constitutional assembly. The last time someone had demanded a constitution from the tsar was in December 1825. Back then, the regime had crushed the revolt of the military officers later known as Decembrists with the help of artillery. The tsar and his government believed that they had to show their resolve once again and not repeat the mistake of Louis XVI of France, whose indecisiveness had, in their opinion, cost him his throne and his life in the French Revolution.

As the demonstrators approached the tsar's Winter Palace—the building that now houses the Hermitage Museum—the army opened fire, killing more than a hundred people on the spot and wounding more than five hundred. Father Gapon survived, but never again would he pray for the tsar or hope for his protection. In the appeal that Gapon wrote that night, he called the tsar a beast. He also called for vengeance: "So let us take revenge, brothers, on the tsar, who is cursed by the people, on all his treacherous tsarist spawn, on his ministers and all robbers of the unfortunate Russian land!" Full revenge would have to wait another thirteen years—Bolsheviks would gun down Tsar Nicholas II and his family in July 1918—but the revolution that the tsar's circle hoped to avoid began right away. It propelled the whole empire, including the Ukrainian provinces, into a new era—the age of mass politics, characterized by the creation of political parties, parliamentary elections, male suffrage, and growing governmental reliance on nationalist support.

THE REVOLUTION CAME to Ukraine three days after the events of Bloody Sunday in St. Petersburg. On Wednesday, January 12, the workers of the South Russian Machine-Building Factory in Kyiv went on strike. Those in the metal works of Katerynoslav, Yuzivka, and the rest of the Donbas soon joined them. The flames of class war now engulfed the economic boom areas of the previous fifteen years. If before January 1905 the workers had merely asked for better conditions, higher pay, and an eight-hour workday, they now backed their demands with strikes, demonstrations, and open resistance to the authorities. When it came to resistance, the overpopulated and impoverished village did not lag far behind the city. The peasants began by cutting down trees in forests belonging to the nobility and went on to attack noble's mansions. There were more than three hundred such attacks, with peasants of the former Cossack territories on the Left Bank of the Dnieper leading the way. The peasants expected the tsar to issue a manifesto transferring the noble lands to them. It never came. Instead, the government used the army to crush the revolts, killing sixty-three peasants in December 1905 in the village of Velyki Sorochyntsi, the birthplace of Nikolai Gogol (Mykola Hohol) in the Poltava gubernia. The Velyki Sorochyntsi tragedy was anything but an exception.

In the summer of 1905, the regime began to lose the unconditional support of men in uniform, most of them former peasants. In June, there was a mutiny on the battleship *Potemkin* of the Black Sea Fleet. Most of its leaders and participants were sailors recruited from Ukraine. Though planned for October, the uprising began in June as the sailors mutinied over *borshch* (beet soup) prepared with spoiled meat. The petty officer Hryhorii Vakulenchuk from the Zhytomyr region appealed to his comrades, according to some accounts, in Ukrainian, with the words, "How long will we be slaves?" After a senior officer shot and killed Vakulenchuk, the leadership of the revolt passed to Opanas Matiushenko, a twenty-six-year-old sailor from the Kharkiv region. The rebels killed the commanding officers, raised the red flag, and headed from the open sea to Odesa, where they supported the workers' strike going on in the city. The arrival of the battleship with the corpse of Vakulenchuk provoked new protests, riots, and skirmishes with the police.

Russian Cossack units blocked points of access to the port from the city, including the famous Potemkin Stairs—depicted as a site of mass killings and high drama in Sergei Eisenstein's classic film *Battleship Potemkin* (1925). There is no proof that anyone actually died on the stairs, but police and army units gunned down hundreds of people all over the city. The battleship eventually left Odesa, avoided an encounter with a flotilla loyal to the regime, and headed for Romania, where the rebel sailors surrendered to authorities. Their leader, Matiushenko, spent some time in Europe and the United States and then returned to Odesa to continue the revolutionary struggle. He was arrested, tried, and executed in Sevastopol, the home base of the *Potemkin*. At the time of his execution, Matiushenko, who became a symbol of revolution but refused to join any political party, was twenty-eight years old.

In October 1905, the wave of workers' strikes reached its peak. A railroad strike paralyzed the whole empire. In Ukraine, workers at the main railway junctions—Kyiv, Kharkiv, and Katerynoslav—stopped work. Industrial workers soon joined them. By mid-October, 120,000 Ukrainian workers and close to 2 million workers throughout the empire had walked off the job. Emperor Nicholas II then changed tactics and offered his rebellious subjects a major concession. In a manifesto issued on October 17, he granted basic civil rights, including freedom of conscience, speech, assembly, and association. His decree introduced universal male suffrage in the empire and stipulated that the conduct of elections to the Duma—the first Russian parliament—would ensure representation of all classes of society. The tsar promised not to adopt any new laws without the approval of the Duma. The absolute monarchy was on the verge of turning into a constitutional one. The liberal intelligentsia received the manifesto with jubilation.

AMONG THOSE WHO stood out in the jubilant crowds that poured into the streets of major Ukrainian cities after the publication of the manifesto were

the Jews. Conservative supporters of the monarchy saw Jews as closely associated with revolution. They also blamed Jews for all the troubles that had
befallen the local population since the onset of industrialization and rapid
urbanization. In many Ukrainian cities, jubilation ended in pogrom. Pogroms were hardly new in Ukraine or the Pale of Settlement in general, which
included the former provinces of Poland-Lithuania and the Ukrainian south.
The first big wave took place in 1881: after revolutionaries assassinated Emperor Alexander II, the Jews were blamed for the tsar's death. In present-day
Moldova, the Chişinău pogrom of 1903 lasted three days and nights and
took the lives of forty-nine people, creating an uproar in the American press
and triggering a new wave of Jewish emigration. But the pogroms of the past
paled in comparison with those of 1905. In October, hundreds of people
died in pogroms in Kyiv, Katerynoslav, and Odesa. Thousands were injured,
and tens of thousands of Jewish homes and enterprises were destroyed.

In Kyiv, the pogrom began after a demonstration that was at once a victory celebration and a denunciation of the tsar's October 17 manifesto as
mere window dressing on the part of the regime. As the demonstrators attacked the city prison, released political prisoners, desecrated the monument
to Nicholas I in front of Kyiv University, removed the imperial insignia from
the facade of the university building, destroyed Russian imperial flags and
replaced them with red ones, and called for the emperor to be hanged, the
conservative public blamed the Jews. The following night, gangs of migrant
workers, Orthodox zealots, and outright criminals began to attack Jews and
their property. "There's your freedom, there is your constitution and revolution, there's your crown and portrait of our tsar," cried one of the attackers.
Twenty-seven people were killed, close to 300 injured, and some 1,800 Jewish houses and businesses destroyed. On Khreshchatyk, Kyiv's main street,
only one of twenty-eight Jewish shops avoided destruction.

After witnessing the pogrom, one of the best-known Jewish authors of
the twentieth century, Sholem Aleichem, left the city and the country for
faraway New York. Anticipation of a pogrom became a major theme in his
last story about Tevye the Dairyman. The subject is also prominent in those
of his stories on which the Broadway classic *Fiddler on the Roof* is based. In
both the story and the musical, the city policeman is sympathetic to the
Jews. That was true of some policemen, but many stood by during the pogroms, encouraging the violence. That seems to have been the case in Kyiv.
By the time the police took action against the perpetrators of the pogrom, it
had been going on for two days.

In many ways, the Kyiv pogrom was representative of those that took place in Ukraine's other big cities. The perpetrators were usually workers—recent migrants to the cities from the impoverished villages of Russia and, to a lesser extent, Ukraine who were competing with Jews for jobs and felt exploited and discriminated against by city and factory officials and entrepreneurs. In the Jews, they found easy prey and a "legitimate" target: by attacking them, the perpetrators could manifest and defend their "true Russian identity" and loyalty to the empire's principles of autocracy, Orthodoxy, and nationality. Peasants would join in to pillage properties in small towns and on the outskirts of big cities. These criminals felt free to attack properties they would not have touched before.

Although the mobs associated revolution with the Jews, the crowds that both celebrated the tsar's manifesto and found it wanting were led by activists of a number of political organizations, only a few of which were Jewish. Vladimir Lenin's Bolsheviks, a radical wing of the Russian Social Democratic Labor Party, were in the forefront of the workers' strikes and demonstrations. They denounced the manifesto. The party aimed to topple the regime by means of an all-empire strike and uprising. The Mensheviks, a branch of the same party that opposed Lenin's dictate, conducted their own propaganda. Also very active was the Russian Party of Socialist Revolutionaries, which established cells in Kharkiv, Zhytomyr, and Chernihiv, among other major Ukrainian cities, before the revolution. Many Jews joined the social democrats, Mensheviks and Bolsheviks alike, but they also had their own political parties. One of the most active in the events of 1905 was the Jewish Labor Bund, a socialist party representing Jewish workers and artisans.

While Jewish participation in the revolution, more often than not under the banners of the Bund, indicated the importance of national and religious minorities in the unfolding revolutionary struggle, the main "all-Russian" parties refused to make any meaningful concessions to the empire's nationalities. Leaders of the Bund were among the organizers of the Russian Social Democratic Labor Party but left it once Lenin questioned the autonomous status of their organization and its exclusive right to represent Jewish workers. The Bolsheviks and the social democrats in general believed in one indivisible workers' movement, as well as one indivisible Russian Empire. The Socialist Revolutionaries were more flexible, recognizing the importance of cultural autonomy and willing to consider a federal structure for the Russian state. But those concessions were insufficient to prevent the national minorities of the empire from forming their own political parties.

UKRAINIANS ON BOTH sides of the Russo-Austrian border had been busy founding their own political parties since the 1890s. It was an age when political forces all over Europe had entered the party-building stage, hitting the streets in an effort to organize the masses in support of their political agendas. In Russian-ruled Ukraine, the first political party was created in 1900. Its mobilization stage began in Poltava and Kharkiv. A group of local students who refused to join all-Russian parties and sought to merge socialist and nationalist ideas established a party of their own, the Revolutionary Ukrainian Party. The activists formed a network of cells in Ukraine and began working among the peasants, calling on them to revolt. They also adopted a program elaborated in a pamphlet written by Kharkiv lawyer Mykola Mikhnovsky, titled *Independent Ukraine* and printed in Galicia. With it the first Ukrainian political party created in the Russian Empire proclaimed independence as its goal.

"The fifth act of a great historical tragedy, the 'struggle of nations,' has begun, and its conclusion is fast approaching," wrote Mikhnovsky, all but predicting the disasters of the coming world war. Mikhnovsky suggested that the way out of the nightmare of great-power antagonism was "shown by newly liberated nations that had risen against all forms of foreign domination." He continued, "We know that our people, too, are in the position of an enslaved nation." He then declared the goal of Ukrainian national liberation and, being a lawyer to boot, developed a legal and historical argument to denounce the Russo-Ukrainian agreement concluded by Bohdan Khmelnytsky in 1654. Mikhnovsky claimed that Russia had violated its conditions by encroaching on the rights and privileges given to the Cossack officers in Khmelnytsky's day. Hetmans Ivan Vyhovsky and Ivan Mazepa had used similar arguments back in the seventeenth and early eighteenth centuries. Unlike them, however, Mikhnovsky called on his countrymen to set themselves completely free, not to accept a Polish or Swedish protectorate.

The pamphlet marked a turning point in Ukrainian political thinking in the Russian Empire. Its acceptance as the program of the first Ukrainian political party boosted Mikhnovsky's ideal. But the party soon split on the question of whether to prioritize nationalism or socialism. Mikhnovsky's thesis about the coming independence of Ukraine was relegated to the background for another seventeen years. It would return in January 1918 in the fires of another revolution. For the time being, in the Revolution of 1905, most Ukrainian politicians sought autonomy in a "liberated" democratic and federal Russia, not outright independence. Indicative of the mood in society was the success of the Spilka (Union)—a social democratic party that emerged from Mikhnovsky's Revolutionary Ukrainian Party but was multiethnic in composition, with close ties to the Russian social democrats and the Jewish Bund. In April 1905, the Spilka had close to 7,000 members. Its success was due in part to its status as a regional branch of Russian social democracy.

The October Manifesto produced further changes in Ukraine's political landscape. In a desperate attempt to recapture the political initiative and split the opposition to the government, the tsar issued his manifesto to grant citizens of Russia civil rights and introduce male suffrage. A monarchist party, the Union of October 17, was established in support of the manifesto. In October, the liberal Constitutional Democratic Party took shape, followed in November by the formation of the nationalist and anti-Semitic Union of the Russian People. The Ukrainian political scene was now split three ways, with socialists and social democrats represented by the Spilka and a number of "all-Russian" parties and groups; the liberal Ukrainophile intelligentsia grouping itself in the somewhat misleadingly named Ukrainian Radical Democratic Party, which cooperated with the Russian constitutional democrats; and the descendants of the Little Russia trend forming the core of monarchist organizations such as the Union of the Russian People.

All three camps, to the degree that they were concerned with the Ukrainian national question, traced their roots to the Ukrainian cultural revival of the 1830s and 1840s and claimed Taras Shevchenko as a predecessor. None of them wanted to see Shevchenko as a St. Petersburg artist and intellectual: everyone thought of him as a "people's poet" with a Cossack moustache, dressed in a peasant sheepskin coat. Shevchenko was their ticket to the peasant masses, and in the new era of mass politics, it could be a winning ticket. But only one camp, the Ukrainian liberals, addressed the people in Shevchenko's language. The Revolution of 1905 finally allowed them to do so after more than forty years of limitations. The breakthrough came in February 1905, when the Russian Imperial Academy of Sciences issued a memorandum that advocated lifting the prohibitions on Ukrainian-language publications. The academic community recognized Ukrainian ("Little Russian") as a language in its own right, not a mere dialect.

In October 1905, on the same day that Emperor Nicholas II issued his manifesto, official restrictions on Ukrainian publications were dropped as well. By December 1905, two Ukrainian-language newspapers were being

printed in Lubny and Poltava. In September 1906, Ukrainian liberals began
to publish the first daily newspaper in Ukrainian—*Rada* (*Council*)—in Kyiv.
In 1907, they began to issue the first Ukrainian-language journal. The first
academic publication in Ukrainian appeared in the following year. By that
time there were nine Ukrainian-language newspapers altogether, with a total
print run of 20,000 copies. That was just the beginning: the following years
saw an explosion of Ukrainian-language publishing. The leading genre was the
illustrated brochure with humorous content, accounting for an overall print
run of close to 850,000 copies between 1908 and 1913, followed by poetry,
with a total print run approaching 600,000 copies. The Ukrainian peasants, it
turned out, preferred to joke and recite poetry in their own language.

The first contest for the hearts and minds of the Ukrainian masses came
in the spring of 1906, with elections to the first Russian Duma. The social
democrats did not participate, and the liberals scored highly. The radical
democrats, who joined forces with the Russian constitutional democrats,
gained a few dozen seats for their members and sympathizers in the Duma.
Upon arrival in St. Petersburg, they formed the Ukrainian Club to promote
Ukrainian cultural and political causes. Forty-four of the ninety-five deputies
elected from Ukraine joined the club. But the First Duma was short-lived:
the tsar found it too revolutionary and dissolved it in two months. Elections
to the Second Duma took place in early 1907 with the active participation of
the social democrats. The Spilka, with its fourteen elected deputies, emerged
ahead of every other Ukrainian party except the monarchists, who got almost
a quarter of the popular vote. The Ukrainian deputies formed a second parliamentary caucus, now with forty-seven members. One of its projects was
the introduction of the Ukrainian language into the public schools. The caucus did not get very far, as the decline of revolutionary activity in the empire
allowed the tsar to dissolve the Second Duma as well. It was in session
slightly longer than the first, from March to June 1907. The dissolution of
the Second Duma marked the end of the revolution.

Ukrainian activists based much of what they did from 1905 to 1907—
from forming parliamentary caucuses to establishing Ukrainian educational
and scholarly institutions—on the accomplishments of their counterparts in
Austria-Hungary, where the age of mass politics had arrived decades earlier.
Instead of an impediment, the Russo-Austrian border served as a boon for the
Ukrainian national movement: when things became difficult on one side, activists from the other picked up the torch and helped their brethren. From the
1860s on, Dnieper Ukrainians who found themselves in trouble because of

prohibitions on Ukrainian publications received help from and gave support to Galician Ukrainophiles. At the turn of the twentieth century, the Galicians found themselves in a position to assist Dnieper Ukraine again.

THE KEY FIGURE in the transfer of the Galician experience to Dnieper Ukraine was a forty-year-old professor of Ukrainian history at Lviv University, Mykhailo Hrushevsky. An alumnus of Kyiv University, Hrushevsky came to Galicia in 1894 and established himself as the leading Ukrainian academic on either side of the Russo-Austrian border. He began writing his multivolume *History of Ukraine-Rus'*, the first academic work to establish the Ukrainian historical narrative as completely distinct from the Russian one. He also served as president of the Lviv-based Shevchenko Scientific Society, turning it into an equivalent of the national academy of sciences that Ukraine did not yet have. Once he heard about the formation of the Ukrainian Club during the First Duma, Hrushevsky left his students in Lviv and moved to St. Petersburg to edit the club's publication and serve as adviser to the Ukrainian deputies. In the next few years, Hrushevsky moved the journal *Literaturno-naukovyi visnyk* (*Literary and Scholarly Herald*), which he had been editing in Lviv, to Kyiv, where he also founded the Ukrainian Scientific Society, modeled on the Shevchenko Scientific Society in Lviv.

Hrushevsky claimed that the "liberation of Russia"—the goal of the broad liberal coalition that had emerged in the Russian Empire on the eve of the revolution—was unattainable without the "liberation" of Ukraine. He sought a democratic and autonomous Ukraine within a democratic federal Russian state. He called on the Ukrainian intelligentsia to join Ukrainian political parties instead of sacrificing their national agenda in the service of "all-Russian" goals. Hrushevsky also aimed to prevent a possible alliance of Russian liberals with Polish nationalists at the expense of Ukrainian political and cultural goals. He argued that there should be no separate deals when it came to nationalities, all of which should be treated equally. He feared that a Russo-Polish agreement on the introduction of the Polish language in the schools of the former Poland-Lithuania would entail the exclusion of the Ukrainian language from the school system. The Polonization of the Ukrainian peasantry would thus replace the Russification of the Ukrainian countryside in the western provinces of the empire. As things turned out, the threat did not materialize.

Hrushevsky's Galician experience very much informed his concern. The Ukrainian National Democratic Party dominated Ukrainian politics there.

Created in 1899 with the help of Hrushevsky and his close ally Ivan Franko, Ukraine's best-known Galician writer, it united Ukrainophile populists and socialist radicals. The national democrats declared Ukrainian independence as their ultimate aim (before Mikhnovsky's Revolutionary Ukrainian Party), but their immediate goals included the division of Galicia into Ukrainian and Polish territories and equality of ethnic groups in the empire. None of this sat well with the Polish political parties. The Polish National Democratic Party, led by Roman Dmowski, sought to assimilate Ukrainians into Polish culture, while the Polish socialists, led by the future head of an independent Polish state, Józef Piłsudski, argued for a federal solution to the Ukrainian question. There was little room for compromise between the Polish and Ukrainian visions of Galicia.

Polish-Ukrainian relations deteriorated beyond repair during the 1907 elections to the imperial and Galician parliaments—the first elections based on the principle of universal male suffrage. The Ukrainians did relatively well in the imperial elections but failed to break the Polish grip on the Galician legislature: the electoral law benefited the Polish upper classes and was further manipulated by Polish officials. The result was a Ukrainian loss and violent clashes that resulted in several deaths. Relations between university students belonging to the two national communities were also highly antagonistic. Hrushevsky felt it necessary to take a handgun when he went to teach evening classes. Polish-Ukrainian relations reached a new low in April 1908, when a Ukrainian student assassinated the Polish viceroy of Galicia.

While the Ukrainian national democrats failed to achieve their major goal—the partition of the province and the attainment of Ukrainian autonomy within Austria-Hungary, they did quite well in promoting their educational and cultural agenda. In the 1890s, during a short-lived reconciliation between the Ukrainophiles and the Polish establishment, Galician schools introduced the Ukrainian phonetic alphabet in the classroom. It maintained that status despite the deterioration of Polish-Ukrainian relations in the first decade of the twentieth century. The first generation of Galician Ukrainians educated en masse—there would be 2,500 elementary schools teaching in Ukrainian by the eve of World War I—was now learning about world affairs in the Ukrainian language as a matter of course. This simple fact would become the foundation of a strong Ukrainian identity in the region for generations to come.

The Russophiles, who promoted a form of the Russian language, lost the battle for the school curriculum. They were also losing the competition at the ballot box. In the elections of 1907, Ukrainian politicians forged alliances with Jewish candidates (at least two Jewish deputies to the Austrian parliament won election with the support of Ukrainian voters), while the Poles tried unsuccessfully to support the Russophiles. The Ukrainian parties won twenty-two seats in the imperial parliament, while the Russophiles took only two. The Russophile movement had ceased to be a serious threat to Ukrainian populism in Galicia.

UKRAINIAN PARTIES IN the Russian Empire found themselves in a very different situation after the Revolution of 1905. If anything, they were losing the battle for influence among their own people. The Ukrainian language was never allowed into the schools, and with the end of the revolution the authorities began to shut down Ukrainian organizations and harass and close Ukrainian-language publications. Russian nationalist organizations, on the other hand, got a free hand to conduct their propaganda among the Ukrainian peasantry.

The government of conservative Russian prime minister Petr Stolypin was building up political support in the western borderlands of the empire by mobilizing radical Russian nationalism. The new electoral law helped pro-nationalist candidates to win election. In Ukraine, as in the rest of the empire, Russian nationalist organizations allied themselves with like-minded hierarchs and priests of the Russian Orthodox Church, spreading Russian nationalism and anti-Semitism among Ukrainian peasants and city dwellers. Kyiv became the site of the most scandalous trial in imperial Russian history—the Beilis affair, in which a Jew stood accused of the ritual killing of a Christian boy. The Pochaiv monastery in Volhynia became a hotbed of Russian nationalism and anti-Semitism in the years leading up to World War I. The largest imperial branch of the Union of the Russian People was based in Volhynia. Members of the union and similar organizations claimed to be defending the interests of Russians (in the Ukrainian case, Little Russians) against "foreign" Polish and Jewish exploiters. Their propaganda represented the "foreigners" as capitalist bloodsuckers and revolutionary radicals.

The results of the Ukrainian elections to the Third Duma (1907–1912) demonstrated the appeal of imperial Russian nationalism. Out of forty-one deputies elected in Ukraine, thirty-six were characterized as "true Russians," a term used at the time to define Russian nationalists. The assassination of Petr Stolypin in Kyiv in September 1911 by a Russian Socialist Revolutionary changed nothing in imperial politics. Russian nationalist parties gained 70 percent of the Ukrainian vote in the elections to the Fourth Duma—a stunning result, given that ethnic Russians made up no more than 13 percent of Ukraine's population. The majority not only of voters but also of those elected on the Russian nationalist ticket were ethnic Ukrainians, such as the founder of the Kyiv Club of Russian Nationalists and a ranking member of the Fourth Duma, Anatolii Savenko. Another ethnic Ukrainian, Dmitrii Pikhno, headed the Kyiv branch of the Union of the Russian People. The Kyiv newspaper *Kievlianin*, which he edited, became the mouthpiece of the nationalist organizations. In the course of the Revolution of 1905, radical Russian nationalism had effectively replaced whatever remained of Ukrainian distinctiveness among the promoters of Little Russian identity.

Although unfinished in more than one sense, the Revolution of 1905 became a turning point in the history of the Ukrainian national movement in the Russian Empire. It marked the first time that Ukrainian activists managed to take their ideas to the masses and test their strength and popularity. For the first time ever, they were allowed to address the masses in the Ukrainian vernacular and use the media to disseminate their ideas. They formed Ukrainian clubs and established Prosvita (Enlightenment) societies all over Ukraine. The Ukrainophiles of older times could only have dreamed of such a breakthrough into public life. The activists accomplished a great deal in a short period. But the end of the revolution, followed by reactionary official policies that found support in the radical brand of Russian nationalism, left the Ukrainian parties in a state of disarray and disillusion. In Austrian-ruled Ukraine, the Ukrainophiles defeated the proponents of the all-Russian idea but were unable to break the hold of the Polish parties on Galician politics. While Ukrainian activists in both empires formulated the goal of Ukrainian independence, even the achievement of local autonomy seemed beyond their means, unless something were to shake the economic, social, and political foundations of the imperial regimes. Realization of Ukrainian dreams of independence or even autonomy would require a major political earthquake. Its first shocks came in August 1914.

IV

THE WARS
OF THE WORLD

CHAPTER 18

THE BIRTH OF A NATION

JUST TWO SHOTS were fired on the morning of June 28, 1914, in the city of Sarajevo. With the first, the nineteen-year-old student Gavrilo Princip wounded Archduke Franz Ferdinand of Austria. With the second, he hit the archduke's wife, Duchess Sophie. Both would die before noon. There would also be major collateral damage. The trigger of the Browning pistol pulled by Princip also triggered World War I.

Gavrilo Princip, a member of a Serbian nationalist organization, hated the Habsburgs and dreamed of a single free Yugoslav state in the Balkans. The Austro-Hungarian government had other dreams. It wanted to preserve the empire and decided to exploit the assassination of the archduke as a reason to go to war with Serbia and punish it as an instigator of Slavic nationalism within the imperial borders. Russia backed Serbia, and Germany stood behind Austria-Hungary, while Britain and France supported Russia. By early August, virtually all of Europe was at war. The Great War, as it was known at the time, cost the world up to 18 million lives, both military and civilian, and more than 22 million wounded.

Historians have long argued about the causes of the first total war in human history. They most often cite the division of the world into two rival military camps: the Triple Entente of Britain, France, and Russia ranged against the Triple Alliance (Central Powers) of Germany, Austria-Hungary, and Italy (later replaced by the Ottoman Empire). Vladimir Lenin emphasized great-power rivalry for control of markets and resources. Other factors include the rise of mass politics in Europe, as well as a military doctrine that stressed the need for speedy mobilization and the power of the first strike. All of them indeed contributed to the outbreak of the conflict and to the warring nations' inability to end it until four long years of slaughter had passed.

In examining the underlying causes of the war, it is important not to lose sight of the reason why Princip fired the shots in Sarajevo and why Austria-Hungary decided to go to war. That reason was the growing conflict between ever more aggressive nationalism and rapidly weakening multiethnic empires. The war triggered by a nationalist activist did serious damage to empires. The losers included not only Austria-Hungary but also the Ottoman and Russian empires: the first disintegrated completely, while the latter two lost their monarchies and some of their territories, surviving in a different form. Among the victors were the numerous national movements that began building their own states on the ruins of the formerly invincible imperial giants. While hardly a victor by any stretch of imagination, Ukraine was among the nations that the war gave a chance to create a state of its own.

IN ITS FIRST months and even years, the war promised nothing good for minority nationalisms. It created a wave of support for ruling dynasties and imperial power. The Russian government used its outbreak to impose further restrictions on the activities of Ukrainophile organizations. The Ukrainian activists, whom government officials often called "Mazepists"—a reference to the eighteenth-century hetman who had joined forces with Sweden against Russia—were treated as potential agents of the Habsburgs. Despite their assurances of loyalty, the government closed Ukrainian organizations, including the Prosvita (Enlightenment) societies, and shut down the remaining Ukrainian publications, including the daily *Rada*—the last remnant of the liberal period inaugurated by the Revolution of 1905. All this dashed the hopes of those Ukrainian leaders who saw the war as an opportunity to create a united autonomous Ukraine within the Russian state. The Ukrainian liberals declared neutrality, refusing to support either of the warring sides. Leftist radicals turned to Austria in the hope of defeating the Russian Empire.

The war began with spectacular victories for the imperial Russian armies. In the north, the Russian troops made their way into Prussia; in the south, they entered Galicia and Bukovyna. In early September they took Lviv, and by the end of the year they controlled the Carpathian mountain passes, advancing into Transcarpathia. The new restrictions on Ukrainian organizations in the empire led to the attacks on Ukrainian activists in Austria-Hungary. The Russian occupation of Galicia and Bukovyna lasted until May 1915—long enough to indicate the future that the Romanov Empire had in store for the Habsburg Ukranians. The occupying authorities raised the banner of the reunification and liberation of the pan-Russian nation, bringing the previously marginalized Russophiles back to the center of Galician politics. The Russian administration replaced Ukrainian with Russian as the language of instruction in the local schools and renamed Austrian and Jewish Lemberg—Polish Lwów and Ukrainian Lviv—as Russian Lvov.

While the Russians supported the Russophiles, the Austrians started persecuting them as soon as the war began. On September 4, 1914, the first Russophile activists rounded up arrived in an open field in the Thalerhof camp near the city of Graz in Styria. Thousands of arrested Russophiles and members of their families soon joined them. Many were community leaders—priests, educators, and members of the educated classes—but most were simple peasants. In the course of the war, close to 20,000 people were incarcerated in Thalerhof, which acquired notoriety as one of the first concentration camps in Europe. Close to 3,000 prisoners died of cold and disease. Today, only the name of a road near Graz airport—Lagerstrasse, or Camp Street—reminds one of the tragedy of the Galician and Bykovynian Russophiles. Others were shipped to the prison camp of Theresienstadt (Terezin), a fortress in the present-day Czech Republic, which counted Gavrilo Princip as one of its inmates. He died there of tuberculosis in late April 1918, slightly more than half a year before the end of the war he helped unleash. In Canada, the authorities interned close to 4,000 Ukrainians and ordered another 80,000 to report regularly to the police, treating them as "aliens of enemy nationality." The nationality ascribed to them was "Austrian," as all were recent émigrés from Austria-Hungary.

Unlike the Russophiles, the leaders of the Ukrainian movement in Austria-Hungary declared their loyalty to the monarchy. In that, they followed most of their peasant supporters, whose favorite song in the years leading up to the war was about the wife of Emperor Franz Joseph, Empress Elizabeth (Sisi), assassinated by an Italian anarchist in 1898. The song addressed Elizabeth as "our lady" and Franz Joseph as "our father." With the start of the war, the Ukrainian activists formed a Supreme Ukrainian Council, whose name reflected that of the Supreme Ruthenian Council of the revolutionary year 1848. The council called into existence the first Ukrainian military formation in the Austrian army. Out of 10,000 volunteers, the authorities formed a corps of 2,500 called the Sich Riflemen—referring, of course, to the Zaporozhian Sich and the Dnieper Cossacks as an expression of the all-Ukrainian identity and aspirations of the Galician volunteers.

The Ukrainian politicians in Austria-Hungary had a twofold political program: to partition Galicia and achieve autonomy for its Ukrainian part and to form an independent Ukrainian state out of Russian-ruled Ukraine. To achieve the second goal, the Austro-Hungarian Ukrainians not only joined the imperial army but also embarked on the project of turning the Little Russians among the Russian prisoners of war into Ukrainians. Leading that effort was the Union for the Liberation of Ukraine, formed in Vienna but staffed largely by émigrés from Dnieper Ukraine, who knew how to talk to their own people. Among them was the future father of the radical Ukrainian nationalism of the 1920s and 1930s, a native of southern Ukraine: Dmytro Dontsov.

In the late spring and summer of 1915, a joint German-Austrian offensive allowed the Austrians to recapture most of Galicia and Bukovyna. As a result, the region was completely cleansed of Russophiles, who retreated eastward with the Russian army. "They went in whole households, led by their village heads, followed by their horses, cows, and the treasures they had managed to snatch up," wrote the newspaper *Kievskaia mysl'* (*Kyivan Thought*) about the Russophile exodus. Most of the refugees ended up in Rostov and the lower Don region on the Russo-Ukrainian ethnic border. It was the final chapter in the history of the Russophile movement as a major political force: those who had avoided Thalerhof were now leaving their land for Russia. In the spring and summer of 1916, the Russian army, led by the talented General Aleksei Brusilov, launched a major offensive that recaptured Volhynia, Bukovyna, and parts of Galicia. But it turned out to be the last hurrah of an empire close to economic and military exhaustion. The all-Russian idea would soon find itself under attack not only in Habsburg-ruled Ukraine but also in the realm of the Romanovs.

THE ROMANOV DYNASTY, if not the empire itself, came to an end in early March 1917. In the previous month, food shortages in Petrograd (the war-era name of St. Petersburg) had sparked workers' strikes and mutiny in the military ranks. The leaders of the Duma convinced Emperor Nicholas II, psychologically exhausted after years of war, to abdicate the throne. He passed the crown to his brother, who refused the honor—the Duma leaders predicted a new revolt if he were to agree. The dynasty was no more: pressure from the street, a soldiers' revolt, and the skillful maneuvering of the formerly loyal Duma had put an end to it. The leaders of the Duma then stepped in to create a provisional government, one of whose tasks was to conduct elections for a constitutional assembly that would decide the future of the Russian state.

The Petrograd events, which became known in history as the February Revolution, took the embattled leaders of the Ukrainian organizations completely by surprise. Mykhailo Hrushevsky, a key figure in the Ukrainian national movement in Galicia and during the Revolution of 1905 in Dnieper Ukraine, was working on an article in the Moscow Public Library when he heard noises and loud voices outside. When he asked the librarian what was going on, he learned that it was a revolution: Muscovites were rushing to the Kremlin to take control of that symbol of Russian statehood. In Kyiv in early March, representatives of Ukrainian political and cultural organizations created a coordinating body that they called the Central Rada. They elected Hrushevsky as its head and awaited his speedy arrival in Kyiv. When he came, he threw his support behind the young generation of Ukrainian activists, most of them students and professionals in their twenties.

Few of Hrushevsky's old colleagues from the moderate branch of the Ukrainian movement (now called the Society of Ukrainian Progressives) wanted to join the young revolutionaries: having experienced the Revolution of 1905, they knew that revolutions end in reaction and were prepared to exchange their loyalty to the regime for concessions in the cultural sphere. Making Ukrainian a language of educational instruction was their highest priority. Hrushevsky believed that they were wrong: the time had come not to ask for educational reform but to demand territorial autonomy for Ukraine in a reformed democratic Russian state. That sounded too ambitious to many veterans of the Ukrainian movement, if not downright unrealistic, given the difficult history of Ukrainian dealings with the imperial government. But Hrushevsky and his young, enthusiastic supporters thought otherwise.

They began their activities in March, working from a room in the basement of the Pedagogical Museum in downtown Kyiv. They created a General Secretariat—a government of autonomous Ukraine—headed by Volodymyr Vynnychenko, a leading modernist writer. Writing in both Ukrainian and Russian, Vynnychenko had become the first Ukrainian since Nikolai Gogol to acquire a significant readership in Russia proper. The new government claimed jurisdiction over a good part of today's Ukraine, including the imperial gubernias of Kyiv, Podolia, Volhynia, Chernihiv, and Poltava. By July, the Provisional Government in Petrograd recognized it as the regional government of Ukraine.

How could all that happen? How could the Ukrainian idea, marginalized after the Revolution of 1905, emerge victorious in competition with visions of the future promoted by Russian liberals and social democrats, as well as by proponents of Great Russian nationalism from the ranks of "true Russian" patriots? In the revolutionary atmosphere of the time, the mixture of liberal nationalism and socialism offered by the young leaders of the Rada turned out to be an addictive ideology. The politically active public came to regard the territorial autonomy of Ukraine advocated by the Ukrainian parties as the only way out of the plethora of military, economic, and social problems besieging the country. The Central Rada led the way as the only institution capable of meeting the two main demands of the moment: land and peace.

The soldiers, who wanted to end the war as soon as possible, enthusiastically backed the Rada en masse. While the Provisional Government in Petrograd was busy launching a new offensive on the eastern front and pleading with soldiers to fight to the end alongside Britain and France, the Central Rada promised peace and became the only hope for it in Ukraine, which the fighting had devastated. The "Ukrainized" army units—detachments formed of recruits from the Ukrainian provinces and sent to the Ukrainian sector of the front in the course of 1917—declared their loyalty to the Rada. There were altogether close to 300,000 recruits. These war-weary peasants in soldiers' uniforms were not only eager to return home but wanted to get there in time for the redistribution of noble land, which the Central Rada promised to carry out despite strong opposition from the landowning classes. The Ukrainian peasantry, politically dominated by the Ukrainian Socialist Revolutionaries, which happened to be the largest political party in the Rada, was solidly in the Rada's corner.

During the summer of 1917, the Central Rada, originally little more than a coordinating committee of Ukrainophile political and cultural organizations, had turned into the country's parliament as all-Ukrainian congresses of peasants, workers, and soldiers sent their representatives to it. The national minorities did likewise. Mykhailo Hrushevsky went out of his way to call on his supporters not to permit the repetition of the pogroms of 1905 and promised Jews, Poles, and Russians cultural autonomy in a self-governing Ukrainian republic federated with Russia. In return, the Jewish socialist parties joined the Rada and backed the idea of Ukrainian territorial autonomy. So did the left-leaning representatives of other minorities. The Rada's membership exceeded eight hundred. Even earlier its leaders created a smaller standing body, the Little Rada, to coordinate the work of the new revolutionary parliament.

Dozens of prominent Ukrainians returned to Kyiv from Petrograd and Moscow, which the Bolsheviks had made the new capital of Russia in March 1918, to take part in building the new Ukraine. One of them, Heorhii Narbut, a talented artist with an international reputation, became a founder of the Ukrainian Academy of Fine Arts. He also became the principal designer of the Ukrainian coat of arms and the country's first banknotes and stamps. The coat of arms included two historical symbols, a trident borrowed from the coinage of Prince Volodymyr of Kyiv, and the image of a Cossack: the new state claimed Kyivan Rus' and the Cossack Hetmanate as its two predecessors. The two colors of the coat of arms, blue and yellow, came from Galicia, where they had been part of its coat of arms for centuries. The colors symbolized the unity of the Ukrainian lands on both sides of the eastern front in the world war.

Not everything was rosy in the newly created Ukrainian autonomy. The Rada had failed to establish a viable state apparatus or create reliable armed forces out of the hundreds of thousands of officers and soldiers who pledged their allegiance to it. Writers, scholars, and students, who found themselves at the helm of the new parliament, were busy living the romantic dream of national revolution and destroying the old state machine. The lack of a functioning government and a loyal army became an issue in the fall of 1917, when the Central Rada began to lose control of the situation on the ground because of its inability to fulfill its earlier promises. In the cities, where support for the Rada dropped between 9 and 13 percent (the only exception was Kyiv, with 25 percent), power was shifting toward the Bolshevik-dominated soviets (councils). The countryside was growing ever more restless as the Central Rada failed to deliver either land or peace. The peasants began seizing state and noble lands on their own initiative.

THE BOLSHEVIK COUP in Petrograd, subsequently known as the October Revolution, had a major impact on the developments in Ukraine. In direct response to the coup, the Central Rada proclaimed the Ukrainian People's Republic—a state in its own right, but one that would remain in federal union with Russia. It also claimed new territories Katerynoslav, Kharkiv and Kherson gubernias, as well as parts of the Tavrida, Kursk, and Voronezh gubernias settled by ethnic Ukrainians. These actions spelled the end of the short-lived cooperation between the Central Rada and the Bolsheviks, who had coordinated their actions in Kyiv to defeat the troops loyal to the Provisional Government. The confrontation between the Ukrainian government in Kyiv and the Bolshevik government in Petrograd had begun.

The Bolsheviks gained power in Russia by taking control of the soviets—a new form of government created by representatives of workers, peasants, and soldiers and contested by various political parties. The October coup, which brought down the Provisional Government, was rubber-stamped by the Second All-Russian Congress of Soviets, which met in Petrograd during the coup and was dominated by the Bolsheviks and their allies. They tried the same tactic in Ukraine, calling a session of the Ukrainian Congress of Soviets to take place in Kyiv in December 1917. But most of the delegates turned out to be peasant supporters of the Central Rada: the planned Bolshevik coup in Kyiv failed.

That turned out to be a temporary setback. The Bolshevik organizers left Kyiv for Kharkiv, where a congress of soviets from the industrial east of the country met in late December. It declared the creation of a virtual state, the Ukrainian People's Republic of Soviets, on December 25, 1917. At the beginning of January 1918, Bolshevik troops from Russia entered Ukraine and moved on Kyiv under the banner of the virtual state proclaimed in Kharkiv, which would later become the capital of Soviet Ukraine. Led by the Russian officer Mikhail Muraviev, they advanced by railroad and took control of major industrial centers, where workers' detachments mobilized by the Bolsheviks backed them. The Central Rada had effectively lost control of the industrial towns, where it held sway over the liberal intelligentsia but not over the workers. It also had very few troops to protect itself against the Russian invasion. Those military units that declared support for Ukrainian independence in the summer of 1917 had been sent to the front. Now the leaders of the Central Rada found themselves constrained to declare their country's complete independence of Russia, but they had no troops to defend it.

On January 22, 1918, the Central Rada issued its fourth, and last, universal (decree), which proclaimed the independence of Ukraine. It became a law on January 24. "The Ukrainian People's Republic hereby becomes an independent, free, and sovereign state of the Ukrainian people, subject to no one," read the text. In introducing the bill to the Rada, Mykhailo Hrushevsky stressed its two immediate goals: to facilitate the signing of a peace treaty with Germany and Austria—only an independent country could do that—and to protect Ukraine from the Bolshevik invasion and the insurgency of the Red Guards, workers' units organized by the Bolsheviks in the large industrial centers. But the historical significance of the Fourth Universal went far beyond its immediate objectives. It was Ukraine's first open break with Russia since the times of Ivan Mazepa. The idea of an independent Ukrainian state, first formulated in Dnieper Ukraine only seventeen years earlier, had acquired broad political legitimacy. The genie of independence was now out of the imperial bottle.

"We want to live in peace and friendship with all neighboring states: Russia, Poland, Austria, Romania, Turkey, and others, but none of them has the right to interfere in the life of the independent Ukrainian republic," read the universal. This was, of course, easier said than done. Russian troops were converging on Kyiv from the north and east, while in the city itself, the Bolsheviks staged a workers' uprising at the Arsenal, the major military works whose buildings serve today as Kyiv's art center and exhibition hall. There was a shortage of reliable troops, as Bolshevik promises of land, peace, and the revolutionary transformation of society had lured many away. The Rada called for mobilization. At the railway station of Kruty in the Chernihiv region, a detachment of approximately four hundred Ukrainian students and cadets engaged advancing Bolshevik forces consisting of sailors from the Baltic Fleet and a military unit from Petrograd. Twenty-seven of the Ukrainian fighters ended up in enemy hands and were shot in retaliation for the stubborn resistance they had put up to the Bolshevik advance for five long hours. In Ukrainian historical memory, they became celebrated as the first martyrs for the cause of national independence. More would follow.

ON FEBRUARY 9, 1918, the Central Rada abandoned Kyiv and retreated westward. That night, in the town of Brest on today's Polish-Belarusian border, its representatives signed a peace treaty with the Central Powers: Germany, Austria-Hungary, and their allies. Having refused to form a regular army in the summer and fall of 1917, the Central Rada now had no choice but to look beyond Ukraine's borders for protection. The Ukrainian delegates agreed to German and Austrian military intervention, which began almost immediately: exhausted by the long war, the armies and economies of the Central Powers needed agricultural products, and Ukraine already had a reputation as the breadbasket of Europe. The parties agreed to "reciprocal exchange of the surplus of . . . more important agricultural and industrial products." In exchange for Ukrainian grain, the Central Powers offered their well-armed and well-oiled military machine. It rolled into Ukraine within ten days after the signing of the treaty. By March 2, it had driven the Bolsheviks out of Kyiv, the Central Rada was back in the building of the Pedagogical Museum, and the students who died at Kruty had been buried with military honors at Askold's Mound, the legendary burial place of the first Viking ruler of Kyiv.

The Bolsheviks were in retreat, and unable to stop the advancing German and Austrian troops (about 450,000 men) by military force, they tried to do so by diplomatic and legal means. They began to create on paper and declare the independence of virtual people's republics in southeastern Ukraine. The Odesa People's Republic and the Donets-Kryvyi Rih Republic, formed to oppose the Central Rada, were now joined by the Taurida Republic. The Central Powers paid no attention. With the help of Ukrainian troops, they even took the Crimea—which the Central Rada had never claimed—but did not annex it to the Kyiv-based Ukrainian People's Republic. Soon the Bolsheviks found themselves outside Ukraine, whose independence they were forced to recognize in order to conclude a peace treaty of their own with the Central Powers.

The new Ukrainian state was now independent of Russia not only de jure but also de facto. But its independence of the Central Powers, to whom the Central Rada had agreed to supply 1 million tons of grain, was anything but a given. This became perfectly apparent in late April 1918, when the German military authorities dissolved the Rada, not trusting its socialist-dominated government to fulfill their "pump out grain" agenda. The dissolution took place only a few days after the Rada agreed to supply its allies with the aforementioned million tons of grain, as well as significant quantities of other agricultural products. The coup engineered by the Germans brought to power the government of General Pavlo Skoropadsky, a descendant of an eighteenth-century Cossack hetman, deeply conservative in his views, who represented the interests of Ukraine's landowning class. He declared himself hetman of the new state, appealing to the historical memory of the masses. In the tradition of the hetmans of old, he ruled as a dictator, his power limited only by foreign authority—the German and Austrian command.

A product of the Russian cultural milieu, Skoropadsky had undergone rapid Ukrainization in the revolutionary year 1917, when the Provisional Government put him in charge of its new Ukrainian military formations—a desperate attempt to continue the war by appeasing the nationalities. He embraced the

Ukrainian idea first in autonomous and then in pro-independence form, remaining dedicated to it (and to his German backers) to the end of his life, which came in April 1945, when an Allied bomb killed him in Germany. Skoropadsky's rule turned out to be a great boon for Ukrainian state and institution building. For the first time, the country got its own banks and a functioning financial system. The hetman recruited imperial-era officials to run ministries and establish local government offices, and the former imperial officers created military units. In the realm of education, Ukraine acquired its own Academy of Sciences, its first national library, and a national archives. It also got three new universities, in Katerynoslav, Kamianets-Podilsky, and Kyiv. Although Skoropadsky never fully mastered the Ukrainian language, he helped fulfill the old dream of the Ukrainophile intelligentsia—the introduction of Ukrainian into the school system, which the Central Rada had initiated.

Whatever Skoropadsky's achievements in the institutional sphere, his rule was anathema to the socialist leaders of the Central Rada. They refused to cooperate with the new regime, which they considered, often for very good reason, a creation of and safe haven for Russian conservatives driven out of Russia by the Bolshevik revolution. Many socialist leaders went underground and plotted a political comeback. An uprising against the hetman was in the air. The regime was anything but popular among laborers, whose working day it extended to twelve hours, or peasants, whose harvests the authorities confiscated. By the end of the summer of 1918, thousands of workers were on strike, and close to 40,000 peasants had joined armed detachments—post–World War I Ukraine now had no shortage of trained military personnel. The punitive expeditions carried out by German troops made things even worse. By early fall, the regime was in a death spiral. It tried to save itself by raising the banner of federalism with non-Bolshevik Russia, but this belated attempt to appease the Entente, which supported the idea of a united Russian state, backfired. The symbolic surrender of Ukrainian independence only angered the socialist leaders of the Central Rada, who were working actively to overthrow the hetman. But more than anything else, the end of the world war spelled the end of the Skoropadsky regime.

ON NOVEMBER 11, 1918, in the forest of Compiègne north of Paris, representatives of the German military command signed an armistice with their French and British counterparts. The end of hostilities meant that the German and Austrian troops would leave Ukraine. Three days later, on November 14, the Directory, a revolutionary committee named after the government of eighteenth-century revolutionary France and chaired by Volodymyr Vynnychenko, former head of the Rada government, rose openly against the hetman. The Directory allowed the Germans and Austrian troops to leave, and on December 15 its troops, composed of rebel peasants and military units that had deserted the hetman, entered Kyiv. The Hetmanate was no more. A creation of the war, backed by one of the warring parties, it proved unable to survive on its own. The Ukrainian People's Republic was back, gladly taking over the institutions created by its predecessor. But its control of Kyiv was by no means firm. The Bolsheviks, who had had to retreat before the German and Austrian advance earlier that year, were now preparing to retake Ukraine.

In Galicia, on the other side of the front line, the end of the world war precipitated the creation of another Ukrainian state that would soon be known as the Western Ukrainian People's Republic. Its formation began in October, after the declaration of the new emperor, Charles I, on the federalization of the Austro-Hungarian Empire. The Ukrainian leaders claimed their ethnic territories of Galicia, Bukovyna, and Transcarpathia. Austria-Hungary was living out its final days: its last act, the signing of the armistice agreement with the Entente, now joined by the United States, took place on November 3, 1918. The nationalities ruled from Vienna and Budapest were eager to leave the imperial cage, but the fall of the Dual Monarchy, which did not survive the month of November, unleashed a flood of competing territorial claims. The Ukrainians and Poles in particular were at each other's throats for control of Galicia. Despite numerous promises, the Vienna government had failed to divide the province into eastern and western parts, and now the Poles claimed all of it.

The Ukrainians struck first on the morning of November 1, 1918, taking control of Lviv—a city surrounded by a Ukrainian-populated countryside but itself largely Polish and Jewish in ethnic composition. They declared the independence of the brand-new Ukrainian state that day. The Poles fought back, reclaiming the city twenty days later. The leadership of the Western Ukrainian People's Republic, headed by the prominent lawyer and civic leader Yevhen Petrushevych, had to move its headquarters eastward, first to Ternopil and then to Stanyslaviv (today's Ivano-Frankivsk). It was the beginning of a prolonged and bloody Ukrainian-Polish war. On December 1, 1918, representatives of the two Ukrainian republics, eastern and western, decided to join forces and create a single state. They needed as much unity as they could muster. The future was by no means bright for either of them. World War I, which many hoped would end all wars, set off new ones the moment it ended.

The Great War had begun with Austria trying to maintain its hold on its Slavic nationalities and Russia, acting as the pan-Slavic protector of the Balkans, and trying to extend its pan-Russian identity into Austria-Hungary. Both imperial governments lost. In eastern and central Europe, the war weakened and then destroyed empires, while social revolution did away with the old order. Like the rest of Europe, Ukraine emerged from the calamities of war a very different place—shell-shocked and with a ruined economy, a diminished population, mobilized ethnic identities, and more antagonistic ideologies than ever before. But the collapse of empires gave Ukrainians a new identity, produced a Ukranian state with its own government and army, and placed Ukraine on the political map of Europe. The new politics born of war gave Ukrainians on both sides of the former imperial border a clear political goal—independence. Little more than a fantasy before the war broke out, it became part of an ideology shared by socialist leaders of the Rada, conservative backers of Skoropadsky, and the fighters of the Western Ukrainian People's Republic in Galicia. More often than not, the cause of independence mobilized Ukrainians while antagonizing minorities and alienating neighbors. It was one thing to proclaim independence and quite another to achieve it. Ukrainians would have to fight for it on more than one front.

CHAPTER 19

A SHATTERED DREAM

I N KYIV, WEDNESDAY, January 22, 1919, turned out to be a fine winter day, with some frost but no snow. We know this because a film crew was in the city that day for one of the first filmings of a public event in the capital of Ukraine. A year had passed since the Central Rada's proclamation of Ukrainian independence in its Fourth Universal. Now back in power, some of its former leaders used the occasion for another important proclamation—the unification into one independent state of the former Russian- and Austrian-ruled parts of the country. They built a triumphal arch leading from Volodymyr Street to St. Sophia Square, choosing the Kyivan Rus'–era cathedral as the backdrop for a mass rally, church service, and military parade—elaborate formalities to celebrate what had seemed a few months earlier nothing more than the dream of a small circle of Ukrainian intellectuals on both sides of the Russo-Austrian border.

As the bells of St. Sophia began to ring the noon hour, the camera captured images of happy faces, women holding flowers, and crowds of men in military uniforms. At the center of attention were the members of the Directory—the new revolutionary government—led by a tall man with a goatee wearing a dark leather overcoat and sporting a broad-brimmed wool hat. This was the head of the Directory and the former premier of the Central Rada government, Volodymyr Vynnychenko. To his right marched the representatives of western Ukraine, authorized by the popular assemblies of Ukrainian lands formerly under Habsburg rule to conclude the unification of the two Ukrainian states. But neither Vynnychenko nor Lev Bachynsky, the deputy chairman of the parliament of the Western Ukrainian People's

Republic, attracted most of the cameraman's attention. The greatest amount of "air time" went to a middle-aged man of medium build wearing a sheepskin hat of the kind worn by most of the officers around him. At one point he was filmed standing next to Vynnychenko and smoking a cigarette, then fixing his belt and attire. This was Symon Petliura, the chief *otaman*, or commander in chief, of the Directory's army.

Born in the city of Poltava in 1879, Petliura was thirty-nine years old at the time of the filming. Like Joseph Stalin, who was half a year older, Petliura began his revolutionary activities as a student at a theological seminary. He rose through the ranks to become one of the leaders of the Ukrainian Social Democratic Labor Party. After the defeat of the Revolution of 1905, he edited a number of Ukrainian journals and newspapers, first in Kyiv, then in St. Petersburg and, from 1911, in Moscow. In 1917, as head of the Ukrainian General Military Committee and then as the Central Rada's general secretary for military affairs, he led the formation of Ukrainian units in the ranks of the Russian army. The imperial authorities would entrust one such unit to the command of future hetman Pavlo Skoropadsky.

The film made in Kyiv on January 22, 1919, shows Petliura standing together with Volodymyr Vynnychenko but not conversing with him. There was no love lost between the two politicians. Their rivalry went back to prewar times, when both were leading members of the Ukrainian Social Democratic Labor Party. Vynnychenko, who had strong pro-Bolshevik sympathies, blamed Petliura for provoking the Bolshevik invasion of Ukraine. In December 1917, on the verge of that invasion, Petliura was forced to resign from the government. Although Petliura and Vynnychenko teamed up to lead the uprising against the hetman, their rivalry continued within the Directory. By March 1919, Vynnychenko, whose attitude was still pro-Soviet and pro-Bolshevik, would be out of the Directory, out of Ukraine, and pretty much out of politics. After the departure of Vynnychenko, Petliura would become the sole head of the Directory.

There were important political and military reasons for the rise of Petliura at a time when not only Vynnychenko but also Mykhailo Hrushevsky, another major figure of 1917, went into the emigration. Petliura gained prominence as his offices of government secretary for military affairs and then commander in chief became critically important, with the Ukrainian revolution passing from its parliamentary to its military stage. By early 1919, with Ukraine once again under Bolshevik attack, Petliura was the government's key minister. On February 2, 1919, less than two weeks after celebrating the Act of Union, the Directory was forced out of Kyiv. It moved first to Vinnytsia and then established its headquarters in Kamianets-Podilskyi, once close to the former Russo-Austrian border and now on the border with the Western Ukrainian People's Republic.

There was no alternative to retreat because the Ukrainian army was again in disarray. The peasant detachments that Petliura had led in the last months of 1918 against Hetman Skoropadsky had all but evaporated: out of 100,000 peasant soldiers, only a quarter stayed with Petliura, while others departed for their villages, believing that they had accomplished their mission and the rest was up to the government they had helped to install. Most of those who stayed were led by *otamans*—a Cossack-era word for commanders now applied to independent warlords. Petliura's title of chief *otaman* reflected a sad reality: he presided over a group of unruly warlords, not a disciplined army. Petliura and his officers never managed to make the transition from an insurgent force to a regular army. Successful rebels, the Ukrainian politicians turned out to be amateurs at building a state and organizing armed forces.

THE ONLY RELIABLE units in the service of the Ukrainian People's Republic were those composed of Galician soldiers—Ukrainians in the Austrian service captured by the Russian army during World War I who joined the forces of the republic after the February Revolution of 1917. They turned out to be the most disciplined formations of a number of successive Ukrainian governments. In July 1919, Petliura got new reinforcements from Galicia. The Ukrainian Galician army, 50,000 strong, crossed the Zbruch River, which had earlier divided the Habsburg and Romanov empires, and joined Petliura's troops in Podolia. The unity of eastern and western Ukraine, declared half a year earlier in Kyiv, seemed to be bearing its first fruits. But the circumstances of unification were dire indeed—both Petliura's forces and the Galician army were on the verge of defeat, with the latter being driven out of Galicia by the advancing Polish army.

How and why did that happen? Despite losing Lviv to the Poles in November 1918, the western Ukrainian government had managed to establish effective control over most of Ukrainian-populated eastern Galicia. It created a functioning administrative system, proposed a set of reforms that included the redistribution of land, which benefited the peasantry, and mobilized the Ukrainian population around the idea of independence from Poland. The turning point in the Polish-Ukrainian war was the arrival in Galicia in April 1919 of an army of 60,000 led by General Józef Haller von Hallenburg. It

had been formed in France out of Polish prisoners of war (they had originally fought on the Austrian side) and armed by the Entente. Part of the army's officer corps was French. The army was sent to the eastern front to fight
the Bolsheviks, but Haller deployed it against the Ukrainian troops in Galicia. The French protested and sent telegrams to that effect, while the Poles,
driving the ill-equipped Ukrainian army eastward, assured the French that
the Ukrainians were all Bolsheviks. In the summer of 1919, the Ukrainian
Galician army retreated to the Zbruch and crossed it to join Petliura's forces
in Podolia.

Between the 50,000-strong Galician army, 35,000 troops loyal to Petliura, and some 15,000 men fighting under the leadership of allied *otamans*,
the Ukrainian armed forces constituted a major fighting force. The arrival of
the Galicians gave Petliura a chance to reclaim territories lost to the Bolsheviks in central and eastern Ukraine. But the unity of the two Ukraines turned
out to be less firm than imagined. The conservative leadership of the Western Ukrainian People's Republic had difficulty making common cause with
the leftist members of the Directory government, the Galician commanders
could not comprehend the lax discipline of the former insurgents, and the
two groups looked in different directions for possible allies.

Not only the Ukrainian government in Kyiv but also nationalist governments in other parts of the empire, especially the Baltics and the North Caucasus, resisted the Bolshevik coup in Petrograd in October 1917. In southern
Russia, former imperial officers and the Don Cossacks joined forces to create
the White Army, which fought for the restoration of the pre-Bolshevik political and social order. The Western powers, including Britain and France,
threw their support behind the White Army under the leadership of General
Anton Denikin, who began an offensive against the Bolsheviks in Ukraine in
the early summer of 1919. The appearance of Denikin in southern Ukraine
and his northward drive posed a new question for the Ukrainian government
and its military forces. Should they ally themselves with Denikin against the
Bolsheviks or shun him, since he aimed not only to undo the social revolution advocated by the Ukrainian leaders but also to restore the one and indivisible Russian state?

The Galicians and the Dnieper Ukrainians responded differently to that
question. The westerners saw no problem in allying themselves with the anti-
Bolshevik and anti-Polish White Army. The easterners, for their part, regarded the Poles, whom the Galicians despised, as potential allies against the

Bolsheviks and the Whites, while the *otamans* were not above joining the Red Army. Brought together by ideology and circumstance, the two sides were still fighting their own wars. In August, when the Whites and the Galician units simultaneously entered Kyiv, the Galicians graciously retreated, leaving the city to the Whites, causing a major conflict between Petliura and the Galician commanders. A complete rupture came about in November 1919, when a major epidemic of typhus all but wiped out both armies, forcing the remaining Galicians to join the Whites, while Petliura made a deal with the Poles.

The year 1919, which had begun on a high note, with great hopes for the two Ukrainian states, was ending in disaster. By the end of the year, the Ukrainian armed forces were no more, and with them went statehood. The eastern Ukrainians were defeated because they were politically divided and ill organized, whereas the Galicians lost because, outnumbered and outgunned, they got no help from their eastern brethren. The unification of the two states and armies had resulted more in a military alliance than in the creation of a united state or armed force. A long period of existence in separate states under different political and social orders had strongly affected the political and military cultures of the two Ukrainian elites and their followers, who believed that they belonged to the same nation. Despite the disasters of 1919, they were not prepared to give up that idea.

As THE UKRAINIAN armies left the battlefield and the idea of Ukrainian independence seemed to be fading away, three major forces clashed in the fight for control of Ukraine. The Polish armies, driven by the vision of reestablishing a Polish state with borders as close to those of the prepartition commonwealth as possible, held sway over Galicia and moved into Podolia and Volhynia. The White armies, backed by the Entente, pushed northward from southern Ukraine into Russia with the goal of reestablishing the one and indivisible Russian state of tsarist times. Then there were the Bolsheviks, whose long-term goal was world revolution, while their immediate imperative was military survival. They could achieve neither without Ukrainian coal and bread, as Vladimir Lenin openly admitted.

Of all the regimes and armies that fought in Ukraine in 1919, the Bolsheviks left the largest footprint and kept Kyiv in their hands longest—from February to August, and then again in December. But holding the capital and controlling the large industrial cities of the Ukrainian steppe did not mean controlling Ukraine as a whole. The countryside was in revolt against the new Bolshevik masters. Their rule antagonized Ukrainian liberals and socialists, many of whom were prepared to welcome Soviet power in principle but not at the expense of their nation-building program. The same was true of the peasants, who took Bolshevik promises to give them land at face value, only to have their crops requisitioned at gunpoint. Led by a variety of warlords, the peasants rebelled, and their revolts became as much a factor in the Bolshevik loss of Ukraine as the White armies of Denikin and the Galician and eastern Ukrainian armies of Petliura. After the defeat of Denikin and the recapture of Kyiv in December 1919, the Bolsheviks decided to learn from their mistakes of the previous year.

Vladimir Lenin himself spelled out the "lesson of 1919" for his followers. According to Lenin, the Bolsheviks had neglected the nationality question. Consequently, the Bolshevik army returned to Ukraine in late 1919 and early 1920 under the banner of the formally independent Ukrainian Socialist Soviet Republic and tried to address the Ukrainians in their native language. Russification was out; cultural accommodation of the national revolution in Ukraine was in. In a move reminiscent of imperial co-opting of local elites, the Bolsheviks opened their party's door to the Ukrainian leftists; these former Socialist Revolutionaries had accepted the idea of a Soviet organization of the future Ukrainian state and became known as Borotbists after the title of their main periodical, *Borot'ba* (*Struggle*). Accepted into the Bolshevik Party on an individual basis, they provided the Bolsheviks with badly needed Ukrainian-speaking cadres and a cultural elite. Peasants, too, were finally accommodated and given the land they had been promised for so long: in the spring of 1920, the Bolsheviks postponed their plans for establishing big collective farms on lands confiscated from the nobility and allowed the peasants to divide the land of their former masters.

The new strategy worked. In the course of 1920, the Bolsheviks were able to establish control over central and eastern Ukraine and fend off the last real threat in the region. In late April 1920, the Polish armies of Józef Piłsudski, supported by the remnants of Petliura's army, launched an advance on Kyiv from the front line in Volhynia and Podolia. Piłsudski's goal was the creation of a Ukrainian buffer state between Poland and Soviet Russia. The offensive met with initial success. On May 7, Petliura once again entered Kyiv as head of the Ukrainian government, but this time there was no Galician army at his side. The price he had to pay for the support of his Polish allies was hardly of much importance in practical terms, but it had enormous symbolic significance. The chief *otaman* agreed to recognize Polish control over

Galicia, delivering the final blow to the troubled relations between the two Ukrainian states.

Petliura's success was short-lived. The Soviets launched a counteroffensive, forcing the joint Polish-Ukrainian army out of Kyiv on June 13. The First Cavalry Army, led by one of the best-known Soviet cavalry commanders of the war, Semen Budenny, broke through the defenses, headed off the retreating troops, and wreaked havoc behind the Polish and Ukrainian lines. The Red Army was advancing along the entire front, not only in Ukraine but also in Belarus, covering up to twenty miles per day. It soon neared the city of Lviv, which Joseph Stalin, then a commissar of one of the Red Army fronts, was determined to take in order to make a name for himself. Ironically, not only Polish but also Ukrainian troops, the latter being Petliura's men from eastern Ukraine, defended Lviv against the Red Army's onslaught. Their successful defense of the city turned out to be a major factor leading to ultimate Soviet defeat in the war with Poland.

The fortunes of war changed yet again in mid-August 1920. Armed with the help of the Entente and advised by British and French officers (among the latter was the future French president Charles de Gaulle), the Polish units stopped the Red Army's offensive on the outskirts of Warsaw, defeating it in a battle that became known as the Miracle on the Vistula. One of those responsible for the miracle on the Soviet side was Stalin. He encouraged Budenny to disobey the orders of his commanders and try to take Lviv instead of proceeding against Warsaw. Now the Red Army found itself in a chaotic retreat. By October, when the two sides signed an armistice, the Polish-Soviet border had been pushed back deep into Belarus in the north and Ukraine in the south. In Ukraine, the Poles were once again in control of Volhynia and parts of Podolia. Despite this gain, the Polish attempt to create a Ukrainian buffer state with its capital in Kyiv failed, as did Ukrainian hopes for the revival of independent statehood. The Miracle on the Vistula also put an end to Soviet plans to bring their revolution into the heart of Europe.

BY FAR THE best-known "chronicler" of the Polish-Soviet War was the Odesa-born Russian Jewish writer Isaac Babel. He fought in the ranks of Budenny's First Cavalry Army and kept a diary that he later used to write a collection of short stories titled *Red Cavalry*. The collection, which Budenny criticized for distorting the heroic image of his soldiers, describes the brutality of war, the violence of Red cavalrymen, and the tragic plight of the Jewish population of Ukraine in conditions of permanent warfare. With numerous armies fighting one another for almost three years, constantly changing front lines, the civil population of Ukraine suffered new terror and destruction without having had a chance to recover from the devastation of the world war. No group fared worse than the Jews, who became subject to attack from all sides, by Reds, Whites, Ukrainian armies, and warlords.

Pogroms were hardly a new phenomenon in Ukraine and the Pale of Settlement in general, but now armed aggressors were carrying them out. The casualties of the pogroms grew exponentially, passing the 30,000 mark in Ukraine alone. To the usual causes of pogroms—the desire to loot, economic rivalry, Christian anti-Judaism, and modern anti-Semitism—yet another was added: the ideologies and politics of the revolutionary era, which viewed the Jews on the one hand as capitalist exploiters, hated by communist and socialist propagandists, and, on the other, as ardent supporters of Bolshevism.

Major pogroms began in the spring of 1918, the last year of the war, when German and Austro-Hungarian armies moved into Ukraine. The perpetrators, however, were not the advancing Germans or the troops of the Central Rada but the retreating Bolsheviks, who replaced Christian zeal with communist righteousness and justified their assault on the Jews of Novhorod-Siverskyi and Hlukhiv—the capital of the former Hetmanate—as an attack on the bourgeoisie. In the spring of 1919, when the Petliura army was retreating westward under Bolshevik attacks, the Ukrainian units unleashed a series of pogroms, the largest of which, in the town of Proskuriv (today's Khmelnytskyi), took the lives of close to 1,700 Jews. Later that year, warlords and their unruly bands, who did not care much about slogans and were interested mainly in loot, plundered Jewish settlements. In the fall came the Denikin forces, who conducted their own pogroms under the new anti-Semitic slogan "Beat the Jews, save Russia." The largest of those took place in the town of Fastiv south of Kyiv, killing close to 1,000 innocent victims. Overall, the Whites were responsible for up to 20 percent of the pogroms, the Reds for up to 10 percent, the warlords for up to 25 percent, and Petliura's forces for up to 40 percent; the latter carried out the largest number of pogroms during the war years. The White Army was the only organized armed force whose soldiers conducted pogroms with the explicit approval of their commanding officers. The only soldiers who seemed to steer clear of pogroms were the Galician Ukrainians.

The Jews of the Ukrainian shtetls organized self-defense units, which were quite effective at stopping warlords but could not do much about large armies. Jewish youths also joined the Red Army en masse: its political commander, Leon Trotsky, was a native of Ukraine and often regarded as a symbol of Jewish Bolshevism. But the Red Army's popularity among Jews went far beyond Trotsky. Jewish revolutionaries had always been active in social democratic movements, whether Bolshevik or Menshevik. Moreover, young Jews were joining the army that, judging by the number of pogroms, seemed the friendliest to them. From that point of view, the story of Isaac Babel, who after a short stint in the Cheka—Lenin's secret police—joined Budenny's Cavalry Army as a political commissar and reporter, was hardly atypical for a Jewish youth from Odesa.

The pogroms of 1919 ended the Ukrainian-Jewish alliance of the first months of the revolution. They also turned Symon Petliura into a dreadful symbol of Ukrainian anti-Semitism, an identification only strengthened when, in 1926, while he was living in emigration in Paris, a former Red Army soldier named Sholom Schwartzbard gunned him down. Many believed that Schwartzbard had eliminated the leader of the Ukrainian political émigrés on behalf of the Soviet secret police. But Schwartzbard claimed that he had acted on his own and killed Petliura to avenge his Jewish relatives, who had died in the Ukrainian pogroms. A Paris court set the perpetrator free.

Was Petliura indeed responsible for the pogroms? A social democrat in his prerevolutionary years and a leader of the leftist Directory, Petliura himself was as internationalist in his outlook as in his political milieu. He shared the view of Mykhailo Hrushevsky and other leaders of the Central Rada that the Jews were natural allies of the Ukrainians in the struggle against national and social oppression. That motif made its way into the orders that he issued to his troops. "It is time to realize that the world Jewish population—their children, their women—was enslaved and deprived of its national freedom, just as we were," he wrote in an order of August 1919. "It should not go anywhere away from us; it has been living with us since time immemorial, sharing our fate and misfortune with us. I resolutely order that all those who incite you to carry out pogroms be expelled from our army and tried as traitors to the Fatherland."

In Petliura's mind, attacking Jews was equivalent to betraying Ukraine. The problem was that while he issued decrees, he only rarely or belatedly punished perpetrators. Otaman Ivan Semesenko, whose detachment conducted the Proskuriv pogrom in February 1919, was tried and shot on Petliura's orders only in March 1920—too late to have a broader impact on the army at the height of the pogroms. Petliura was reluctant to enforce his orders, as he had limited control over his army. The reasons for the army's engagement in pogroms were the same as those for its loss of the struggle for independence—its units were unruly and disorganized. The socialist Ukrainian leaders, such as Petliura, were riding the wave of peasant revolution, which came too early from the perspective of the Ukrainian national movement. Before their country went up in the flames of revolution, foreign intervention, and civil war, the Ukrainian activists never had a chance to work with the peasant masses and educate them in the basics of their socialist faith. The parties that had a free hand to conduct propaganda in Ukraine on the eve of World War I were the proponents of the Little Russian idea and the activists of Russian nationalist organizations, for whom anti-Semitism was a key ideological factor. Right-Bank Ukraine, the bastion of Russian nationalism on the eve of the war, also became the scene of the most horrendous pogroms of 1919.

THE ONLY WARLORD who tried, though with mixed success, to restrain his troops from conducting pogroms and fought anti-Semitism in the ranks of his peasant army was Nestor Makhno. A short, frail man with a feminine face and long hair, he was the charismatic commander of the largest "private" army in the former Russian Empire, which numbered 40,000 at its height. A peasant by origin and an anarchist according to his political views, Makhno was the most ideologically driven of the warlords. His home base and area of operation was the town of Huliaipole in southern Ukraine—a peasant heartland between the coal mines of the Donbas and the iron mines of Kryvyi Rih. At the turn of the twentieth century, a railroad that crossed the Moscow-Sevastopol line in the city of Aleksandrovsk (today's Zaporizhia), not far from Makhno's hometown, linked the two regions. The location of the railroads placed Makhno and his army at the center of the fighting.

Makhno's peasant fighters shared few of his anarchist principles and dreams and looked down on the ideologically motivated anarchists around their *bat'ko*, or father, as they referred to him in the tradition of peasant paternalism. The peasants hated state control of any kind—an attitude that appealed to Makhno's anarchist ideologues—and wanted expropriation and redistribution of land. Like the Zaporozhian Cossacks of the early modern era, Makhno's army, which operated on the former Cossack-Tatar borderland, kept its distance from the Ukrainian governments to the north and often fought with them. While the absolute majority of Makhno's fighters were ethnic Ukrainians, and the Ukrainian national agenda was not entirely foreign to Makhno—his teacher wife actively promoted it—the warlord's vision of anarchist revolution was basically internationalist.

Of all the forces that fought over Ukraine, Makhno regarded the Bolsheviks alone as potential candidates for an alliance, but they turned against him immediately after he helped them defeat their main enemy, General Petr Wrangel's White Army, whose remnants had turned the Crimea into their last bastion. Wrangel's was the eighth Crimean government in less than three years. The Crimean Tatars had established the first as the Crimean People's Republic on December 25, 1917. After two major waves of emigration to the Ottoman Empire, the Tatars constituted close to 30 percent of the peninsula's population (the rest were Russians, Ukrainians, Greeks, Bulgarians, Jews, and representatives of other nationalities). Their republic represented one of the first attempts of any Islamic group to build a secular state—a result of the cultural and educational activities of the previous generation of Crimean Tatar activists, led by Ismail Gaspirali, the father of the modern Crimean Tatar nation. But the Crimean People's Republic was short-lived. In January 1918, power on the peninsula passed to the Bolsheviks, who declared an independent Taurida (Crimean) Republic but were soon overrun by Ukrainian and German forces.

Under German rule, the Crimea remained independent of Ukraine, but in September 1918 Hetman Skoropadsky declared an economic blockade of the peninsula and forced the Crimean government to join the Ukrainian state as an autonomous region. This arrangement did not last long, as the German retreat brought to power a new government led by a liberal politician of Karaite origin, Solomon Krym. His minister of justice was Vladimir Nabokov, father of the famous writer. But the Bolsheviks were already on the march. They executed Emperor Nicholas II and his immediate family in the Urals in July 1918. On April 7, 1919, surviving members of the Romanov imperial family left their mansions near Yalta and were brought to the safety of the West by the British dreadnought *Marlborough*. From June 1919, the Crimea was under the control of the White Army, first under the leadership of General Denikin and, once he resigned in April 1920, then under General Wrangel.

Wrangel claimed to lead the government of southern Russia, but in fact he controlled only the Crimean Peninsula and a strip of steppeland north of it. He and his ministers wanted to recover the whole Russian Empire, which was easier said than done. Despite the support offered by the Entente, Wrangel was losing the war with the Bolsheviks. On November 8, 1920, the Red Army and allied detachments of Makhno's forces began their attack on the Crimea from the mainland, marching in freezing weather through the shallow waters of the Syvash lagoon and storming the White Army's fortifications on the four-mile-wide Perekop isthmus connecting the peninsula with the mainland. On November 17 they entered Yalta. General Wrangel evacuated the remnants of his army to Istanbul. Those who stayed behind—close to 50,000 officers and soldiers—were massacred in the largest mass killing of the war. It turned out to be not only the last slaughter of the bloody revolutionary war but also a prelude to the no less bloody rule of the Bolsheviks over a vast country, of which most of Ukraine was forced to be a part.

IN MARCH 1921, representatives of Soviet Russia, Soviet Ukraine, and Poland signed a peace treaty in Riga, Latvia, that established a new Polish-Soviet border. Under the terms of the treaty, Poland not only retained Galicia but also took over previously Russian-ruled Volhynia. Ukraine found itself divided not between two countries, as before World War I, but among four. Bukovyna, occupied by Romania in 1918, remained under the control of Bucharest, while Transcarpathia was taken away from defeated Hungary and handed over to the newly created Czechoslovak state. Czechs and Slovaks, Poles and Lithuanians—the western neighbors of Ukraine—all got independent states, while the Ukrainians, despite repeated efforts to secure one for themselves, received little more than autonomy within a Russian-led polity.

How to explain such an outcome? The reasons are numerous. One is the presence of more powerful and aggressive neighbors that claimed Ukrainian territories for themselves. But the key factor was the immaturity of the Ukrainian national movement and the late arrival of the idea of independent statehood in both Habsburg- and Romanov-ruled Ukraine. Whereas in Austrian Galicia the division between proponents of Ukrainian and all-Russian identity had been overcome by 1918, in Dnieper Ukraine it continued throughout the war and the revolution. Regionalism, which resulted from the different historical trajectories of individual parts of Ukraine, was a major obstacle both in Austrian Ukraine, where the dynamics of nation building differed significantly between Galicia, Bukovyna, and Transcarpathia, and in Dnieper Ukraine, where the idea of Ukrainian statehood gained much greater support in the former Hetmanate and the formerly Polish-ruled Right Bank than in the steppe regions of the east and south. Cities, especially big cities populated by non-Ukrainians, remained beyond the scope of the Ukrainian drive for independence, which relied almost exclusively on the support of the peasant masses.

Given these constraints on the Ukrainian national project, another important question arises: How could the nascent national movement, which first formulated the political goal of independence at the turn of the twentieth century and did not embrace it until 1918, get as far as it did in a political landscape dominated by former imperial powers and much more developed national movements? The revolutionary impact of World War I and the collapse of two empires created unexpected opportunities for the Ukrainian movement in 1917 and 1918, and it took full advantage of them. The Ukrainian national project emerged from the bloody turmoil of World War I and the struggle for independence much more mature than it had been previously. Despite the failed effort to create one functioning state out of Habsburg and Dnieper Ukraine, the ideal of unified and independent statehood became central to the new Ukrainian credo.

CHAPTER 20

COMMUNISM AND NATIONALISM

DURING THE INTERWAR period (1918–1939), the Ukrainians emerged as the largest nation in Europe with an unresolved national question. Ukraine lacked a state of its own, and four European states had divided its territories: Bolshevik Russia, Poland, Romania, and Czechoslovakia. Soviet Ukraine, which became part of the Russia-led Soviet Union in 1922, included the central and eastern Ukrainian lands; it had a common border with Poland in Volhynia and Podolia, as agreed at the peace talks in Riga in 1921, and with Romania along the Dniester River. The erstwhile Entente had recognized the latter border in its 1920 Treaty of Paris with Romania, but the Soviet authorities challenged it.

Each of the governments that found itself in control of Ukrainian territory tried to solve its Ukrainian question in a different way, using a number of strategies ranging from accommodation to suppression. The two competing ideologies and belief systems throughout the twentieth century in eastern Europe were communism and nationalism. In the Ukrainian case, as in many others, nationalism and communism not only opposed each other but also sought accommodation in the hybrid form of national communism. As a result of different ways of mobilizing Ukrainian political and cultural identity, a number of Ukrainian national projects emerged that attempted to replace the Ukrainian liberal and socialist projects of the prewar era. The two most influential new projects turned out to be the Soviet variant of national communism in Soviet Ukraine (the Ukrainian Socialist Soviet Republic, or Ukrainian SSR) and radical nationalism, based largely in Polish-ruled Galicia and Volhynia. The interaction between these two models of Ukrainian identity would define much of the country's twentieth-century history.

In December 1922, the Ukrainian Socialist Soviet Republic (its name would change to the Ukrainian Soviet Socialist Republic in 1937), a communist polity that included the central and eastern lands of Ukraine, initiated a formal agreement with Soviet Russia and the republics of Belarus and Transcaucasia to create the Union of Soviet Socialist Republics (USSR). The creation of the USSR resulted from Vladimir Lenin's intervention in the debate between Joseph Stalin, who held the newly created position of general secretary of the Central Committee of the Russian Communist Party, and the leaders of Ukraine and Georgia. Stalin wanted Ukraine and other republics to join the Russian Federation with rights of autonomy within it. The Ukrainian communist leaders resisted. They included old Bolsheviks and Ukrainian socialists who embraced the idea that social revolution implied national liberation and that creating a union of sovereign Soviet republics would best achieve both. Lenin, who dreamed of world revolution and envisioned China, India, Germany, France, and the United States joining the union in the future, supported the Ukrainian position.

The union was created with Ukraine very much in mind. Its immediate purpose was to keep the Ukrainians in, the Poles out, and the Russians down. Moscow considered the Ukrainians, whose leaders, most notably Symon Petliura, had shown themselves capable of unleashing mass peasant uprisings, the most restive and rebellious ethnic minority under its rule, while it saw Russian nationalist aspirations as a major threat to the unity of the multiethnic state. Poland was, of course, an adversary that, with Western support, might launch another offensive against the union and tear away part of Ukraine. Between the federalism of the union treaty and the centralism of the ruling Communist Party, Ukraine enjoyed de facto autonomy, arguably with broader prerogatives than those imagined by mainstream Ukrainian politicians of the decades leading up to World War I or even the leaders of the Central Rada in the first months of the 1917 revolution.

Ukraine would realize this new stage in its nation building within the political and legal framework established by the Soviet regime, which referred to itself as the "dictatorship of the proletariat." In the early 1920s, as the regime tried to solidify its control of a country devastated by war, revolution, and civil strife, it allowed some elements of the market to reenter the highly centralized Soviet economy through the back door of the New Economic Policy. In the political and cultural sphere, the Soviet leaders looked for new ways to hold on to the imperial possessions of the Romanovs. They found a provisional solution to the latter problem in the policy of *korenizatsiia*, or indigenization, which emphasized the economic development of the non-Russian peripheries, as well as the support and development of local cultures. The Twelfth Party Congress, which took place in April 1923, a few short months before the formal creation of the Soviet Union, adopted *korenizatsiia* as official party and government policy.

One goal that Moscow tried to achieve through its indigenization policy was the creation of loyal local elites. The policy of the Romanovs, who had extended Russia's territory by incorporating local elites into the imperial apparatus, was not applicable in the revolutionary era. The inclusion of local revolutionary elites took place in 1920 with the admission to the party of members of the Ukrainian Communist party (*Borot'ba*), but that strategy undermined the ideological uniformity of the party and could go only so far. Meanwhile, Ukraine lacked an indigenous communist elite in numbers sufficient to ensure the stability of the Bolshevik regime. The population of Soviet Ukraine in the mid-1920s was less than 30 million, with Ukrainians constituting roughly 80 percent, Russians less than 10 percent, and Jews 5.5 percent. The ethnic composition of the party was very different. In 1922, out of almost 55,000 members of the Communist Party of Ukraine, Russians made up an absolute majority, with more than 53 percent, while Ukrainians accounted for barely 24 percent—the same percentage as representatives of all other nationalities, most of whom were ethnic Jews. Rural Ukrainians regarded the new administration as little more than an occupying force. The party regime in Moscow wanted to change that perception in order to establish its control over the Ukrainian peasantry.

The national communists—a group in the Ukrainian party leadership that saw revolution as a vehicle for both social and national liberation of the Russian-ruled minorities—argued that in order to overcome differences between the proletarian city and the petty bourgeois world of the village, the party had to adopt the language and culture of the majority of the Ukrainian population, which happened to be Ukrainian. With communist ideology remaining largely an urban phenomenon, the village emerged in communist thinking about Ukrainization as a major challenge—as, of course, it had been during the revolution and civil war. The Ukrainian national communists advocated a strategy akin to that adopted by Byzantine proselytizers at the end of the first millennium—embracing the local language and culture with the goal of promoting the new religion, in this case communism. The victory of the Byzantine approach over the Roman one, which insisted on one lingua franca for all true believers, allowed the position advocated by the national communists to prevail as the official party line. But they were fighting an uphill battle at best.

The most solid resistance came from the party itself, most of whose members were non-Ukrainian. According to one report, only 18 percent of party members in the civil service could claim a good knowledge of Ukrainian, as opposed to 44 percent of the service as a whole. The Ukrainian national communists, led by Oleksandr Shumsky, demanded a harder line on Ukrainization. Shumsky wanted to replace Stalin's Ukrainian-born protégé Lazar Kaganovich, an ethnic Jew who found the Ukrainian language a struggle, with the ethnic Ukrainian Vlas Chubar, head of the Ukrainian government, as general secretary of the Communist Party of Ukraine. Shumsky also demanded that Stalin promote linguistic Ukrainization of the workers. From the outset, the policy had been limited to ethnic Ukrainians, excluding the Russians of Ukraine, as well as other ethnic groups, which had their own indigenization programs. The party was highly reluctant to alienate the Russian or highly Russified working class with a language policy that it was likely to resist. Shumsky was contending against heavy odds.

Stalin refused to remove Kaganovich, claiming that the proposal was badly timed. He remained obdurate even though the loyalty of the Ukrainian party organization, the largest in the Soviet Union, was essential to him in his ongoing struggle for control of the party after Lenin's death in January 1924. Stalin also refused to budge on the issue of the Ukrainization of the working class. "Our party, state, and other apparatuses serving the population can and must be Ukrainized at a certain rate," wrote Stalin in April 1926 to the Ukrainian Politburo—the top Bolshevik leaders of Ukraine. "But the proletariat cannot be Ukrainized from above. The Russian working masses cannot be *forced* to renounce the Russian language and Russian culture and adopt Ukrainian as their language and culture." Stalin was especially critical of the calls for distancing Ukrainian culture from Russian culture that he associated with the writings of Mykola Khvyliovy, a Ukrainian author of Russian ethnic origin (born Nikolai Fitilev). "While West European proletarians and their communist parties are full of sympathy for 'Moscow,' the citadel of the international revolutionary movement and Leninism; while West European proletarians gaze with sympathy on the banner waving in Moscow, the Ukrainian communist Khvyliovy can say nothing more in favor of Moscow than exhort Ukrainian activists to flee 'Moscow . . . as quickly as possible,'" wrote Stalin.

Deciding to retake the initiative from the Ukrainian national communists, Stalin ordered his own man, Kaganovich, to lead the Ukrainization drive and address Shumsky's concerns about the slow pace of Ukrainization. Kaganovich obliged, turning what had been Ukrainization "by decree" before 1926 into a much more effective and comprehensive policy. In 1927, he managed to deliver his report to the Ukrainian party congress in Ukrainian. He also took a hard line when it came to the use of Ukrainian in educational institutions and in propaganda and cultural work among the working class. After Kaganovich's recall to Moscow in 1928, his successor, Stanislav Kosior, an ethnic Pole, continued his policies. According to official figures, Ukrainian-language instruction in institutions of higher learning increased from 33 percent in the 1926–1927 academic year to 58 percent in 1928 and 1929. The percentage of Ukrainian-language newspapers grew from 30 percent of all newspapers in Ukraine in 1926 to 92 percent in 1932. In June 1932, 75 percent of all lectures given to miners in Ukraine were in Ukrainian.

While Ukrainization was central to the indigenization policy in Ukraine, it did not involve only ethnic Ukrainians. Russian, Jewish, Polish, and German ethnic regions were created in Ukraine with their own administrations. Publishing houses printed books in national languages, and schoolchildren were educated in the languages of their ethnic groups. But the effects of this policy remained limited mainly to the countryside. In the cities, ethnic minorities were being Russified even more quickly than Ukrainians. In 1926, 62 percent of ethnic Ukrainians in Kharkiv gave Ukrainian as their mother tongue, but only 41 percent of Jews did so. Some Jewish intellectuals, such as Grigorii Kerner (Hrytsko Kernerenko), a native of Nestor Makhno's capital of Huliaipole, embraced Ukrainization and chose to write in Ukrainian, but most opted for Russian as a more direct route to modernity. Many left for Moscow and made prominent careers there. The writers Ilia Ilf (Fainzilberg) and Vasilii Grossman—natives of Ukraine's two best-known Jewish centers, Odesa and Berdychiv—both took this route.

STALIN'S SUPPORT FOR Ukrainization was tactical and temporary. He believed that Russians and Ukrainians were one and the same people, and at the end of the 1920s, the party decided that the survival of the regime depended on support from the largest ethnic group—the Russians. It would have to keep Ukrainian ambitions to create a fully independent culture in check.

In 1929, the Soviet secret police began a wave of arrests in preparation for one of the first show trials to take place in the Soviet Union. Staged in Kharkiv, the trial largely targeted the leadership of the Ukrainian intelligentsia, accused of belonging to a bogus organization called the Union for the Liberation of Ukraine. Prosecutors alleged that members were in touch with Ukrainian émigrés and the Polish government and planning an uprising ultimately aimed at creating an independent Ukrainian state. At the top of the list of supposed plotters were the vice president of the Ukrainian Academy of Sciences and former deputy head of the Central Rada, Serhii Yefremov, and the former prime minister of the Ukrainian People's Republic, Volodymyr Chekhivsky. The latter was also a leading figure in the Ukrainian Autocephalous Orthodox Church, which was independent of Moscow and identified by the prosecutors as a branch of the plotters' organization. The accusations were false, but the judges sentenced 15 people to death, 192 to various terms of imprisonment, and 87 to internal exile. The trial directly attacked the intellectuals at the forefront of the Ukrainization drive. The party was changing its policy, signaling by means of the trial that it was no longer targeting Russian great-power chauvinism and instead had local nationalism in its sights. The Ukrainian national communists, including the influential minister of education, Mykola Skrypnyk, lobbied Moscow to organize a similar trial against Russian "great-power chauvinism" but failed.

Linguistic and cultural Ukrainization failed to change the culture of the industrial east and south of the republic. Nowhere was that more apparent than in the new capital of Ukraine, the city of Kharkiv. There, the percentage of those giving Ukrainian as their mother tongue only grew between 1926 and 1939 from 24 to 32 percent—an insignificant increase, given the efforts to Ukrainize the city—but even more troubling was the fact that the percentage of those giving Russian as their mother tongue remained the same, around 64 percent. That remained the case even as the city's population doubled during the same period from 417,000 to 833,000, and the share of Ukrainians grew from 39 to 49 percent. The upswing of the Ukrainization policy stalled before it could claim the city for the Ukrainian cultural cause—a failure that had profound long-term consequences for the self-identification of the Ukrainian east. But that policy also left another mark on Ukrainian society. It created conditions in which more and more urban Ukrainians claimed Ukrainian rather than Russian as their nationality, despite their predominant use of the Russian language. As Russian-speaking Ukrainians kept growing in number, they forged an all-important cultural link between Ukrainian-speaking Ukrainians and Russian-speaking Russians. In fact, all three groups had a lingua franca, called *surzhyk*, a mixture of the two languages.

In THE 1920s, Soviet leaders were bent on world revolution and conducted an active undercover campaign among Ukrainians in neighboring states, trying to destabilize and weaken the multiethnic countries of eastern Europe. France and the other Western powers, for their part, were trying to turn the same countries into a buffer zone to prevent the spread of Bolshevism in Europe. The leaders of Soviet Ukraine portrayed their republic as a new Ukrainian Piedmont—a state that would bring national and social liberation to Ukrainians temporarily under foreign bourgeois rule. The term itself harked back to the era of Italian unification, when the Piedmont had led other Italian regions toward the formation of a nation-state. The Poles and then Ukrainians applied the Piedmont metaphor to Galicia, which both regarded as the center of their respective national movements, and then the Ukrainian Bolsheviks picked it up. With the Ukrainization drive under way, presenting Soviet Ukraine as a beacon of Ukrainian nationhood was not difficult. Many of the Ukrainian-populated regions to the west found themselves under de facto occupation and experienced oppression of almost all forms of their communal and cultural life.

An exceptionally difficult political and cultural situation was that in Polish-ruled Galicia. Its population was about 5 million, with Ukrainians constituting close to 4.4 million. The Versailles and Riga peace treaties, as well as the Polish constitution, guaranteed the Ukrainian minority in Poland legal equality and the right to establish its own schools and use the Ukrainian language in the public sphere. But actual conditions were not in keeping with the international obligations undertaken by the young Polish state. Bitter memories of the Polish-Ukrainian war were still fresh, with the Polish authorities having interned close to 70,000 Ukrainians during and immediately after the war. Ukrainians boycotted the Polish institutions in the region: they opened and ran their own underground university and ignored the 1920 Polish census and the 1922 elections. But these tactics proved ineffective after March 1923, when the Conference of Ambassadors created by the Paris Peace Conference decided to recognize Polish rule over Galicia. That decision deprived Ukrainians in Galicia of their last hope that Western intervention could improve their situation and left them to cope with the new political circumstances as best they might.

The Conference of Ambassadors made its decision on the understanding that the Ukrainians would get some form of autonomy. This never materialized, as the new Polish state intended its nationality policy to bring about not only the political but also the cultural assimilation of the minorities. The authorities viewed minorities—which, apart from the Ukrainians, included Belarusians, Germans, and Jews—as the main internal challenge to the stability of the regime, which in 1926 turned from a republic into a form of dictatorship. The discriminatory policies against the Ukrainian majority in Galicia manifested in the so-called *Lex Grabski* of 1924, a law named after the future minister of education, who imposed restrictions on the use of the Ukrainian language in the educational system and began the practice of turning Ukrainian schools into bilingual Polish-Ukrainian ones.

Language became a key factor in the policy of cultural Polonization of minorities. In Eastern Galicia, where in 1910 Ukrainians had accounted for 65 percent and Poles for 21 percent of the population, by the early 1930s the percentage of Ukrainians, or, rather, those who claimed Ukrainian as their mother tongue, had dropped to 59 percent, while the Polish share had grown to 29 percent. These changes resulted partly from the educational policies of the regime, which promoted Polish-language schools and discriminated against Ukrainian ones. In 1930, there were fifty-eight state-run Polish gymnasiums (high schools) in the Ukrainian part of Galicia, as opposed to six Ukrainian gymnasiums. Although the Ukrainians established private gymnasiums, they were outnumbered there as well: in the same year, there were twenty-two private Polish gymnasiums versus fourteen Ukrainian ones. New teaching positions went almost exclusively to Poles. Out of almost 12,000 teachers in Galicia, fewer than 3,000 were ethnic Ukrainians, while the rest were Poles. Close to six hundred Ukrainian teachers who could not find employment at home were transferred to Polish-settled areas of the state.

The increase in the number of Poles in census statistics resulted not only from official support for the Polish language but also from government policies encouraging Polish migration to Eastern Galicia, now called Eastern Little Poland. Soon after gaining independence, the Polish leadership decided to break up large landholdings and distribute the pieces among peasant farmers. In Galicia and other parts of the state settled by Ukrainians, this meant that Polish landowners, who possessed most of the land, lost as a result of the reform, while Ukrainian peasants gained. In response, the government introduced policies that privileged Polish military veterans and farmers resettling in Galicia. The same policies applied to Volhynia, a former

Russian imperial possession where Poles historically constituted a lesser portion of the population than in Austrian Galicia. In Volhynia, the government allocated 40 percent of all land that became available as a result of the reform to Polish colonists. During the interwar period, close to 300,000 ethnic Poles moved to the Ukrainian lands of the Polish state—Galicia, Volhynia, and Podlachia.

Further developments encouraged Ukrainians, who constituted the absolute majority in the villages, and Jews, who made up more than 70 percent of the population in the small towns of Galicia, to leave the region and the country. Economic stagnation and neglect of the eastern borderlands were largely responsible for increasing emigration. The extraction of oil in Galicia fell 70 percent from its peak on the eve of World War I, but no other industry, short of the small forestry and agricultural sectors, existed to replace it. In the early 1930s, the working class of the Drohobych district did not exceed 45,000. The Ukrainian peasants tried to improve their situation by reviving the cooperative movement that had existed under Austrian rule. By far the most successful was the Dairy Union, which not only competed successfully at home but also exported its products to Czechoslovakia, Austria, Germany, and other European countries. Almost every Ukrainian farmer joined the Dairy Union. But the cooperatives could only do so much to improve the plight of the Ukrainian village. With urban jobs almost unavailable, the land-hungry peasants (about half of peasant farms did not exceed five acres) often had no choice but to leave the country.

During the interwar period, as many as 200,000 Ukrainian peasants emigrated from Poland. Many of them ended up in the United States and, after immigration there was closed in the mid-1920s, in Canada and Argentina. Approximately the same number of Jews left Poland, with most of them (up to 75,000) going to Palestine and the rest to Argentina and the United States. Both worsening economic conditions (most Jews in Galicia and the rest of Poland lived in poverty) and rising anti-Semitism, which resulted in the boycott of Jewish shops initiated by Polish nationalists and attacks on Jewish communities, drove Jewish emigration. In the latter half of the 1930s, after the death of Józef Piłsudski, the head of state, who tried to curb anti-Semitism, dozens of Jews were killed and hundreds injured in riots and skirmishes throughout Poland. The Polish government tried to "solve" the "Jewish question" by asking the Western powers and their Jewish communities to help the impoverished Jews of Poland or to take Jewish refugees. Western governments were not responsive, to say the least.

THE ECONOMIC AND cultural policies implemented by the Polish authorities in the Ukrainian lands in the 1920s ran directly counter to those pursued at the time by the Bolsheviks in Soviet Ukraine. Instead of promoting rapid industrial development, Polish authorities relied on agriculture; instead of integrating Ukrainians into the state apparatus, they encouraged emigration and promoted the influx not only of Polish administrators but also of Polish colonists into the region. But the Polish state had one feature that the Soviet Union never possessed—a political system built on the principles of electoral democracy. Even after Józef Piłsudski's coup of 1926, the Polish state maintained elements of political pluralism and religious toleration that allowed Ukrainians to establish their own political parties, churches, and cultural organizations.

After the defeat of Ukrainian statehood in Galicia in 1919, the Greek Catholic Church reclaimed its role there as the main national institution, while its head, Metropolitan Andrei Sheptytsky, assumed the status of generally recognized national leader. If the former was not a new phenomenon—the church had performed that function at least since the Revolution of 1848—Sheptytsky's undertaking the role of national leader was quite a novelty. A descendant of a Ruthenian noble family that had given the church a metropolitan back in the eighteenth century, Sheptytsky was born Roman Catholic to a family that had been culturally Polonized for more than one generation. Many in Ukrainian society regarded his adherence to the Greek Catholic Church, followed by his ascension at the turn of the twentieth century to the highest position in its hierarchy, as a Polish attempt to take over the last Ukrainian "national" institution in the land. But Sheptytsky, who felt himself more a loyal subject of Austria-Hungary than a son of Poland, did his best to protect his church and its members from the Polonizing efforts of the new Polish state. With the spread of the Polish language and the authorities' refusal to introduce nationality as a census category, religion, in this case Greek Catholicism, became one of the main markers of Ukrainian identity in interwar Galicia.

A party with deep prewar roots, the National Democratic Alliance, dominated Ukrainian politics in interwar Galicia; its leaders came from the ranks of the Ukrainian National Democratic Party of Austrian times. Galician politics entered a new era in 1929 when the Ukrainian Military Organization, a clandestine network led by Colonel Yevhen Konovalets, who had been active in the struggle for independence in eastern Ukraine in 1918 and 1919, turned into a political party called the Organization of Ukrainian Nationalists (OUN). The new organization inherited from its predecessor the goal of Ukrainian independence and irredentism, as well as the conspiratorial structure and terrorist tactics employed to achieve its goals. New was the ideology of radical nationalism, which the veterans of the wars for independence from 1918 to 1921 had simply lacked. The new ideology condemned the liberal nationalism of the leaders of the prewar Ukrainian movement, whom the OUN accused of limiting themselves to issues of language and fostering a culture of defeatism. It proclaimed the nation as its supreme value and aimed at the creation of a "new man." Dmytro Dontsov, a native of eastern Ukraine and a former social democrat, formulated this ideology. Dontsov never joined the OUN but shaped the new generation of its leaders and activists through his writings.

Almost immediately, the OUN, at best a marginal force on the Ukrainian political scene, proved its ability to influence that scene far beyond its actual political weight. The OUN scored big in June 1934, when its members assassinated the Polish minister of the interior, Bronisław Pieracki, claiming that he had played a critical role in the Pacification—a series of repressive measures taken against Ukrainian activists in the fall of 1930. The killing of Pieracki followed the assassination of a Soviet diplomat in Lviv in the fall of 1933 in retaliation for the 1932–1933 famine in Soviet Ukraine. The same man organized both assassinations: a twenty-five-year-old student at the Lviv Polytechnical Institute, Stepan Bandera, who became head of the OUN network in Galicia in June 1933. The public learned more about Bandera and OUN ideology after his arrest and prosecution by the Polish police. Bandera's trial for the assassination of Pieracki took place in Warsaw; a second trial followed in 1936 in Lviv for the killing in July 1934 (after Bandera's arrest) of a respected Ukrainian director of a Lviv gymnasium whom the OUN had accused of cooperating with the Polish police.

In his closing statement at the Lviv trial, Bandera explained why he and his comrades not only took the lives of others but also risked their own: "The OUN values the lives of its members very highly, but as we understand our idea, it is so grand that when it comes to its realization, not only individual sacrifices but hundreds and thousands must be offered in order to realize it." Bandera was talking about the goal of an independent Ukraine. For his role in the assassination of Pieracki, Bandera received the death sentence, later commuted to seven life terms. He would go free in September 1939, when the

German and Soviet invasion of Poland created chaos in Polish jails, allowing many prisoners, Bandera among them, simply to walk through their gates.

THE ORGANIZATION OF Ukrainian Nationalists had distinct Galician roots, but in the 1930s it made inroads into Ukrainian territories beyond Galicia, especially in the former Russian province of Volhynia. Ethnic relations there were quite different from those in Galicia. According to the 1931 census, 68 percent of Volhynians claimed Ukrainian as their mother tongue, while 17 percent gave Polish and 10 percent Yiddish. Before World War I, Volhynia was a hotbed of Russian nationalism, with local Ukrainian peasants lacking a distinct national identity and sending to the Russian Duma members of the Union of the Russian People and its sister organizations. After its incorporation into the Polish state, the province had become an object of intensive Polish colonization as well as a sphere of competition between two Ukrainian nation-building projects. Both were Ukrainian, but one, modeled on Galicia, was strongly anti-Polish, while the other was culturally and linguistically Ukrainian but politically loyal to the Polish regime.

The Polish government did its best to seal off Volhynia from the "harmful" influence of Galician nationalism. It introduced the so-called Sokal border, named after a town on the boundary between Galicia and Volhynia, to limit the territorial extent of the activities of Galician Ukrainian institutions. The Ukrainian Greek Catholic Church was allowed no representation in Volhynia, Polisia, Podlachia, or the Kholm region, as Greek Catholics there were subordinate to the Polish Roman Catholic Church. In areas north of the Sokal border, the government prohibited the activities of the Prosvita (Enlightenment) Society and limited the distribution of literature from Galicia. It made special efforts to prevent the OUN from establishing its network in Volhynia.

One of the strongest supporters and enforcers of the Sokal border was Henryk Józewski, onetime Polish interior minister and governor of Volhynia from 1928 to 1938. An ethnic Pole born and educated in Kyiv, Józewski had served as deputy minister of interior in the Ukrainian government of Symon Petliura. He became a promoter of the Petliura-Piłsudski alliance in 1921 and, as head of Piłsudski's chancellery and interior minister, championed the cause of Polish-Ukrainian accommodation. He considered such a prospect realistic if Volhynia were shielded from the destructive influences of Galicia. Józewski worked closely with "good Ukrainians," representatives of the

Petliura emigration in Poland—his former comrades in arms from Dnieper Ukraine—to foster a version of Ukrainian nationalism in Volhynia loyal to Poland. He supported an Orthodox Church independent of Moscow under the jurisdiction of the metropolitan of Warsaw and the patriarch of Constantinople. He also supported moderate Ukrainian politicians in parliamentary elections. Among them was Petliura's nephew Stepan Skrypnyk, a member of the Polish parliament and future Orthodox bishop, who would win election as patriarch of the Ukrainian Orthodox Church independent of Moscow after Ukraine gained its independence in 1991.

Nationalist and anti-Polish ideas came to Volhynia not only from Galicia with members of the OUN but also from Soviet Ukraine with adherents of the Communist Party of Western Ukraine (CPWU). The latter were significantly more numerous than the former. In the mid-1930s, the CPWU had approximately 1,600 members and the OUN about 800. Both groups offered Ukrainian peasants an ideological product that combined social and national revolution. In the late 1930s, the authorities stepped up repression against communists and nationalists alike, again with many more arrests among the communists: the police detained close to 3,000 supporters of communist organizations and about 700 nationalists. Despite political persecution unleashed by the Stalin regime in the 1930s, on the eve of the Soviet invasion of Poland in September 1939, Volhynian youth continued to listen to Soviet radio and look up to Soviet Ukraine.

Józewski counteracted Soviet influence by attempting to close the Polish-Soviet border to Bolshevik incursions and clamp down on pro-Soviet peasant insurrections in Volhynia, but he also found inspiration in the Soviet Ukrainization policy and sought to turn Volhynia into a Ukrainian Piedmont. In a major departure from the educational policies adopted by the Polish government in Galicia, Józewski supported the establishment of Ukrainian schools in Volhynia. He also helped make Ukrainian an obligatory subject in bilingual Polish-Ukrainian schools. The Volhynian experiment came to an end in 1938 with Józewski's resignation as governor and a general hardening of the Polish attitude toward national minorities after Piłsudski's death in 1935. Despite all his efforts, Józewski failed to stop the spread of nationalist ideas in Volhynia. His toleration of the Ukrainian language and identity helped turn the province, strongly influenced by Russian imperialist currents before 1914, into a stronghold of Ukrainian nationalism with powerful anti-Polish overtones.

Nationalists and communists managed to cross both internal barriers (like the Sokal border in Poland) and international ones, represented by the boundaries of interwar states. The case of Ukrainians in interwar Romania attests to the ability of both groups to do just that—ignore international boundaries. Under a million ethnic Ukrainians lived in interwar Romania, settled in northern Bukovyna, southern Bessarabia, and Maramureş. Like Poland in that period, Romania varied its policies toward different groups of Ukrainians.

The Romanian government welcomed former veterans of the Petliura army and gave formerly Russian-ruled territories of Ukraine, southern Bessarabia in particular, Ukrainian schools. Official policy was quite different vis-à-vis the formerly Austrian-ruled territories, with their much higher level of ethnic mobilization. In the former Austrian region of northern Bukovyna, the increasingly dictatorial Romanian regime imposed restrictions on Ukrainian cultural and political activities that exceeded those introduced by the Polish regime in Galicia. Besides introducing an agricultural reform that favored Romanian settlement in the region at the expense of Ukrainian peasants, the government undertook a major Romanization of Ukrainians, treating them as Romanians who had somehow forgotten their native language. Romanian became the sole language of administration and education in northern Bukovyna, and even the Orthodox liturgy (the region was predominantly Orthodox) was supposed to be served in Romanian instead of Church Slavonic.

The Romanian regime was anything but popular among the Ukrainians, who looked for alternative ideologies and political parties to represent their interests. If southern Bessarabia was more open to communist propaganda, northern Bukovyna became fertile ground for the spread of nationalist ideas. The largest Ukrainian political party in northern Bukovyna, the national democrats, did their best to develop cultural organizations and defend the interests of the Ukrainian population in parliament. They had some success in the late 1920s but were generally unable to change government policies. This opened the door to more radical groups, including members of the OUN, who formed their first cell in Bukovyna in 1934. The nationalists, most of whom were students, soon became active in Bessarabia and Maramureş and published the popular newspaper *Svoboda* (*Liberty*), which had 7,000 subscribers before the Romanian authorities banned it in 1937. Repressive measures against the nationalists that year forced them underground, where the organization survived the outbreak of World War II.

IN THE 1920s and early 1930s, the communists turned out to be more effective than nationalists in crossing one more European border, that of Czechoslovakia. The breakup of the former Habsburg Monarchy caught approximately half a million Ukrainians in Transcarpathia, part of the Hungarian realm of Austria-Hungary, before they had managed to decide who they really were—Russians, Ukrainians, or a separate ethnic group called Ruthenians. They faced the same choices as the Galician Ruthenians in the second half of the nineteenth century, but the process here took much more time and effort. In 1919, the region voluntarily joined the newly created pan-Slavic state of Czechoslovakia, where it adopted the name Subcarpathian Rus'. The Czechoslovak government, while originally neutral with regard to the identity issue, eventually backed the development of a politically neutral Ruthenian identity. This was an improvement over Austro-Hungarian times, when Budapest had attempted to Magyarize the local population. Prague also supported economic development of the region, which was an agricultural backwater, accounting for only 2 percent of national manufacturing output. As in Poland and Romania, however, the Czechoslovak government gave most administrative positions not to Ukrainians but to ethnic Czechs and Slovaks and supported a program of resettlement to the region, reserving much of its land for colonists.

Czechoslovakia was the only eastern European country that not only declared but acted according to democratic values in the interwar period. In the case of Transcarpathia, that meant free and fair elections. Given the difficult economic situation in the region, the land hunger among the peasants, and the corresponding rise of social tensions, the major beneficiaries of the democratic freedoms granted by Prague were the communist and radical leftist parties: in 1924, the communists got 40 percent of the vote. The nation builders in Transcarpathia were hopelessly split. Proponents of the three strands of Ukrainian national identity—Russophile, Ukrainophile, and Ruthenian—competed with one another. The strongest were the Russophile and Ukrainophile factions. The pro-Ukrainian Prosvita (Enlightenment) Society had 96 reading rooms in the region versus 192 established by the Russophile Dukhnovich Society. The Orthodox Church was in the hands of the Russophiles, while the Ukrainophiles made inroads into the Greek Catholic Church, traditionally controlled by pro-Hungarian elements. Modern Ukrainian identity was a latecomer to Transcarpathia, but in the 1920s it became the most dynamic political force in the region, linking it with other Ukrainian territories in a diverse but cohesive project to build a modern Ukrainian nation.

OF ALL THE regimes that controlled parts of Ukrainian territory during the interwar period, only the communist authorities in Moscow allowed the Ukrainian national project some form of statehood and offered support for the development of Ukrainian culture. The communist project of Ukrainian nation building had broad appeal both in Soviet Ukraine and in the neighboring eastern European countries with large Ukrainian communities. But national communism as a means of resolving the Ukrainian question encountered serious obstacles to its implementation. In eastern Europe, proponents of a communist Ukraine encountered a variety of hurdles: anticommunist as well as anti-Ukrainian policies implemented by national governments; opposition from mainstream Ukrainian parties seeking a modus vivendi with existing regimes; and rising competition from the radical Ukrainian nationalist ideology. But the main reason for the failure of national communism lay in the dramatic changes in Soviet policy that occurred in the 1930s. They turned Soviet Ukraine, once imagined as a communist Piedmont, into a communist Pompeii: the eruption of the Stalinist volcano reduced to ashes the high hopes that Ukrainian nation builders had once cherished with regard to the revolutionary regime in Moscow.

CHAPTER 21

STALIN'S FORTRESS

O N DECEMBER 21, 1929, Joseph Stalin celebrated his fiftieth birthday. The event was marked as a state occasion, leaving no doubt within the Soviet Union or abroad that a new supreme leader had emerged from almost a decade of struggle among the heirs of Vladimir Lenin. During the years leading up to his triumph, Stalin had turned the secondary post of general secretary of the party into the most powerful position in the land, using the party machine to take control of the government and its repressive apparatus embodied in the Chief Political Directorate (GPU), a euphemism for the secret police.

Never before in peacetime had so much depended on the thoughts, actions, and whims of one individual. Stalin's power and influence surpassed that of Lenin and every one of his imperial predecessors, including Peter I. While it would be a mistake to explain all that happened in the Soviet Union in the 1930s by pointing to Stalin alone—he often reacted to events instead of shaping them—there is little doubt that Stalin and a narrow circle of aides made all crucial decisions of the period. Most of those aides were under the spell of Stalin's authority and intellect; as time went on, they often became fearful of raising their voices in opposition to their leader, whose cult of personality grew steadily throughout the 1930s. In their eyes, Stalin was the best hope for the survival of the revolutionary regime, which they believed to be under siege from abroad by the capitalist West and from within by the peasant majority of the population, whose mentality they regarded as petty bourgeois.

In a special edition of the newspaper *Pravda* issued on the occasion of Stalin's jubilee, numerous articles written by his loyal lieutenants lauded him not only as the continuator of the cause initiated by Karl Marx, Friedrich Engels, and Vladimir Lenin but also as the "organizer and leader of socialist industrialization and collectivization." The first term, "socialist industrialization," referred to a Soviet-type industrial revolution, a government-funded and state-run program intended to bring about a revolutionary increase in industrial production, with priority given to the development of heavy industry, production of energy, and building of machinery. The second term, "collectivization," meant the creation of state-run collective farms based on the plots of land distributed to the peasants in the successful effort to win their support for the Bolshevik cause during and after the revolutionary wars. The implementation of both these programs in the late 1920s effectively spelled the end of the New Economic Policy, which had limited state control to leading industries and allowed elements of the market economy in agriculture, light industry, and services.

The Soviet leadership deemed the industrialization and collectivization programs, coupled with the Cultural Revolution—a set of policies designed to train a new generation of cadres to replace the old managerial and bureaucratic class—the best means of ensuring the survival of the communist regime in a hostile capitalist environment. The three programs were key elements of the Bolshevik plan for transforming a traditional agricultural society into a modern industrial power, with the proletariat replacing the peasantry as the dominant class. Throughout the 1920s, Soviet leaders argued about the pace at which to implement their vision. It became clear early on that they could fund industrialization only from within—the West was not eager to finance a country bent on world revolution—and the only internal source for the so-called socialist accumulation of capital was agriculture, in other words, the peasantry. Stalin had initially advocated "natural," evolutionary industrialization but then shifted position to insist on faster economic and social transformation.

THE KREMLIN REGARDED Ukraine, the second most populous Soviet republic, with slightly more than 2 percent of the Soviet Union's territory and close to 20 percent of its population, both as a source of funds for industrialization, given its agricultural output and potential, and as an area for investment, given the preexisting industrial potential in the east and south of the republic. But with the center fully in control of resources, the Ukrainian leadership had to lobby Moscow to invest capital, originally extracted from Ukrainian villages, in the Ukrainian cities. Ukraine did relatively well during the first five-year plan (1928–1933), receiving approximately 20 percent of all investment, which matched its share of the total Soviet population. But Ukraine found itself shortchanged after 1932, with the redirection of resources toward the industrialization of the Urals and Siberia, deeper in the Soviet East, away from the dangerous border with Poland. Most of the capital allocated to Ukraine went to the traditional southeastern industrial areas, farther from the border. The Right Bank of the Dnieper remained agricultural—most of the investment channeled there was for the construction of Red Army defense lines.

By far the largest construction project launched in Ukraine during the first five-year plan was Dniprohes, the Dnieper dam and electric power station built immediately beyond the Dnieper rapids. The site was chosen near the city of Oleksandrivsk, renamed Zaporizhia (Site Beyond the Rapids) in 1921—a reminder of the region's Cossack past and an acknowledgment of the importance of the Cossack myth during the revolutionary years. Once a small, sleepy town, Zaporizhia became a major industrial center, with metallurgical complexes growing around the power plant, which was the main supplier of energy for the industrialized Donbas and Kryvyi Rih regions. Apart from helping to produce electricity, the dam resolved a major problem that had hampered economic development by increasing the depth of the Dnieper sufficiently to drown the rapids and open the river fully to shipping. Dniprohes became the showpiece of the first Soviet five-year plan, while the population of Zaporizhia more than quadrupled in the course of a decade, growing from 55,000 in 1926 to 243,000 in 1937.

Like most Marxists of his time, Lenin believed in the transforming power of technology and once went on record as saying that communism meant Soviet rule plus the electrification of the whole country. Soviet propaganda claimed that Dniprohes was the first major step toward communism, but people at the top knew that they needed not only Soviet rule but also the efficiency of capitalism to get there. "The combination of Russian revolutionary sweep with American efficiency is the essence of Leninism in party and state activity," asserted Stalin in 1924. A number of American consultants, who lived in newly built brick cottages in an "American garden city" complete with two tennis courts and golf links, provided American expertise to the Dniprohes managers and engineers. The chief American consultant was Colonel Hugh Lincoln Cooper, a civil engineer who had cut his teeth on the construction of the Toronto Power Generating Station at Niagara Falls and the

Wilson Dam, which was part of the Tennessee Valley Authority. A proponent of free enterprise who once testified before Congress against direct US government involvement in development projects, Cooper agreed to the Bolsheviks' offer when they deposited the sum of $50,000 into his account even before the start of negotiations on the scope of his services to the project.

The "Russian revolutionary sweep" that Stalin wanted to combine with American efficiency came to Dniprohes with tens of thousands of Ukrainian peasants unqualified to do the job but eager to make a living. The number of workers employed in the construction of the dam and the electric power station grew from 13,000 in 1927 to 36,000 in 1931. The turnover was extremely high, even though the Soviets abandoned the earlier policy of equal pay for all categories of workers, and the top managers received up to ten times as much as unqualified workers; qualified workers made three times as much as the latter. Peasants had to turn into workers not only by learning trades but also by getting accustomed to coming in on time, not taking breaks at will, and following the orders of their superiors. It was a tall order for many new arrivals at the construction site of communism. In 1932, the Dniprohes administration hired 90,000 workers and released 60,000.

On May 1, 1932, after five years of construction, engineers ran the first tests on the turbines and generators produced by American companies, including the Newport News Shipbuilding and Drydock Company and General Electric. In October the brand-new plant, whose original estimated cost of $50 million had increased eightfold by the time of completion, was officially inaugurated for operation. The formal head of the Soviet state, Mikhail Kalinin, chairman of the Supreme Soviet, came to the site to preside over the ceremony. Speeches were made; communism was praised. Somewhat later, Colonel Cooper and five other American consultants received the Order of the Red Banner of Labor for their contribution to the construction of communism.

The construction of Dniprohes made history in more than one way. For the first time since the beginning of industrial development in Ukraine, the main workforce consisted not of ethnic Russians but of Ukrainians. The latter constituted approximately 60 percent of employees, while the former amounted only to 30 percent. The reasons for this shift would have been obvious to anyone who had left the Dniprohes construction site in October 1932 and explored the countryside, which was bracing itself for the coming man-made famine.

IN THE LATE 1920s, the Ukrainian village became as inhospitable to its inhabitants as the Russian village had been before the revolution, if not more so. It was not poor soil or bad weather but the dramatically changed political climate that made the Ukrainian village a living hell for the peasants, driving them out of their homes to construction sites such as Dniprohes. That was the result of Stalin's policy of forced collectivization, which expelled the peasants from their natural habitat in the process of squeezing all possible resources out of the village.

In the fall of 1929, with the support of Lazar Kaganovich, the former general secretary of the Communist Party of Ukraine recalled to Moscow the previous year and placed in charge of the agricultural sector, Stalin stepped up the collectivization of land and households, demanding an all-out drive to enforce the policy. Waged throughout the USSR, this campaign hit hardest in the grain-producing areas, of which Ukraine was among the most productive. Tens of thousands of GPU officers, party officials, and rank-and-file party members arrived in the countryside to coerce the peasants to join the collective farms, which meant giving up their private parcels of land, as well as their horses and agricultural equipment. In March 1930, the authorities reported the collectivization of up to 70 percent of all arable land—a more than tenfold increase from the previous year, when less than 6 percent of all land had belonged to collective and state farms. Most of the peasants were bullied into joining the collective farms, but many resisted. By the spring of 1930, a wave of peasant uprisings engulfed the Ukrainian countryside. In March 1930 alone, the authorities registered more than 1,700 peasant revolts and protests. Rebels killed dozens of Soviet administrators and activists and attacked and assaulted hundreds more. In regions of Ukraine bordering on Poland, whole villages rose up and marched toward the border to escape the terror of Stalin's collectivization campaign.

With peasants in strategically important borderlands in revolt and the wave of peasant unrest spreading to other parts of the Soviet Union, the government used the army and the secret police to go after the rebels. They mainly targeted the well-to-do peasantry, which had no incentive to join the collective farms and often led protests against the forced collectivization of peasant property. The authorities not only arrested and imprisoned leaders of the revolts but also expelled from Ukraine and forcibly resettled anyone branded a *kurkul'* (Russian: *kulak*)—a term applied originally to well-off peasants but then extended to include anyone who did not belong to the poorest stratum of the village population. In 1930, the Soviets deported up to 75,000 alleged *kurkul'* families from Ukraine to remote parts of Kazakhstan and Siberia. Many were taken to remote forests by train and left to die of disease and malnutrition.

But opposition in the village was too great to counter with repression alone, and the authorities decided to make a tactical retreat. In March 1930, Stalin published an article with the telling title "Dizziness with Success," in which he blamed forced collectivization on overzealous local officials. The party activists interpreted the article as a party order to stop forced collectivization, and over the next few months half the previously collectivized land reverted to peasants leaving collective farms. But the retreat was temporary. By the fall of 1930, the forced collectivization campaign had resumed. This time the peasants opted largely for passive forms of resistance, including refusal to grow more grain and agricultural produce than necessary for survival, the slaughter of domestic animals to preclude their confiscation by the state, and flight from the village, often to industrial centers such as Zaporizhia, where they joined the new socialist proletariat.

Faced with this new form of peasant resistance, Stalin and his aides refused to admit defeat and accused the peasants of sabotage and attempting to starve the cities and undermine industrialization. The authorities declared that the peasants were hiding grain and demanded greater quotas both from the collectivized peasantry and from those who refused to join the collective farms. The regime singled Ukraine out for especially harsh treatment, as it was crucial to the fulfillment of Moscow's economic plans. By mid-1932, 70 percent of Ukraine's households were collectivized, as opposed to an average of 60 percent across the Soviet Union. The republic that produced 27 percent of Soviet grain became responsible for 38 percent of all grain deliveries to the state. The new policy brought famine and mass starvation to Ukraine in the winter and spring of 1932, hitting the most populous agricultural areas of the forest-steppe zone.

Hundreds of thousands starved, and more than 80,000 died of hunger in 1932 in the Kyiv region alone. Especially hard hit were the sugar-beet production areas southwest of Kyiv, around the cities of Bila Tserkva and Uman. Vlas Chubar, head of the Ukrainian government, admitted in June 1932 that excessive requisitions, which left the peasants nothing to eat, had caused the famine. He wrote to Stalin, "Given the overall impossibility of fulfilling the grain-requisition plan, the basic reason for which was the lesser harvest in Ukraine as a whole and the colossal losses incurred during the harvest (a result of the weak economic organization of the collective farms and their utterly inadequate management from the districts and from the center), a system was put in place of confiscating all grain produced by individual farmers, including seed stocks, and almost complete confiscation of all produce from the collective farms."

According to Chubar, the famine most severely affected individual non-collectivized peasants whose property the state had requisitioned for their failure to meet procurement quotas. Next on the list were members of collective farms with large families. By March and April 1932, thousands of people were either starving or dying of hunger in hundreds of villages. In May 1932, a representative of the Kyiv Central Committee of the Communist Party picked seven villages in the Uman district at random. There were 216 registered deaths from hunger that month, and 686 individuals were expected to die in the next few days. In one of those villages, Horodnytsia, wrote the party official to his bosses in Kharkiv, the capital of the Ukrainian SSR, "up to 100 have died; the daily death toll is 8–12; people are swollen with hunger on 100 of 600 homesteads." Chubar asked Stalin to provide Ukraine with famine relief, but the general secretary would not hear of it. He denied the reality of the famine and banned the word itself from official correspondence.

Stalin attributed the failure of his policies not only to peasant resistance to collectivization and procurement quotas but also to covert resistance on the part of the Ukrainian party cadres. "*Most important* now is Ukraine," wrote Stalin to Kaganovich in August 1932.

> They say that in two oblasts of Ukraine (Kyiv and Dnipropetrovsk, I think), about 50 district committees have come out *against* the grain-procurement plan, calling it *unrealistic*. . . . If we do not start fixing the situation in Ukraine right away, we may lose Ukraine. Bear in mind that Piłsudski is not dawdling. . . . Also bear in mind that in the Communist Party of Ukraine (500,000 members, ha-ha), there is no lack (yes, no lack!) of corrupt elements, committed and latent Petliurites, and, finally, outright agents of Piłsudski. As soon as things get worse, those elements will not hesitate to open a front within (and outside) the party, *against* the party.

The master of the Kremlin was clearly concerned about the regime's prospects of survival. He had never gotten over the surprise attack of Polish and Ukrainian troops on Kyiv in the spring of 1920. At that time, former Ukrainian Socialist Revolutionaries had joined the advancing forces of Józef

Piłsudski and Symon Petliura. Stalin feared a recurrence of 1920 on a larger scale. In the early 1930s, party membership in Ukraine was approaching half a million, with 60 percent consisting of ethnic Ukrainians—the result of the Ukrainization policy. Would those cadres remain loyal to Stalin if Piłsudski invaded again? He had serious doubts. In July 1932, the Soviet Union signed a nonaggression pact with the selfsame Piłsudski, ensuring that there would be no attack from the West for the next three years. In Stalin's mind, the time had come to "secure Ukraine" by requisitioning grain, teaching the peasants who had resisted collectivization a lesson, and purging the Ukrainian party apparatus of those who refused to follow his orders.

Stalin's August 1932 letter to Kaganovich included a detailed plan for avoiding the "loss" of Ukraine. He suggested replacing the current leaders of the Ukrainian party and government, as well as the leadership of the secret police, with new cadres. "We should set ourselves the goal of turning Ukraine into a real fortress of the USSR, a truly model republic," he wrote. In November, Stalin sent a plenipotentiary to Ukraine to take over the secret police apparatus. In December, he turned a Politburo meeting on grain procurement into a platform to attack the Ukrainian party leadership for not only failing to fulfill quotas but also distorting the party line on Ukrainization. "The Central Committee and the Soviet of People's Commissars note," stated the resolution prepared on Stalin's orders, "that instead of correct Bolshevik conduct of nationality policy in a number of districts of Ukraine, Ukrainization was conducted mechanically, without taking account of the concrete particulars of each district, without careful selection of Ukrainian Bolshevik cadres, which made it easier for bourgeois nationalist elements, Petliurites, and others to create their legal covers, their counterrevolutionary cells and organizations."

The Politburo resolution spelled the end of Ukrainization in regions of the North Caucasus and the Far East settled by Ukrainians. It also served as the basis for an attack on the Ukrainization policy and its cadres in Ukraine itself, leading to the dismissal or arrest of thousands of party functionaries and the suicide of Mykola Skrypnyk, the people's commissar of education and main promoter of Ukrainization at the state level. Stalin blamed Ukrainian nationalists at home and abroad for causing the Ukrainian peasantry to sabotage party policy and hide grain from the state, thereby undermining the industrialization campaign. The attack on the Ukrainian peasantry went hand in hand with the attack on Ukrainian culture. The famine that was beginning in Ukraine when the Politburo issued its resolution on procurements and Ukrainization resulted not only from Stalin's policy toward the peasantry and the party apparatus but also from his shift of nationality policy that equated resistance to the grain requisitions with nationalism.

In December 1932, Stalin sent Kaganovich and the head of the Soviet government, Viacheslav Molotov, to Ukraine to ensure that the unrealistic grain-procurement quotas would be met. Led by Moscow plenipotentiaries and terrorized by the GPU, Ukrainian party cadres took all they could from the starving and, in many cases, dying peasantry. The authorities punished those villages that failed to fulfill their quotas by cutting off supplies of basic goods, including matches and kerosene, and confiscating not only grain but also livestock and anything else that could be used as food. The first deaths caused by the new famine were reported in December 1932; by March 1933, death from starvation was a mass phenomenon. The party bosses, now alarmed, bombarded Kharkiv and Moscow with requests for assistance. It came in insufficient quantities, too late to save millions of starving peasants. Most of the victims died in late spring and early summer, when food supplies ran out completely. Many died because they ate grass or early vegetables—their stomachs could not digest raw foodstuffs after months of starvation.

Hardest hit were the Ukrainian parklands in the Kyiv and Kharkiv oblasts that had suffered from famine earlier in the spring—too weak to do proper sowing, the peasants there had little in the way of supplies and were the first to die. By the end of 1933, the Kyiv and Kharkiv oblasts had each lost up to a million inhabitants. The major grain-producing oblasts in the Ukrainian steppes, Odesa and Dnipropetrovsk, both lost in excess of 300,000 people. Less affected was the industrial Donbas, where 175,000 people died of hunger in 1933. The steppe areas suffered less from the famine than did the parklands because they had not experienced famine the previous year; also, if things got really bad, the peasants could find refuge at the construction sites of Zaporizhia, Kryvyi Rih, and the Donbas. Besides, in the spring of 1933 the Moscow government was much more willing to supply relief grain to the south than to central Ukraine: Moscow needed more grain, and keeping people alive in the major grain-producing areas to harvest crops was the only way to get it. Others could be left to die, and they did. Altogether, close to 4 million people perished in Ukraine as a result of the famine, more than decimating the country—every eighth person succumbed to hunger between 1932 and 1934.

The famine produced a different Soviet Ukraine. Stalin managed to keep it in his embrace by purging the party and government apparatus of those who would not go against their own people and take the last food supplies from the starving: of more than three hundred secretaries of district party committees, more than half lost their positions in the first half of 1933, many of them arrested and exiled. The rest would toe the party line no matter what. Those were the cadres Stalin wanted to keep, at least for the time being. He also got a new "socialist" peasantry. Those who survived the famine had learned their lesson: they could survive only by joining the party-controlled collective farms, which were taxed at a lower rate and, in the spring of 1933, were the only farms to receive government relief. The collectivization of the absolute majority of households and land, now an accomplished fact, dramatically changed the economy, social structure, and politics of the Ukrainian village.

Was the Great Ukrainian Famine (in Ukrainian, the Holodomor) a premeditated act of genocide against Ukraine and its people? In November 2006, the Ukrainian parliament defined it as such. A number of parliaments and governments around the world passed similar resolutions, while the Russian government launched an international campaign to undermine the Ukrainian claim. Political controversy and scholarly debate on the nature of the Ukrainian famine continue to this day, turning largely on the definition of the term "genocide." But a broad consensus is also emerging on some of the crucial facts and interpretations of the 1932–1933 famine. Most scholars agree that it was indeed a man-made phenomenon caused by official policy; while it also affected the North Caucasus, the lower Volga region, and Kazakhstan, only in Ukraine did it result from policies with clear ethnonational coloration: it came in the wake of Stalin's decision to terminate the Ukrainization policy and in conjunction with an attack on the Ukrainian party cadres. The famine left Ukrainian society severely traumatized, crushing its capacity for open resistance to the regime for generations to come.

STALIN USED THE Great Famine to turn Ukraine into an "exemplary Soviet republic," as he called it in his letter to Kaganovich. The transfer of the capital in 1934 from Kharkiv to Kyiv, whose intelligentsia, decimated by purges, no longer presented a challenge to the Soviet regime in Ukraine, completed the transformation of the autonomous and often independently minded republic into a mere province of the Soviet Union.

As the master of the Kremlin had wanted, Ukraine became a model of Soviet industrialization and collectivization. By the end of the 1930s, the industrial output of Ukraine exceeded that of 1913 eightfold, an achievement only slightly less impressive than that of the union's largest republic—Russia. The agricultural sector was fully collectivized, with 98 percent of all households and 99.9 percent of all arable land listed as collective property. The problem was that impeccable collectivization statistics belied agriculture's dismal performance. In 1940, Ukraine produced 26.4 million tons of grain, only 3.3 million more than in 1913, posting an increase in agricultural production that amounted to less than 13 percent. The village, devastated by the Great Famine and collectivization, could not keep pace with the rapidly growing industrial city. Although Ukraine underwent rapid industrialization and modernization, it paid a tremendous price for that "leap forward." Between 1926 and 1937, the population of Soviet Ukraine fell from 29 to 26.5 million, rising to slightly more than 28 million in 1939.

Many Ukrainians of all ethnic backgrounds perished in the Great Purge— the multiple waves of arrest, execution, and exile that engulfed the Soviet Union from 1936 to 1940, taking their greatest toll in 1937. As many as 270,000 people were arrested in Ukraine in 1937 and 1938, and close to half of them were executed. The Great Purge had the same objective as many of Stalin's other policies of the 1930s—to ensure the survival of the regime and Stalin's position as its supreme leader. Those of his former allies and enemies who still survived, including Lev Kamenev, Georgii Zinoviev, and Nikolai Bukharin, he had shot. In Ukraine, the same fate befell the leaders of the party, state, and secret police apparatus who had shown their loyalty to Stalin during the Great Famine. The regime wanted docile new cadres unaware of the crimes of the past who would serve the leader faithfully. Aside from party cadres, the terror hit former members of non-Bolshevik parties and national minorities hardest. Ukraine, as a border republic with numerous minorities whose loyalty the regime questioned, again came under severe scrutiny. Ethnic Poles and Germans topped the hierarchy of enemies. Poles accounted for close to 20 percent of those arrested, and Germans for about 10 percent. The USSR targeted both groups, whose portion of the overall population did not exceed 1.5 percent, as potential spies and "fifth columnists" of its main adversaries at the time, Poland and Germany.

In 1938, Stalin sent his new lieutenant, Nikita Khrushchev, to Ukraine to carry out the last repressive measures and prepare the republic for what he believed to be a coming war. Khrushchev's task was the same as that of his predecessors: to turn Ukraine into a socialist fortress. "Comrades," declared Khrushchev to delegates at the Ukrainian party congress in June 1938, "we shall bend every effort to ensure that the task and directive of the Central

Committee of the All-Union Communist Party (Bolshevik) and Comrade Stalin—to make Ukraine a fortress impregnable to enemies—is fulfilled with honor." The next few years would test the strength of the Ukrainian redoubt.

In October 1938, the government of the rump Czechoslovakia (then being dismembered by Adolf Hitler) appointed a Ukrainian activist, the Reverend Avhustyn Voloshyn, to lead the government of autonomous Transcarpathia, renamed from Subcarpathian Rus' to Carpatho-Ukraine. The decision followed the transfer of the Hungarian-populated regions of Transcarpathia, along with its two main urban centers, Uzhhorod and Mukacheve, to Hungary. The new government replaced a short-lived administration of Russophile orientation and adopted Ukrainian as the official language. It also created its own paramilitary units to resist Hungarian and Polish militias. Called the Carpathian Sich—a reference to the Sich Riflemen of Galicia and Sich Cossacks of Dnieper Ukraine—those units often consisted of young members of the Organization of Ukrainian Nationalists (OUN), who came from Poland to fight for the cause of Ukrainian statehood.

The year 1939 began with rumors in European foreign ministries that Hitler planned to use Carpatho-Ukraine as a springboard to attack Soviet Ukraine and "reunite" all ethnic Ukrainian territories. In January, Hitler offered the visiting Polish foreign minister, Józef Beck, an exchange of Danzig and the Polish corridor to the Baltic Sea for new territories in Ukraine to be acquired as a result of the German invasion of the USSR. Beck declined the offer. Irrespective of Beck's position, Hitler decided not to play the Ukrainian card against Stalin, at least not immediately. When his troops moved into Prague in March 1939 to end the existence of Czechoslovakia, Hitler decided against the creation of an independent Ukrainian state and gave Transcarpathia to his ally, Hungary. The government of autonomous Transcarpathia met this decision with surprise and disappointment.

On March 15, the day Hitler's forces moved into Prague, the parliament of Carpatho-Ukraine proclaimed the independence of its land. The new country chose blue and yellow as the colors of its national flag and adopted the Ukrainian national anthem, "Ukraine Has Not Yet Perished." The declaration of independence did not stop the Hungarian army, which moved into the region without encountering resistance from Czechoslovak forces. The only troops fighting the advancing Hungarians were members of the Carpathian Sich units. "At a time when eight million Czechs submitted to the rule of the German state without offering the least resistance, thousands of Ukrainians came out against a Hungarian army of several thousand," wrote a

Ukrainian reporter at the time. Altogether the Carpathian Sich had about 2,000 fighters. As the forces were unequal, Ukrainian resistance was soon crushed. The government of the Reverend Voloshyn left the country, and Hungarian soldiers or Polish border guards captured many surviving members of the OUN on their way back to Galicia. This was the first baptism of fire for the nationalist fighters: more would come.

Stalin was sufficiently worried by the developments in Transcarpathia to ridicule the idea of German support for Ukrainian independence in a speech to a party congress in Moscow in March 1939. The existence of significant Ukrainian territories outside the Soviet Union that could be used by Hitler to challenge Stalin's control over Soviet Ukraine became a major concern of his "fortress builders" on the eve of World War II. The defensive bulwark seemed to have developed a large crack—the threat of Ukrainian irredentism.

CHAPTER 22

HITLER'S *LEBENSRAUM*

A DOLF HITLER PRESENTED his views on the future of the world in *Mein Kampf* (*My Struggle*), the book he dictated in the Landsberg Prison in Bavaria during his incarceration for his role in the Munich Beer Hall Putsch in November 1923. In his prison cell, the former Habsburg subject pledged to fight against the so-called Jewish conspiracy to dominate the world and propounded the creation of a German empire that would provide the Aryan race with *Lebensraum* (living space) in eastern Europe. Hitler spent only a year in prison. From 1933, when he became chancellor of Germany and his Nazi Party came to power, he had enough resources to begin implementing his plans. Hitler's ideas, spelled out for the first time in 1923, had a profound impact on the world, but in few places was their impact as destructive and their consequence as tragic as in Ukraine—the centerpiece of Hitler's vision of *Lebensraum.*

The idea of *Lebensraum* for the Germans was not Hitler's creation. First formulated before World War I, it envisioned the acquisition of German territory all over the world. Germany's defeat in the war made colonial expansion across the British-controlled seaways all but impossible, and Hitler saw room for growth in eastern Europe alone. "It would have been more practical to undertake that military struggle for new territory in Europe rather than to wage war for the acquisition of possessions abroad," he wrote in *Mein Kampf.* The Treaty of Brest-Litovsk (1918), which included the recognition of a Ukraine independent of Russia and occupied by German and Austrian troops, provided one model for German eastward expansion. But Hitler had little appetite for nation building in the east. His goal was different: to wipe out the existing population all the way to the Volga and settle the fertile lands of eastern Europe—Ukraine in particular—with German colonists. "Too much importance cannot be placed on the need to adopt a policy that will make it possible to maintain a healthy peasant class as the basis of the national community," wrote Hitler in *Mein Kampf.* "Many of our present evils have their origin exclusively in the disproportion between the urban and rural portions of the population."

Hitler's rural utopia for the Germans required not only the acquisition of new territory but also its deurbanization and depopulation. His vision for eastern Europe differed greatly from the one introduced by the Bolsheviks and promoted by Joseph Stalin. Both dictators were prepared to use brute force to build their utopias, and both needed Ukrainian territory, soil, and agriculture to achieve their goals, but they had dissimilar attitudes toward the cities and the population at large. Ukraine would learn what that meant in practice and assess the degree of difference between the two regimes during its three-year occupation by Nazi Germany from 1941 to 1944. With its pre-1914 reputation as the breadbasket of Europe and one of the highest concentrations of Jews on the continent, Ukraine would become both a prime object of German expansionism and one of the Nazis' main victims. Between 1939 and 1945 it would lose almost 7 million citizens (close to 1 million of them Jewish), or more than 16 percent of its prewar population. Only Belarus and Poland—two other countries within the sphere of Hitler's *Lebensraum*—sustained higher proportional losses.

IN *MEIN KAMPF*, Hitler envisioned an alliance with Britain to defeat France and a pact with Russia to annihilate Poland. Ultimately, Russia— or, rather, the Soviet Union—was supposed to provide Hitler with what he wanted: land for settlement and a wealth of natural resources that would turn Germany into a continental empire whose links with its colonies the British navy could not disrupt. The alliance with Britain never materialized, but by the fall of 1939 Hitler had indeed accomplished an accord with the Soviet Union and the annihilation of Poland.

When World War II began with a German attack on Poland on September 1, 1939, Hitler and Stalin had already agreed on a partition of the Polish lands on the basis of the Molotov-Ribbentrop Pact, signed less than ten days earlier. As Stalin delayed Soviet entrance into the war, concerned about the reaction of Britain and France as well as the ongoing Soviet-Japanese conflict in Mongolia, German diplomats used the Ukrainian card to speed up the Soviet attack on Poland. They claimed that if the USSR continued to delay its invasion, Germany would have no choice but to create separate states in the territories assigned to the Soviet Union. The formation of a German-backed Ukrainian state in Galicia and Volhynia was the last thing Stalin wanted to see in that area. When he finally sent his troops across the Polish border, they marched under the pretext of defending the "fraternal" Ukrainian and Belarusian peoples.

By early October 1939, the Polish army had ceased to exist, destroyed by the attacks of the two powerful neighbors. The Soviets captured but then released most of its rank-and-file soldiers. The officers, however, met a different fate. The USSR detained close to 15,000 of them in three detention camps, one in Ukraine and two in Russia. In the spring of 1940, most of them would perish in Katyn Forest near Smolensk and other sites of mass murder. Initially, however, few people, especially among the non-Poles, suspected the Soviets of evil intentions. The Red Army, which was no match for the Germans in mechanization, demonstrated its superiority to the Polish troops in the quality of its armaments, which included new tanks, aircraft, and modern guns—all products of Stalin's industrialization effort. But to the surprise of many, the Soviet officers and soldiers were often badly dressed, poorly fed, and shocked by the relative abundance of food and goods in the Polish shops. The locals found Soviet officers ideologically indoctrinated, uncultured, and unsophisticated. For years, they would tell and retell stories about the wives of Red Army officers who allegedly attended theaters in nightgowns, believing them to be evening dresses. But the non-Polish citizens of the former Polish state were prepared to live with the well-armed and uncultured "liberators" as long as they promised to improve their lives, and for a while it seemed that they would.

Once the Red Army had taken Lviv and other major centers in Galicia and Volhynia, the occupiers held Soviet-style elections to the National Assembly of Western Ukraine, which in turn asked Kyiv and Moscow to annex Galicia and Volhynia to Soviet Ukraine. Nikita Khrushchev, the newly appointed party boss in Kyiv, insisted that the northern Polisia, including the city of Brest, also be transferred to Ukraine, but Stalin decided to assign that territory to the Belarusian republic. The new authorities made it possible for local Ukrainians and Jews to enter government service and take the positions in educational, medical, and other institutions denied them under Polish rule. They treated local Jews well but often turned those the Germans expelled from Poland back at the border. The authorities launched a comprehensive Ukrainization campaign, turning the Polish-language university, schools, theaters, and publishing houses into Ukrainian ones. They also nationalized large landholdings and distributed the land among the poor peasants. Pro-Soviet sympathies, always strong among members of communist and leftist parties and organizations in the region, grew even stronger.

But the honeymoon in relations between the Soviet authorities and the local Ukrainians did not last long. Never well disposed to organized religion—the institutional basis of Ukrainian identity in the former Polish republic—the Soviets confiscated the landholdings of the Greek Catholic Church and tried to limit the role of the traditional churches, both Orthodox and Greek Catholic, in public life. More surprising was the Soviet treatment of former leaders and rank-and-file members of the Communist Party of Western Ukraine, who were generally suspected of nationalism and eventually targeted by the Soviet secret police. The same suspicion soon fell on Ukrainian cadres promoted to senior positions in local government and education.

In 1940, the occupation authorities began mass arrests and deportations of the local population to the Far North, Siberia, and Central Asia. Former Polish government and police officials, members of Polish political parties, and military settlers brought to the region during the interwar period headed the list of "enemies of the people." In February 1940, the NKVD, Stalin's secret police, carried out the first mass deportation of close to 140,000 Poles. Nearly 5,000 deportees did not reach their destinations, dying of cold, disease, and malnutrition on the way. Altogether, between the fall of 1939 and June 1941, when Germany attacked the USSR, the Soviet secret police deported close to 1.25 million people from Ukraine. The NKVD also hunted members of the Organization of Ukrainian Nationalists (OUN), whose leaders, including Stepan Bandera, fled to the German-controlled part of Poland. Stalin saw them as a clear and present danger to his regime.

The fall of Paris to the advancing German armies in June 1940 caught Stalin by surprise and made him think that Hitler would soon turn eastward to attack the Soviet Union. The regime had to solidify its control over the newly acquired territories and remove potential "fifth columnists." Stalin also decided to occupy all parts of eastern Europe assigned to his sphere of influence by the Molotov-Ribbentrop Pact. These included the Baltic states of Estonia, Latvia, and Lithuania and parts of Romania, which comprised Bessarabia and Bukovyna. The Soviet leader annexed southern Bessarabia and northern Bukovyna, settled largely by Ukrainians, to Soviet Ukraine in August 1940. There the Soviet authorities introduced the same policies as they had earlier in Galicia and Volhynia, including the nationalization of land, promotion of local non-Romanian cadres, and Ukrainization of institutions. Arrests and deportations followed.

STALIN WAS PREPARING for an attack by his ally, Adolf Hitler. He expected it to take place in 1942, but it came a year earlier, catching the Soviet dictator by surprise. Hitler needed Soviet resources, including Ukrainian wheat and coal, as soon as possible, especially as he was still at war with Britain, and behind the British lion cornered on its islands loomed the much larger United States—the most powerful economy in the world. Hitler attacked the USSR against the objections of the Reich's leading economists, who argued that the invasion would solve none of Germany's problems and become a drain on the German economy. But the military brass preferred war with the Soviets to war with the West, and Hitler was happy to oblige.

In December 1940 he signed a directive ordering preparations for war with the Soviet Union. The operation was code-named Barbarossa after the twelfth-century German king and Holy Roman emperor who had led the Third Crusade. He had drowned while trying to cross a river in heavy armor instead of taking the bridge used by his troops. It was certainly a bad omen, but at the time those in the know paid no attention to historical precedent. Like Barbarossa before him, Hitler was prepared to take risks and cut corners. The planners aimed to defeat the Soviets and drive them beyond the Volga in the course of a campaign that would last no longer than three months. Hitler wanted his armies to take Leningrad first, capture the Donbas coal mines second, and then take Moscow. The Wehrmacht sent German soldiers to the front with no provision for winter clothing. This turned out to be a mistake, although it had the short-term benefit of misleading Stalin, who refused to believe that the Germans would attack without preparing for a winter campaign and was thus caught off guard when they invaded.

The invasion began in the early hours of June 22, 1941, along a front stretching from the Baltic Sea in the north to the Black Sea in the south. Germany and its allies, including Romania and Hungary, fielded some 3.8 million soldiers. Germany's Army Group South attacked Ukraine, advancing from positions in Poland and marching along the ancient route between the northern slopes of the Carpathians and the Prypiat marshes. The Romanians attacked in the south, moving into Ukraine between the southern slopes of the Carpathians and the Black Sea. The Huns had used these routes in the fifth century and the Mongols in the thirteenth when they invaded central Europe. Now the troops moved in the opposite direction, but they proceeded along the same unpaved roads, with mechanized divisions, not cavalry, raising dust. On the Soviet front, the Germans concentrated some 4,000 tanks and more than 7,000 artillery pieces. Over 4,000 aircraft covered the advance. The Germans had almost complete control of the air—a surprise Luftwaffe attack destroyed the bulk of Soviet military planes on the airfields before they could become airborne.

The Red Army had approximately the same number of men on the Soviet western border as the Germans and significantly more tanks, guns, and aircraft. The USSR's materiel, however, was inferior to the latest German models, and inexperienced officers, who had only recently replaced the more experienced commanders purged by Stalin, led its men into battle. Commanders abandoned their units, while the morale of the soldiers, many of them peasants who had survived the famine and collectivization, was low. It fell further with every passing day as the Germans took advantage of their surprise attack, gained territory rapidly, and inflicted devastating casualties on the retreating Soviet troops. What Stalin had considered his success—the acquisition of new territory after the signing of the Molotov-Ribbentrop Pact—turned out to be a trap. In the month preceding the invasion, he had moved his troops west of the defense lines built over the previous decade so as to protect the new borders, and now they had to defend a border that they had had no time to fortify. As envisioned by the planners of blitzkrieg warfare, the German panzer divisions cut through the Soviet defenses, encircling entire armies and creating havoc behind Red Army lines.

In western Ukraine, Red Army commanders launched a major counteroffensive in the region of Lutsk, Brody, and Rivne, sending all their tank formations into battle, only to be outmaneuvered and defeated by a much smaller Wehrmacht tank force. It would be all downhill after that. In three weeks, the Wehrmacht managed to advance eastward anywhere from three hundred to six hundred kilometers. Not only Galicia and Volhynia, recently occupied by Soviet forces, but also large parts of Right-Bank Ukraine were lost. More than 2,500 Soviet tanks and close to 2,000 aircraft were destroyed. Casualties were hard to count. In August, German divisions surrounded and imprisoned more than 100,000 Red Army soldiers near the city of Uman in Podolia, but they took the greatest prize near Kyiv the following month. Contrary to the advice of Red Army commanders, including the leading Soviet military strategist, Georgii Zhukov, Stalin refused to withdraw his troops from the Kyiv region, given the city's symbolic importance, and caused probably the greatest Soviet military disaster of the entire war.

Red Army units led by a native of the Chernihiv region, General Mykhailo Kyrponos, resisted the advance but could do little against German mechanized divisions. Kyiv fell to the Germans on September 19, 1941. General Kyrponos died in battle the next day near the town of Lokhvytsia. The Wehrmacht surrounded and took prisoner more than 660,000 Red Army soldiers in the Kyiv pocket. In October, the same fate befell close to 100,000 men between Melitopol and Berdiansk in southern Ukraine, and another 100,000 surrendered near Kerch in the Crimea in November. By the end of the year, when the Red Army was forced to abandon almost all of Ukraine, more than 3.5 million of its officers and soldiers were in enemy hands. The retreating Soviets followed a scorched-earth policy, removing industrial equipment, livestock, supplies, and people from areas they were about to leave. Altogether, they evacuated approximately 550 large factories and 3.5 million skilled laborers to the east.

MANY IN UKRAINE welcomed the German advance in the summer of 1941, hoping for the end of the terror unleashed by the Soviet occupation authorities in the years leading up to the war. This was true not only for the recently occupied regions of western Ukraine but also for central and eastern Ukraine, where the population never forgave the regime for the horrors of the famine and collectivization. Some expected that "national socialism" would bring true socialism. Others simply hoped for improved living standards. With Soviet salaries insufficient to buy even a pair of shoes, it was not difficult to nourish false hopes and imagine that the "European" Germans would make life better for the population they were "liberating" from Moscow's control. Many remembered the Austrians of the pre–World War I period and the German occupation of Ukraine in 1918, which was benign by the standards of the Stalinist terror. Some saw the return of the Germans as a prelude to the restoration of a Ukrainian state as it had been under Hetman Pavlo Skoropadsky. Those who awaited the Germans with such expectations were soon proved wrong, often dead wrong, irrespective of what had fed their hopes for a better life under German occupation.

The German minister for the occupied eastern territories, Alfred Rosenberg, a Baltic German educated in Moscow, among other places, originally put together German plans for Ukraine. He wanted to support Ukrainian,

Baltic, Belarusian, Georgian, and other Soviet nationalities' aspirations for independent statehood in order to undermine the Soviet Union. In his vision, a Ukrainian polity independent of Russia would become a client state of the Reich along with a Baltic federation, Belarus, and Finland. Indeed, Rosenberg's experts advocated the expansion of Ukrainian territory all the way to the Volga. But Rosenberg lost the political contest to head of the German security forces and later minister of the interior Heinrich Himmler, Reichstag president and aviation minister Hermann Göring, and other Nazi leaders eager to implement their racial ideology and squeeze the newly conquered territories for every economic resource they had. The 1918 Brest-Litovsk vision of eastern European states, Ukraine among them, controlled by Germany gave way in the summer of 1941 to a model, rooted in Hitler's *Mein Kampf*, of colonial dismemberment and exploitation.

The Germans divided the Ukrainian territories under their control into three parts: Galicia was lumped together with what had been Western Galicia and the Warsaw region into an entity called the General Government; most of Ukraine from Volhynia in the northwest to Zaporizhia in the southeast, along with southern Belarus around the cities of Pinsk and Homel, became the Reichskommissariat Ukraine; and eastern Ukraine, from Chernihiv in the north to Luhansk and Stalino (Yuzivka, Donetsk) in the south, remained under military command as an area too close to the front lines to be assigned to civilian administration. The division of Galicia and Volhynia and the aggregation of Volhynia with Dnieper Ukraine reflected German thinking about the region in terms of the divide established by the Russo-Austrian border in the late eighteenth century. The partitioning of Ukraine was not the only disappointment that befell those previously terrorized by the Soviets. They would soon discover that the Germans of 1941 were anything but the Germans of 1918.

The first to experience disappointment with the Nazi regime were the members of the Organization of Ukrainian Nationalists. The OUN had split in 1940, soon after one of its most radical leaders, Stepan Bandera, walked out of a Polish prison in September 1939. Bandera led a revolt against the old cadres and soon found himself at the helm of the OUN's largest faction and most radical members. In February 1941, they made a deal with the leaders of German military intelligence (Abwehr) to form two battalions of special operations forces from their supporters. One battalion, Nachtigall, was among the first German troops to enter Lviv on June 29. The next day it took part in the proclamation of Ukrainian independence by members of the Bandera faction of the OUN. This spelled the end of German cooperation with Bandera's followers. The Germans, who had very different plans for Ukraine, turned on their former allies, arresting scores of members of the Bandera faction, including Bandera himself, whom they told to denounce the declaration of independence. He refused and was sent to Sachsenhausen concentration camp, where he would spend most of the war. Two of his brothers were arrested as well and died in Auschwitz.

The Bandera faction of the OUN went overnight from the Germans' loyal ally to their enemy. The more moderate OUN faction, headed by Colonel Andrii Melnyk, tried to take advantage of the German conflict with its competitors and moved its expeditionary groups into central and eastern Ukraine to set up its network, influence the selection of Ukrainian cadres for the occupation administration, and conduct educational work and propaganda among the local population. The faction's operations came to a halt in late 1941, with the German administration taking ever stricter control over the Reichskommissariat Ukraine. Nazi police had hundreds of OUN members shot in Kyiv and other cities and towns of Ukraine. By early 1942, both factions of the OUN were at war with the Germans.

NAZI TREATMENT OF Soviet prisoners of war sent another signal, this time to the citizens of central and eastern Ukraine, that the Germans of 1941 bore no resemblance to the Germans of 1918. If the former were just occupiers, the latter were colonizers who treated the conquered as subhuman.

Before the war, Stalin had refused to sign the Geneva Convention of 1929 that regulated the treatment of prisoners of war—the USSR was a revolutionary power that did not abide by capitalist rules of conduct. When he tried to do so in the summer of 1941, it was too late: the Germans would not agree to extend to Soviet prisoners the treatment they offered POWs from the West. Whereas they treated the latter with a degree of respect, recognizing rank and providing access to medical attention, as well as to parcels of food and clothing, they denied Soviet prisoners of war all of that. Besides, they did not leave everyone who wanted to surrender alive; many they shot on the spot. On June 6, 1941, more than two weeks before the invasion, the headquarters had issued the order for troops to shoot on capture commissars and Red Army political officers, as well as NKVD men and Jews. Muslims who failed to prove that their circumcision had nothing to do with the Jewish religion also often met their end, as did, occasionally, Red Army commanders who fell into captivity. Those left alive got sent to makeshift concentration camps— old factories, schoolyards, often fields surrounded by barbed wire.

During forced death marches to those concentration camps, guards shot those wounded, ill, and weary prisoners who could no longer walk. The locals tried to feed the exhausted POWs and help them in any way they could, the assumption being that others were feeding and helping their own sons, husbands, and fathers mobilized into the Red Army before the war and probably facing the same ordeals. Once in camp, the prisoners often went without food and water, which caused hunger, starvation, and, ultimately, cannibalism. Disease took care of those who managed to survive on the meager rations. Nazi propaganda portrayed the Soviet POWs as subhuman, and their treatment was inhuman indeed. Ideology was only partly responsible for that. The Germans had not planned on taking hundreds of thousands, indeed millions, of prisoners. In the first months of the war, the more people died in captivity, the less trouble there was for the Wehrmacht. Not until November 1941 did the masters of the Reich economy begin to consider the POWs as a workforce, which was in short supply in Germany. In the course of the war, more than 60 percent of those captured on the eastern front died in captivity.

Ukrainians, like members of other Soviet-ruled nationalities of the western USSR, generally fared better in the camps than Russians and Muslims. At first the Germans even allowed them to go free, considering them a lesser threat than the Russians. Thus, in September 1941, the Nazis issued a directive allowing the release of Ukrainians, Belarusians, and Balts. Inmates could leave the camps if a relative claimed them (sometimes women claimed strangers as their husbands) or if they came from a particular region. The policy was reversed in November, but probably tens, if not hundreds, of thousands of Ukrainian men drafted into the Red Army and captured by the Germans in the summer and fall of 1941 managed to survive the ordeal and return to their families. Later in the war, Ukrainians, Belarusians, and Balts were more likely than Russians to be recruited into police battalions and trained to secure eastern European territory cleansed of local inhabitants and settled by German colonists. The Nazis sent some to guard concentration and extermination camps in Poland once the leadership of the Third Reich realized that the promised German colonial paradise in eastern Europe was being postponed indefinitely.

In the twisted world of the Nazi occupation, the Holocaust turned former Soviet POWs from victims into perpetrators. In Auschwitz, by far the best-known Nazi concentration camp, the first to die in the gas chambers were Soviet POWs—the Germans tested Zyklon-B gas on them in September 1941. Later, guards recruited from the POW camps—the so-called Trawniki men, named for the place where they were trained—helped conduct Jews arriving at the camp to the gas chambers. Jewish men selected from the previous transports then gathered and sorted the clothes of the victims. In the camps, survival too often meant participating in the destruction of fellow humans. Ukraine under German occupation became a large-scale model of a concentration camp. As in the camps, the line between resistance and collaboration, victimhood and criminal complicity with the regime became blurred but by no means indistinguishable. Everyone made a personal choice, and those who survived had to live with their decisions after the war, many in harmony, some in unending anguish. But almost everyone suffered survivor's guilt.

THE HOLOCAUST WAS the single most horrific episode of the Nazi occupation of Ukraine, which had no shortage of horror. Most Ukrainian Jews who became victims never made it either to Auschwitz or to any other extermination camp. Heinrich Himmler's *Einsatzgruppen*, with the help of local police formed by the German administration, gunned them down on the outskirts of the cities, towns, and villages in which they lived. The shooting began in the summer of 1941 in all territories taken by the Wehrmacht from the retreating Soviets. By January 1942, when high Nazi officials gathered in the Berlin suburb of Wannsee to coordinate the implementation of the Final Solution—the eradication of European Jewry—Nazi death squads had killed close to 1 million Jewish men, women, and children. They did so in broad daylight, sometimes in plain sight and almost always within earshot of the local non-Jewish population. The Holocaust in Ukraine and the rest of the western Soviet Union not only destroyed the Jewish population and its communal life, as was the case in Europe generally, but also traumatized those who witnessed it.

Every sixth Jew who died in the Holocaust—altogether close to a million people—came from Ukraine. By far the best-known massacre, with the greatest number of victims, took place in Babi Yar (in Ukrainian, Babyn Yar, or Old Woman's Ravine) on the outskirts of Kyiv. There, in the course of two days, the automatic fire of Sonderkommando 4a of Einsatzgruppe C, assisted by the German and local police, killed 33,761 Jewish citizens of Kyiv. The shootings took place on September 29 and 30, 1941, on the orders of Major General Kurt Eberhard, the military governor of Kyiv, who would commit suicide while in American custody after the end of the war.

Eberhard ordered the mass execution in retaliation for acts of sabotage carried out by Soviet agents. Five days after Kyiv fell to the Germans on September 19, bombs planted before the Soviet retreat blew up a number of landmark buildings in the city's downtown. As expected, the German military command occupied the structures, and the explosions killed quite a few senior German officers. Nazi propaganda claimed that the Germans were fighting the war in the east against the Jewish Commune, as the propagandists referred to the Soviet regime, linking the Jewish origins and communist beliefs of some of its early leaders. As the German authorities saw it, there was a direct association between Soviet agents and Jews. They had already made that link explicit in Lviv, Kremianets, and other cities and towns of western Ukraine. There the NKVD had shot tens of thousands of prisoners, many of them local Ukrainians and Poles, before leaving the cities and retreating eastward. Back then, the Germans had encouraged anti-Jewish pogroms "in retaliation" for the Soviet atrocities. Beginning in August, however, they had changed their policy—the *Reichsführer* of the SS (Schutzstaffel), Heinrich Himmler, had authorized the killing of Jewish women and children and the annihilation of entire Jewish communities. Pogroms no longer sufficed. The Jews had to die.

"Jews of the city of Kiev and vicinity!" read a leaflet distributed in Kyiv in late September. "On Monday, September 29, you are to appear by 8:00 a.m. with your possessions, money, documents, valuables, and warm clothing at Dihtiarevska Street, next to the Jewish cemetery. Failure to appear is punishable by death." The Jewish citizens of Kyiv—largely women, children, and the elderly, as the men had been summoned to military service—thought that they were being assembled for resettlement and would not be harmed. The next day was Yom Kippur, the Day of Atonement. Those who responded to the call were escorted to the gates of the Jewish cemetery, forced to surrender their documents and valuables, stripped naked, and then shot in groups of ten on the slopes of a ravine. The Babi Yar massacre stands out in history, as it was the first attempt to annihilate the entire Jewish community of a major urban center anywhere in Europe. But numerous other massacres of horrendous proportions preceded and followed it. In late August, a German police battalion gunned down more than 23,000 Jews, largely refugees from Hungarian-ruled Transcarpathia. In October, close to 12,000 Jews of Dnipropetrovsk were shot in a ravine on the outskirts of the city—the future site of the Dnipropetrovsk National University. In December, about 10,000 Jews of Kharkiv met the same fate on the premises of the city's tractor factory—the pride of the Soviet industrialization project.

Romanian dictator Ion Antonescu—who took back northern Bukovyna and Bessarabia, which Stalin had forced him to surrender in 1940, and brought Odesa and parts of Podolia under his control—treated Jews with the same contempt and brutality as his Nazi masters. In October 1941, in an episode replicating the Babi Yar massacre, Antonescu ordered 18,000 Jews executed in retaliation for the Soviet demolition of the building that housed Romanian military headquarters in Odesa and killed a senior Romanian commander. In all, between 115,000 and 180,000 Jews died under Romanian occupation in Odesa and environs. Furthermore, between 100,000 and 150,000 Bukovynian and Bessarabian Jews perished in the Romanian version of Hitler's Holocaust. Most of the Galician Jews, like Polish Jews residing in the General Government, died in the course of 1942 after spending months isolated from the rest of the population in ghettos created on Nazi orders. Acting on instructions of German police commanders, the Jewish and Ukrainian police rounded them up and shipped them to extermination camps. Motivated more often by greed than anti-Semitism, locals often tried to take advantage of the misfortunes of their Jewish neighbors, either denouncing them to the authorities or seizing their property. But the majority simply looked the other way.

The Holocaust in Ukraine also differed from the Holocaust in central and western Europe in that those who tried to rescue Jews were subject not only to arrest but also to execution. So were the members of their families. Still, many did try to save their Jewish neighbors. To date the State of Israel has recognized more than 2,500 citizens of Ukraine as "Righteous Among the Nations" for sheltering Jews during the Holocaust. The list is incomplete and still growing. One person missing from it is Metropolitan Andrei Sheptytsky of the Ukrainian Catholic Church, who hid hundreds of Galician Jews in his residence and in monasteries. In February 1942 he sent a letter to Himmler protesting the use of Ukrainian police in the rounding up and extermination of Galician Jewry. The letter had no effect. Those who delivered Himmler's response told the metropolitan that if it were not for his age, he would have been shot. A few months later, Sheptytsky issued his best-known pastoral letter, "Thou Shall Not Kill," on the sanctity of human life. It was read in all Ukrainian Catholic churches and understood as his condemnation of the Holocaust. Sheptytsky's name does not appear on the list of the "righteous" because in the summer of 1941 he welcomed the German takeover of Galicia after two years of Soviet occupation. Whatever Sheptytsky's and his fellow countrymen's hopes for German rule, they vanished very quickly.

THE SEVERITY OF the occupation regime differed from one part of Hitler's Ukrainian *Lebensraum* to another. The Romanians, who never wanted Odesa and its environs but dreamed of exchanging it for Hungarian-held northern Transylvania, simply robbed southern Ukraine of everything they could lay their hands on. German policies were somewhat milder and the treatment of Ukrainians somewhat more humane under military command and in the former Austrian possessions.

The worst was in the Reichskommissariat Ukraine. The man responsible for some of the most heinous crimes committed by the Nazi occupation regime in Ukraine was the *Reichskommissar* of Ukraine, Erich Koch. Stocky and loudmouthed, sporting a Hitler-style moustache, the forty-five-year-old Koch was the party administrator for East Prussia. He had a reputation for brutality and for getting things done. In Ukraine he was tasked with exploiting resources and depopulating the conquered territory. He treated the Ukrainian population as European colonizers treated blacks and Asians in their overseas colonies, asserting, "No German soldier will ever die for that nigger people." Koch did not want Ukrainians progressing beyond the fourth grade of elementary school and shut down universities and schools for students above fifteen years of age. "If I find a Ukrainian who is worthy of sitting at the same table with me, I must have him shot," he declared on one occasion. His subordinates did a great deal of shooting indeed, some of it in the Babi Yar ravine, the same place where a few months earlier the Germans had killed nearly 34,000 Kyiv Jews. By the time the occupation of Kyiv ended in November 1943, another 60,000 Nazi victims—Soviet prisoners of war, Ukrainian nationalists, members of the Soviet underground, and Roma—had found their final resting place in Babi Yar.

Koch established his Ukrainian headquarters in the town of Rivne in Volhynia, which had been part of interwar Poland. It was the third capital of the polity called "Ukraine" in slightly more than twenty years: whereas the Soviets had chosen industrial and highly Russified Kharkiv over "nationalist" Kyiv in the 1920s, the Germans preferred provincial Rivne, with a population of 40,000, over the large and now heavily Sovietized Kyiv. Blockaded and starved, Kyiv was witnessing its first cases of famine since 1933. The Nazis' vision of *Lebensraum* included the pastoralization of Ukraine and the elimination of major urban centers, whose population they otherwise had to feed, diverting resources from the Reich and its army. Thus the policy was to starve the cities, whose inhabitants, driven by hunger into the countryside, would become a productive force, feeding themselves and the German Reich. The Germans left collective farms intact, taking advantage of the Soviet invention for extracting resources from the rural population. They also refused to privatize large enterprises, regulating whatever was left of Ukraine's economy with a new bank, colonial currency, and price controls. They controlled the movement of population with identity cards.

Starting in January 1942, the Nazis exploited Ukraine as a source not only of agricultural products but also of forced labor. That month the first train of so-called *Ostarbeiter* (eastern workers) left Kyiv for Germany, carrying young Ukrainians attracted by the promise of jobs, good living conditions, and the chance to get acquainted with Europe. "Germany calls you! Go to beautiful Germany!" ran one ad in a Kyiv newspaper. One poster, titled "The Wall Has Come Down," portrayed Ukrainians looking through an opening in the wall isolating the Soviet Union from Europe. On the horizon were the skylines of German cities. "Stalin placed a high wall around you," read the caption. "He well knew that anyone who saw the outside world would fully grasp the pitiful state of the Bolshevik regime. Now the wall has been breached, and the way to a new and better future has been opened." It was an opportunity for the younger generation to leave the villages and see the world. Many responded with interest and even enthusiasm.

The ads turned out to be a trap. Whether they worked in factories or the households of individual Germans, young men and women ended up as slave laborers, forced to wear a badge reading "OST" and regarded as subhuman by the German authorities and a good part of German society. As news of exploitation in Germany began to reach Ukraine, the occupation authorities had more and more difficulty fulfilling monthly quotas of 40,000 Ukrainian laborers: they began rounding up people arbitrarily and packing them off to Germany by force. Altogether, close to 2.2 million Ukrainians were apprehended and sent to Germany in 1942 and 1943. Many died of malnutrition, disease, and Allied bombing of the military and munitions factories where they worked. Those who survived and were liberated by Red Army soldiers in late 1944 and 1945 (only 120,000 individuals registered as displaced persons at the end of the war) were often treated as traitors, and some were shipped directly from German concentration camps to Soviet ones in the Gulag system. Ukraine was not the only part of the Soviet Union where the Germans engaged in slave-hunting expeditions, but it was by far the largest hunting ground. Citizens of Ukraine constituted close to 80 percent of all *Ostarbeiter* taken from occupied areas of eastern Europe to Germany in the course of the war.

BY THE SUMMER of 1943, little remained of the original German plan to establish a paradise for German farmers in Ukraine. Hitler had spent a good part of the summer and autumn of 1942 in Ukraine, where German engineers, using the forced labor of Soviet POWs, built his farthest eastern headquarters, code-named Werwolf, in a pine forest near the city of Vinnytsia. He was also there in the spring of 1943, but on September 15 of that year, he left Werwolf forever. That day he ordered his troops in Ukraine to retreat to the Dnieper defensive line. A week later, Soviet troops crossed the Dnieper north of Kyiv, cracking Hitler's eastern wall for the first time. The Germans would detonate the entire underground structure of Werwolf before retreating from the area in the spring of 1944.

The dream of conquest and *Lebensraum* had ended, but the horror it unleashed remained. Ukraine became a graveyard for millions of Ukrainians, Russians, Jews, and Poles, to list only the largest affected ethnic groups. The Holocaust eradicated most of Ukrainian Jewry. Gone, too, were the German and Mennonite settlers of southern Ukraine and Volhynia—if the Soviets had not deported them in 1941, they now fled with the retreating Wehrmacht. The Polish population of Volhynia and Galicia was under attack from Ukranian nationalists. As the Red Army began its advance into Ukraine after the victorious Battle of Kursk in July 1943, the Soviet leaders confronted a very different country from the one they had left in haste in the summer and fall of 1941. The cities were empty and their industrial enterprises completely destroyed.

The survivors greeted Red Army troops as liberators, but Soviet officials had doubts about their sincerity. The people who welcomed them had managed to survive under enemy rule and lived outside Soviet control long enough to have doubts about the Stalinist system. Orthodox believers had become accustomed to the only freedom Hitler brought them—freedom of worship. Those who did not think of themselves primarily in ethnonational terms began to do so after living under the Nazi occupation, when life and death was often decided on the basis of ethnicity. All of that threatened the victorious communist regime. Until the 1980s, Soviet citizens would fill out numerous forms that included questions about whether they or their relatives had lived in German-occupied territory. Those questions were next to the ones about the individual's criminal record.

CHAPTER 23

THE VICTORS

S OVIET TROOPS RECAPTURED Kyiv from the retreating Germans on November 6, 1943. Forty-nine-year-old Lieutenant General Nikita Khrushchev, political commissar of the First Ukrainian Front—the group of armies that entered the city—was overcome with joy. As party leader of Ukraine before the war, he knew the city and environs well and now entered Kyiv by the road he had used before the war to go to and from his country house. Khrushchev found the buildings in downtown Kyiv intact—the Germans, unlike the retreating Soviets in 1941, had not tried to blow them up—but the city completely deserted, as he had ordered it shelled the previous day in order to speed up the German retreat.

As Khrushchev, accompanied by Ukrainian party leaders, approached the Opera House in downtown Kyiv, which had miraculously survived the Soviet attempt to blow it up in 1941, he noticed a screaming man running toward him. "I am the only Jew left! I am the only Jew in Kyiv who is still alive!" screamed the man. Khrushchev tried to calm him down and asked how he had survived. "I have a Ukrainian wife," came the answer, "and she kept me hidden in the attic. She fed me and took care of me." People began to emerge from their hiding places, and a few minutes later another citizen of Kyiv, an old man with a huge beard, hugged and kissed Khrushchev, who later remembered being "very touched." The soldiers of the regime, for whom many in the summer of 1941 had wished nothing but defeat, now returned as saviors. It was not so much what the Soviets did after their return but what the Germans had done during the occupation that changed the attitude of those who survived, leading them to welcome the Red Army soldiers not only as victors but also as liberators. Those who thought otherwise, including a good part of the Ukrainian intellectual elite, had left with the Germans.

The Red Army would spend the next year liberating the rest of the Ukrainian territories from German occupation, but the Soviets would fully secure control over those lands only after the final Allied victory over Germany in May 1945. In June of that year, the Soviet government would draw a new western Ukrainian border by annexing to the USSR not only the lands claimed in the Molotov-Ribbentrop pact but also the Transcarpathian region of interwar Czechoslovakia. It was victor's justice in its characteristically ruthless Soviet rendition.

NIKITA KHRUSHCHEV HAD dreamed of returning to Kyiv ever since the loss of the city to the Germans in September 1941. In the spring of 1942, soon after the Red Army stopped the Germans at the approaches to Moscow, he pushed for a Soviet counteroffensive in Ukraine with the goal of capturing its old capital, Kharkiv, and advancing on the industrial center of Dnipropetrovsk. The offensive, which began on May 12, 1942, saw Soviet tank formations break through enemy lines and push beyond Kharkiv into the steppes of Left-Bank Ukraine. But as the troops moved further southwest, meeting little if any resistance from the Germans, they realized that they were walking into a trap. The Germans had closed ranks, creating an encirclement akin to those that the Red Army had suffered the previous year. Khrushchev pleaded with Stalin to stop the offensive, but Stalin refused. It was too late to remedy the situation anyway. In a disastrous operation that lasted eighteen days, the Soviets lost 280,000 men killed, missing in action, and captured. When Stalin asked Khrushchev whether the figure of 200,000 POWs reported by the Germans was a lie, Khrushchev said that it was about right. Stalin blamed him for the defeat; only the presence of other Politburo members when Stalin refused to follow his advice and halt the clearly doomed operation saved Khrushchev from possible execution.

The battle for Ukraine turned out to be prolonged and bloody. The tide turned at Stalingrad in February 1943, as the Red Army defeated the million-man army of Germany and its allies. Immediately after Stalingrad, the Red Army continued its offensive and retook Kursk, Belgorod, and Kharkiv from the Germans. But Field Marshal Erich von Manstein launched a counteroffensive, retaking Kharkiv and Belgorod and routing fifty-two Soviet divisions. Not until August 23, 1943, after the victory at Kursk, did the Red

Army manage to take Kharkiv once again. On September 8, the Soviets raised the red banner over the city of Stalino (the former Yuzivka and future Donetsk). In the next few months, Soviet forces took the rest of Left-Bank Ukraine. They breached the Eastern Wall, the defensive line established by Hitler to stop the Soviet advance on the Right Bank of the Dnieper, in numerous places on a front extending more than 1,400 kilometers. The Red Army managed to field more than 2.5 million men against some 1.25 million Germans. The fighting was ferocious: according to conservative estimates, the Soviets lost over a million killed and wounded and the Germans more than half a million. No one counted the losses among the civilian population. They were enormous.

As the party leader of occupied Ukraine, Khrushchev was deeply involved in organizing partisan units behind the German lines. The Nazi occupation policies provoked resentment, outrage, and eventually defiance, which drove people into the ranks of the resistance. While there were numerous urban resistance cells, the countryside provided a natural habitat for large groups of partisans, who waged a long and exhausting war against the occupiers. Ecology was the key. Since the steppes provided poor cover for resistance fighters, they fought in the woods of the northern Kyiv and Chernihiv regions, the forests and marshes of northern Volhynia, and the foothills of the Carpathian Mountains. Apart from their habitat, their professed Ukrainian patriotism and hatred of the Nazi occupation united the partisans. The former Soviet-Polish border and ideology, however, divided them. West of the border, nationalists led the partisans, while communists predominated east of it.

As a rule, the Soviet secret police organized the communist guerrillas, who received orders and supplies from a body called the Ukrainian Staff of the Partisan Movement, headed by an NKVD general and part of the Moscow-based Central Staff of the Partisan Movement. One of the best-known partisan leaders of Ukraine, Sydir Kovpak, had headed a city council before the war. Apart from his experience as a guerrilla commander during the German occupation of Ukraine in 1918, he had graduated from an NKVD school that trained cadres for partisan warfare. The Soviet partisans began their activities in early 1942 with attacks on German units behind the lines and centers of occupation administration. As time went on and the Red Army began its westward advance after the Battle of Stalingrad, the activities of Soviet partisans increased in number and scope. If there were 5,000 fighters in 1942, their numbers had increased almost tenfold by 1944.

The Germans tried to deal with the growing partisan movement, which not only challenged their control over Ukraine but also disrupted communications and deliveries of supplies, by unleashing a reign of terror on the local population. This included burning villages that the occupation authorities believed to be under partisan control or suspected of supporting the partisans. With German manpower in short supply, the authorities relied on police battalions recruited from the local population. Their members rarely joined the police for ideological reasons and included many former members of the Communist Party and the Komsomol (communist youth organization) seeking to escape persecution or even extermination by the occupation authorities. As there were locals on both sides of the divide, partisan warfare often turned into a brutal vendetta in which relatives of the partisans and policemen paid the ultimate price for choices made by their kinsmen. With the war turning against the Germans in 1942, more and more policemen changed sides and joined the partisans. At times it was difficult to tell a collaborator from a resistance fighter. It was a long war, and many shifted from one role to the other over its course.

AFTER THE CAPTURE of Kyiv, Khrushchev immediately immersed himself in administration, reintegrating the former Soviet territories into the Ukrainian Soviet Socialist Republic (Ukrainian SSR) and reincorporating the lands that the Soviets had not controlled before the war. It turned out to be a long and formidable task that would take most of his time and energy. By early 1944, the front had moved west of the Dnieper. By March, Soviet troops had retaken Right-Bank Ukraine and crossed the prewar border, pushing into Romania. In October 1944, the Red Army crossed the Carpathians and gained control of Transcarpathia, which official propaganda hailed as the final act in the reunification of the Ukrainian lands. There was no talk of a possible return of the territory either to Hungary or to Czechoslovakia. More than half a million Red Army soldiers died in the fighting for western Ukraine.

"As we pushed the Germans west, we encountered an old enemy— Ukrainian nationalists," recalled Khrushchev as he described his efforts to reincorporate western Ukraine into the Soviet state in 1944 and 1945. The Soviet authorities often referred to these nationalists generally as "Banderites," given the overall control of the nationalist insurgency by the Stepan Bandera faction of the Organization of Ukrainian Nationalists (OUN). Eventually, this term came to denote anyone who fought in the ranks of the Ukrainian Insurgent Army (UPA), controlled by Bandera's followers.

The name was misleading in more than one sense. First, not all the UPA fighters shared the nationalist ideology or belonged to the OUN. Second, Bandera himself never returned to Ukraine after his arrest by the Germans in the summer of 1941 and had no operational control over the forces that bore his name. He became a symbolic leader and a proverbial father of the nation, imprisoned by the Germans for most of the war and then living as an émigré in West Germany.

The Ukrainian Insurgent Army, which had close to 100,000 soldiers at its height in the summer of 1944, was fighting behind the Soviet lines, disrupting Red Army communications and attacking units farther from the front. A number of commanders led the insurgents, the most prominent being the former commander of the Nachtigall battalion, Roman Shukhevych. Like Shukhevych, many UPA commanders had German training, which they received as members of auxiliary police units. They abandoned those units with their weapons in early 1943. While they regarded the Germans as their main enemies, in 1943 the UPA mostly fought the Polish insurgency. The long history of animosity between Ukrainians and Poles in Volhynia and Galicia, exacerbated by each side's mounting suspicions of the other's intentions, led in the spring and summer of 1943 to mass actions of ethnic cleansing involving the burning of villages and mass murder of innocent civilians.

The influx into Volhynia, soon after the Soviet victory at Stalingrad in February 1943, of Soviet partisan units led by Sydir Kovpak triggered the Ukrainian-Polish conflict. They received support from some Polish settlers in Volhynia, who viewed the Soviets as potential allies against the Ukrainians. Ukrainian and Polish historians still argue over whether the OUN leadership sanctioned Ukrainian attacks on Polish villages and, if so, on what level. There is no doubt, however, that most victims of the ethnic cleansing were Poles. Estimates of Ukrainians killed as a result of Polish actions in Galicia and Volhynia vary between 15,000 and 30,000, whereas the estimates for Polish victims are between 60,000 and 90,000—two to three times as high. The Germans originally tried to stop the military conflict at the rear, but ended up supplying weapons to the combatants. If they could not control the countryside, they could at least keep their enemies divided. They also benefited from UPA operations against the advancing Red Army.

Among the UPA's major successes was the killing of a leading Soviet commander, General Nikolai Vatutin. On February 29, 1944, UPA fighters ambushed and wounded Vatutin as he was returning from a meeting with subordinates in Rivne, the former capital of the Reichskommissariat Ukraine.

He died in Kyiv in mid-April. Khrushchev, who attended Vatutin's funeral, buried his friend in the government center of Kyiv. After the war, he came up with an inscription for the monument: "To General Vatutin from the Ukrainian people." Khrushchev believed that the inscription would infuriate the Ukrainian nationalists, but party officials in Moscow treated it as an expression of the selfsame Ukrainian nationalism. Khrushchev appealed directly to Stalin, who allowed him to go ahead with his original plan. The Ukrainian-language inscription was placed on the monument, which was erected in 1948 and still stands in downtown Kyiv—one of many reminders of the complexity of Ukrainian memory of World War II.

In World War II, Ukrainians found themselves on more than one side of the conflict. The absolute majority fought in the ranks of the Soviet army. Moscow enlisted more than 7 million Ukrainians of various nationalities— every fifth or sixth Soviet soldier came from Ukraine. Over 3.5 million were called up at the start of the war, and roughly as many again were drafted in the course of it. Many soldiers who survived the German onslaught and imprisonment in 1941 were released to their families and then seized and drafted immediately after the Red Army retook the areas where they lived. They became known as "men in black jackets," as most were thrown into battle immediately after being drafted—without proper uniforms, training, ammunition, or even arms. As people who had stayed under German occupation, the military command regarded them as traitors and considered them expendable. Most of the "men in black jackets" died in combat on the outskirts of their towns and villages days after the long-awaited "liberation."

While the Soviets had no qualms about taking Ukrainians into the army and sending them into battle, the Germans long refused to enlist the men from the conquered territories in their regular units. They were welcomed, however, as auxiliaries—*Hilfswillige* (willing helpers), or Hiwis. An estimated 1 million former Soviet citizens joined Hiwi auxiliary units, with Ukrainians and natives of Ukraine constituting roughly one-quarter of that number. The policy began to change after Stalingrad as the Germans started running out of manpower. The newly formed non-German units came under the direct supervision of Heinrich Himmler and became part of the Waffen-SS— the military branch of the SS (Schutzstaffel), Himmler's brutal police force. Among Waffen-SS divisions were units recruited from almost every European nationality, including Frenchmen, Swedes, Russians, and Ukrainians.

Close to 20,000 Ukrainians served in the course of the war in the 14th Waffen-SS Grenadier Division, known as the Division Galizien.

The German governor of the District of Galicia, Otto von Wächter, promoted the idea of creating the division. A native of Vienna, Wächter played the old Austrian game of supporting the Ukrainians against the Poles, and his rule witnessed an increase in the number of Ukrainian schools in the district. His German regime banned political organizations and hunted down OUN operatives but tolerated Ukrainian welfare, cultural, and even academic institutions—a striking difference from all other parts of Ukraine. Wächter believed that the Ukrainians were loyal enough to entrust with arms. In Berlin, however, many doubted both their loyalty and their racial status. Eventually the leadership decided to call the division Galician rather than Ukrainian, deeming Galicians, as former Austrian subjects, a more "civilized" and reliable group than Ukrainians in general. Berlin not only divided Ukraine along the old Russo-Austrian boundary but also conducted its policy toward different parts of the country following the old Austrian patterns. The division would consist only of Galicians, and its name and symbols would make no reference to Ukraine and Ukrainians.

The recruitment of volunteers for the division, announced in April 1943, immediately caused a split in the nationalist underground: the Bandera faction was vehemently opposed, while followers of Bandera's opponent, Colonel Andrii Melnyk, supported it. Mainstream Ukrainian political leaders, including bishops of the Catholic Church, were also divided. Those who supported the formation of the division thought as much in terms of Galicia's Austrian past as did the Germans in deciding to create it. Back in 1918, the existence of a Ukrainian legion in the Austrian army had allowed the Ukrainians to train cadres and acquire arms that they used in the war for independence. Many in the Ukrainian community thought that history might repeat itself. Few were happy with German rule in Ukraine, even fewer shared the Nazi ideology, and no one believed in a German future after Stalingrad and Kursk. Apart from hard-nosed calculation, only their shared anticommunism brought the Ukrainian politicians and the German authorities together.

Backed by mainstream Ukrainian politicians and presented to Ukrainian youth as an alternative to going to the forest to join the Bandera insurgents or staying under imminent Soviet occupation, enrollment in the division seemed a lesser evil to parents who sent their sons to join its ranks. Most would soon have reason to regret their choice. Trained and commanded by

German officers, the division got its baptism by fire in July 1944 near the Galician town of Brody. It was both a christening and a wake. Soviet forces surrounded the Division Galizien, together with seven other German divisions. Total casualties reached almost 38,000, with 17,000 taken prisoner. The Division Galizien, which numbered close to 11,000 men, was virtually wiped out: only about 1,500 managed to escape. The Battle of Brody spelled the end of the division as a fighting force. Later that year, replenished with new recruits, it was sent first to Slovakia and then to Yugoslavia to fight partisans. There history repeated itself as farce, if not as tragedy—vintage 1918 memories of Ukrainian units in Austrian uniform securing Ukrainian independence gave way to 1944 realities of Ukrainians wearing Nazi swastikas and putting down the liberation movements of fellow Slavs.

ON JULY 27, 1944, the Red Army recaptured Lviv. The seizure of that city and western Ukraine presented Nikita Khrushchev and the political leadership of Soviet Ukraine with a new set of challenges. The main concern with Lviv was the possible formation of a Polish city government that would declare loyalty to the Polish government-in-exile in London. Khrushchev rushed into the city left open by the retreating Germans. "We were afraid that some local bodies might arise there that would turn out to be hostile to Soviet rule," he remembered later. "We had to move quickly to put our people in charge of the city. And that is what we did." In 1944, Lviv was a largely Polish city surrounded by a largely Ukrainian countryside. It became a bone of contention between Stalin on the one hand and the Polish government-in-exile, supported by the Western Allies, on the other. Khrushchev's installation of Soviet administrative bodies meant that Stalin was not going to accommodate Polish hopes of keeping the city.

Two days before the capture of Lviv, Stalin had bullied the members of the Polish Committee of National Liberation—the communist government-in-waiting created by the Soviets to replace the Polish government-in-exile in London—into agreeing to the future borders of the Polish state, which would roughly follow the Molotov-Ribbentrop line of 1939 and leave Lviv on the Soviet side of the border. A letter Stalin had received a few days earlier from Khrushchev helped him in this effort. The Ukrainian party boss wanted to attach to his republic not only Lviv and other areas east of the Molotov-Ribbentrop line but also the city of Kholm (Chełm), located in a predominantly Ukrainian-populated region—Khrushchev's wife, Nina Petrivna Kukharchuk, came from that area. Stalin threatened his Polish clients with Khrushchev's request, giving them to understand that if they did not agree to give up Lviv, he would push for Kholm as well. They caved in, taking Kholm and abandoning their claims to the Galician capital. Kholm, captured by the Red Army on July 23, became the first town west of the Molotov-Ribbentrop line taken by the Soviets and the first seat of the Polish government dependent on Moscow.

In September 1944, the communist-dominated Polish government and the Khrushchev-led administration of Soviet Ukraine signed an agreement on the new borders and an exchange of population intended to make the borders not only political but also ethnic boundaries. The idea behind the agreement was quite simple: Poles were to go west, to areas beyond the Molotov-Ribbentrop line, while Ukrainians would go east of that line. Stalin was eager to move not only borders but also peoples in order to stabilize future frontiers, get rid of minorities, and thereby forestall any possibility of irredentist movements in the Soviet territories. While the nationalists had planned to bring prewar borders into line with ethnic boundaries, Stalin took a further step, adjusting ethnic boundaries to fit the borders he established by force of arms.

In February 1945, when President Franklin Delano Roosevelt of the United States and Prime Minister Winston Churchill of Britain came to Yalta in the Crimea to discuss the future of the postwar world with Stalin, the Soviet leader insisted on drawing a new boundary between the Soviet Union and Poland along the Molotov-Ribbentrop line. The Western leaders agreed, giving retroactive legitimacy to the movement of population that had already taken place. Stalin also made sure that Ukraine and Belarus, with their new western borders, would become members of the United Nations, additionally legitimizing the new Soviet boundaries. The Potsdam Conference, which again featured the leaders of the United States, Britain, and the Soviet Union and took place in the summer of 1945, after the defeat of Germany and the end of hostilities in Europe, accommodated Stalin's demand to assign former German lands in the west to Poland as compensation for the territories it had lost in the east. Moscow expelled more than 7.5 million ethnic Germans from the territory of the new Polish state, making room for Poles resettled from the east. The Soviets began to ship Poles westward even before Red Army troops captured the eastern German territories. Thus, in September 1944, Polish citizens of Lviv who were supposed to go to Breslau (Polish: Wrocław) were temporarily "parked" in the former Nazi concentration and extermination camp of Majdanek near the city of Lublin. Only later would they reach their final destination on former German territory.

Given the open warfare between the Ukrainian and Polish undergrounds and the ethnic cleansing that accompanied it, many Poles and Ukrainians were indeed more than ready to leave their homes and save their lives, if not their possessions. But some refused to move. In the end, it did not matter much. Stalin and his Polish clients were only too eager to use the experience the NKVD had acquired in the course of mass deportations of the war era to achieve their goal of creating minority-free states. Soviet officials called the deportation campaign "repatriation." The "patrias" were imagined, as most of the deportees were not returning to but leaving their homelands. About 780,000 Poles were "repatriated" west of the Molotov-Ribbentrop line from Ukraine alone. Approximately the same number were moved from Belarus and Lithuania to the territory of the new Polish state. The deportees included close to 100,000 Jews who had survived the Holocaust in the Soviet Union. Most of those resettled ended up in the former German lands assigned to Poland by Stalin with the reluctant agreement of the Western leaders.

As Poles and Jews went west, Ukrainians headed east. In two years, between 1944 and 1946, close to half a million Ukrainians were deported from lands west of the Molotov-Ribbentrop line to the Ukrainian SSR. Around the same time, more than 180,000 Ukrainians from western Ukraine were arrested and deported to Siberia and the Soviet interior for real or alleged collaboration with the nationalist underground. An additional 76,000 Ukrainians were deported in October 1947. The deportations aimed mainly to curb Ukrainian nationalist resistance, which continued in western Ukraine long after the end of the war. Nikita Khrushchev later claimed that Stalin had been prepared to deport all Ukrainians to the east, but there were too many of them.

That seemed to be an option open to the Polish communist authorities, though on a smaller scale. In 1947, in an operation code-named Vistula, they deported from their eastern borderlands the entirety of the Ukrainian population still remaining in Poland—altogether 140,000 men, women, and children—and replaced them with ethnic Poles. They expelled the deportees from their homes and resettled them in the former German territories in western and northern Poland. The checkered Polish-Ukrainian boundary, with its ethnically and religiously mixed population, was becoming a clear-cut Soviet-Polish border, with Poles on one side and Ukrainians on the other. Ukraine itself, a multiethnic territory for most of its history, was turning into a Ukrainian-Russian condominium as a result of the extermination of the Jews and the deportation of the Poles and Germans.

Stalin moved populations around not to appease the nationalists but to fight nationalism and cement his control over the borderlands. He was sealing the Soviet borders not only with new demarcation lines and border guards but also with a neverending campaign against the capitalist West—closing the Ukrainian gates to Europe more tightly than during the interwar period or, indeed, any previous time in history. The reality of the Nazi occupation of Ukraine had crushed the Ukrainian intelligentsia's dream of joining Europe. The Europe that the Germans brought to Ukraine came in the form of a colonial empire, its agents driven by notions of race, exploitation, and the extermination of "subhumans" (*Untermenschen*). The Soviets took advantage of this recent disappointment with the West to fuel the propaganda of the Cold War era. For years they would link Ukrainian nationalism with German fascism by constantly referring to the Ukrainian insurgents as "German-Ukrainian nationalists."

The Soviet regime was also intent on erasing age-old cultural boundaries. In March 1946, working through its agents, the NKVD convoked a special council of the Ukrainian Catholic Church at which the participants were forced to dissolve their church and join the Russian Orthodox Church instead. The council took place in the absence of bishops, whom the NKVD had arrested a year earlier. The decision to destroy the church came immediately after the Yalta Conference and was carried out within the borders defined by the meeting of the Big Three. As Transcarpathia was not yet officially part of Soviet Ukraine, the Catholic Church there was allowed to exist for another three years until it was crushed with the start of the Cold War in 1949. The Soviets suspected the Catholic Church as a whole of doing the bidding of the Vatican and the Western powers. All institutional, religious, and cultural links with the West had to be cut, destroying an institution that had long served as a bridge between the Catholic West and the Orthodox East. In a few short years, more than 5 million Ukrainian Catholics became nominally Orthodox.

By 1945 THE victorious Soviet Union, using its military force, had moved its boundaries deep into east-central Europe. The Soviets took a page from the book of Ukrainian nationalism by expanding the nominally Ukrainian republic to include Polish, Czechoslovak, and Romanian territories traditionally settled by Ukrainians.

These territorial acquisitions presented new challenges to the Soviet regime in Ukraine. After the Revolution of 1917, the Soviets had managed to anchor Dnieper Ukraine to the USSR by recognizing the Ukrainian claim to the industrial centers of eastern and southern Ukraine, often settled by ethnic Russians. By taking over largely Ukrainian-inhabited parts of the former Austria-Hungary claimed during the interwar period by Poland, Romania, and Czechoslovakia, Stalin brought into Soviet Ukraine fairly well-developed traditions of autonomy, parliamentary democracy, and communal and national self-organization that had been all but absent in the central and eastern Ukrainian lands. The Soviet regime also encountered a new ideological threat—radical nationalism, represented by a well-organized political structure with its own partisan military force, the Ukrainian Insurgent Army.

The full incorporation of those territories, which included their economic, social, and cultural integration into Soviet Ukraine and the USSR, would take decades to accomplish. Moscow still had to pacify those areas by driving the nationalist insurgency underground and then destroying it—a process that lasted into the 1950s. To become fully Soviet, those lands would have to undergo collectivization and industrialization, and their youth would have to be indoctrinated in the basics of Soviet Marxism. But even with the passing of time, the historical ties between the newly acquired Soviet territories and central and western Europe did not cease to exist. The westward shift of Soviet borders turned the formerly non-Soviet parts of Ukraine into internal borderlands, where for decades the regime imposed policies different from those that it pursued in the rest of Ukraine.

The Soviets used the Ukrainian card not only to legitimize possession of the region but also to Sovietize it. Moscow returned to its Ukrainization policy of the 1920s, offering the region the opportunity to join Soviet society through the Ukrainization of its political and cultural life. But the regime was slow to integrate local cadres, whom it did not trust, and therefore brought in Ukrainians from eastern and central parts of the republic. This delayed the full integration of the region. At the same time, the offer of Ukrainian culture in exchange for political loyalty helped slow down Russification in the rest of Ukraine. This policy of grudging Ukrainization, coupled with the historical tradition of high national mobilization within the boundaries of Austria-Hungary and then Poland, as well as memories of the nationalist insurgency, would turn western Ukraine, in particular Galicia, into Ukraine's center of national culture and political activism for the rest of the Soviet era.

V

THE ROAD TO
INDEPENDENCE

CHAPTER 24

THE SECOND SOVIET REPUBLIC

UKRAINE'S MEMBERSHIP IN the United Nations, which admitted the republic as a founding member at the San Francisco Conference in April 1945, raised its international status to one comparable with the British dominions of Canada and Australia or even sovereign states like Belgium or Brazil. Nevertheless, it would take almost half a century to match the promise of UN membership with the attainment of national independence. In taking that path, Ukraine contributed to the disintegration of empires and the formation of new nation-states on their ruins—a process that almost tripled the number of independent states in the world from about 70 in 1945 to more than 190 today.

Its United Nations seat and enhanced status aside, at the end of the war Ukraine presented a sorry picture. Although the map made it seem like one of the main beneficiaries of the war—Ukraine's territory increased by more than 15 percent—the republic was in fact one of the war's main victims. It lost up to 7 million of its citizens, who had constituted more than 15 percent of its population. Out of 36 million remaining Ukrainians, some 10 million didn't have a roof over their heads, as approximately 700 cities and towns and 28,000 villages lay in ruins. Ukraine lost 40 percent of its wealth and more than 80 percent of its industrial and agricultural equipment. In 1945, the republic produced only one-quarter of its prewar output of industrial goods and 40 percent of its previous agricultural produce.

With its industrial base devastated by Soviet scorched-earth tactics, the deindustrialization and deurbanization policies of the Germans, and the relentless fighting between the two armies, in some places Ukraine had to be rebuilt almost from scratch. Western advisers suggested that it was easier to build new plants than to restore old ones, but the authorities decided to reconstruct the plants they had built with such huge sacrifices in the 1930s. As had been the case then, they prioritized heavy industry. As far as the Kremlin was concerned, the rest could wait.

By 1948, the wartime Soviet alliance with the United States and Britain had given way to the Cold War between Moscow and the West. At stake was Soviet control over central and eastern Europe, as well as Western positions in Iran, Turkey, and Greece. With the Soviet army stationed as far west as Germany, Ukraine was no longer a border republic facing what was considered the hostile West, as it had been during the interwar period, but its importance to the union's industrial and agricultural potential remained as great as it had been before the war. Ukraine had to produce arms, food, and soldiers to fight what many deemed an imminent conflict between the communist East and the capitalist West. For Ukrainians, that meant a lot of guns and very little butter. Ukraine had rebuilt its economic potential by 1950, but agricultural production lagged behind, with prewar levels not reached until the 1960s.

THE FIRST POSTWAR decade in Ukraine largely entailed reconstructing the shattered economy, rehabilitating a shocked and traumatized society, and restoring the party's ideological and political control over lands temporarily lost to Germany and its allies in the course of the war. In western Ukraine—the former Polish, Romanian, and Czech provinces of the country—the restoration of party control in fact meant its introduction, as the Soviet regime had lasted less than two years before the German invasion. Throughout Ukraine, this period saw the (re)implementation of the political, social, and economic models developed in the 1930s. In his last years, Stalin was not eager to engage in experimentation—late Stalinism was clearly running out of revolutionary zeal. The experience of the war that had just ended and preparations for war with the West, which the Kremlin believed was about to begin, informed most of the political, social, and cultural decisions made by Stalin and his aides.

Among the reconstruction projects given high priority by those at the very top of the Soviet political pyramid was one of the giants of Soviet industrialization of prewar years: the Dnieper electric power station in Zaporizhia. The retreating Soviets had blown up part of the Zaporizhia dam in 1941, but they saved the remains in 1943, when the Germans tried to finish the job—Soviet scouts cut the wire that was supposed to detonate the explosives. The reconstruction of the dam and the electric power station became a priority for the newly appointed party boss of the Zaporizhia region and future leader of the Soviet Union, Leonid Brezhnev, who came to the city in 1946 to find the power station and the industrial enterprises built around it completely destroyed. "Grass was already growing among the bricks and iron, the howling of dogs gone wild could be heard from afar, and all around there were nothing but ruins, with black crows' nests hanging from the branches of burned trees," wrote Brezhnev, recalling his first impressions on visiting what remained of the Zaporizhia industrial complex in the summer of 1946. "I had had occasion to see something similar after the Civil War, but then it was the dead silence of the factories that was frightening, while now they had been completely reduced to dust."

According to the report of a government commission, the city of Zaporizhia had no electricity or running water. More than 1,000 apartment buildings, 74 schools, 5 cinema theaters, 2 universities, and 239 stores had been destroyed. But Moscow sent Brezhnev to Zaporizhia not so much to rebuild the city as to get the power station and the steelworks, called Zaporizhstal, working again. He did what he was asked to do in record time. The electric power station generated its first electricity in March 1947, with the first steel produced in September of that year. In November 1947, in recognition of Brezhnev's accomplishments, the Kremlin recalled him from Zaporizhia and promoted him to party boss of the neighboring Dnipropetrovsk region, one of the main economic powerhouses of Ukraine. Brezhnev left Zaporizhia producing electricity and steel but still in ruins. That was the model for rebuilding Ukraine after the war: industrial enterprises took priority. People were left to suffer and even die.

In his memoirs, first published in 1978, Brezhnev writes about difficult times in the cities but says nothing about the villages, which in 1946 and 1947 witnessed the return of famine on a scale comparable to that of 1932 and 1933. Close to a million people died as a result of the new famine that hit southern Ukraine especially hard, including the Dnipropetrovsk and Zaporizhia regions led by Brezhnev. Not surprisingly, Brezhnev remained silent about the new crime of the regime in which he held a prominent office—the starving to death of hundreds of thousands of its citizens. A prominent official who refused to stay silent was Brezhnev's boss at the time, Nikita Khrushchev. In memoirs smuggled to the West and published in the United States in 1970 but unknown to the readers in the USSR until the late 1980s (Brezhnev's, by contrast, appeared in print runs approaching 15 million copies in the 1970s), Khrushchev described not only the famine but also the inability of the republican leadership to do anything to save the victims—Moscow still made life-and-death decisions affecting Ukraine exclusively.

Khrushchev blamed the new Ukrainian famine on Stalin, as he did much else that happened in the 1930s and 1940s. In this case, he was clearly on target. In the summer of 1946 the worst drought in half a century hit Ukraine, but the authorities in Moscow kept demanding grain from the Ukrainian countryside, devastated by the war and a bad harvest. This time they needed grain for the reindustrialization of the cities and for Soviet-occupied eastern Europe, where Stalin shipped millions of tons of grain to keep the new communist regimes going. To prevent the impending catastrophe, Khrushchev appealed directly to Stalin, asking for the introduction of ration cards for the peasants like the ones introduced for city dwellers. His pleas went unanswered. Moreover, someone began spreading rumors accusing Khrushchev of Ukrainian nationalism—he was too protective of his republic and its people. Khrushchev soon fell out of favor with Stalin and was demoted: although left in office as head of the Ukrainian government, he lost his position as party leader. His new boss and replacement as party leader of Ukraine was Lazar Kaganovich, the promoter of the Ukrainization policy of the 1920s and an organizer of the Great Famine of the 1930s.

Kaganovich saw his new task in Ukraine as reinforcing Moscow's ideological control. Maksym Rylsky, a neoclassical poet and head of the Ukrainian Writers' Union, became the main victim of Kaganovich's ideological witch hunt. He was attacked in the press for Ukrainian nationalism and removed from his position in the fall of 1947. Although Stalin soon recalled Kaganovich to Moscow, and Khrushchev got his old party office back, attacks on Ukrainian cultural figures continued. They were part of an all-union campaign associated with Stalin's ideological watchdog Andrei Zhdanov, who attacked Soviet writers and artists for "bourgeois individualism," "lack of ideological clarity," and "kowtowing to the West." Among the victims of Zhdanov's campaign were the satirists Mikhail Zoshchenko in Russia and Ostap Vyshnia in Ukraine. Writers could depict only one conflict in their work—that between the good and the better—which put satirists out of a job. The search for ideological deviants that began with writers spread to musicians and historians. In Ukraine, a hunt for "nationalists" reached its peak in 1951 with an attack in *Pravda* on Volodymyr Sosiura's poem "Love Ukraine," a patriotic text written by that prominent poet in

1944. The regime came to see what was good for mobilizing Ukrainian patriotism against German aggression during the war as nationalistic when it sought to consolidate control over the formerly occupied territories.

The Great Patriotic War, as the Soviet-German war of 1941–1945 became known in the Soviet Union, provided new legitimacy for the regime that had managed to survive and repel foreign invasion. But the war had also changed the political landscape of the Soviet Union, giving people agency to a degree unmatched since the revolution. Moscow's efforts to reimpose ideological uniformity and the degree of central control that existed before the war were only partly successful, especially in a republic like Ukraine, where nationalist resistance to the Soviet regime lasted well into the 1950s. Western Ukraine, Galicia and Volhynia in particular, remained under de facto military occupation for years after the war and received different treatment than the rest of the republic.

THE UKRAINIAN INSURGENT Army continued to challenge Soviet rule in the Galician countryside into the 1950s—significantly longer than any other armed resistance in Soviet-occupied eastern Europe. Around 1947, the commanders of the Ukrainian Insurgent Army changed tactics by splitting large formations into smaller units of no more than fifty fighters, and then even into smaller groups with a maximum of ten members. They avoided large-scale military confrontations with the much more numerous Soviet troops, saving their forces for a new war between the USSR and the West that they expected to break out at any moment. Meanwhile, even the smaller insurgent units continued to create problems for the Soviet regime, attacking representatives of the party and state apparatus and undermining efforts at collectivization of agriculture and Sovietization of the region through the educational system. The regime responded with repressive measures that included forced deportations of hundreds of thousands of Ukrainians suspected of supporting the underground.

It took the Soviet security services until the spring of 1950 to track down and kill the commander in chief of the Ukrainian Insurgent Army, Roman Shukhevych. Another commander replaced him, but in the next few years organized resistance was largely crushed, and small underground units lost contact with one another. Some of the insurgent units made their way through Polish and Czechoslovak territories to the West and joined the émigré nationalists led by Stepan Bandera in West Germany. In 1951, the British and the Americans started to airdrop members of the Bandera and other nationalist organizations back into Ukraine with the goal of collecting intelligence. The Soviets responded by stepping up their attempts to assassinate Bandera and other leaders of the Ukrainian emigration in Germany. They succeeded in the fall of 1959, when a Soviet agent killed Bandera with a KGB-made spray gun loaded with cyanide. The assassin defected to the West in 1961 and confessed to killing Bandera and another Ukrainian émigré leader back in 1957. His testimony in a West German court left no doubt that the orders to kill émigré leaders had come from the top echelon of the Soviet government.

Ukrainian nationalists, whether real or perceived, were not the only target of Soviet propaganda and the secret police in the last years of Stalin's rule. At that time a new group, Soviet Jewry, emerged at the top of the hierarchy of enemies. Jews had been among the victims of the Stalinist purges of the 1930s, but not until the late 1940s were they targeted as a group. That change came with the onset of the Cold War and the founding of the State of Israel. Now Jewish citizens of the USSR came under suspicion for double loyalty and siding with the West against their Soviet motherland.

In January 1948 a leader of Soviet Jewry, renowned actor and artistic director Solomon Mikhoels, was killed on Stalin's orders. By the end of the year, Stalin had imprisoned the Jewish wife of his right-hand man, Viacheslav Molotov—Polina Zhemchuzhina, a native of southern Ukraine and a strong supporter of Mikhoels. The Soviet media declared war on "cosmopolitans"—a euphemism for Jews—purging many Jews from the party and security apparatus. The Jews of Ukraine found themselves among the primary targets of discrimination. In 1952, the anti-Semitic campaign reached new heights with the arrest of a number of Jewish doctors, accused, along with Slavic colleagues, of killing members of the Soviet leadership, including Andrei Zhdanov, who had died of natural causes in 1948. Only Stalin's death put an end to the anti-Semitic campaign. The Soviet leadership stopped the campaign in its tracks and released the surviving doctors from prison, but anti-Semitism remained in the corridors of power in Moscow, Kyiv, and other Soviet centers.

JOSEPH STALIN DIED on March 5, 1953, ending the most dreadful era in Soviet history and leaving a legacy that would haunt his successors and the country they ruled for generations to come. The anti-Semitic campaign was one of many aspects of that legacy. The struggle against Stalin's inheritance became one of the defining features of Nikita Khrushchev's rule as Stalin's successor. But it took time for the former Ukrainian party boss to gain full power in the party and the state and to develop his anti-Stalinist orientation.

Nikita Khrushchev's rise to the pinnacle of Soviet power began in December 1949, when Stalin summoned him from Lviv, where he was at war with the nationalist underground, to Moscow and handed him his old position as head of the Moscow party organization. He arrived in the Soviet capital a few days before the lavish celebrations of Stalin's seventieth birthday. During the official ceremony, the dictator seated Khrushchev next to himself, with a visiting dignitary from China, Mao Zedong, on his other side.

Immediately after Stalin's death, Khrushchev emerged as one of the four most powerful Soviet leaders. In June 1953 he masterminded the arrest of his most dangerous competitor, security tsar Lavrentii Beria. In February 1955 he got rid of Beria's one-time ally, the head of the Soviet government, Georgii Malenkov. In June 1957 he crushed the opposition of Stalin's former aides Viacheslav Molotov and Lazar Kaganovich, and in March 1958 he became head of both the Communist Party and the Soviet government. The help of his clients in Ukraine made Khrushchev's success possible. The republic had the largest (in terms of membership) party organization in the union, given that the Russian communists did not have their own party, and thus the largest voting bloc in the all-union Central Committee.

Khrushchev rewarded his Ukrainian clients handsomely by bringing them to Moscow. Among the first to make the move was Oleksii Kyrychenko, the first ethnic Ukrainian in the position of party boss of Ukraine since the revolution. In 1957 he became secretary of the all-union Central Committee and the second most powerful man in the country. Khrushchev's protégés also included former party secretary from Zaporizhia and Dnipropetrovsk Leonid Brezhnev, who became head of the Supreme Soviet and de jure head of the Soviet state under Khrushchev. Another product of the Ukrainian party machine was Nikolai Podgorny (Mykola Pidhorny), the former first secretary of the Communist Party of Ukraine, appointed by Khrushchev to the all-union Central Committee in 1963. These and dozens of other Khrushchev protégés from Ukraine brought clients of their own to the center. Whereas Stalin had relied on cadres from the Caucasus for a good part of his career, Khrushchev relied on people from Ukraine. By promoting Ukrainian party cadres to positions of power in Moscow, Khrushchev made the Ukrainian communist elite a junior partner of the Russian party and government bosses in running the multiethnic Soviet empire. Its members gained influence on decisions made in the center, as well as more autonomy in deciding their internal Ukrainian affairs.

The rise of Ukraine to honorary second place in the hierarchy of Soviet republics and nationalities began in January 1954 with all-union celebrations of the tercentenary of the Pereiaslav Council (1654). Official party propaganda hailed the council, which approved the passing of the Cossack Hetmanate under the protection of the Muscovite tsar, as the "reunification of Ukraine with Russia." That formula had its roots in the nineteenth-century imperial paradigm of the "reunification of Rus'" through the efforts and under the auspices of the autocratic Russian state. A special document officially approved by the Central Committee in Moscow, the "Theses on the Tercentenary of the Reunification of Ukraine with Russia," explained what that formula meant under the new circumstances. The document built on the Stalinist policy of treating the Russians as the "leading force of the Soviet Union among all the peoples of our country"—the formula coined by Stalin in a toast he delivered at the banquet celebrating the end of the Soviet-German war in May 1945. It also elevated the Ukrainians to the status of the second most important Soviet nationality. According to the document, Russians and Ukrainians were separate peoples, albeit closely related in history and culture.

The Soviet authorities ordered the construction of a number of monuments to mark the anniversary and gave the long, awkward name "Tercentenary of the Reunification of Ukraine with Russia" to a number of institutions, including a university in the city of Dnipropetrovsk. Ironically enough, Hetman Pavlo Skoropadsky had founded the university in 1918 at a time when Russian forces had been driven out of Ukraine and the country was under German control. But the most lavish symbolic gesture, celebrating the "eternal friendship" of the two East Slavic peoples, was the transfer of the Crimean Peninsula in February 1954 from the jurisdiction of the Russian Federation to that of Ukraine. Ten years earlier, the Crimean Tatars had been deported from the Crimea, as the entire nation was accused of collaborating with the Germans. Despite the propagandistic effort to represent the transfer of the peninsula as a manifestation of fraternal amity between the two nations, the real reasons were more prosaic. The key factor was geography. Cut off from Russia by the Kerch Strait and linked by communication lines to the Ukrainian mainland, the Crimea needed assistance from Ukraine to rebuild its economy, which not only the war and German occupation but also the expulsion of the Crimean Tatars had undermined.

In 1950, the Crimea delivered to the state five times less grain than it had in 1940, three times less tobacco, and twice fewer grapes. The settlers sent to the peninsula from the Russian Federation were unaccustomed to southern conditions and of little help in rebuilding the economy. When in the fall of 1953 Nikita Khrushchev visited the peninsula, distressed settlers besieged his car and demanded assistance. From the Crimea he went directly to Kyiv to begin negotiations on the transfer of the peninsula to Ukraine, believing that the republic was in a position to help the economically depressed region and that its agricultural experts knew how to deal with droughts and produce grain in steppe conditions. Khrushchev's clients in Kyiv went along, as did his colleagues in Moscow. By February 1954, the Ukrainian, Russian, and all-union Supreme Soviets had signed off on the deal.

The Crimea became part of Ukraine—the first and last enlargement of the republic's territory based not on ethnic but geographic and economic considerations. Of the 1.2 million inhabitants of the Crimea, Russians constituted 71 percent and Ukrainians 22 percent. The peninsula benefited from the new arrangement and the investments and expertise provided by the Ukrainian government. The production of Crimean wines doubled between 1953 and 1956, and production of electricity increased by almost 60 percent. But the major boost to the Crimean economy came in the following decade with the construction of the North Crimean Canal, whose first stage was completed in 1963. As construction continued in subsequent years, the canal made it possible to bring as much as 30 percent of all Dnieper water to the peninsula and irrigate more than 6,000 square kilometers of agricultural land. It also supplied water to the cities of Feodosiia, Kerch, and Sudak.

Nikita Khrushchev's secret speech at the Twentieth Party Congress, held in Moscow in February 1956, opened a new era in the life of the Soviet Union and its constituent republics. The new leader attacked Joseph Stalin for violating the principles of socialist legality by instigating purges of party members. He did not mention the persecution of millions who did not belong to the party, the Great Famine of 1932 and 1933, and the deportations of entire nations. As the de-Stalinization drive launched by Khrushchev's speech continued, many former leaders of Ukraine, including Stanislav Kosior, Vlas Chubar, and Mykola Skrypnyk, were politically rehabilitated. The

Ukrainian KGB—the Committee for State Security, a new name for the secret police—and Ukraine's general prosecutor's office reviewed close to a million cases of victims of political terror, rehabilitating under 300,000 people. Charges and sentences remained in effect for those accused of Ukrainian nationalism, taking part in the nationalist underground, or collaborating with the Germans. Still, tens of thousands of members of the Ukrainian nationalist underground were released from the Gulag, as were surviving bishops and priests of the Ukrainian Catholic Church. The KGB placed most of these people under surveillance upon their release.

Khrushchev was a believer. He had faith in communism as a superior social order. In the early 1960s, he publicly declared to his own people and the world that the basis for a communist society would be established in the next twenty years. In Marxist-Leninist parlance of the time, that meant ability to produce an abundance of consumer goods, which were in short supply in the USSR. Khrushchev also adopted a new party program of communist construction. The promotion of the new secular religion, now with a firm date for the advent of the communist paradise, went hand in hand with struggle against traditional religion. In a reversal of postwar Stalinist policy, Khrushchev unleashed new repressions against religious groups, promising the extinction of religion before the arrival of communism and pledging to show the last religious believer on television in the not too distant future. Thousands of Orthodox churches, mosques, synagogues, and prayer houses were closed as part of this revival of the antireligious campaign of the 1920s and 1930s. In Ukraine, the number of Orthodox churches fell by almost half, from 8,207 to 4,565, between 1960 and 1965. Especially hard hit were the regions of eastern and central Ukraine—in Galicia, the authorities were careful not to close too many churches in order not to drive the newly converted Orthodox believers into the ranks of the clandestine Ukrainian Catholic Church.

While it was clear to many that the advertised arrival of communism was little more than a propaganda ploy, the end of the Stalinist terror, the release of some categories of political prisoners, and the publication of works exposing the crimes of Stalin's regime (including the writings of Aleksandr Solzhenitsyn, a prisoner of the Gulag between 1945 and 1953) created an atmosphere of relative freedom known as the "Khrushchev thaw." In Ukraine it was marked by a return to public life of the generation of writers and artists whose works had been proscribed under late Stalinism. Among them was Ukraine's best-known filmmaker, Oleksandr Dovzhenko, who was able to leave his Moscow exile and resume work in his homeland. The poets Maksym Rylsky and Volodymyr Sosiura, who had been under attack in the 1940s and 1950s, were active again. They helped raise a new generation of Ukrainian poets—Ivan Drach, Vitalii Korotych, and Lina Kostenko, among others—who became leading figures of the "sixties generation," which was pushing the limits of socialist-realist literature and culture.

The new party line was sold to worried cadres as a return to "Leninist norms," which meant, among other things, the end of mass purges of the party apparatus and some decentralization of power. Both changes empowered the regional and republican elites, and the Ukrainian cadres were more than happy to embrace the new opportunities. With the creation of regional councils charged with economic development (another return to the policies of the 1920s), the Ukrainian authorities found themselves in control of more than 90 percent of enterprises located on their territory and all of their agricultural facilities. They were now much more independent of the center than their predecessors. From the early 1950s, local officials ran Ukraine with virtually no influx of party and government personnel from Russia or any other Soviet republic. The local cadres were organized in client networks, with the position of an individual party boss depending on his (there were very few women in the party apparatus) personal loyalty to his superior. The Ukrainian party networks extended all the way to the Kremlin, becoming more stable and independent than most other republican networks in the union.

Khrushchev's reforms contributed to the spectacular expansion of Soviet industry and the increasing urbanization of Soviet society. His program of constructing cheap five-story apartment buildings that became known as *khrushchevki* changed the skyline of every Soviet city and allowed hundreds of thousands of citizens to move from temporary shelters and cramped communal apartments to individual apartments with heat, running water, and indoor toilets. Although most state resources went to the development of the Virgin Lands of Kazakhstan and the natural resources of Siberia in the Khrushchev years, Ukraine became one of the main beneficiaries—and victims—of the new industrial growth.

In the 1950s and 1960s, three new hydroelectric power stations went up on the Dnieper, diverting the natural flow of the river, creating gigantic artificial lakes, flooding agricultural lands and nearby mines, and forever changing the ecology of the region. The construction of chemical complexes designed to produce pesticides for agriculture and consumer goods for the masses enhanced the economic potential of the republic but also increased pressure on its ecological system. Ukraine was also deeply involved in the Soviet atomic and space projects, both products of the arms race that accompanied most of the Cold War. In the town of Zhovti Vody, close to the site of the first battle between Bohdan Khmelnytsky and the Polish royal army in 1648, uranium was discovered and mined. The largest missile-producing facility in all of Europe was built in the nearby city of Dnipropetrovsk. Ukraine's contribution to the Soviet breakthrough into outer space was enormous. In recognition of that contribution and Ukraine's symbolic place in the hierarchy of Soviet republics, a Ukrainian became the first non-Russian launched into space by a Soviet rocket. Pavlo Popovych, a native of the Kyiv region, made his first trip into space in 1962. His second flight would take place in 1974.

As might have been expected, the growth of the Soviet space program and the military-industrial complex did little for the well-being of the population, which in the early 1960s again found itself on the verge of famine. The immediate cause of food shortages was a number of droughts that hit Soviet agriculture. This time, instead of exporting grain as in 1932 and 1933 and in 1946 and 1947, the government decided to buy grain abroad, avoiding a repetition of the disasters of those years. It was a marked departure from Stalin's times. Khrushchev tried to improve the plight of the peasants and the productivity of collective farms by dramatically raising purchase prices for agricultural products (the price for grain increased sevenfold). He also reduced the individual plots of collective farmers by half, believing that this would free them from extra effort at home and leave more time and energy for work on the collective farms.

But Khrushchev's well-intentioned policies did not bring the results he had hoped for. He continued to dictate what the collective farms should cultivate and how, promoting the increased production of corn, which could not and did not grow in the places designated by the party apparatchiks in Moscow. His attempt to provide the peasants with more time to relax undermined the production of agricultural products on individual lots. Between 1958 and 1962, the number of domestic animals in individual ownership decreased by more than half, from 22 million to 10 million. The reforms that were supposed to increase productivity and improve living standards in the village made products much more expensive in the cities, where prices for butter went up by 50 percent and meat by 25 percent. Many city dwellers recalled the 1950s as a paradise lost. The peasants preferred the 1960s.

IN OCTOBER 1964, when the members of Khrushchev's inner circle, including his Ukrainian protégés Leonid Brezhnev and Nikolai Podgorny, removed him from power in a palace coup, few Soviet citizens had anything good to say about one of the Soviet Union's greatest reformers. They took full advantage, however, of the opportunity provided by his de-Stalinization policies to complain publicly about their ousted leader and his economic initiatives, which had left store shelves empty and driven prices for agricultural products through the roof.

The new leaders, who had arranged the coup partly out of fear that Khrushchev would blame them for economic difficulties and remove them from power, decided to play it safe. They returned to the centralized model of the Soviet economy created in the 1930s by abolishing regional economic councils and reinstating all-union ministries in Moscow as the main governing bodies of the Soviet economy. But they left in place the relatively high purchase prices for agricultural products, turning agriculture from a source of revenue, as in Stalin's times, into an economic black hole that demanded ever new subsidies. The living conditions of collective farmers, which had never been easy, improved somewhat, but their productivity did not; moreover, the new leaders never reinstated the original sizes of individual plots and continued to suppress personal initiative in the agricultural sector. Like Khrushchev, they made it an official goal to improve living standards for the population but feared the power of private ownership and private initiative.

The ouster of Khrushchev and his replacement as party leader by a less ideologically motivated Leonid Brezhnev led to the scaling down of his "communism tomorrow" propaganda campaign. It also brought about the reinstatement of Stalin-era controls on public debate and a return to political repression. The new leadership signaled the change, of course, by arresting and putting on trial Andrei Siniavsky and Yulii Daniel—two writers who published their works in the West and stood accused of anti-Soviet activities. The arrests came in the fall of 1965, a year after Khrushchev's dismissal. In early 1966 the two intellectuals were sentenced to seven and five years of hard labor, respectively. The trial marked the end of the Khrushchev thaw.

In Ukraine, arrests began a few months earlier, in the summer of 1965. The KGB targeted young intellectuals in Kyiv and Lviv who had begun their literary and cultural activities during the thaw. An early activist of the Ukrainian dissident movement, Yevhen Sverstiuk, later characterized it as essentially cultural and driven by "youthful idealism . . . a search for truth and honesty . . . rejection, resistance, and opposition to official literature." While concerned with the fate of the Ukrainian nation and its culture, young intellectuals presented their arguments in Marxist-Leninist terms, pushing the limits of Khrushchev's de-Stalinization and "return to Leninism" campaigns. That was especially true of one of the first *samvydav* (Russian: *samizdat*, or self-published) texts of the Ukrainian dissident movement, titled *Internationalism or Russification?* Written soon after the first arrests of Ukrainian dissidents in 1965 by the young literary critic Ivan Dziuba, the treatise argued that under Stalin Soviet nationality policy had lost its Leninist bearings, rejected internationalism, and become hostage to Russian chauvinism.

Despite the growing political rigidity of the regime and its increased intolerance toward any form of opposition, the "Khrushchev thaw" did not end in Ukraine with the first arrests of young intellectuals and continued in some respects until the early 1970s. This was certainly true of the revival of national communism, which found a strong supporter in Petro Shelest, the first secretary of the Central Committee of the Communist Party of Ukraine and a member of the all-union Politburo. The son of peasants from the Kharkiv region of eastern Ukraine, he had joined the party in the 1920s. Like the national communists of that era (one of whom, Mykola Skrypnyk, was not only rehabilitated but also celebrated in Ukraine in the 1960s), Shelest believed that his main task was not to follow orders from Moscow but to promote the economic development of Ukraine and support its culture. The Ukrainian language was under ever-increasing pressure from Russian: the number of students in Ukrainian-language schools had been falling since the prewar years, with the proportion of students in Russian schools increasing from 14 percent in 1939 to 25 percent in 1955 and to more than 30 percent in 1962.

These figures disturbed Petro Shelest, who presided over the formation of a new type of Ukrainian identity that took pride in the republic's role in defeating German aggression and in its enhanced status in the union, combining elements of loyalty to the socialist experiment with local patriotism and celebration of Ukrainian history and culture. This new identity was an amalgam of the Soviet identity formed in the 1920s and the national identity that had taken shape in interwar Poland, Romania, and, to some extent, Transcarpathia. While dominant, the Soviet component had to adjust and become more culturally Ukrainian and self-assertive than it would otherwise have been.

The political situation in Moscow, which somewhat resembled that of the 1920s, helped Shelest's return to the ideas of national communism and his ability to pursue them long after the ouster of Khrushchev. A number of political cliques were fighting for control of the party and government, and the support of Ukrainian party cadres was as essential in Moscow in the 1960s as it had been in the 1920s. Shelest was only too happy to trade support for the Brezhnev group, which was competing with cadres led by former KGB head Aleksandr Shelepin, for limited Ukrainian political and cultural autonomy. The informal deal came to an end in 1972 when Brezhnev, having marginalized Shelepin, decided to move against Shelest. The latter was transferred to Moscow in May 1972 and, while still a member of the Moscow Politburo, accused of nationalist deviations on the basis of his book *O Ukraine, Our Soviet Land*, which was full of pride in Ukrainian history and the republic's achievements under socialism.

Brezhnev replaced Shelest with his own loyalist, Volodymyr Shcherbytsky, who came from Brezhnev's native Dnipropetrovsk region. The Dnipropetrovsk faction was pushing aside other Ukrainian cadres in Moscow and Kyiv and taking ever greater control of the Soviet party and state machine. Shelest's departure from Ukraine was followed by a purge of his loyalists and an attack on Ukrainian intellectuals. Ivan Dziuba, author of the "national communist" *Internationalism or Russification?*, was sentenced to five years in labor camp and five years of internal exile for the work he had written back in 1965. Purged from institutions of the Ukrainian Academy of Sciences were Mykhailo Braichevsky and scores of other historians and literary scholars working on the pre-1917 history of Ukraine, especially the "nationalistic" Cossack era. The KGB was catching up on work it had been unable to complete in Ukraine under Petro Shelest. But repressions could do only so much and last only so long. The next time the Ukrainian party elites and Ukrainian intellectuals established a common front against Moscow, it would no longer be under the slogan of a return to Leninist ideals.

CHAPTER 25

GOOD BYE, LENIN!

O<small>N</small> N<small>OVEMBER</small> 15, 1982, the citizens of Ukraine, along with their counterparts in other republics of the Soviet Union, were glued to their
television screens. All channels were transmitting a report from Moscow: the
leaders of the Soviet Union, representatives of numerous foreign countries
and international organizations, and tens of thousands of Muscovites were
gathered in Red Square to bid farewell to Leonid Brezhnev, a native of
Ukraine who had ruled the world superpower for eighteen long years. Having been chronically ill for a considerable period, he had died in his sleep a
few days earlier. Many television viewers who had known no other leader
found it hard to believe that "Leonid Ilich Brezhnev, the indefatigable fighter
for peace throughout the world," as official propaganda hailed him, was
gone. His regime of septuagenarians had frozen upward mobility in Soviet
society, disappointed all hopes for change, and seemed able to stop time.
The operational term was "stability." Soon the Brezhnev era would become
known as the period of stagnation.

In Ukraine, in the course of the two decades from 1966 to 1985, the annual industrial growth rate had decreased from 8.4 to 3.5 percent; in agriculture, which had never done well, it fell from 3.2 to 0.5 percent. Those were
the official numbers, which did not mean much in an era of falsified reports.
The reality was even grimmer. The Soviet Union was becoming ever more
dependent on hard currency from the sale of oil and gas abroad. In the early
1970s, while Soviet and Western engineers were busy constructing pipelines
to bring gas to Europe from Siberia and central Asia, Ukrainian gas from the
Dashava and Shebelynka fields was taken away from domestic consumers

and shipped to central Europe to bring in hard currency. With its gas fields depleted, Ukraine would in time become a gas-importing country.

Khrushchev's promise to the Soviet people that they would live under communism never materialized, and the regime's propagandists had completely forgotten it. The standard of living was in free fall, slowed only by high oil prices on the world markets. By the time of Brezhnev's death, cynicism among both the elites and the general population with regard not only to communism but even to "developed socialism"—the term that replaced communism as the definition of the Soviet social order—had reached an all-time high. As Brezhnev's casket was lowered into a freshly dug grave near the Kremlin wall, the clocks on the Kremlin towers struck another hour, and the guns fired salvos signaling the end of one era and the beginning of a new one. It would bring an attempt at radical reform, dramatic economic decline, and the political fragmentation of the mighty Soviet Union—a process in which Ukraine would lead the way toward its own independence and that of less decisive Soviet republics.

AMONG THE MEMBERS of the Politburo who gathered on the podium of the Lenin mausoleum to deliver eulogies for the deceased Brezhnev, one man stood out from the rest. Volodymyr Shcherbytsky, the silver-haired party boss of Ukraine, remained hatless on that cold November day in a show of respect. A client of Brezhnev's for most of his career, Shcherbytsky had special reason to grieve. Before Brezhnev's unexpected death, there had been a rumor in the halls of the Kremlin that at the forthcoming plenum of the Central Committee he would step down and transfer his powers to Shcherbytsky, ensuring the continuing preeminence of the Dnipropetrovsk faction in the country's leadership. Shcherbytsky, a native of that region, had been the party boss of Dnipropetrovsk before coming to Kyiv. But Brezhnev died before the plenum took place. The new party leader, former KGB chief Yurii Andropov, had nothing to do with the Dnipropetrovsk clique and would soon go after Brezhnev's cronies for corruption.

After the funeral, Shcherbytsky would go back to Ukraine and dig in there, trying to survive the uncertain times. In good health at sixty-four, he was a youngster among the members of the Politburo. His immediate competitors were older and in poor condition. Besides, during his years at the helm of the Ukrainian party machine, Shcherbytsky had managed to establish a loyal clientele. He survived Andropov, who died in December 1984, and his successor, Konstantin Chernenko, who passed away in March 1985.

But his chances of rising to the top in Moscow were now a thing of the past. The partnership between the Russian and Ukrainian elites established by Nikita Khrushchev and cemented by Brezhnev was all but gone. The energetic new leader of the Soviet Union, Mikhail Gorbachev, who came to power in March 1985, had no ties to the Ukrainian party machine. The son of a Russian father and a Ukrainian mother, Gorbachev grew up in the North Caucasus—a territory with a mixed Russian and Ukrainian population—and learned Ukrainian folk songs as a child. But he was first and foremost a Soviet patriot with no special attachment to any republic except Russia. He saw the client pyramids created by Brezhnev's allies in the republics as a major threat to his own position and to the reform program that he launched soon after coming to power

The conveyor that had brought Ukrainian cadres to Moscow for the previous thirty years soon stopped functioning. Gorbachev was bringing in new people from the Russian regions. Among them was his future nemesis, Boris Yeltsin. In December 1986, Gorbachev violated the unofficial agreement between the center and the republics that had existed since Stalin's death—the party boss in charge of each republic had to be a local belonging to the titular nationality. Gorbachev "parachuted" an ethnic Russian, Gennadii Kolbin, into Kazakhstan to replace a Brezhnev loyalist, the ethnic Kazakh Dinmukhamed Konayev. The appointment of Kolbin, a product (like Yeltsin) of the Sverdlovsk (currently Yekaterinburg, an industrial city in the Urals) party machine who had no ties with Kazakhstan and had never worked there, brought Kazakh students into the streets in the first nationalist riot in the postwar history of the USSR.

The rift between the new leadership in Moscow and the leaders of Ukraine came to the fore soon after the worst technological disaster in world history— the April 1986 explosion at the Chernobyl nuclear power plant located less than seventy miles north of Kyiv—hit Ukraine. The idea of bringing nuclear energy to Ukraine belonged to Ukrainian scientists and economists; Petro Shelest, who wanted to create new sources of electrical energy for the rapidly developing Ukrainian economy, had lobbied for it in the 1960s, during his tenure as party boss of the republic. By the time the Chernobyl nuclear power station went online in 1977, Ukrainian intellectuals, including one of the leading lights of the sixties generation, Ivan Drach, were welcoming the arrival of the nuclear age in their country. For Drach and other Ukrainian patriots, Chernobyl represented a step toward the modernization of Ukraine. He and other enthusiasts of nuclearization failed to notice, however, that the project was run from Moscow, with most of the power plant's skilled personnel and management coming from outside Ukraine. The republic was getting electrical energy but had little control over what was going at the plant, which, like all Soviet nuclear facilities, and indeed most of Ukraine's industrial enterprises, was under the jurisdiction of all-union ministries. The plant itself and the accident that occurred there became known to the world under the Russian spelling of the name of the nearest city—Chernobyl, not Chornobyl.

When on the night of April 26, 1986, the fourth reactor of the Chernobyl power station exploded as a result of a turbine test that went wrong, the Ukrainian leaders suddenly realized how little control they had over their own destinies and that of their republic. Some Ukrainian officials were invited to join the central government commission dealing with the consequences of the accident but had little influence there, finding themselves obliged to follow instructions from Moscow and its representatives at the site. They organized the resettlement of those dwelling in a thirty-kilometer zone around the station but were not allowed to inform the population of the republic about the scope of the accident and the threat that it posed to the health of their fellow citizens. The limits of the republican authorities' power over the destiny of Ukraine became crystal-clear on the morning of May 1, 1986, when the winds changed direction and, instead of blowing north and west, turned south, bringing radioactive clouds to the capital of Ukraine. Given the quickly changing radiological situation in a city of more than 2 million people, the Ukrainian authorities tried to convince Moscow to cancel a planned parade marking International Workers' Day. They failed.

As party organizers brought columns of students and workers to downtown Kyiv to begin the parade on the morning of May 1, one man was conspicuously missing from the group of republican leaders: Volodymyr Shcherbytsky. For the first time in his long career, he was running late for the May Day parade. When his limousine finally reached Khreshchatyk, Kyiv's main street and the focal point of the parade, the Ukrainian party leaders saw a clearly upset Shcherbytsky. "He told me: You will put your party card on the table if you bungle the parade," said the Ukrainian party boss to his aides. No one doubted the identity of the unnamed "he"—only one person in the country, Mikhail Gorbachev, was in a position to threaten Shcherbytsky with expulsion from the party. Despite the rapidly increasing radiation level, Gorbachev ordered his Ukrainian underlings to carry on as usual in order to show the country and the world that the situation was under control and that the Chernobyl explosion presented no danger to the health of the population. Shcherbytsky and other party leaders knew otherwise but felt they had no choice other than to follow the orders from Moscow. The parade went on as scheduled. They could only shorten it from four hours to two.

The explosion and partial meltdown of the fourth reactor at the Chernobyl nuclear plant released about 50 million curies of radiation into the atmosphere—the equivalent of five hundred Hiroshima bombs. In Ukraine alone, more than 50,000 square kilometers of land were contaminated—a territory larger than Belgium. The exclusion zone around the reactor alone accounted for 2,600 square kilometers, from which more than 90,000 inhabitants were evacuated in the first weeks after the explosion. Most of them would never see their homes again. The city of Prypiat, which housed close to 50,000 construction workers and operational personnel of the power plant, remains deserted even today—a modern-day Pompeii memorializing what would become the last days of the Soviet Union. Images of Vladimir Lenin and the builders of communism, along with slogans celebrating the Communist Party, still remain on the walls of Prypiat.

In Ukraine, the radiation fallout directly affected 2,300 settlements and more than 3 million people. The explosion endangered close to 30 million people who relied on the Dnieper and other rivers for their water supply. The accident was a disaster for the forest areas of northern Ukraine—the oldest settled regions of the country, where for millennia the local population had found refuge from steppe invaders. Now the forests that had provided shelter from the nomads and food for survivors of the Great Famine of 1932 and 1933 became sources of destruction. Their leaves emitted radiation—an invisible enemy from which there was no refuge. It was a disaster of global proportions, and with the exception of neighboring Belarus, nowhere felt more acutely than Ukraine.

The Chernobyl accident sharply increased discontent with Moscow and its policies across all party and social lines—radiation affected everyone, from members of the party leadership to ordinary citizens. As the Ukrainian party bosses mobilized the population to deal with the consequences of the disaster and clean up the mess created by the center, many asked themselves why they were risking their own lives and those of their family members. Around their kitchen tables, they grumbled about the center's failed policies and shared their frustration with the people they trusted. Only the Ukrainian writers would not remain silent. At the meetings organized by the members of the

Ukrainian Writer's Union, many of those who had welcomed the arrival of nuclear power a decade earlier now condemned it as an instrument of Moscow's domination of their republic. Among those leading the charge was Ivan Drach, whose son, a student in a Kyiv medical school, had been sent to Chernobyl soon after the accident without proper instructions or protective gear and was now suffering from radiation poisoning.

The Chernobyl disaster awakened Ukraine, raising fundamental questions about relations between the center and the republics, the Communist Party and the people, and helping to start the first major public debate in a society struggling to regain its voice after decades of Brezhnev-era stagnation. The generation of the 1960s was in the forefront. Among them was writer Yurii Shcherbak, who organized an environmental group in late 1987 that evolved into the Green Party. The ecological movement, which presented Ukraine as a victim of Moscow's activities, became one of the first forms of national mobilization in Ukraine during the years of the Gorbachev reforms. The new man in the Kremlin not only alienated the Ukrainian party leadership but also empowered democratically minded intellectuals and the nationally conscious intelligentsia to mobilize against that elite. As things turned out, the two conflicting groups in Ukraine—the communist establishment and the nascent democratic opposition—would discover a common interest in opposing Moscow in general and Gorbachev in particular.

MIKHAIL GORBACHEV WAS in many ways a member of the sixties generation, his worldview strongly shaped by Khrushchev's de-Stalinization campaign and inspired by ideas of socialist reform promoted in the 1960s by liberal economists and political scientists both in the USSR and in eastern Europe. One of the principal ideologists of the Prague Spring of 1968, Zdeněk Mlynář, was Gorbachev's roommate in the dormitory of Moscow University Law School in the 1950s. Gorbachev and his advisers wanted to reform socialism in order to make it more efficient and "user-friendly," or, as people said in Prague before the Soviet invasion of 1968, to create socialism with a human face.

Gorbachev began with a program of "accelerating" Soviet economic development that did not call for fundamental reform but emphasized the more efficient use of available institutions and resources. But the Soviet economy was in no condition to accelerate anything other than rates of decline. "We were on the edge of an abyss," went a political joke of Brezhnev's times, "but since then we have made a huge step forward." The rhetoric of "acceleration" soon gave way to the policy of "perestroika," or restructuring, which took decision-making authority away from ministries in Moscow and invested it not in the regions and republics, as under Khrushchev, but in individual enterprises. This upset the central bureaucracies and local bosses, who were also antagonized by Gorbachev's policy of "glasnost," or openness, which exposed them to criticism from below, which the Moscow-based media now encouraged. Perestroika originally mobilized support for the new leader and his reformist ideas among the intellectuals and the urban intelligentsia, who were fed up with Brezhnev-era controls on public life and the lies of official propaganda.

Gorbachev's reforms created opportunities for political mobilization from below. In Ukraine, dissidents of the 1960s and 1970s freshly released from the Gulag were among the first to take advantage of the new political and social climate. In the spring of 1988 they founded the Ukrainian Helsinki Union, the first openly political organization in perestroika-era Ukraine. Most of its members—including the head of the union, Moscow-trained lawyer Levko Lukianenko, who had spent more than a quarter century in prison and internal exile—had previously belonged to the Brezhnev-era Ukrainian Helsinki Group. That dissident organization, created in 1976, took on the task of monitoring the Soviet government's observance of its human rights obligations as defined at the Helsinki Conference on Security and Cooperation in Europe, which took place in the Finnish capital in the summer of 1975. If many members of the group, and then the union, began in the 1960s as Marxists who wanted to reinstate "Leninist norms" of nationality policy, the arrests unleashed in 1972 in conjunction with the removal from Ukraine of Petro Shelest put an end to their communist ideals. The Helsinki movement provided the Ukrainian dissidents with a new ideology—that of human rights, including the rights both of individuals and of nations, defined in political and cultural terms.

The defense of national culture, especially language, was among the key issues that galvanized Ukrainian society during the first years of perestroika. The first truly mass organization to be created in Ukraine was the Society [for the Protection] of the Ukrainian Language, which by the end of 1989, the year of its creation, numbered 150,000 members. Ukrainian intellectuals considered their language and culture—the very foundations of the Ukrainian nation—to be under threat. Language presented a special challenge. According to the census of 1989, Ukrainians constituted 73 percent of the republic's population of 51 million, but only 88 percent of them claimed Ukrainian as their mother tongue, and only 40 percent used it as a language of convenience. This was largely the outcome of an urbanization process in which rural Ukrainians moved to the cities only to become culturally Russified. By the 1980s, there were large ethnic Ukrainian majorities in most Ukrainian cities (Donetsk, where Russians were still in the majority, was a rare exception), but the language of convenience in all major cities, with the notable exception of Lviv in western Ukraine, was Russian. The Ukrainian Language Society wanted to reverse the process, addressing first and foremost those ethnic Ukrainians who did not speak Ukrainian on a daily basis but had a pronounced Ukrainian identity and believed that they or their children should speak the language. It was an uphill battle.

In the late 1980s, the Soviet Union was sometimes portrayed as a country not only with an unpredictable future but also with an unpredictable past. The Ukrainians, like the other non-Russian nationalities, were trying to recover a past concealed from them by decades of official Soviet historiography and propaganda. The "recovery" began with the return to the public sphere of the historical writings of Mykhailo Hrushevsky, issued in hundreds of thousands of copies. Also reprinted were the works of writers and poets of the 1920s, representatives of the so-called Executed Renaissance of Ukrainian culture, many of whom did not survive the terror of the 1930s. As in Russia and other republics, the Memorial Society took the lead in uncovering Stalin's crimes of the Great Purge period. In that regard, Ukrainian intellectuals had stories to tell that were unique to their country. The first of them was the history of the Great Famine of 1932 and 1933, which the regime had covered up completely. The second was the story of armed resistance to the Soviet regime in the late 1940s and early 1950s conducted by the Organization of Ukrainian Nationalists and the fighters of the Ukrainian Insurgent Army.

The famine was part of eastern Ukrainian experience, while nationalist resistance and insurgency had characterized western Ukraine, but revived fascination with one historical narrative was capable of uniting east and west—the story of the Cossack past. After the removal of Petro Shelest in 1972, the authorities instituted a purge of so-called Cossackophiles among historians and writers, treating an interest in Cossack history as tantamount to an expression of nationalism. Now, with the collapse of the official historical worldview, the Cossack myth made its way back into the public arena, and indeed, as Brezhnev's propagandists maintained, it was closely linked to the national idea.

In the summer of 1990 Ukrainian activists, many of them from Galicia and western Ukraine, organized a "march to the east"—a mass pilgrimage to Zaporizhia and Cossack sites along the lower Dnieper. The march aimed to "awaken" Ukrainian identity in the eastern regions of the republic. It was a huge success, mobilizing tens of thousands of people and popularizing a version of Ukrainian history opposed to the one dominant in still very pro-communist southern Ukraine. In the following year the authorities, who had originally opposed the march, decided to jump on the bandwagon of the rising Cossack mythology. They sponsored their own Cossack events in both eastern and western Ukraine but failed to reap the expected political dividends. The party and its credibility were in precipitous decline.

"What idiot invented the word 'perestroika'?" Shcherbytsky asked his staffers when he heard the term for the first time. When Gorbachev, on a visit to Kyiv, asked people preselected by the KGB to apply pressure to local leaders, Shcherbytsky, who was present at the meeting, turned to his aides and pointed a finger at his head, indicating that Gorbachev's mind was addled, and asked, "Whom, then, is he going to rely on?" In September 1989, Gorbachev felt strong enough to take on the last holdover of the Brezhnev regime in the Politburo—Shcherbytsky himself. That month Gorbachev came to Kyiv to tell the party elite that the all-union Politburo had voted to remove Shcherbytsky from his position. The Ukrainian Central Committee had no choice but to depose him as its first secretary as well. Less than half a year later, Shcherbytsky would succumb to illness, unable to deal not only with the end of his own career but also with the end of the political and social order he had served all his life.

THE YEAR 1989 became a turning point in Ukrainian political history in more ways than one. It saw the arrival of mass politics, with the first semifree elections to the new Soviet parliament; the creation of the first political mass organization, called Rukh—the Popular Movement for Perestroika—whose membership approached the 300,000 mark in the fall of 1989 and more than doubled by the end of the following year; and the legalization of the Ukrainian Catholic Church, which the Stalin regime had driven underground but whose supporters now numbered in the millions. In 1990, elections to the new Ukrainian parliament dramatically changed the political scene in Kyiv. Pro-democratic deputies formed a bloc called the People's Council that managed to change the tone of Ukrainian politics, although only a quarter of the parliamentary deputies belonged to it. In the summer of 1990, the Ukrainian parliament followed in the footsteps of its counterparts in the Baltic republics and Russia, declaring Ukraine a sovereign country. The declaration did not stipulate the republic's secession from the USSR but gave its laws precedence over those of the union.

The center was powerless to stop the republics' assertion of sovereignty. Gorbachev, the father of the Soviet reforms, was by now in serious trouble. He had alienated the communist elites and lost the support of the intelligentsia in the center and the republics. His economic reforms unbalanced the economic system, sending production figures into a tailspin and worsening already low living standards. The party bosses were unhappy with reforms that threatened their power and struck them as doomed to fail, further endangering their position. Intellectuals, by contrast, considered the reforms insufficiently radical and tardily implemented. Ironically, these mutually hostile groups found a common enemy in Gorbachev and the center as a whole. Sovereignty, and finally complete independence, became a common platform enabling cooperation between these opposing forces in the Ukrainian political spectrum.

Mass mobilization in Ukraine followed a variety of regional patterns defined by history. In Galicia, Volhynia, and to some extent Bukovyna—areas attached to the Soviet Union on the basis of the Molotov-Ribbentrop Pact— mobilization was similar to that in the Baltic states, which the USSR had also annexed at the start of World War II. There, former dissidents and intellectuals led the movement under the banner of democratic nationalism, and took control over local governments. In the rest of the country, the party elites, whose survival Gorbachev made dependent on their ability to get elected to the republican and regional councils, were confused, but hung on to power. When the Ukrainian Supreme Soviet elected as its new chairman a native of Volhynia, the fifty-six-year-old Leonid Kravchuk, the arrival of this new leader originally from western Ukraine did not appear to count for much. But times were changing. Gorbachev's reforms made parliament by far the most important branch of government. By the end of 1990, the wily Kravchuk had emerged as the most powerful and popular leader in Ukraine. He was the only Ukrainian official who could talk to the rising opposition movement, based largely in the western lands. He also had a significant following among the party elite, the group of so-called pro-sovereignty communists who wanted political and economic autonomy for Ukraine.

In the course of the following year, Kravchuk showed real political talent in maneuvering among various groups of deputies and steering parliament toward the achievement of sovereignty and then independence. The first test of his skills came in the fall of 1990. Alarmed by the Lithuanian declaration of independence in March of that year and responding to the growing pro-independence movement in the other republics, Gorbachev succumbed to the pressure of hard-liners in his government and gave tacit approval for the rollback of democratic freedoms. In Ukraine, the communist majority in parliament passed a law prohibiting demonstrations near the parliament building and approved the arrest of a member of the People's Council in parliament. But the communist hard-liners were in for a surprise. On the morning of October 2, 1990, dozens of students from Kyiv, Lviv, and Dnipropetrovsk descended on October Revolution Square in downtown Kyiv— the future Independence Square, known as Maidan—and began a hunger strike. Among other things, they demanded the resignation of the prime minister and Ukraine's withdrawal from negotiations on the new union treaty—Gorbachev's initiative to save the union by giving its constituent republics greater autonomy.

The authorities were divided in their reaction to the student strike. Whereas the government brought in the police to disperse the protesters, the Kyiv city council gave permission for the protest to continue. Over the next few days, the number of hunger strikers grew to 150. When the government organized its supporters to dislodge the protesters, close to 50,000 Kyivans marched on the square to protect the students. Soon all the city universities were on strike. The protesters marched on parliament, occupying the square in front of the parliament building. Under pressure from the street and urged to yield by Kravchuk and the parliamentary moderates, the communist majority decided to retreat. They gave the student leaders television time to present their demands and dismissed the head of government, who had taken part in negotiations for a new union. It was a major victory for the Ukrainian students and Ukrainian society as a whole. The events of October 1990 in downtown Kyiv would later become known as the First Maidan (*maidan* is Ukrainian for "square"). The second would come in 2004 and the third in 2013 and 2014.

When on August 1, 1991, President George H. W. Bush of the United States flew to Kyiv from Moscow to urge Ukraine to stay in the USSR, the Ukrainian political class was divided with regard to its goals. The national democratic minority wanted outright independence, demands for which had been growing in Ukraine ever since Lithuania declared its own independence in March 1990. The communist majority in the Ukrainian parliament wanted broad autonomy within a reformed union. That was also Gorbachev's aim. After failing to stop the independence drive of the Baltic republics of Lithuania, Latvia, and Estonia by using military force in early 1991, Gorbachev called a referendum on the continuing existence of the union. It took place in March 1991, and 70 percent of those who took part voted in favor of a reformed union. Gorbachev also renewed his negotiations with the republican leaders, including Boris Yeltsin of Russia and Nursultan Nazarbaev of Kazakhstan, trying to convince them to form a looser union. He reached a deal with them in late July 1991, but Ukraine was not ready to sign. Leonid Kravchuk and his group were pushing for a different solution: a confederation with Russia and other republics that Ukraine would join on its own terms.

Bush took Gorbachev's side in his address to the Ukrainian parliament, dubbed by the American media his "Chicken Kiev speech" because of the American president's reluctance to endorse the independence aspirations of the national democratic deputies. Bush favored setting the Baltic republics free but keeping Ukraine and the rest together. He did not want to lose a reliable partner on the world stage—Gorbachev and the Soviet Union that he represented. Moreover, Bush and his advisers were concerned about the possibility of an uncontrolled disintegration of the union, which could lead to wars between republics with nuclear arms on their territory. Apart from Russia, these included Ukraine, Belarus, and Kazakhstan. In his speech to the Ukrainian parliament, President Bush appealed to his audience to renounce "suicidal nationalism" and avoid confusing freedom with independence. The communist majority applauded him with enthusiasm. The democratic minority was disappointed: the alliance of Washington with Moscow and the communist deputies in the Ukrainian parliament presented a major obstacle to Ukrainian independence. It was hard to imagine that before the month was out, parliament would vote almost unanimously for the independence of Ukraine and that by the end of November, the White House, initially concerned about the possibility of chaos and nuclear war in the post-Soviet state, would endorse that vote.

THE EVENT THAT triggered the change of heart among the conservative deputies of the Ukrainian parliament and, in time, throughout the world was the hard-liners' coup against Mikhail Gorbachev in Moscow on August 19, 1991.

The coup had in fact begun a day earlier in Ukraine, more specifically in the Crimea, where Gorbachev was taking his summer vacation. On the evening of August 18, the plotters showed up on the doorstep of his seaside mansion near Foros and demanded the introduction of martial law. Gorbachev refused to sign the papers, forcing the plotters to act on their own. On the following day, in Moscow, the plotters, led by the KGB chief and the ministers of defense and interior, declared a state of emergency throughout the USSR. The Ukrainian leadership, headed by Kravchuk, refused to implement the emergency measures in their republic but, in striking contrast to Russian president Boris Yeltsin in Moscow, did nothing to challenge the coup. While Kravchuk called for the people of Ukraine to stay calm, Yeltsin brought his supporters into the streets and forced the military to withdraw from Moscow after the first skirmishes between the army and the protesters resulted in fatalities. The plotters blinked and lost. In less than seventy-two hours, the coup was over and the plotters under arrest. Muscovites poured into the streets to celebrate the victory not only of freedom over dictatorship but also of Russia over the union center.

Gorbachev returned to Moscow but proved incapable of regaining power. In fact, he fell victim to another coup, led this time by Yeltsin, who took advantage of the weakening of the center to start Russia's takeover of the union. He forced Gorbachev to rescind decrees appointing his people as heads of the army, police, and security forces, and then suspended the activities of the Communist Party, leaving Gorbachev no choice but to resign as its general secretary. Russia was effectively taking over the union—an unexpected turn of events that diminished interest in the union among those republics that had wanted to be part of it until August 1991. Ukraine was now leading the way out.

On August 24, 1991, the day after Yeltsin took control of the union government, the Ukrainian parliament held a vote on independence. "In view of the mortal danger hanging over Ukraine in connection with the coup d'état on 19 August 1991, and continuing the thousand-year tradition of state building in Ukraine," read the declaration of independence drafted by Levko Lukianenko, the longest-serving prisoner of the Gulag and now a member of parliament, "the Supreme Soviet of the Ukrainian Soviet Socialist Republic solemnly declares the independence of Ukraine." The results of the vote came as a surprise to everyone, including Lukianenko himself: 346 deputies voted in favor, 5 abstained, and only 2 voted against. The communist majority that had opposed independence since the first session of parliament in the spring of 1990 was no longer in evidence. Kravchuk and his "pro-sovereignty communists," under attack from the opposition for not having opposed the coup, closed ranks with the national democrats and brought along the hard-liners, who felt betrayed by Moscow and threatened by Yeltsin's attack on the party. Once the result of the vote appeared on the screen, the hall exploded in applause. The crowds outside the parliament building were jubilant: Ukraine was free at last!

Lukianenko's declaration referred to the thousand-year history of Ukrainian statehood, meaning the tradition established by Kyivan Rus'. His declaration was in fact the fourth attempt to proclaim Ukrainian independence in the twentieth century: the first occurred in 1918 in Kyiv and then in Lviv, the second in 1939 in Transcarpathia, and the third in 1941 in Lviv. All those attempts had been made in wartime, and all had come to grief. Would this one be different? The next three months would tell. A popular referendum scheduled for December 1, 1991, the same day as the previously scheduled election of Ukraine's first president, would confirm or reject the parliamentary vote for independence. The referendum provision was important for more than one reason. On August 24, it helped those members of the communist majority who had doubts about independence to vote in favor of it—theirs, after all, was not the final decision and could be reversed in the future. The referendum also gave Ukraine a chance to leave the union without open conflict with the center. In the previous referendum organized by Gorbachev in March 1991, about 70 percent of Ukrainians had voted to stay in a reformed union. Now another referendum would enable it to make a clean break.

Gorbachev believed that support for independence in Ukraine would never reach 70 percent. Yeltsin was not so sure. In late August 1991, soon after the Ukrainian parliament had voted for independence, he instructed his press secretary to make a statement that if Ukraine and other republics declared independence, Russia would have the right to open the question of its borders with those republics. Yeltsin's press secretary indicated the Crimea and eastern parts of Ukraine, including the Donbas coal region, as possible areas of contention. The threat was partition if Ukraine insisted on independence. Yeltsin then sent a high-powered delegation led by his vice president, General Aleksandr Rutskoi, to force Ukraine to reverse its stance. But the Ukrainians stood their ground, and Rutskoi returned to Moscow empty-handed. Blackmail had failed, and Yeltsin had neither the political will nor the resources to deliver on his threat.

In September 1991, Ukraine entered a new political season. Six candidates were contending for the presidency, and all of them were campaigning for independence. Kravchuk convinced the Crimean authorities to shelve their plans for a separate referendum on the peninsula's independence from Ukraine. Polling numbers showed growing support for independence among all national groups and in all regions of the country. The two largest minorities— the Russians, who numbered more than 11 million, and the Jews, whose numbers approached 500,000—were expressing support for the idea of Ukrainian independence. In November 1991, 58 percent of ethnic Russians and 60 percent of ethnic Jews were in favor. The minorities now embraced the Ukrainian cause, as they had not done in 1918, regarding Moscow with greater concern and suspicion than the capital of their republic.

On December 1, 1991, Ukrainians of all ethnic backgrounds went to the polls to decide their fate. The results were mind-boggling for even the most optimistic proponents of independence. The turnout reached 84 percent, with more than 90 percent of voters supporting independence. Western Ukraine led the way, with 99 percent in favor in the Ternopil oblast of Galicia. But the center, south, and even the east were not far behind. In Vinnytsia, in central Ukraine, 95 percent voted for independence; in Odesa, in the south, 85 percent; and in the Donetsk region, in the east, 83 percent. Even in the Crimea, more than half the voters supported independence: 57 percent in Sevastopol and 54 percent in the peninsula as a whole. (At that time, Russians constituted 66 percent of the Crimean population, Ukrainians 25 percent, and the Crimean Tatars, who had just begun to return to their ancestral homeland, only 1.5 percent.) In the center and east of the country, many voted for independence while supporting Leonid Kravchuk's bid for the presidency. He won 61 percent of the popular vote, obtaining a majority in all regions of Ukraine except Galicia. There, victory went to the longtime Gulag prisoner and head of the Lviv regional administration Viacheslav Chornovil. Ukraine voted for independence and entrusted its future to a presidential candidate who, many believed, could strike a balance between Ukraine's various regions and nationalities, as well as between the republic's communist past and its independent future.

The vote for Ukraine's independence spelled the end of the Soviet Union. Those participating in the referendum had changed not only their own fate but the course of world history. Ukraine freed the rest of the Soviet republics still dependent on Moscow. Yeltsin made a final attempt to convince Kravchuk to sign a new union treaty when he met with him at a Belarusian hunting lodge in Belavezha Forest on December 8, 1991. Kravchuk refused, citing the results of the referendum in all oblasts of Ukraine, including Crimea and the east. Yeltsin backed off. If Ukraine was not prepared to sign, Russia would not do so either, he told the newly elected Ukrainian president. Yeltsin had explained to the president of the United States more than once that without Ukraine, Russia would be outnumbered and outvoted by the Muslim republics. A union including neither Ukraine nor Russia, with its huge energy resources, had no political or economic attraction for the other republics. At Belavezha the three leaders of the Slavic republics—Yeltsin, Kravchuk, and Stanislaŭ Shushkevich of Belarus—created a new international body, the Commonwealth of Independent States, which the Central Asian republics joined on December 21. The Soviet Union was no more.

On Christmas Day, December 25, 1991, Gorbachev read his resignation speech on national television. The red banner of the Soviet Union was run down the flagpole of the Kremlin's senate building, to be replaced with the Russian tricolor—red, blue, and white. Kyiv's colors were blue and yellow. There was no longer a symbolic link between Moscow and Kyiv. After four unsuccessful attempts, undertaken by different political forces under various circumstances, Ukraine was now not only united but also independent and free to go its own way. What had seemed impossible only a few months earlier had become a reality: the empire was gone, and a new country had been born. The old communist elites and the leaders of the young and ambitious national democrats had joined forces to make history, with Ukraine as the gravedigger of the last European empire. They now had to find a way to create the future.

CHAPTER 26

THE INDEPENDENCE SQUARE

MIKHAIL GORBACHEV'S RESIGNATION speech marked the official end of the Soviet Union, but its dissolution only got under way on that date. The USSR bequeathed not only an economy in ruins but also a socioeconomic infrastructure, army, way of thinking, and political and social elite bound by a common past and shared political culture. The entity that would take the place of the vanished empire—whether a community of truly independent states or the reincarnation of a Russia-dominated polity—was anything but a given. The first challenge facing the newly elected president of Ukraine, Leonid Kravchuk, and his aides after Gorbachev's resignation entailed convincing their Russian counterparts that the Commonwealth of Independent States was anything but a reincarnation of the USSR. That was no easy task.

On December 12, 1991, speaking to the Russian parliament upon its ratification of the commonwealth agreement, Boris Yeltsin stated, "In today's conditions, only a Commonwealth of Independent States can ensure the preservation of the political, legal, and economic space built up over the centuries but now almost lost." Yeltsin's successor, Vladimir Putin, echoed his former boss's sentiments when he said in March 2014, on the occasion of Russia's annexation of the Crimea, "Many people in both Russia and Ukraine, as well as in other republics, hoped that the Commonwealth of Independent States, which arose then, would become a new form of joint sovereignty." If there were some in Ukraine who wished for that at the time, they were not in the Ukrainian parliament, which on December 20, 1991, issued an appeal that stated the opposite: "According to its legal status, Ukraine is an independent state—a subject of international law. Ukraine opposes the transformation of the Commonwealth of Independent States into a state formation with its own ruling and administrative bodies."

Whatever Yeltsin's intentions, Ukraine took its independence seriously and planned to use the forum established by the commonwealth to negotiate the terms of divorce, not remarriage. The tensions between Russia, which viewed the commonwealth as an instrument for the reintegration of the post-Soviet space, and Ukraine, which insisted on full independence from Moscow, came to the fore in January 1993, when Ukraine refused to sign the Statute of the Commonwealth and thus declined to become a full member of the organization it had helped create two years earlier. The country would take an active part in the economic program and initiatives of the commonwealth but not in military ones. Ukraine never signed the statute. In the course of the 1990s, Kyiv also refused to sign numerous agreements on collective security with other commonwealth members. Kyiv had serious disagreements with Moscow regarding the future of the Soviet armed forces, control over nuclear arsenals, and the disposition of the Soviet Black Sea Fleet.

EARLY ON, THE Ukrainian leadership decided to form its own armed forces and navy on the basis of units of the Soviet army and navy stationed on Ukrainian territory. Whereas the Baltic states had asked the Soviet army to leave and created their own armed forces from scratch, the Ukrainians could not do likewise: the huge army, whose personnel exceeded 800,000 officers and men, would not leave of its own free will. It had nowhere to go, as Russia was already struggling to accommodate hundreds of thousands of troops returning from central and eastern Europe, whose constituent states were leaving Moscow's sphere of influence for good in order to become fully sovereign.

The leadership entrusted the task of turning the Soviet military into a Ukrainian one to forty-seven-year-old General Kostiantyn Morozov, the commander of an air force army in Ukraine who became Ukraine's first minister of defense in the fall of 1991. A native of the Donbas region in eastern Ukraine and half Russian by birth, Morozov tied his fate to the future of Ukrainian independence when he took the oath of allegiance to Ukraine on December 6, 1991, immediately before the Belavezha meeting and the creation of the commonwealth. On January 3, 1992, the first group of Soviet officers swore allegiance to independent Ukraine. The Ukrainian takeover of the 800,000-strong Soviet ground forces was complete by the spring of 1992.

Officers had the choice of swearing allegiance to Ukraine and staying in service or moving to Russia or other parts of the former Soviet Union. In all, there were 75,000 ethnic Russians in the Soviet forces stationed in Ukraine. About 10,000 officers refused to take the oath and either retired or were transferred. Soldiers and noncommissioned officers conscripted into the Soviet army returned home, wherever that might be. New conscripts now came from Ukraine alone.

In January 1992, elements of the Soviet Black Sea Fleet also began taking the oath of allegiance to Ukraine. But the Ukrainian takeover of the fleet encountered a major problem when its commander, Admiral Igor Kasatonov, ordered all personnel to board their ships and put out to sea. This caused the first major crisis in Russo-Ukrainian relations in May 1992. In September, Presidents Kravchuk and Yeltsin agreed to divide the fleet, avoiding direct conflict between the two countries. It turned out to be a lengthy process. For some time the entire fleet, with more than eight hundred ships and close to 100,000 servicemen, remained under Moscow's control. In 1995, Russia turned over 18 percent of the fleet's ships to Ukraine but refused to leave Sevastopol. In 1997 the two countries signed a set of agreements providing legal justification for the continuing presence of the Russian fleet, including more than three hundred ships and 25,000 servicemen, in Sevastopol until 2017. Although Ukraine had lost the battle over the fleet, the deal opened the door to a Russo-Ukrainian friendship treaty that guaranteed Ukrainian territorial integrity. The parties signed the treaty in 1997, but the Russian parliament took two years to ratify it. Once that process was over, it appeared that Ukraine had completed its "civilized divorce" from its Russian neighbor and former imperial master.

BY THE END of the 1990s, Ukraine had settled its border and territorial issues with Russia, created its own army, navy, and air force, and established diplomatic and legal foundations for integration with European political, economic, and security organizations. The idea of Ukraine as a constituent of the European community of nations and cultures had long obsessed Ukrainian intellectuals, from the nineteenth-century political thinker Mykhailo Drahomanov to the champion of national communism in the 1920s, Mykola Khvyliovy. In 1976, the European idea had made its way into the first official declaration issued by the Ukrainian Helsinki Group. "We Ukrainians live in Europe," read the first words of the group's manifesto. Ukraine, officially a founding member of the United Nations, had not been invited to take part in the Helsinki Conference on Security and Cooperation in Europe. The Ukrainian dissidents believed nevertheless that the human rights obligations undertaken by the Soviet Union in Helsinki applied to Ukraine as well. They went to prison and spent long years in the Gulag and internal exile defending that point of view.

The emergence of an independent Ukrainian state in 1991 created the conditions for turning the dissidents' dream into reality. In institutional terms, that meant joining the European Union and parting ways with the Soviet past, reforming the Ukrainian economy and society, and counterbalancing the enormous political, economic, and cultural sway that Moscow continued to have over its former province. The realization of full sovereignty for Ukraine became closely associated with the aspiration to join the European community of nations. These interrelated tasks would test the political skills of the Ukrainian elites, the unity of the Ukrainian regions, and the Soviet-era discourse about Ukraine's fraternal ties with its largest and historically most important neighbor, Russia.

Ukraine's political engagement with the West began in earnest in January 1994 with the signing of a deal brokered by the United States, according to which Ukraine gave up the nuclear weapons it had inherited from the USSR—potentially the world's third-largest nuclear arsenal. In the Budapest Memorandum signed in December of that year, the United States, Russia, and Great Britain provided security assurances to Ukraine, which joined the Treaty on the Non-proliferation of Nuclear Weapons as a nonnuclear state. While many in Kyiv questioned the prudence of giving up nuclear weapons (the invasion of Ukraine by Russia, one of the Budapest Memorandum guarantors of Ukraine's sovereignty and territorial integrity, would strengthen their case in 2014), there were significant benefits to be gained at the time. Ukraine ended its de facto international isolation as a country previously refusing to join the Nuclear Non-proliferation Treaty and became the third-largest recipient of US foreign aid, after Israel and Egypt.

In June 1994, the Ukrainian government signed a cooperation agreement with the European Union (EU), the first such agreement that the EU had offered a post-Soviet state. In the same year, Ukraine became the first country among the members and associate members of the Commonwealth of Independent States to enter into the Partnership for Peace agreement with the North Atlantic Treaty Organization (NATO). The Western military alliance, which had come into existence in 1949 at the start of the Cold War to defend western Europe from the Soviet Union, was now reinventing itself. NATO began building institutional bridges with former adversaries in eastern Europe, including Russia, which signed the agreement a few months after Ukraine. In 1997, Ukraine deepened its cooperation with the alliance by signing the Charter on Distinctive Partnership and opening a NATO information center in Kyiv. In 1998, the cooperation agreement signed four years earlier with the European Union became functional. Things looked promising. Major obstacles, however, stood in the way of Ukraine's becoming a European nation as envisioned by its intellectuals. Most of them were within Ukraine itself.

Like many post-Soviet countries, during its first years of independence Ukraine underwent a major political crisis caused by economic decline and social dislocation and focused on relations between the presidency and parliament, both institutions having been created in the political turmoil of the last years of the Soviet Union. Russia resolved the conflict in September 1993 when President Yeltsin ordered tanks to fire on the Russian parliament building and the Russian authorities arrested Russia's vice president and the head of parliament, both accused of instigating a coup against the president. Yeltsin's advisers rewrote the constitution to limit the power of parliament, turning it into something more of a rubber stamp than an active agent in the Russian political scene. Ukraine resolved the emerging conflict between the president and parliament with a compromise. President Kravchuk agreed to call early presidential elections, which he lost, and in the summer of 1994 he peacefully transferred power to his successor, Leonid Kuchma, the former prime minister and erstwhile rocket designer heading Europe's largest missile factory.

Throughout the tumultuous 1990s, Ukraine not only managed its first transfer of power between two rivals for the presidency but also maintained competitive politics and created legal foundations for a viable democracy. In 1996, President Kuchma rewrote the Soviet-era constitution, but he did so together with parliament, which secured a major role for itself in the Ukrainian political process. One of the main reasons for Ukraine's success as a democracy was its regional diversity—a legacy of both distant and more recent history that translated into political, economic, and cultural differences articulated in parliament and settled by negotiation in the political arena. The industrialized east became a stronghold of the revived Communist Party. Western Ukraine, formerly ruled by Austria and Poland, sent deputies to parliament who populated the ranks of the national democratic Rukh, led by former Gulag prisoner Viacheslav Chornovil. But whoever gained a majority in parliament acquired it as a result of a coalition agreement and had to deal

with an opposition that was not easy to satisfy or co-opt. No political grouping was strong enough to destroy or sideline another. At the time, Ukraine's
democracy was often called democracy by default. That turned out to be a
good thing. In the post-Soviet space, democracies created purely by design
did not last long.

As often happens with former colonial administrators, a strong inferiority
complex afflicted the Kyiv elites vis-à-vis their Russian counterparts, and they
initially followed models developed in Russia to deal with their own political,
social, and cultural challenges. It took them a while to realize that the Russian
models did not work in Ukraine. Ukraine was different. Nowhere was this
clearer than in the Ukrainian religious scene. By 1992, the Ukrainian Orthodox Church, which accounted for 60 percent of all Orthodox communities
in the former Soviet Union, had split four ways: there were Greek Catholics
who had emerged from the underground, Orthodox who remained under
Moscow's jurisdiction, adherents of an independent Ukrainian Orthodox
Kyiv Patriarchate, and, finally, the Autocephalous (self-ruling) Ukrainian Orthodox Church, which had its roots in the 1920s and also did not recognize
the authority of Moscow. President Kravchuk's efforts to turn the Kyiv Patriarchate into a de facto state church, as Russia had done with the Moscow
Patriarchate, failed. So did President Kuchma's attempts to do the same with
the Ukrainian branch of the Orthodox Church of the Moscow Patriarchate.

The Ukrainian scene remained as pluralistic at the turn of the twenty-first
century as it had been after the declaration of independence. If anything, it
became even more diverse. Eventually, all political forces had to accept the
reality that Russian political solutions generally did not work in Ukraine.
President Kuchma explained why in a book published in 2003, close to the
end of his second term in office. The title was telling indeed: *Ukraine Is Not
Russia*.

THE MAJOR CHALLENGE to the democratic nature of the Ukrainian political
process was the catastrophic economic decline that followed the declaration
of independence and was often blamed on it, making not only the Leonid
Brezhnev era but also the period of Mikhail Gorbachev's reforms look like a
paradise lost. In six years, between 1991 and 1997, Ukrainian industrial production fell by 48 percent, while the gross domestic product (GDP) lost a
staggering 60 percent. The biggest loss (23 percent of the previous year's
GDP) occurred in 1994, the year of presidential elections and the signing of
the first cooperation agreement with the European Union. These were figures

comparable to but more significant than American economic losses during the Great Depression, when industrial production fell by 45 percent and GDP by 30 percent.

The 1990s brought terrible hardship to Ukraine. By the end of the decade, close to half of Ukrainians claimed that they had barely enough money to buy food, while those who were leading relatively comfortable lives amounted to barely 2 or 3 percent of the population. This translated into higher mortality rates and lower birth rates. The former overtook the latter for the first time in 1991. Ten years later, when the government of independent Ukraine conducted its first census, it found 48.4 million Ukrainians in the country, 3 million fewer than the 51.4 million counted in the last Soviet census of 1989.

Once again, Ukraine became a source of emigration. Many left for a few months or even years to make the kind of money they could not make at home. They headed mainly to Russia, with its oil and gas wealth, and the countries of east-central Europe and the European Union. Others left forever. Ukrainian Jews led the way. Many of them had not been allowed to leave the Soviet Union in the 1980s, becoming "refuseniks" whom the Soviet authorities denied exit visas and turned into second-class citizens by firing them from the universities and barring them from government jobs. Now they could leave and did so in astonishing numbers. Between 1989 and 2006, more than 1.5 million Soviet Jews left their countries of residence, including a good many Jews of Ukraine. Whereas the Ukrainian population as a whole fell by roughly 5 percent between 1989 and 2001, the Jewish population fell by a staggering 78 percent, decreasing from 487,300 to 105,500. Among those who left were the families of the cofounders of Paypal (Max Levchin) and WhatsApp (Jan Koum). But not only Jews wanted to leave. Many of the emigrants were Ukrainians, Russians, and members of other ethnic groups. Ukraine also became a transit point for illegal immigrants from the rest of the commonwealth and countries such as Afghanistan and Pakistan.

The reasons for the steep economic decline were numerous. The collapse of the Soviet economy not only disrupted economic ties between different republics but also spelled the end to procurement for the ex-Soviet military. Ukraine, home to a highly developed military-industrial complex, suffered disproportionately in this regard. Unlike Russia, Ukraine had no oil and gas revenues to soften the blow. Moreover, the Ukrainian metallurgical complex—the industrial sector that survived the crash and provided most of the funds for the Ukrainian budget—depended entirely on Russian natural gas supplies and had to pay ever increasing prices for that precious commodity. But by far the most important reason for the economic decline was the Ukrainian government's delaying of badly needed economic reforms and continuing to subsidize money-losing state enterprises by issuing credits and printing more money. Runaway inflation, which reached a staggering 2,500 percent in 1992, set the seal on the rapid economic decline.

During the first years of independence, the government was reluctant to give up ownership and thus control over Soviet-era industrial and agricultural enterprises that required more and more state subsidies. Once it finally decided to do so, it faced opposition in parliament, largely from the "red directors" who managed the large enterprises. In 1995, parliament exempted 6,300 state-owned enterprises from privatization. By that time, fewer than one-third of industrial enterprises had been transferred to private ownership. The first stage of privatization was carried out with vouchers issued to the entire population of the country. It benefited largely the "red directors," who now had assets but few incentives to change anything. But privatization without new approaches and restructuring could not revive the Ukrainian economy. By 1999, when close to 85 percent of all enterprises were privately owned, they accounted for less than 65 percent of all industrial output. Half the industrial enterprises in the country were in deficit. Most of the large enterprises remained in the hands of Soviet-era managers and people close to the government. They maintained monopolies, restrained competition, and deepened the economic crisis.

Ukraine needed new owners and a new class of managers to revive its economy. The country got both in a group of young, ambitious, and ruthless businessmen who had no roots in the old planned economy of Soviet times and had made their way up from the economic chaos of the perestroika years and mafia wars of the 1990s. Known in Ukraine, as in Russia, as oligarchs, they emerged as the main beneficiaries of the second stage of privatization, which amounted to the sale of government assets at a fraction of their actual value. The oligarchs made their fortunes by being innovative and opportunistic, but also by ingratiating, bribing, and shooting their way into the offices of the "red directors." With the military-industrial complex in steep decline, the Ukrainian metallurgical industry became the richest prize in the 1990s and early 2000s. At that time, more than half the country's industrial output came from four eastern oblasts—Dnipropetrovsk, Zaporizhia, Donetsk, and Luhansk—that were rich in iron ore and coal and produced Ukraine's primary export product: steel.

The new "men of steel" included the leader of the Donetsk group, Rinat Akhmetov, who in the early 1990s took over leadership of a company called Lux, known to the Ukrainian authorities for its criminal origins and connections. In the Dnipropetrovsk region, two local businessmen divided major metallurgical assets: Viktor Pinchuk, who married into President Kuchma's family, and Igor Kolomoisky, who established one of the first major private banks in Ukraine. Others also shared the loot of post-Soviet Ukrainian privatization. Still, the corrupt and often criminal nature of the privatization process aside, the "oligarchization" of the Ukrainian economy coincided with the end of economic decline. Ukraine began the new millennium with a rapid economic recovery, and, for better or worse, the oligarchs were important figures in that new success story.

MOST OF THE privatization of Ukrainian industry took place on the watch of President Leonid Kuchma between 1994 and 2004. Kuchma, who had been a "red director" himself, presided over the process that ultimately benefited the oligarchs, gaining him their economic and political support. Kuchma won his second term in 1999 by presenting himself as the only candidate capable of defeating the communists, who were exploiting economic decline and hardship to attempt a revival, and by splitting the national democratic bloc: his main opponent on the "right," Rukh leader Viacheslav Chornovil, died under suspicious circumstances in a car crash a few months before the elections. During his second term in office, which began in 1999, Kuchma emerged as the supreme arbiter of relations between the new oligarchic clans in economics and politics. He also tried to consolidate his personal power and marginalize parliament. It did not work as planned: Ukraine, indeed, was not Russia.

President Kuchma's downfall began in the autumn of 2000 with the release by opposition leader Oleksandr Moroz, head of the Socialist Party of Ukraine, of tape recordings made secretly in Kuchma's office by one of his bodyguards. The tapes documented Kuchma's dealings with local officials involved in privatization schemes, his bribe taking, and his efforts to suppress opposition media. One journalist whose name was mentioned on the tapes was Heorhii Gongadze, the thirty-one-year-old founder of the web newspaper *Ukraïns'ka pravda* (*Ukrainian Truth*). Kuchma wanted him detained and sent to Chechnia, where insurgents were fighting the Russian army. In September 2000, Gongadze's corpse was found beheaded in a forest near Kyiv. Kuchma's complicity in the murder was never proved in court, but those who listened to the released tapes had no doubt that the president himself had ordered the minister of the interior to threaten and kidnap the journalist.

Kuchmagate, as the tape scandal became known in Ukraine, was a turning point in Ukrainian politics. It ended the rise of authoritarian tendencies in the presidential office. The scandal exposed the corrupt side of the policies of the president, who had been credited during his first term with solving the dispute over the Black Sea Fleet, securing the Crimea, convincing Russia to recognize Ukraine's borders, turning his country toward the West, and launching the long-delayed privatization. Now it turned out that the president was also a crook, perhaps even a murderer. The opposition, which included former national democrats, socialists, and even communists, launched a political campaign under the slogan "Ukraine without Kuchma." Citizens responded positively to calls for a clampdown on political and economic corruption. The emerging middle class that was replacing the Soviet-era intelligentsia, which the economic collapse had wiped out, was fed up with official corruption, the suppression of political activity, and restrictions on freedom of speech. Ukraine wanted change.

Kuchma managed to survive the immediate fallout from the tape scandal but was unable to stop the rise of political activism. A new generation, coming not from outside the political establishment, as in Soviet times, but from within, led opposition to his regime. Those who wanted to end government corruption, improve relations with the West tarnished by Kuchmagate, and launch a program of integration with the European Union found their leader in handsome forty-seven-year-old former prime minister Viktor Yushchenko, who had no ties with the political and economic clans of eastern Ukraine and came from the rural northeast.

VIKTOR YUSHCHENKO HAD presided over the beginning of economic recovery. During his short stay in the prime minister's office, from December 1999 to May 2001, Yushchenko, together with his deputy prime minister, Yulia Tymoshenko, closed loopholes that allowed the oligarchs to avoid taxation. The state lowered taxes on medium and small business, bringing a good part of the Ukrainian economy out of the shadows and increasing state revenues. This allowed Yushchenko's government to pay wage and pension arrears. On Yushchenko's watch, Ukraine's GDP stopped falling and showed solid 6 percent growth in 2000, which also saw industrial production increase by 12 percent. The trend would continue for most of the decade. Dismissed from his position in the middle of Kuchmagate, Yushchenko soon emerged as the leader of the Our Ukraine Party, which got almost a quarter of the popular vote in the parliamentary elections of 2002.

Whereas pro-reform Ukraine pinned its hopes on Yushchenko, the former governor of Donetsk oblast and Kuchma's last prime minister, Viktor Yanukovych, championed President Kuchma's oligarchic regime. He was also the choice of the Russian president, Vladimir Putin, who took over from Yeltsin in 2000 and was eager to have an ally, if not a client, in Kyiv. In 2004, Yushchenko and Yanukovych faced each other in the most strongly contested presidential elections Ukraine had seen since independence. In early September 2004, Yushchenko, who was leading the race, fell suddenly and violently ill. With the diagnosis unclear and his life in danger, his aides brought him to a clinic in Vienna, where the doctors came to a shocking conclusion. The Our Ukraine presidential candidate had been poisoned, and the poison was of a particular kind—a dioxin of a strain produced in a handful of countries, including Russia and excluding Ukraine. The correct diagnosis saved Yushchenko's life. With his face disfigured by the poison and a reliance on heavy medication to deal with the excruciating pain, Yushchenko returned to the election trail, gaining more support.

In late October 2004, when Ukrainians went to the polls to choose among twenty-four presidential candidates, Yushchenko was in the lead, with Yanukovych a close second: each received close to 40 percent of the vote. They then proceeded to the second round, with Yushchenko gaining the support of most of the voters whose candidates did not make it to that stage. Following the second round of voting on November 21, independent exit polls showed Yushchenko clearly in the lead, with 53 percent of the popular vote against Yanukovych's 44 percent. But when the government-controlled electoral commission announced the official results, most Ukrainian voters were in for a surprise. According to the official report, Yanukovych had won with 49.5 percent of the vote over Yushchenko's 46.9 percent. The official results were rigged. As telephone intercepts of discussions between members of Yanukovych's campaign staff showed, they had tampered with the server of the state electoral commission to falsify election results submitted to Kyiv.

Yushchenko's supporters were outraged. An estimated 200,000 Kyivans came to the Maidan, Kyiv's Independence Square, to protest the election fraud. The Orange Revolution, which received that name after the official colors of Yushchenko's presidential campaign, had begun. In the following

days and weeks, with protesters coming from the rest of Ukraine, the number of participants in rallies swelled to half a million. As television cameras
transmitted images of the Maidan protests all over the world, European
viewers discovered Ukraine for themselves, seeing it for the first time as
something more than a distant region on the map. The images left no doubt
that its inhabitants wanted freedom and justice. Europe and the world could
not stand aside. Backed by voters, European politicians involved themselves
in the Ukraine Crisis and played an important part in its resolution. The key
role went to Polish president Aleksander Kwaśniewski, who convinced President Kuchma to throw his support behind the decision of the Constitutional
Court to annul the official results of the elections as fraudulent.

On December 26, 2004, Ukrainians went to the polls for the third time
in two months to elect their new president. As expected, Yushchenko won
with 52 percent over Yanukovych's 44 percent—results close to those of the
independent exit polls conducted during the second round of the elections.
The Orange Revolution got its president. But could he fulfill the promise of
the revolution—to bear down on crony capitalism, free the country from
corruption, and bring it closer to Europe? Yushchenko believed that he could.
His road to the transformation of Ukraine led through the European Union.

PRESIDENT YUSHCHENKO MADE foreign policy his priority and confided to
one of his aides that joining the EU was a goal worth living for. Ukrainian
diplomats did their best to capitalize on the positive image of Ukraine created
in the West by the Orange Revolution and to jump on the departing train of
EU enlargement—in 2004, the European Union accepted ten countries as
members, seven of them former Soviet satellites and republics. It was too late:
the train had left the station. While the European Parliament voted in January 2005 in favor of establishing closer relations with Ukraine with an eye to
future membership, the European Commission, which made decisions on
enlargement, was much more cautious. Instead of starting negotiations on
accession to the union, it offered Ukraine a plan for closer cooperation.

The locomotive of history did not take Ukraine into the EU along with
some of its western neighbors in the wake of the Orange Revolution for several reasons. Some of them were beyond Kyiv's control. Germany and other
major stakeholders in the union were worried about the economic and political consequences of the enlargement that had already taken place. They
added insult to injury by questioning Ukraine's status as a "European state."

But the main reasons for Kyiv's failure to join the European club of democratic nations had to do with Ukraine itself. The post-Orange years were full of internal contradictions. Major achievements mixed with spectacular failures of government policy.

The new government stopped the persecution of political opponents and provided guarantees of freedom of expression for citizens and the media. Economically, Ukraine was doing better than might have been expected. Between 2000 and 2008, when its economy felt the impact of the global recession, the country's GDP doubled, reaching $400 billion and surpassing GDP figures for 1990, the last full year of the USSR's existence. But the Yushchenko government failed to make Ukraine a fairer place in which to live and conduct business. It did precious little about rampant corruption. On top of that, the constitutional changes to which the Yushchenko camp agreed in December 2004 to cancel the fraudulent elections made the country difficult to govern. According to the amendments demanded by Yanukovych's supporters and accepted by Yushchenko, the president lost the right to appoint the prime minister, who, now elected by parliament, emerged as an independent actor in Ukrainian politics. Neither the president nor the prime minister had enough power to implement reforms on his or her own, and Yushchenko had a hard time finding common ground with Prime Minister Yulia Tymoshenko, his former revolutionary ally.

By the time Yushchenko's term came to an end in early 2010, there was broad disappointment with his rule. His rivalry with Tymoshenko had turned Ukrainian politics into an interminable soap opera, discrediting the cause of reform and European integration. The president's attempt to build a strong Ukrainian national identity by promoting the memory of the 1932–1933 Great Ukrainian Famine and celebrating the fighters of the Ukrainian Insurgent Army against the Soviet regime failed to translate into broad electoral support. In fact, memory politics divided Ukrainian society. Especially controversial was Yushchenko's posthumous "Hero of Ukraine" award to Stepan Bandera, leader of Ukrainian radical nationalism in the 1930s and 1940s. The Bandera affair provoked a strong negative reaction not only in the east and south of the country but also among the Ukrainian liberal intelligentsia in Kyiv and Lviv and alienated European friends of Ukraine. Yushchenko, observers said at the time, was trying to bring Ukraine into Europe, but he had in mind the Europe of the turn of the twentieth, not the twenty-first, century.

Not only Ukraine but the whole post-Soviet region was lagging behind, trying to manage the transition from imperial subject to independent state that the countries of central Europe had resolved nearly a century earlier. Very soon, Ukraine would find itself in a crisis that reminded many of the problems of the nineteenth century. That crisis would bring foreign intervention, war, annexation, and the idea of the division of the world into spheres of influence. It would also test Ukraine's resolve to remain independent and challenge the key elements of its national identity.

CHAPTER 27

THE PRICE OF FREEDOM

Bohdan Solchanyk came to Kyiv from Lviv by train early in the morning of February 20, 2014. A twenty-eight-year-old historian, sociologist, and budding poet, he taught at the Ukrainian Catholic University in Lviv and was working on a doctoral dissertation on electoral practices in Ukraine with an adviser at the University of Warsaw. Solchanyk was not on a research trip when he stepped onto the pavement of the Kyiv railway station on that cold day in February. Elections were not taking place in Kyiv: revolution was. He had dreamed about it back in 2008, when he wrote the poem "Where Is My Revolution?" in which he expressed his generation's disappointment with promises made during the Orange Revolution of 2004 but never fulfilled.

Now a new revolution had come to Ukraine, with hundreds of thousands of people once again pouring into the streets of downtown Kyiv in late November 2013 to demand reform, the end of government corruption, and closer ties with the European Union. Solchanyk felt that his place was among the protesters in Kyiv. February 20 marked his fourth foray into the revolution, which turned out to be his last. A few hours after his arrival in Kyiv, sniper fire killed Solchanyk along with dozens of other protesters. In death, he would become one of the "Heavenly Hundred"—more than one hundred protesters killed in Kyiv in January and February 2014. Those killings ended twenty-two years of generally nonviolent politics in Ukraine and turned a dramatic new page in its history. The democracy peacefully acquired in the final days of the Soviet Union and the independence won at the ballot box in December 1991 would now require defense not only with words and marches but also with arms.

THE EVENTS LEADING up to the mass killings of protesters on the Maidan began in February 2010 with the victory of Viktor Yanukovych, the main target of the Maidan protests of 2004, in the presidential elections. The new president began his tenure by changing the rules of the political game. His ideal was a strong authoritarian regime, and he tried to concentrate as much power in his own hands and those of his family as possible. He rewrote the constitution by forcing parliament to cancel the 2004 amendments and yield more power to the presidency. Then, in the summer of 2011, he put on trial and jailed his main political opponent, former prime minister Yulia Tymoshenko, for signing a gas deal with Russia that was harmful to the Ukrainian economy. With power concentrated in his hands and the political opposition silenced or intimidated, Yanukovych and his appointees focused their attention on the enrichment of the ruling clan. In a brief period, Yanukovych and the members of his family and entourage accumulated huge fortunes, transferring up to $70 billion into foreign accounts and threatening the economic and financial stability of the state, which by the autumn of 2013 found itself on the verge of default.

With the opposition crushed or co-opted, Ukrainian society once again pinned its hopes on Europe. Under President Viktor Yushchenko, Ukraine had begun negotiations with the European Union on an association agreement, including the creation of a free economic zone and visa liberalization for Ukrainian citizens. The hope was that, once signed, the agreement would save and strengthen Ukraine's democratic institutions, protect the rights of the opposition, and bring European business standards to Ukraine, reining in the rampant corruption spreading from the very top of the state pyramid. Some oligarchs, fearing the growing power of the president and his clan and wanting to protect their assets by establishing clear political and economic rules, supported the EU association agreement. Big business also wanted access to European markets and dreaded the possibility of being swallowed by Russian competitors if Ukraine were to join the Russia-led Eurasian Customs Union.

Everything was ready for a signing ceremony at the EU summit in Vilnius scheduled for November 28, 2013. Then, a week before the summit, the Ukrainian government suddenly changed course, proposing to postpone the signing of the association agreement. Yanukovych went to Vilnius but refused to sign anything. If the European leaders were disappointed, many Ukrainian citizens were outraged. The government had broken promises given throughout the previous year, dashing hopes for a better European future. Those were the feelings of the men and women, many participants of the earlier protests who gathered on the Maidan, Ukraine's Independence Square, on the evening of November 21, after the government announced its refusal to sign the agreement. Yanukovych's aides wanted to put an end to the protests as soon as possible in order to head off a new Orange Revolution. On the night of November 30, riot police brutally attacked the students who gathered on the Maidan. That was the one thing Ukrainian society was not prepared to tolerate. The next day, more than half a million Kyivans, some of them parents and relatives of the students beaten by the police, poured into downtown Kyiv, turning the Maidan and its environs into a space of freedom from the corrupt government and its police forces.

What had begun as a demand to join Europe turned into the Revolution of Dignity, which brought together diverse political forces, from liberals in mainstream parties to radicals and nationalists. Once again, as in 2004, the protesters refused to leave the streets. In mid-January 2014, after the government tried to outlaw the protests, bloody clashes began between police and government-hired thugs on the one hand and protesters on the other. The violence reached its peak on February 18. In three days, at least seventy-seven people died—nine police officers and sixty-eight protesters. The killings caused a sea change both in Ukraine and in the international community. The threat of international sanctions forced members of the Ukrainian parliament, many of whom were concerned that the sanctions would affect them as well, to free themselves from fear of presidential reprisal and pass a resolution prohibiting the use of force by the government. On the night of February 21, with parliament against him and the riot police gone from downtown Kyiv, President Yanukovych fled revolutionary Kyiv. The protestors prevailed. The tyrant was gone; the revolution had won. The Ukrainian parliament voted to remove Yanukovych, appoint an interim president, and install a new provisional government headed by the leaders of the opposition.

THE PROTESTS IN Kyiv surprised political observers, as they presented an unusual case of mass mobilization inspired by issues of foreign policy. The protesters wanted closer ties with Europe and opposed Ukraine's accession to the Russia-led customs union.

Russian aspirations to dominate Ukraine were an important factor in the protests on the Maidan. President Vladimir Putin, who had led the Russian government since 2000, first as president, then as prime minister, and then again as president, had gone on record characterizing the collapse of the USSR as the greatest geopolitical catastrophe of the twentieth century. Before returning to the presidential office in 2012, Putin proclaimed the reintegration of post-Soviet space as one of his primary tasks. As in 1991, that space was incomplete without Ukraine. Putin wanted Yanukovych, whom he had supported in the presidential elections in 2004 and 2010, to join the Russia-led customs union—the basis for a future, more comprehensive economic and political union of the post-Soviet states. Yanukovych had made concessions to Russia by prolonging the Russian lease of the Sevastopol navy base for twenty-five years, but he was not eager to join any Russia-led union. Instead, in a failed attempt to counterbalance growing Russian influence and ambition, he edged toward association with the European Union, preparing to sign the agreement.

Russia responded in the summer of 2013 by initiating a trade war with Ukraine and closing its markets to some Ukrainian goods. Moscow used both sticks and carrots to stop Ukraine's westward drift. Among the carrots was the promise of a $15 billion loan to save the cash-strapped and corruption-ridden Ukrainian government from imminent default. The first tranche of that money arrived after Yanukovych refused to sign the EU association agreement. But the protests on the Maidan changed the Kremlin's plans. According to an investigation conducted later by the Ukrainian security service, the Russian security officials were present on the Maidan in the days leading to the killing of dozens of protestors. The killings eventually led to the ouster of President Yanukovych. In early February 2014, a suggestion to take advantage of the internal Ukrainian crisis in order to annex the Crimea, then destabilize and eventually annex parts of eastern and southern Ukraine to Russia, was making its way through the Russian presidential administration. Judging by subsequent events, the proposal did not languish in obscurity. According to President Putin, he personally made a decision to "return" the Crimea to Russia at a meeting with his political advisers and military commanders on the night of February 22, 2014.

Four days later, on the night of February 26, a band of armed men in unmarked uniforms took control of the Crimean parliament. Under their protection, Russian intelligence services engineered the installment of the leader of a pro-Russian party, which had obtained only 4 percent of the vote in the previous parliamentary elections, as the new prime minister of the Crimea. Then Russian troops, along with mercenaries and Cossack formations brought from the Russian Federation at least a week before the start of the operation, blocked Ukrainian military units at their bases with the assistance of locally recruited militias. As the new Ukrainian government struggled to take control of the police and security forces previously loyal to Yanukovych, the Kremlin sped up preparations for a complete takeover of the peninsula by hastily organizing a referendum on its fate. The new government of the Crimea cut off Ukrainian television channels, prevented the delivery of Ukrainian newspapers to subscribers, and unleashed propaganda for the separation of the Crimea from Ukraine. Opponents of the referendum, many of them belonging to the Crimean Tatar minority, were intimidated or kidnapped.

In mid-March 2014, the citizens of the Crimea were called to polling stations to vote for reunification with Russia. The results of the Moscow-endorsed referendum were reminiscent of Brezhnev-era polls, when the turnout was reported as 99 percent and the same figure was given for the percentage of voters supporting government candidates. It was now claimed that 97 percent of voters had supported the unification of the Crimea with Russia. In Sevastopol, local officials reported a pro-Russian vote amounting to 123 percent of registered voters. The new Crimean authorities declared the total turnout to be 83 percent, but according to the Human Rights Council attached to the office of the Russian president, less than 40 percent of registered voters had taken part in the referendum. On March 18, two days after the referendum, Vladimir Putin called on the Russian legislators to annex the Crimea as an act of historical justice, undoing part of the damage done to Russia by the disintegration of the USSR.

The Ukrainian government in Kyiv did not recognize the referendum but was in no position to do much about it. It ordered its troops to withdraw from the peninsula, unwilling to risk war in a country still divided by the political turmoil of the Revolution of Dignity. The Ukrainian army, underfunded for decades and with no experience of warfare, was no match for the Russian Federation's well-trained and equipped troops, who had fought a prolonged war in Chechnia and mounted the Russian invasion of Georgia in 2008. Kyiv was also busy trying to stop Moscow's destabilization of other parts of the country. The Kremlin demanded the "federalization" of Ukraine, with the provision that every region would have veto power over the signing of international agreements. Russia did not just want the Crimea; it was trying to stop Ukraine's movement toward Europe by manipulating local elites and populations in the east and south of the country.

If Ukraine refused to follow the Russian "federalization" scenario, there was another option: the partition of the country by turning eastern and southern Ukraine into a new buffer state. A Russian-controlled polity called New Russia was supposed to include Kharkiv, Luhansk, Donetsk, Dnipropetrovsk,

Zaporizhia, Mykolaiv, Kherson, and Odesa oblasts, allowing Russia overland access to the newly annexed Crimea and the Russian-controlled Transnistria region of Moldova. It did not look plausible, as in April 2014 only 15 percent of the population of the projected New Russia supported unification with Russia, while 70 percent were opposed. But the southeast was not homogenous. Pro-Russian sentiment was quite high in the industrial Donbas region of eastern Ukraine, where 30 percent of those polled supported unification with Russia, and low in Dnipropetrovsk oblast, where supporters of Russia accounted for less than 7 percent of the population.

Russian intelligence agencies initiated the destabilization of Ukraine from the Donbas in the spring of 2014. The Donbas stood out as one of the most economically and socially troubled regions of Ukraine. Part of the rust belt of the Soviet Union and then of Ukraine, it had received huge subsidies from the center to support the dying coal-mining industry. Donetsk, the main regional center, was the only major Ukrainian city where ethnic Russians constituted a plurality—48 percent of the population. Many citizens of the Donbas were attached to Soviet ideology and symbols, with monuments to Lenin (largely demolished in central Ukraine in the course of the Revolution of Dignity) emblematizing the region's Soviet identity. The government of President Yanukovych came to power and held it by mobilizing its eastern Ukrainian electorate, stressing its linguistic, cultural, and historical differences from central and especially western Ukraine. It claimed that the regionally dominant Russian language was under threat from Kyiv, as was the historical memory of the Great Patriotic War, allegedly in jeopardy from proponents of the Ukrainian Insurgent Army in western Ukraine. While the linguistic divide and opposing historical memories indeed drove a wedge between Ukraine's east and west, politicians exaggerated the differences far beyond their actual importance in order to win elections. Such political opportunism created fertile ground for Russian intervention in Ukraine.

Paramilitary units often trained and financed by the Russian government and close to the Kremlin oligarchs showed up in the Donbas in April 2014. By May, they had taken control of most of the region's urban centers. The ousted President Yanukovych used his remaining political ties and substantial financial resources to help destabilize his home region. Gangs in the pay of the exiled president attacked supporters of the new government in Kyiv, while corrupt policemen helped them by supplying names and addresses of potential victims. The local elites, led by Rinat Akhmetov, a business partner of the ousted Yanukovych and Ukraine's richest oligarch, played along, hoping to

shield themselves from the revolutionary changes coming from Kyiv by turning the Donbas into something of an appanage principality under the flag of
the self-proclaimed Donetsk and Luhansk people's republics, which corresponded to the two oblasts that constituted the industrial region of Donbas.
They miscalculated and by the end of May had lost control of the region to
Russian nationalists and local activists, who launched an antioligarchic revolution. As in Kyiv, people in Donetsk were fed up with corruption, but many in
the Donbas oriented themselves on Russia, not Europe, and hoped not for a
corruption-free market economy but for a Soviet-era state-run economy and
social guarantees. If the protesters on the Maidan saw their country as part of
European civilization, the pro-Russian insurgents imagined themselves as participants in a broader "Russian World" and their war as a defense of Orthodox values against the advance of the corrupt European West.

THE LOSS OF the Crimea and the turmoil in the Donbas, as well as Russian
efforts to destabilize the situation in Kharkiv and Odesa, led to a new mobilization of Ukrainian civil society. Tens of thousands of Ukrainians, many of
them participants in the Maidan protests, joined army units as well as new
volunteer formations and went to fight the Russia-led insurgency in the east.
Since the government was able to supply the soldiers only with weapons, volunteer organizations sprang up all over Ukraine, collecting donations, buying
supplies, and delivering them to the front lines. Ukrainian society was taking
up the task that the Ukrainian state was not in a position to perform. Between January and March 2014, according to data from the Kyiv International Institute of Sociology, the share of those who supported Ukrainian
independence jumped from 84 percent to 90 percent of the adult population.
The share of those who wanted Ukraine to join Russia fell from 10 percent in
January 2014 to 5 percent in September. Even most of those polled in the
Donbas saw their region as part of the Ukrainian state. The percentage of
"separatists" wanting either independence or union with Russia grew from
under 30 percent to more than 40 percent of those polled in Donbas between
April and September 2014 but never reached a majority, giving most pro-
European Ukrainians hope of retaining those territories but also pointing to
future problems in forming a common national identity.

In the presidential election of May 2014, in a show of political unity,
Ukrainian voters gave a first-round victory to one of Ukraine's most prominent businessmen and an active participant in the Maidan protests, forty-nine-
year-old Petro Poroshenko. With the end of the legitimacy crisis generated by

the ouster of Yanukovych, Ukraine was ready to stand up to both open and covert aggression. In early July, the Ukrainian army achieved its first major success—the liberation of the city of Sloviansk, which had served as the headquarters of the best-known Russian commander, a former lieutenant colonel of military intelligence, Igor Girkin (Strelkov). In a desperate attempt to stop the Ukrainian advance, Russia began to supply the insurgents with new armaments, including antiaircraft missiles. According to Ukrainian and American officials, one such missile shot down a Malaysian Airlines Boeing 777 with 298 people on board on July 17, 2014. The victims came from the Netherlands, Malaysia, Australia, Indonesia, Britain, and a number of other countries, giving the Ukrainian conflict a truly global character.

The tragedy of the Malaysian airliner mobilized Western leaders in support of Ukraine, leading them to impose economic sanctions on Russian officials and businesses directly responsible for the aggression. It turned out to be too little, too late. In mid-August, as the two Russian-backed separatist people's republics of Donetsk and Luhansk found themselves on the verge of defeat, Moscow stepped up the offensive and sent regular troops into battle along with mercenaries.

More than a thousand Ukrainian military servicemen and members of volunteer battalions were surrounded in the city of Ilovaisk by the advancing Russian forces. As they reached an agreement with the Russian commanders for withdrawal from the city and began their retreat, the Russian officers made new demands and opened fire at the retreating troops, causing massive casualties on the Ukrainian side. In early September 2014, with the Ukrainian advance in the Donbas halted and Russian troops going on the offensive, the newly elected president of Ukraine, Petro Poroshenko, met with his Russian counterpart, Vladimir Putin, in the Belarusian capital of Minsk to discuss an end to hostilities. Also taking part in the talks were Chancellor Angela Merkel of Germany and President François Hollande of France. On September 5 the conflicting parties signed the Minsk Protocol, a complex agreement that produced a ceasefire but little else.

By January 2015, the two sides were at war again. The Russians tried to repeat their success of the previous year and encircle Ukrainian troops at the key railway junction of Debaltseve. This time the Ukrainians were prepared. The battle continued into February, allowing Germany and France to intervene once again. On February 14, the leaders of Germany, Russia, France, and Ukraine agreed on a new protocol that became known as Minsk II. Although one of its key conditions was a ceasefire, shooting continued after the signing of the protocol. The battle of Debaltseve continued to rage until February 20, when Ukrainian forces retreated from the city. Other conditions of the protocol proved no less difficult to implement. They included a Ukrainian pledge to conduct elections in the breakaway region and a Russian pledge to cede control over the Ukrainian-Russian border to Ukrainian troops. The question of which should come first would remain a bone of contention for years to come.

The Kremlin saved the self-proclaimed republics from collapse but failed to realize its original plan of creating a New Russia—a Russian-controlled polity extending from Donetsk in the east to Odesa in the west that would provide a land bridge from Russia to the Crimea. Russia also failed to stop Ukraine from enhancing its political and economic ties with the West. With Ukraine refusing to accept any loss of its territory or give up its goal of political, economic, and cultural integration with the West, with Russia refusing to let Ukraine leave its sphere of influence, and with the West concerned about the threat to international order but divided over the best strategy to check growing Russian ambitions, the war in eastern Ukraine turned into a prolonged conflict with no end in sight.

CHAPTER 28

A NEW DAWN

THE WORDS OF the Ukrainian anthem, "Ukraine Has Not Yet Perished," turned out to be prophetic and took on optimistic rather than pessimistic overtones in the wake of the military conflict with Russia and its proxies. The Ukrainian forces' heroic defense of the Donetsk airport from May 2014 to January 2015 against overwhelming Russia-backed forces gave the nation a new mythology—the defenders became widely known as "cyborgs"—and a new lease on life.

Ukraine's demonstrated capacity to hold its own in the conflict with the Russian Federation and preserve its independence set the country on a new trajectory. The stabilization of the front in the Donbas made it possible for President Petro Poroshenko and his two subsequent governments, led by Arsenii Yatseniuk and Volodymyr Groisman, to put forward an ambitious agenda defined by the expectations and demands of those who had taken part in the Maidan protests. The country wanted the new government to put an end to the growth of authoritarian tendencies at the top of the state pyramid, hasten Ukraine's integration into Western political and economic structures by signing an association agreement with the European Union, and, last but not least, root out the corruption that had metastasized far beyond Ukraine's central government.

The association agreement with the European Union, whose abrupt abandonment had sparked protests in the fall of 2013, was signed by Ukrainian officials in March 2014, soon after the end of the protests and the Russian annexation of the Crimea. The EU agreed to provide financial and logistical assistance to Ukraine, but a far more important consequence of the agreement was the creation of a free trade area that helped reorient Ukraine not only politically but also economically toward the West. Between 2013 and 2018 Ukraine's exports to Russia would fall from 26 to 12 percent of its trade volume, while exports to the European Union would grow from 28 to more than 40 percent. In 2017 visa-free travel to the European Union—a symbolically important development in light of the pro-European aspirations of the 2013 protests—became a reality, with Ukrainians making 49 million trips to the EU in the course of the next three years.

The revolt against authoritarianism, along with the unresolved problem of regionalism and sporadic separatism highlighted by the war, promoted badly needed decentralization and reform of local government. By mid-2019, more than 28 percent of the population was encompassed by the new system of local government, which redistributed decision-making prerogatives and financial powers from the center to the municipal and local levels. These new powers and responsibilities were assigned to newly formed communities, known in Ukrainian as *hromady*. The formation of *hromady* was done on a voluntary basis and dramatically reduced the dependence of local governments on the center. From now on, local communities will decide how to spend their hard-earned local taxes. This arrangement, considered a norm in the European Union, was now becoming a norm in Ukraine.

While reorientation toward the European Union boosted Ukrainian morale, resistance to Russian military aggression and hybrid warfare increased appreciation of the importance of national culture as a source of unity. In 2017 the Ministry of Foreign Affairs initiated the creation of the Ukrainian Institute—a government body charged with the promotion of Ukrainian culture and Ukraine's image abroad. The creation of the Ukrainian Cultural Foundation and the Ukrainian Book Institute initiated a modest government investment—the first in decades—in the promotion of Ukrainian culture and publishing. As a result of these and other measures, the Ukrainian film industry was revived, and the shelves of Ukrainian bookstores, previously dominated by Russian publications, were stocked with books issued by Ukrainian publishing houses.

The demolition of monuments to Vladimir Lenin, popularly known as the "Leninfall," which began during the Maidan protests in late 2013 and continued in 2014, marked a symbolic breach with the communist past. Governmental institutions, such as the Institute of National Memory, headed by Maidan activist Volodymyr Viatrovych, initiated parliamentary approval of so-called decommunization laws, which mandated the removal of monuments to Lenin and other communist leaders throughout the country. Some 1,300 Lenin monuments out of 5,500 present in the country before 1990 were removed as a result. Streets, villages, cities, and entire regions were stripped of their communist-era names, and local communities were given a freedom to choose new ones. The city of Dnipropetrovsk, named after Ukrainian communist leader Hryhorii Petrovsky, became Dnipro, while the city of Kirovohrad, named after Sergei Kirov, a Soviet leader with no connection to Ukraine, became Kropyvnytsky, named after Marko Kropyvnytsky, a nineteenth-century playwright and actor native to the region. The map of Ukraine was literally changed overnight.

Historic changes took place also on the Ukrainian religious scene. President Poroshenko played a key role in merging two independent Ukrainian Orthodox churches in December 2018 and facilitating recognition of the new church by the patriarch of Constantinople. This was done over the protests of the Moscow Patriarchate, which controlled most of the existing Ukrainian Orthodox parishes and prohibited them from joining the new church. For the first time since the seventeenth century, the leading Eastern patriarchs recognized an Orthodox church outside the jurisdiction of Moscow. This was the culmination of a long process that had begun with the formation of the first autocephalous (independent) Ukrainian Orthodox Church back in 1921 and the restoration of independent branches of the church on the eve and after the fall of the Soviet Union.

Not all these changes were accepted without controversy. The decommunization laws were criticized at home and abroad for attempts to legislate history and promote a nationalist narrative. The role of the government in the creation of the new church was questioned, and concerns were raised about the future of the Russian language and culture in Ukraine. Such criticism came not only from proponents of the old regime and its policies but also from Ukrainian liberal circles, who had supported the Maidan protests and were now concerned with the potential rise of nationalism in the country. Although the war and the new political course strengthened Ukrainian national identity and promoted the Ukrainian language and culture, they did not result in a noticeable rise of nationalism. The nationalist parties failed to attain the 5 percent threshold in the Ukrainian parliamentary elections of 2014 and 2019 and were not represented in parliament—a striking difference from Ukraine's neighbors to the east and west. Patriotism, or civic nationalism, remained the dominant ideology in war-torn Ukraine.

THE WAR IN the Donbas made clear to the country's elites that the continuing existence of Ukraine as an independent state depended less on international agreements such as the Budapest Memorandum than on the ability of the country's armed forces to withstand further aggression.

Ukraine needed a well-trained and battle-ready army, which entailed a transition from a conscripted to a contract-based military force. The demobilization or integration of the volunteer battalions, which had saved the day in 2014, into the regular armed forces or structures of the Ministry of Interior was another urgent task. Both were accomplished by 2016. Conscription was abolished in that year, as 63,500 contracts were signed by officers and soldiers joining the Ukrainian armed forces. The army grew from 140,000 to 250,000 men and women. The volunteer battalions were turned into disciplined fighting units, in spite of resistance from some of their commanders and their business and political backers.

Despite a twofold increase in security spending, Ukraine would not have managed such a transformation on its own. The military reform was backed by the United States and some North Atlantic Treaty Organization countries, with the United States contributing $1.6 billion in security assistance to Ukraine during the first four years of the conflict. American and Canadian officers helped train their Ukrainian partners, and joint land- and sea-based military exercises were introduced. The goal was to help the Ukrainian armed forces defend their country, not to recapture occupied territories or launch offensives against foreign countries. That goal was emphasized by the category of weapons that the United States delivered to Ukraine after long debate: they were Javelins—antitank missiles carried by individual soldiers—weapons of the kind that the Ukrainians had lacked in 2014 and 2015.

International assistance aside, the rebuilding, often from scratch, of the Ukrainian armed forces could not happen without the revival of the country's economy. Russian annexation of the Crimea and the loss of major urban centers in the Donets basin to the puppet "people's republics" of Donetsk and Luhansk were major blows to the Ukrainian state, society, and economy. The annexation of the Crimea meant a loss of 3 percent of the nation's territory and 5 percent of its population. Losses in the Donbas amounted to an additional 7 percent of territory and significant (but hard to calculate) loss of population. The number of internally displaced persons in Ukraine reached 1.7 million people. The war and the loss of territory, people, and industrial enterprises had a crippling effect on the rest of the country's economy.

In 2014 Ukraine's gross domestic product (GDP) contracted by 6.6 percent. Almost 10 percent more was lost in 2015. Up to 2 million Ukrainians who could not find well-paid jobs at home went to work abroad, mostly in the EU countries. To make things worse, Ukraine depended for the functioning of its remaining economy on Russia, which had just taken away part of its territory. The Russian market accounted for 26 percent of Ukrainian exports. Imports from Russia approached 29 percent. The lion's share of those imports consisted of natural gas, with which Ukraine covered more than half its consumption needs.

The political, social, and economic shock of the war meant that Ukraine had to find a way to reform and restructure its chronically ailing economy, especially its financial sector, notoriously open to corruption and abuse. Backed by a mobilized civil society, the Ukrainian leadership was able to convince the leaders of the European Union and other developed economies to provide Ukraine with substantial financial aid. In the first few years of the crisis, the EU alone managed to mobilize up to €14 billion, including €1 billion in grants, to assist the Ukrainian economy. The United States granted $2.2 billion, Canada chipped in $785 million, and Japan came up with a loan of $1.5 billion. Western donors and Ukrainian civil society wanted reforms that went beyond the economic sphere and would deal with the corruption that crippled the Ukrainian economy. The government, which depended on Western grants, was responsive.

The first task was cleaning up the Ukraine's banking system, in which, as one commentator observed, banks often functioned as ATM machines for their owners. Money deposited by savers and investors would be channeled to companies belonging to owners of the banks, which would go out of business, forcing the state to make up the depositors' losses. The financial system did not work, and budgetary shortfalls became commonplace. A reform championed by the governor of the National Bank of Ukraine, Valeria Hontarieva and her team, ended the ATM/laundromat stage in Ukrainian banking history. Owners were required to show the origins of their capital and capitalize their banks. Many refused to return the money, forcing the government to shut them down. Out of 185 banks, only 85 survived the reform.

In 2016 the government nationalized Ukraine's largest bank, PryvatBank, which happened to be co-owned by Igor Kolomoisky, an oligarch who had played a key role in stopping a Russian takeover of Ukraine's eastern and southern regions in 2014. PryvatBank's losses amounted to $5.5 billion.

Kolomoisky fought the government tooth and nail from his self-imposed exile in Switzerland, using his media empire, political influence, and even the paramilitary units he helped to fund during the early stage of the war, but he lost. The badly needed restructuring of the financial sector and refinancing of the banks cost the country 12 percent of its GDP, but it was accomplished. Without this, the restoration of Ukraine's macroeconomic stability and the recovery and further development of its economy would have been all but impossible.

Next came the reform of Ukraine's energy sector, the main source of oligarchic fortunes in the 1990s and arguably the most corrupt sector of the Ukrainian economy prior to 2014. Differential pricing of natural gas (half of it exported from Russia) for commercial enterprises and households created endless opportunities for corruption. According to some estimates, up to $3 billion was stolen annually from the state-owned oil and gas company Naftohaz. In 2014 the company's deficit amounted to 5.5 percent of Ukraine's GDP. The sector was reformed by ending direct gas purchases from Russia and switching to reverse supply of the same gas from eastern European countries. The task of increasing the consumer price—on average, households were paying no more than 12 percent of the actual cost—was politically all but unpalatable to the government but was eventually achieved in 2018, the last full year of Poroshenko's term of office.

Reforms, coupled with economic dislocations caused by the war, significantly changed the ownership structure of the Ukrainian economy. The power of the oligarchs as measured by their wealth was significantly diminished. Between 2013 and 2018 the wealth of the richest one hundred Ukrainians fell from 52 percent of GDP to 20 percent, while the wealth of the ten richest Ukrainians declined from 29 percent to 10 percent. The structure of the Ukrainian economy, a factor partly responsible for the redistribution of wealth, changed as well. The share of mining, designated as part of the rent-seeking economy and associated with the old oligarchic clans, declined, while the share of the technology and telecommunications industries, belonging to the profit-seeking segment of the economy and not associated with the traditional oligarchic groups, increased significantly.

Several reforms specifically targeted corruption. The introduction of mandatory e-declarations of income by government officials, creation of special anticorruption investigative bodies, and establishment after long delays of an anticorruption court became the direct outcomes of the joint efforts of Ukrainian civil society and Western donors. One of the most effective anticorruption reforms, ProZorro (a play on the Ukrainian word for "transparent"), resulted in the introduction of arguably the world's most transparent system of government procurement, drastically reducing opportunities for corruption in that sphere. But with the passage of time, the anticorruption reforms that picked up in the first years of President Poroshenko's tenure encountered numerous problems. The judicial system remained largely unchanged, with reforms blocked at the very top of the government pyramid.

IN THE SPRING of 2019, when citizens voted in the next presidential election, the foremost question on the political agenda was the ability of the country to continue on the path toward the European Union and internal reform while managing to defend itself against Russia.

The incumbent president, Petro Poroshenko, under whose rule the country was stabilized after the virtual collapse of 2014 and subsequent reforms were initiated, was in trouble. The war in the Donbas continued to drain national resources and claim the lives of Ukrainian soldiers and civilians. Although financial and economic reforms helped to improve the situation, they turned out to be very painful for average citizens, who were stunned by large price increases for gas, electricity, and other utilities. With almost a quarter of the population living at or below the poverty line, 5.5 million Ukrainian citizens qualified for government subsidies. President Poroshenko, whose entourage became enmired in corruption scandals during the run-up, did not manage to convince the electorate that his administration's reforms had cleaned up corruption in key sectors of the economy.

In May 2019 Ukraine welcomed a new president, the forty-one-year-old Volodymyr Zelensky, a comedian and businessman with a law degree. To a population exhausted by continuing warfare and economic hardship, Zelensky promised to put an end to war, poverty, and corruption. Like voters in a number of countries affected by a wave of populism, Ukrainian electors chose to register their protest and opted for a political outsider. With his victory in the presidential race, Volodymyr Zelensky made history in more than one way. At the age of forty-one he became the youngest president of Ukraine. He was also the first Jewish president of the country. In the summer of 2019, Ukraine, for a short time, had both a Jewish president and a Jewish prime minister—quite a fit for a country with a long and often tragic history of Jewish-Ukrainian relations.

When it came to electoral politics, the 2019 presidential election demonstrated more continuity than change, showing that the war had turned

Ukraine into a more homogenous country. If opposing candidates in prewar elections had repeatedly divided the country almost evenly between east and west, the new election revealed a very different geography. Both Poroshenko in 2014 and Zelensky in 2019 carried most of the country. The electorate now supported Zelensky almost as overwhelmingly as it had supported Poroshenko in 2014. That trend continued in July 2019, when in the new parliamentary elections, the presidential party, the Servant of the People, a brand-new political entity named after the satirical television series in which Zelensky had played the president of Ukraine, won a majority of seats.

Despite the change of the political guard in Kyiv, the key challenges facing Ukrainian society remained the same: security, institutional reform, and the continuing dominance of the oligarchs in Ukraine's economy and politics. In the first months of his presidency, Volodymyr Zelensky concluded an alliance with Ukraine's "Young Turks," a group of young and ambitious reformers who approached him out of discontent with the pace of reforms initiated under his predecessor. The government, headed by the thirty-five-year-old prime minister Oleksiy Honcharuk, set itself the tasks of continuing economic reform and the war on corruption. Privatization of government-owned assets seemed the fastest way to achieve both goals. The list of state enterprises up for sale was dramatically extended, and the bill lifting the moratorium on the sale of agricultural land, which had been in place since 2001, was sent to parliament for adoption in 2020.

The "Young Turks" were dismissed in March 2020 after less than half a year in office, as their reforms made the oligarchic clans unhappy, while their inexperience contributed to a 7 percent fall in the country's industrial production. Anticorruption measures in the customs service backfired, dramatically reducing government revenues and raising questions about the new president's commitment to anticorruption reforms. The most immediate challenge to the anticorruption program was the influence of Igor Kolomoisky, former owner of the nationalized PryvatBank, who returned to Ukraine immediately after Zelensky's victory and demanded the bank back. The Western governments and institutions that backed Ukraine's banking reform sounded the alarm. The International Monetary Fund's condition for continuing cooperation with Ukraine was the adoption of a law making it impossible to return banks to owners who had made them insolvent.

In May 2020 parliament passed a law prohibiting court challenges to the National Bank's insolvency rulings against corrupt banks. Hailed as a victory for anticorruption forces in Ukraine, the law highlighted the major problem with the government's struggle against corruption: it could not rely on the Ukrainian courts. In October 2020, the Constitutional Court of Ukraine removed criminal responsibility for inaccurate declaration of assets by Ukrainian officials, delivering a major blow to the anticorruption efforts of the previous years and causing a constitutional crisis. The crisis highlighted the need for reform of the judicial system as the major challenge facing Ukraine at the beginning of the new decade. On its successful implementation depends the fate of Ukraine's movement toward a prosperous law-based society.

THE UNFINISHED WAR in the Donbas, which by 2020 had claimed more than 14,000 lives on both sides of the divide, remains Ukraine's most immediate foreign-policy problem, followed by the reintegration of the Donbas and reclamation of the Crimean Peninsula.

Irrespective of Kyiv's wishes, Russia holds the keys to resolving the conflict and continues to apply pressure on Ukraine for a resolution on its own terms. Those terms, which include the return to Ukraine of the economically devastated Donbas while Russia retains de facto control of the region's political life, would destabilize Ukraine and slow down, if not completely derail, its reform agenda and movement toward the European Union. Those were the original goals of Russian aggression. They were not achieved, and the war failed to stop Ukraine's transformation into a well-functioning market democracy. To continue on the path of reform and Eurointegration, Ukraine will need not only to mobilize its own resources but also to ensure continuing support from the international community.

No country is more important for securing Ukraine's political sovereignty in its current conflict with Russia than the United States of America. Since 2014, the United States has taken a leading role in providing political, military and, to a significant degree, economic support for the Ukrainian state. But in order to maintain and strengthen that alliance, the two countries will have to overcome a number of problems that have developed in their relations during the last decade. The common denominator of those problems is corruption, which has held the future of American-Ukrainian relations hostage on both sides of the Atlantic.

Ukraine had first gained notice in American domestic politics during Donald Trump's presidential campaign of 2016. At that time, damaging information from Ukraine caused the resignation of Trump's campaign chairman, Paul Manafort. A US-based political consultant, Manafort had begun working years earlier for a future president of Ukraine, Viktor Yanukovych, after completing a number of contracts with one of Russia's leading oligarchs. Manafort helped bring Yanukovych to office in 2010, but the Revolution of Dignity, which forced Yanukovych to leave the country in 2014, also helped uncover records of secret multi-million-dollar payments by the former presidential party, which were never reported to the Ukrainian or American tax authorities. Manafort was forced to resign as chairman of Trump's presidential campaign and later was sentenced, on charges related to his activities in Russia and Ukraine, first to forty-seven and then to an additional forty-three months' imprisonment.

If the Manafort scandal damaged Trump's presidential campaign of 2016, there were hopes in the White House that a new Ukrainian scandal, this time involving the leading Democratic presidential candidate, Joseph Biden, could help Trump's 2020 reelection campaign. The vice president in Barack Obama's administration, Biden had served from 2014 to 2016 as the administration's point man on Ukraine and played a key role in convincing Kyiv to get rid of a prosecutor general believed by Western governments to be corrupt. In the first half of 2019, with Biden announcing his bid for the White House, Ukrainian officials displeased with Biden's anticorruption campaign struck back, accusing the former vice president of trying to stop the investigation of a Ukrainian company that had offered a place on its board of directors to his son, Hunter Biden.

President Trump raised the issue of Biden's involvement in Ukraine with President Zelensky during a telephone conversation in July 2019. Zelensky used the opportunity offered by the call to ask for the sale of more Javelins for the Ukrainian army. Trump asked for a favor in return. "There is a lot of talk about Biden's son," Trump told the Ukrainian president, "that Biden stopped the prosecution and a lot of people want to find out about that. So whatever you can do with the [US] attorney general would be great." The Ukrainian president promised to help: "Since we won the absolute majority in our parliament, the next prosecutor general will be 100 percent my person," declared Zelensky.

The Ukrainian authorities never launched an investigation: they delayed long enough to be saved by public revelations of a whistle-blower's complaint about Trump's attempt to use the military help to Ukraine for the political gain, and Ukraine received its assistance without meeting Trump's conditions. The first impeachment of President Trump, which focused on that particular episode in Ukrainian-American relations, put them to a new test. To the credit of the key players in Washington and Kyiv, the close relations between the two capitals and countries survived the turmoil. Kyiv's alliances with the United States and the European Union remain essential not only for the survival of Ukraine as a fully independent state but also for the restoration and strengthening of international order, which Russia's aggression against Ukraine and annexation of its territory have undermined.

For Ukraine, Russian aggression raised fundamental questions about its continuing existence as a unified state, its independence as a nation, and the democratic foundations of its political institutions. No less important are questions about the nature of Ukraine's nation-building project, including the role of history, ethnicity, language, and culture in the forging of Ukraine's political nation. Could a country whose citizens represented different ethnicities, spoke (often interchangeably) more than one language, belonged to more than one church, and inhabited a number of diverse historical regions withstand not only the onslaught of a more militarily powerful imperial master but also its claim to the loyalty of everyone who spoke Russian or worshipped at an Orthodox church?

Russian aggression sought to divide Ukrainians along linguistic, regional, and ethnic lines. While that tactic succeeded in some places, most of Ukrainian society united around the idea of a multilingual and multicultural nation joined in administrative and political terms. That idea, born of lessons drawn from Ukraine's difficult and often tragic history of internal divisions, rests on a tradition of coexistence of different languages, cultures, and religions over the centuries. The Ukrainians managed to read their troubled history in a way that secured their future as a political nation.

EPILOGUE
The Meanings of History

HISTORY HAS BEEN used and abused more than once in the Ukraine Crisis, informing and inspiring its participants but also justifying violations of international law, human rights, and the right to life itself. The Russo-Ukrainian conflict, while arising unexpectedly and taking many of those involved by surprise, has deep historical roots and is replete with historical references and allusions. Leaving aside the propagandistic use of historical arguments, at least three parallel processes rooted in the past are now going on in Ukraine: Russia's attempts to reestablish political, economic, and military control in the former imperial space acquired by Moscow since the mid-seventeenth century; the formation of modern national identities, which concerns both Russians and Ukrainians (the latter often divided along regional lines); and the struggle over historical and cultural fault lines that allow the participants in the conflict to imagine it as a contest between East and West, Europe and the Russian World.

The Russo-Ukrainian conflict reminded the world of the Russian annexation of the Crimea in the last decades of the eighteenth century and the creation in southern Ukraine of the short-lived imperial province of New Russia. This memory of Russian imperial expansion into the area was brought to the fore not by outside observers trying to portray current Russian behavior as imperial but by ideologues of the Russian hybrid war in Ukraine, who came up with the New Russia project. They sought to develop their historical ideology on the foundations of imperial conquest and

Russian dominance in lands originally inhabited by the Crimean and Noghay Tatars and Zaporozhian Cossacks. This pertains especially to the trope of Sevastopol as a city of Russian glory—a historical myth rooted in the 1853–1856 Crimean War (a disaster for the Russian Empire) that attributes the heroism of the multiethnic imperial army defending the city to Russians alone.

The formation of the Donetsk and Luhansk "people's republics," along with the attempts to proclaim Odesa and Kharkiv republics—building blocks of a future New Russia—also had its roots in historical memory. It went back to Bolshevik attempts to maintain control over Ukraine's east and south soon after the signing of the Treaty of Brest-Litovsk with Germany (February 1918), which assigned those regions to Ukraine. At that time the Bolsheviks were using self-proclaimed states, including the Crimean and Donetsk–Kryvyi Rih Soviet republics, to claim that they were not part of Ukraine and thus not covered by the treaty. The founders of the new Donetsk republic claimed to use the symbols of the Donetsk–Kryvyi Rih republic of 1918, as, like the old one, theirs would not have arisen or survived without Moscow's sponsorship and support.

While allusions to the Russian imperial and revolutionary past became part of the historical discourse justifying the Russian aggression against Ukraine, its historical motivation is more recent. The rapid and unexpected disintegration of the Soviet Union, recalled by President Vladimir Putin in his speech on the annexation of the Crimea, provides the most immediate historical background to the crisis. The current Russian government keeps claiming that Ukraine is an artificial formation whose eastern territories were allegedly a gift to the country from the Bolsheviks, as was the Crimea after World War II. According to this narrative, the only genuine and thus historically legitimate polity is the empire—first the Russian Empire and then the Soviet Union. The Russian government actively combats and suppresses any historical traditions and memories that undermine the legitimacy of the empire, such as commemoration of the 1932–1933 Great Ukrainian Famine or the Soviet government's 1944 deportation of the Crimean Tatars; such was the case with the ban on public commemoration of the seventieth anniversary of the Crimean Tatar deportation imposed by the Russian authorities in the Crimea in May 2014.

Russia today seems to be following in the footsteps of some of its imperial predecessors who continued to harbor nostalgia for their empires long after they were lost. The collapse of the Soviet Union left Russian elites bitter about their loss of imperial and superpower status, nourishing illusions that what had happened was an accident brought about by the ill will of the West or by politicians like Mikhail Gorbachev and Boris Yeltsin foolishly bickering for power. Such a view of the end of the Soviet Union makes it hard to resist the temptation to rewrite history.

THE RUSSO-UKRAINIAN CONFLICT also brought to the fore another important issue with historical roots and ramifications: the unfinished process of building the modern Russian and Ukrainian nations. The Russian annexation of the Crimea and the propaganda intended to justify Russian aggression in the Donbas have proceeded under the slogan of defending the rights of ethnic Russians and Russian speakers in general. The equation of the Russian language not only with Russian culture but also with Russian nationality has been an important aspect of the worldview of many Russian volunteers who have come to Donbas. One problem with that interpretation of Russianness is that while ethnic Russians indeed make up a majority of the population in the Crimea and large minorities in parts of the Donbas, most of the population of the projected New Russia consists of ethnic Ukrainians. While Russian and separatist propaganda has had an appeal for many ethnic Ukrainians, most have refused to identify themselves with Russia or with Russian ethnicity even as they continue to use the Russian language. That was one of the main reasons for the failure of the New Russia project, which came as a complete surprise to its authors.

The view of Ukrainians as constituents of the Russian nation goes back to the founding myth of modern Russia as a nation conceived and born in Kyiv, the "mother of Russian [rather than Rus'] cities." The *Synopsis* of 1674, the first printed "textbook" of Russian history, compiled by Kyivan monks seeking the protection of the Muscovite tsars, first formulated and widely disseminated this myth in Russia. Throughout most of the imperial period, Ukrainians were regarded as Little Russians—a vision that allowed for the existence of Ukrainian folk culture and spoken vernacular but not a high culture or a modern literature. Recognition of Ukrainians as a distinct nation in cultural but not political terms in the aftermath of the Revolution of 1917 challenged that vision. The aggression of 2014, backed by the ideology of the "Russian World," offers Ukrainians today a throwback in comparison with Soviet practices. Nation building as conceived in a future New Russia makes no provision for a separate Ukrainian ethnicity within a broader Russian nation. This is hardly an oversight or excess born of the heat of battle.

Less than a year before the annexation of the Crimea, Vladimir Putin himself went on record claiming that Russians and Ukrainians were one and the same people. He repeated that statement in a speech delivered on March 18, 2015, to mark the first anniversary of the annexation of the Crimea.

Since the fall of the USSR, the Russian nation-building project has switched its focus to the idea of forming a single Russian nation not divided into branches and unifying the Eastern Slavs on the basis of the Russian language and culture. Ukraine has become the first testing ground for this model outside the Russian Federation.

THE NEW MODEL of Russian identity, which stresses the indivisibility of the Russian nation, closely associated with the Russian language and culture, poses a fundamental challenge to the Ukrainian nation-building project. From its beginnings in the nineteenth century, that project placed the Ukrainian language and culture at its center, but from the outset it also allowed for the use of other languages and cultures, as attested, for example, by the Russian-language writings of Taras Shevchenko, whom many regard as the spiritual founder of the Ukrainian nation. Bilingualism and multiculturalism have become a norm in post-Soviet Ukraine, extending membership in the Ukrainian nation to people of various ethnic and religious backgrounds. This has had a direct impact on the course of the Russo-Ukrainian conflict. Contrary to the Kremlin's expectations, Russian aggression failed to mobilize the support of ethnic Russians outside the areas directly controlled by the Russian army—the Crimea and those parts of the Donbas seized by Russian mercenaries and Russia-backed insurgents.

According to data provided by the respected Kyiv International Institute of Sociology, with Russians constituting 17 percent of the Ukrainian population, only 5 percent of those polled considered themselves exclusively Russian: the rest identified as both Russian and Ukrainian. Even those who considered themselves exclusively Russian often opposed Russian interference in Ukrainian affairs, refusing to associate themselves with Putin's regime. "Ukraine is my Homeland. Russian is my native language. And I would like to be saved by Pushkin. And delivered from sorrow and unrest, also by Pushkin. Pushkin, not Putin," wrote one of Kyiv's ethnic Russians in her Facebook account. The ideology of the "Russian World," which combines Russian nationalism with Russian Orthodoxy and which Moscow and Russian-backed insurgents have promoted as an alternative to the pro-European choice of the Maidan protesters, has helped strengthen the

Ukrainian-Jewish pro-European alliance developing in Ukraine since 1991. "I have said for a long time that an alliance between Ukrainians and Jews is a pledge of our common future," posted a pro-Maidan activist on his Facebook account.

History has left Ukraine united in one state but divided along numerous regional lines that echo the cultural and political boundaries of the past. The line between the parklands of central Ukraine and the southern steppes became a porous border between the predominantly agricultural areas to the north and the urban centers of the mineral-rich steppes to the south. The frontier of Western and Eastern Christianity, after reaching the Dnieper in the seventeenth and eighteenth centuries, retreated to Galicia and now recalls the border between the Habsburg and Russian empires of the pre–World War I era. Within the former Habsburg possessions, Galicia differs from the largely Hungarian-ruled Transcarpathia and the former Moldavian province of Bukovyna. Within the former Russian Empire, Volhynia, which was under Polish rule during the interwar period, is different from Podolia, which stayed under Soviet rule for most of the twentieth century. There is also a difference between the formerly Polish-ruled lands on the Right Bank of the Dnieper and those of the former Cossack Hetmanate on its Left Bank, as well as between the Cossack lands and those colonized largely through the centralized efforts of the Russian Empire in the eighteenth and nineteenth centuries. The borders of those lands also serve as a line between Ukrainians who are more comfortable speaking Ukrainian and those who prefer Russian in everyday speech.

In reality, Ukrainian regionalism is even more complex than the account of it just presented. There are differences between the old Cossack lands of the former Hetmanate and Sloboda Ukraine, while the southern Ukrainian province of Mykolaiv differs greatly in ethnic composition, language use, and voting behavior from the Crimea, which was attached to Ukraine only in 1954. But despite all these differences, Ukraine's regions stick together because the borders indicated above, which were quite distinct in the past, would be almost impossible to reestablish today. Nowadays one sees a patchwork of linguistic, cultural, economic, and political transition zones that link different regions to one another and keep the country together. In practice, there is no easily identifiable cultural boundary dividing the Crimea from the neighboring regions of southern Ukraine or the Donbas from the other eastern regions. None of the historical regions has shown a strong desire to leave Ukraine; nor have elites managed to mobilize citizens in support of secession. True, such mobilization has taken place in the Crimea and the Donbas, but only as a consequence of Russian annexation or intervention.

A SYMBOLIC FAREWELL to the Soviet past—the demolition of remaining monuments to Lenin, more than five hundred altogether, in a few weeks—accompanied the Revolution of Dignity. Among the anti-Kyiv insurgents in the Donbas, there were many defenders of the old Soviet values. But Russian mercenaries and volunteers brought to the region an overarching idea of a different kind. Like the best known of the Russian commanders, Igor Girkin, they came to the Donbas to defend the values of the "Russian World" against the West. In that context, they saw Ukraine as a battleground between corrupt Western values, including democracy, individual freedoms, human rights, and, especially, the rights of sexual minorities on the one hand and traditional Russian values on the other. By that logic, Western propaganda had simply addled the Ukrainians' minds. It was up to the Russians to show them the light.

This interpretation of the conflict has deep roots in the Russian culture and intellectual tradition. While one can hardly imagine modern Russian history without Russian participation in European culture, it is also true that for centuries Russia was cut off from the West or engaged in confrontation with the countries of central and western Europe. Which set of historical experiences best defines Russia's love-hate relationship with the West? In the enduring Russian intellectual debate between Westernizers and Slavophiles, which began in the early nineteenth century and pitted the view of Russia as part of Europe against that of Russia as a distinct civilization with a world mission, the descendants of the Slavophiles and anti-Westerners now have the upper hand.

As for Ukraine, its claim to independence has always had a European orientation, which is one consequence of Ukraine's experience as a country located on the East-West divide between Orthodoxy and Catholicism, central European and Eurasian empires, and the political and social practices they brought with them. This location on the border of several cultural spaces helped make Ukraine a contact zone in which Ukrainians of different persuasions could learn to coexist. It also helped create regional divisions, which participants in the current conflict have exploited. Ukraine has always been known, and lately it has been much praised, for the cultural hybridity of its society, but how much hybridity a nation can bear and still remain united in the face of a "hybrid war" is one of the important questions now being decided in the conflict between Russia and Ukraine.

The pro-European revolution in Ukraine, which broke out a quarter century after the end of the Cold War, took a page from the Cold War fascination with the European West shared by the dissidents of Poland, Czechoslovakia, and other countries of the region, in some cases turning that fascination into a new national religion. The Revolution of Dignity and the war brought about a geopolitical reorientation of Ukrainian society. The proportion of those with positive attitudes toward Russia decreased from 80 percent in January 2014 to under 50 percent in September of the same year. In November 2014, 64 percent of those polled supported Ukraine's accession to the European Union (that figure had stood at 39 percent in November 2013). In April 2014, only a third of Ukrainians had wanted their country to join NATO; in November 2014, more than half supported that course. There can be little doubt that the experience of war not only united most Ukrainians but also turned the country's sympathies westward.

Historically, the shock of war, the humiliation of defeat, and the open wound of lost territories have served as potent instruments for building national solidarity and forging a strong national identity. The partitions of Poland in the second half of the eighteenth century wiped the Polish state off the map of Europe but served as a starting point for the formation of modern Polish nationalism, while the Napoleonic invasion of Germany at the beginning of the nineteenth century gave rise to pan-German ideas and promoted the development of modern German nationalism. Memories of defeat and lost territory have fired the national imaginations of French and Poles, Serbs and Czechs. Invaded, humiliated, and war-torn Ukraine seems to be following that general pattern.

The Russian annexation of the Crimea, the hybrid war in the Donbas, and attempts to destabilize the rest of the country created a new and dangerous situation not only in Ukraine but also in Europe as a whole. For the first time since the end of World War II, a major European power made war on a weaker neighbor and annexed part of the territory of a sovereign state. The Russian invasion breached not only the Russo-Ukrainian treaty of 1997 but also the Budapest Memorandum of 1994, which had offered Ukraine security assurances in exchange for giving up its nuclear weapons and acceding to the Nuclear Non-proliferation Treaty as a nonnuclear state. The unprovoked Russian aggression against Ukraine threatened the foundations of international order—a threat to which the European Union and most of the world were not prepared to respond but one that demands appropriate counteraction. Whatever the outcome of the current Ukraine Crisis, on its resolution depends not only the future of Ukraine but also that of relations between Europe's east and west—Russia and the European Union—and thus the future of Europe as a whole.

ACKNOWLEDGMENTS

I WOULD LIKE TO thank Jill Kneerim for finding an excellent home for the manuscript; Lara Heimert for enthusiastically embracing the challenge of editing and publishing the book; her Basic Books team, especially Roger Labrie, for making that possible; Myroslav Yurkevich for editing different versions of the manuscript; my wife, Olena, for criticizing and eventually endorsing it; Volodymyr Kulyk and Roman Procyk for correcting embarrassing mistakes; my graduate student Megan Duncan Smith for being a fabulous teaching fellow in my course "Frontiers of Europe: Ukraine Since 1500," where I tested some of the ideas presented in the book; the Harvard graduate and undergraduate students who took that course in the fall of 2014 for their questions, e-mails, and course website queries and comments—they have all made their way into this book. My special thanks go to Vladyslav Rashkovan and Dominique Arel for suggesting literature on the latest developments in Ukraine. I am also grateful to Hennady Yefymenko for his comments on the book. Finally, I want to thank everyone who, throughout my long career as a historian and teacher, helped me understand what this book should and should not be about. They do not, of course, bear the blame for any shortcomings.

HISTORICAL TIMELINE

World History: 45,000 BC Humans arrive in southern Europe.

45,000–43,000 BC Neanderthal mammoth hunters build their dwellings in Ukraine.

4500–3000 BC Tribes of the Neolithic Cucuteni-Trypilian culture, producers of clay statues and colored pottery, call lands between the Danube and the Dnieper their home.

Ca. 3500 BC Humans between the Danube and Dnieper Rivers domesticate the horse.

World History: 3500 BC Sumerians migrate to Mesopotamia.

1300–750 BC Cimmerian Kingdom, homeland of the fictional Conan the Barbarian, establishes its rule over the Pontic steppes of southern Ukraine.

750–250 BC Scythian horsemen drive out the Cimmerians.

750–500 BC Greek trading colonies are established on the northern shore of the Black Sea; Greeks imagine that mythical figures such as Amazon female warriors populate the Ukrainian steppes to the north.

World History: 753 BC Legendary founding of Rome.

512 BC Darius the Great of Persia marches through the Pontic steppes in a vain attempt to defeat the Scythian army.

Ca. 485–425 BC Life and times of Herodotus, who described Scythia and classified its population as belonging to various strata, including Royal Scythians and Scythian agriculturalists, the settled population of the forest-steppe borderland.

250 BC–250 AD Sarmatians take control of the steppes from the Scythians.

1–100 Romans establish their presence in the Greek colonies; Strabo identifies the Don River as the eastern border of

Europe, leaving present-day Ukrainian territories on the European side of the Europe-Asia divide.

World History: ca. 30 Jesus enters Jerusalem.

250–375 Goths defeat the Sarmatians and establish their rule over Ukrainian lands.

375–650 Period of migrations: Huns, Avars, and Bulgars make their way through the Pontic steppes.

Ca. 551 Historian Jordanes locates Slavic tribes of Sclaveni and Antes between the Danube and the Dnieper; earlier in the century, the Antes make a name for themselves by attacking the Roman Empire.

650–900 Khazar kaganate collects tribute from Slavic tribes in Ukraine.

World History: 800 Charlemagne is crowned emperor of the Romans.

838 First mention of Rus' Vikings in Western sources.

860 First Rus' attack on Constantinople from the northern shores of the Black Sea.

950 Byzantine emperor Constantine VII Porphyrogenitus describes trade relations with Rus' and the Dnieper–Black Sea route used for both trade and war.

971 Emperor John Tzimisces meets with Prince Sviatoslav of Kyiv on the Danube to negotiate a truce between Byzantium and Rus'.

987–989 Prince Volodymyr of Kyiv besieges the Byzantine fortress of Chersonesus in the Crimea, marries Anna, sister of Emperor Basil II of Byzantium, and accepts Christianity for himself and his realm.

1037 Prince Yaroslav the Wise completes the construction of the St. Sophia Cathedral, seat of the metropolitans of Rus' and site of the first Rus' library.

World History: 1054 Rome and Constantinople divide the Christian Church.

1054 Death of Prince Yaroslav the Wise, dubbed "father-in-law of Europe" by historians because of his daughters' marriages to members of European ruling dynasties, signals the beginning of the disintegration of Kyivan Rus'.

1113–1125 Prince Volodymyr Monomakh temporarily restores the unity of Kyivan Rus' and promotes the writing of the Primary Chronicle, the main narrative source on the history of medieval Ukraine.

1187–1189 A Kyivan chronicler first uses the word "Ukraine" to describe the steppe borderland from Pereiaslav in the east to Galicia in the west.

World History: 1215 Magna Carta is issued by King John of England.

1238–1264   Prince Danylo of Galicia-Volhynia, who received a crown from the pope, establishes control over most Ukrainian territories, playing the Golden Horde in the east against the Polish and Hungarian kingdoms in the west; he founds the city of Lviv.

1240   Kyiv falls to Mongol armies, and Ukraine finds itself within the sphere of influence of the Golden Horde.

1241–1261   Transcarpathia falls under the control of the kings of Hungary.

1299–1325   Metropolitan of Rus' moves his seat from Kyiv, devastated by the Mongols, to Vladimir on the Kliazma and then to Moscow; a separate metropolitanate is established in Galicia.

1340–1392   Once powerful principality of Galicia-Volhynia divides, with Galicia going to Poland and Volhynia, along with the Dnieper region, to the Lithuanian princes.

World History: 1347 Black Death ravages Europe.

1362   Lithuanian and Rus' armies challenge the rule of the khans of the Golden Horde over the Ukrainian steppes in the Battle of Syni Vody; most of the Ukrainian lands become part of the Grand Duchy of Lithuania.

1386   Prince Jogaila of Lithuania marries Queen Jadwiga of Poland, initiating the conversion of the Lithuanian elites to Catholicism and gradual unification of the Kingdom of Poland and the Grand Duchy of Lithuania.

1430–1434   Rus' (Ukrainian and Belarusian) elites of the Grand Duchy of Lithuania rebel against discriminatory policies of the Catholic rulers of the Grand Duchy of Lithuania.

1449–1478   Crimean Khanate becomes independent of the Golden Horde but falls under the control of the Ottoman Empire.

1492   First mention of Ukrainian Cossacks in historical sources.

1514   Prince Kostiantyn Ostrozky defeats the Muscovite army at the Battle of Orsha in the contest between Lithuania and Muscovy for the former lands of Kyivan Rus'.

World History: 1517 Martin Luther issues his Ninety-Five Theses.

1569   Union of Lublin between the Kingdom of Poland and the Grand Duchy of Lithuania creates the Polish-Lithuanian Commonwealth, in which Poland establishes jurisdiction over Ukraine and Lithuania maintains its rule over Belarus, creating the first administrative border between the two East Slavic lands.

1581 First complete Church Slavonic translation of the Bible is published in Ostrih.

1590–1638 Era of Cossack uprisings establishes the Cossacks as a formidable military force and distinct social order.

1596 Union of Brest brings part of the Kyiv Orthodox metropolitanate under the jurisdiction of Rome, dividing Uniates (later Greek Catholics) from Orthodox to the present day.

1632–1646 Metropolitan Peter Mohyla of Kyiv establishes the Kyivan College (future Kyiv Mohyla Academy), reforms his church along the lines of the Catholic Reformation, and presides over the drafting of the first Orthodox Confession of Faith.

1639 French engineer and cartographer Guillaume Levasseur de Beauplan produces his first map of Ukraine, reflecting recent colonization of steppe borderlands.

World History: 1648 Peace of Westphalia establishes a new international order.

1648 Cossack officer Bohdan Khmelnytsky launches an uprising against the Polish-Lithuanian Commonwealth that leads to the expulsion of Polish landowners, massacres of Jews, and creation of a Cossack state known as the Hetmanate.

1654 Cossack officers recognize the suzerainty of the tsars of Moscow, leading to prolonged confrontation between Moscow and Warsaw over control of Ukraine.

1667 Truce of Andrusovo divides Ukraine along the Dnieper between Muscovy and Poland, producing a Cossack uprising against both powers led by Hetman Petro Doroshenko.

1672–1699 Ottomans rule Right-Bank Ukraine.

1674 Monks of the Kyivan Cave Monastery publish the *Synopsis*, a historical text that presents Kyiv as the center of the Russian monarchy and nation, arguing for religious, dynastic, and ethnonational unity of Eastern Slavs in the face of threats from Poland and the Ottoman Empire.

1685 Kyiv metropolitanate transferred from the jurisdiction of the patriarch of Constantinople to that of the patriarch of Moscow.

1708 Upset by Russian assault on Cossack rights, Hetman Ivan Mazepa leads a revolt against Peter I and sides with the advancing army of Charles XII of Sweden.

1709 Battle of Poltava brings victory to the Russian army, leading to the abolition of the hetman's office and further curtailing of Hetmanate autonomy.

World History: 1721 Peace of Nystad makes Russia a European power.

1727–1734 Temporary restoration of the office of hetman under Danylo Apostol.

1740s Rabbi Israel ben Eliezer, better known as Baal Shem Tov, assembles his students and followers in the Podolian town of Medzhybizh and begins the teaching of Hassidism.

1764–1780 Liquidation of the Hetmanate as part of the centralizing reforms of Catherine II of Russia.

1768 Bar Confederation of the Polish nobility and the Haidamaky peasant uprising are accompanied by massacres of Uniates and Jews in Right-Bank Ukraine.

1775 Liquidation of the Zaporozhian Host on the lower Dnieper following the Russo-Turkish War of 1768–1774, in which the Russian Empire is victorious.

1783 Russia annexes the Crimea.

World History: 1789 French Revolution begins.

1772–1795 Partitions of Poland bring Galicia under the control of the Habsburgs and Right-Bank Ukraine and Volhynia under the control of the Russian Empire.

1791 Catherine II creates the Pale of Settlement, prohibiting former Polish and Lithuanian Jewry from moving into the Russian heartland; Ukraine becomes part of the Pale.

1792 Russian Empire wins another war with the Ottomans and consolidates control over southern Ukraine.

1798 Poltava noble Ivan Kotliarevsky publishes *Eneïda*, the first poetical work in modern Ukrainian, ushering in modern Ukrainian literature.

1812 Ukrainian Cossacks fight in the ranks of the Russian imperial army against Napoleon.

1818 First grammar of the Ukrainian language is published.

1819 Rapidly growing city of Odesa becomes a free port, attracting new business and new settlers.

1830 Polish uprising leads to a contest between Polish landowners and Russian government for the loyalty of the Ukrainian peasantry.

1834 Tsar Nicholas I establishes Kyiv University; efforts to turn Kyiv into a bulwark of Russian imperial identity get under way.

1840 Taras Shevchenko, an artist and poet and, in the opinion of many, the father of the Ukrainian nation, publishes *Kobzar*.

1847 Mykola Kostomarov drafts the first political program of the nascent Ukrainian movement, *The Books of the Genesis of the Ukrainian People*, where he calls for the creation of a Slavic federation with Ukraine at its center.

World History: Revolutions of 1848.

1848 The Spring of Nations rocks the Habsburg Empire, causing the mobilization of the Polish and Ukrainian national movements; the Ukrainians unite around the Supreme Ruthenian Council; the imperial authorities decide to emancipate the serfs.

1850s Oil exploration begins in Galicia, turning the Drohobych region into one of the world's most productive oil fields.

1854 British, French, and Ottoman forces land in the Crimea to lay siege to Sevastopol and build the first railroad on the territory of Ukraine, leading from Balaklava to Sevastopol; Russia loses the Crimean War and its Black Sea fleet.

World History: 1861 American Civil War begins.

1861 Emancipation of the serfs in the Russian Empire and liberal reforms of Alexander II transform the economic, social, and cultural landscape of Ukraine.

1863 Alarmed by the new Polish insurrection and the possibility of a split within the "all-Russian nationality," the Russian minister of the interior, Petr Valuev, introduces a ban on Ukrainian-language publications.

1870 Welsh entrepreneur John James Hughes comes to southern Ukraine to establish metal works, initiating development of the Donets industrial basin and inaugurating Russian labor migration to Ukraine.

1876 Ems Ukase, signed by Emperor Alexander II, introduces further restrictions on use of the Ukrainian language; Mykhailo Drahomanov, a young history professor at Kyiv University, emigrates to Switzerland, where he lays the ideological foundations of Ukrainian liberalism and socialism.

1890s Land hunger leads to increased emigration of Ukrainian peasantry from Austria-Hungary to the United States and Canada and from Russian-ruled Ukraine to the North Caucasus and the Russian Far East.

1900 Mykola Mikhnovsky, a Kharkiv lawyer, formulates the idea of the political independence of Ukraine; similar ideas are expressed in Galicia.

1905 Revolution in the Russian Empire ends prohibitions on the use of the Ukrainian language and allows creation of legal political parties; revolutionary upheaval leads to the rise of Russian nationalism and anti-Jewish pogroms; Sholem Aleichem leaves Kyiv for New York.

World History: 1914 World War I begins.

1914 Outbreak of World War I turns Ukraine into a battle-ground between the Russian Empire, Austria-Hungary, and Germany.

1917 Collapse of the Russian monarchy opens the door to the creation of a Ukrainian state, a process led by socialists in the Central Rada, Ukraine's revolutionary parliament.

1918–1920 Ukrainian governments in Russian- and Austrian-ruled parts of Ukraine declare independence but lose the war to their more powerful neighbors, Bolshevik Russia and the newly established Polish Republic.

1920s National communism in Soviet Ukraine.

1921–1923 Ukrainian territories are divided between Soviet Russia, Poland, Romania, and Czechoslovakia.

1927–1929 Bolshevik authorities introduce large-scale industrialization, collectivization, and cultural revolution, policies intended to bring about the communist transformation of economy and society.

World History: 1929 Black Friday inaugurates the Great Depression.

1932–1933 Close to 4 million die in Ukraine as a result of the man-made famine known today as the Holodomor.

1934 Members of the Organization of Ukrainian Nationalists assassinate Polish minister of the interior, Bronisław Pieracki, manifesting both growing dissatisfaction among Ukrainian society with Polish rule and the rising power of radical nationalism.

1937 Stalinist purges, which sent millions to the Gulag and put hundreds of thousands on death row, reach their height.

World History: 1939 World War II begins.

1939 Molotov-Ribbentrop Pact leads to the Soviet occupation of formerly Polish Volhynia and Galicia and formerly Romanian Bukovyna; Czech-ruled Transcarpathia, where Ukrainian activists declare short-lived independence, goes to Hungary.

1941 Nazi invasion of the Soviet Union results in German and Romanian occupation of Ukraine, turning it into one of the main killing fields of the Holocaust and costing millions of Ukrainians of all ethnic backgrounds their lives.

1943 Soviet return to Ukraine brings back communist rule and launches a prolonged war between Soviet security forces and Ukrainian nationalist guerillas in western Ukraine.

1944 Crimean Tatars are deported from the Crimea to Central Asia after being accused of collaboration with the Germans.

1945 Yalta Conference provides international legitimacy for the new Polish-Ukrainian border, leaving Lviv on the Ukrainian side, and makes possible Ukrainian membership in the United Nations; later in the year, Transcarpathia is annexed to Soviet Ukraine as Moscow bullies Prague into submission.

1946 Forcible liquidation of the Ukrainian Greek Catholic Church, whose leaders are accused of following anticommunist policies of the Vatican and maintaining links with the nationalist underground.

World History: 1948 Cold War begins.

1953 Stalin's death ends the rising anti-Semitic campaigns and persecution of Ukrainian cultural figures for alleged nationalist deviations.

1954 Nikita Khrushchev engineers transfer of the Crimea from Russia to Ukraine to facilitate the economic recovery of the peninsula, which depends on the Ukrainian mainland for supplies.

1956 Beginning of de-Stalinization and emergence of the Ukrainian party elite as a junior partner of the Russian leadership in running the Soviet Union.

1964 Ouster of Nikita Khrushchev leads to the end of ideological and cultural concessions by the regime, initiating a partial return to the political norms of late Stalinism.

1970s Era of stagnation unfolds, characterized by slowing of economic growth and mounting social problems.

1975–1981 Helsinki Final Act encourages Ukrainian dissidents to organize in defense of human rights; KGB arrests and imprisons members of the Ukrainian Helsinki Group.

1985 Mikhail Gorbachev comes to power and launches reforms aimed at improving the Soviet political and economic system.

1986 Chernobyl nuclear disaster raises questions about the responsibility of central authorities for the ecological catastrophe and leads to the formation of the Green Party, the first mass political party in Soviet Ukraine.

1990 First competitive elections to the Ukrainian parliament result in the formation of a parliamentary opposition and declaration of the sovereignty of the republic, still within the USSR.

World History: 1991 Soviet Union falls.

1991 After a failed coup in Moscow, Ukraine leads the other Soviet republics out of the union, dealing a deathblow to the USSR in the independence referendum of December 1.

1994 Russian, American, and British assurances with regard to Ukrainian sovereignty and territorial integrity follow Ukraine's transfer of nuclear warheads inherited from the Soviet Union to Russia.

1996 New constitution guarantees democratic freedoms and divides power between the presidential office and parliament, establishing the parliament as a major actor in Ukrainian politics.

1997 Russia and Ukraine sign an agreement on borders recognizing Ukrainian sovereignty over the Crimea and leasing the Sevastopol naval base to Russia.

2004 Democratic Orange Revolution, fueled by widespread rejection of government corruption and Russian interference in the electoral process, brings to power the pro-reform and pro-Western government of President Viktor Yushchenko.

2008–2009 Ukraine declares desire to join the European Union, applies for the NATO Membership Action Plan, and joins the European Union's Eastern Partnership Program.

2013 Russia starts a trade war with Ukraine, forcing the government of President Viktor Yanukovych to back down from signing an association agreement with the European Union, which sparks mass protests that become known as the EuroMaidan and Revolution of Dignity.

2014 As the protests on the streets of Kyiv turn violent, the Ukrainian parliament removes President Yanukovych from office, while Russia launches a hybrid war against Ukraine by taking over the Crimean Peninsula and sending its troops and supplies into the Donbas region.

2015 The Russo-Ukrainian conflict produces the acutest crisis in East-West relations since the end of the Cold War.

WHO'S WHO IN
UKRAINIAN HISTORY

Princes of Kyiv (to 1054)

Helgi (Oleg, Oleh) (? ca. 912)
Ingvar (Ihor, Igor) (? ca. 945)
Olha (Olga, Helga) (ca. 945–962)
Sviatoslav (962–972)
Yaropolk (972–980)
Volodymyr the Great (980–1015)
Sviatopolk the Accursed (1015–1019)
Yaroslav the Wise (1019–1054)

Rulers of Galicia-Volhynia (1199–1340)

Roman the Great (1199–1205)
Danylo of Halych (1205–1264)
Lev (1264–1301)
Yurii (1301–1308)
Andrii and Lev (1308–1325)
Bolesław-Yurii (1325–1340)

Religious and Cultural Leaders (1580–1648)

Ivan Fedorov (ca. 1525–1583), printer of the Ostrih Bible (1581)
Prince Kostiantyn (Vasyl) Ostrozky (1526–1608), Volhynian magnate and promoter of Orthodox reform

Ipatii Potii (1541–1613), a founder and metropolitan of the Uniate Church

Meletii Smotrytsky (ca. 1577–1633), religious polemicist and author of the first grammar of Church Slavonic

Petro Konashevych-Sahaidachny (ca. 1582–1622), Cossack hetman and supporter of the Orthodox Church

Peter Mohyla (1596–1647), Orthodox reformer and metropolitan of Kyiv (1632–1646)

Cossack Hetmans (1648–1764)

Bohdan Khmelnytsky (1648–1657)
Ivan Vyhovsky (1657–1659)
Yurii Khmelnytsky (1659–1663)
Pavlo Teteria (1663–1665)
Ivan Briukhovetsky (1663–1668)
Petro Doroshenko (1665–1676)
Demian Mnohohrishny (1668–1672)
Ivan Samoilovych (1672–1687)
Ivan Mazepa (1687–1709)
Ivan Skoropadsky (1708–1721)
Danylo Apostol (1727–1734)
Kyrylo Rozumovsky (Kirill Razumovsky) (1750–1764)

Figures in the Arts and Letters (1648–1795)

Inokentii Gizel (ca. 1600–1683), archimandrite of the Kyivan Cave Monastery (1656–1683) and publisher of the *Synopsis* (1674)

Nathan Hannover (d. 1663), Talmudist, kabbalist, and author of *Abyss of Despair* (1653)

Samiilo Velychko (1670–1728), Cossack official and historian

Teofan Prokopovych (1681–1736), rector of the Kyivan College and adviser to Peter I of Russia

Rabbi Baal Shem Tov (d. 1760), founder of Hassidism

Hryhorii Skovoroda (1722–1794), philosopher, poet, and composer

Oleksandr Bezborodko (1747–1799), Cossack officer, chancellor of the Russian Empire, and historian of the Hetmanate

National "Awakeners" (1798–1849)

Ivan Kotliarevsky (1769–1838), author of *Eneïda* (Travestied Aeneid)

Oleksandr Dukhnovych (Aleksandr Dukhnovich) (1803–1865), a Transcarpathian priest, poet, and educator

Tadeusz Czacki (1765–1813), founder of the Kremenets Lyceum (1805)

Markian Shashkevych (1811–1843), poet and a publisher of the almanac *Mermaid of the Dniester* (1837)

Mykola Hohol (Nikolai Gogol) (1809–1852), novelist and promoter of Ukrainian history and culture

Taras Shevchenko (1814–1861), artist, poet, and writer often regarded as the father of the Ukrainian nation

Yakiv Holovatsky (1814–1888), historian, ethnographer, a publisher of *Mermaid of the Dniester* (1837), and a leader of the Russophile movement

Mykola Kostomarov (1817–1885), historian, political activist, and author of the first political program of the Ukrainian movement

Administrators and Entrepreneurs (1800–1900)

Armand Emmanuel, Duke of Richelieu (1766–1822), French royalist and governor of Odesa (1803–1814), often considered its true founder

Nikolai Repnin-Volkonsky (1778–1845), Russian military commander and governor of Little Russia (1816–1834), where he helped improve living conditions for serfs and opposed the erosion of Cossack rights

Franz Stadion (1806–1853), Austrian statesman and governor of Galicia (1847–1848), where he freed the serfs and gave impetus to Ukrainian political mobilization

John James Hughes (1814–1889), Welsh entrepreneur, founder of the city of Yuzivka (present-day Donetsk), and initiator of development of the Donets basin industrial region

Platon Symyrenko (1821–1863), entrepreneur and benefactor who financed an edition of Taras Shevchenko's *Kobzar*

Lazar Brodsky (1848–1904), entrepreneur and philanthropist who financed the construction of Kyiv's largest synagogue

Stanisław Szczepanowski (1846–1900), businessman, politician, and author of *Galician Misery* (1888) who contributed to the development of the Galician oil industry by introducing steam drills

Political and Cultural Activists (1849–1917)

Mikhail Yuzefovich (Mykhailo Yuzefovych) (1802–1889), educator and early supporter of the Ukrainophile movement who sponsored the Ems Ukase (1876)

Mykhailo Drahomanov (1841–1895), historian, political activist and thinker, and founder of Ukrainian socialism

Ismail Gasprinski (Ismail Gaspirali) (1851–1914), educator, political activist, and leading figure of the Crimean Tatar national revival

Ivan Franko (1856–1916), poet, writer, publicist, and a founder of the socialist movement in Galicia

Mykola Mikhnovsky (1873–1924), lawyer, political activist, and early promoter of the idea of Ukrainian independence

Writers and Artists (1849–1917)

Yurii Fedkovych (1834–1888), poet and folklorist known for his stories of Bukovynian life

Leopold Ritter von Sacher-Masoch (1836–1895), journalist, writer, and author of romantic stories about Galicia

Mykola Lysenko (1842–1912), composer and founder of the Ukrainian national school in music

Ilia Repin (1844–1930), realist painter best known for his epic painting *Reply of the Zaporozhian Cossacks* (1891)

Sholem Aleichem (Solomon Rabinovich) (1859–1916), leading Yiddish writer best known for his stories about Tevye the Dairyman, which served as a basis for the musical *Fiddler on the Roof*

Olha Kobylianska (1863–1942), modernist writer and early feminist

Heorhii Narbut (1886–1920), graphic artist, a founder of the Ukrainian Academy of Fine Arts (1917), and designer of the Ukrainian coat of arms (1918)

Figures of the Ukrainian Revolution (1917–1921)

Yevhen Petrushevych (1863–1940), lawyer, political activist, and head of the Western Ukrainian People's Republic (1918–1919)

Mykhailo Hrushevsky (1866–1934), prominent historian and president of the Central Rada, the Ukrainian revolutionary parliament (1917–1918)

Pavlo Skoropadsky (1873–1945), descendant of a prominent Cossack family, imperial officer, and hetman of Ukraine in 1918

Symon Petliura (1879–1926), journalist, political activist, secretary of military affairs of the Central Rada, and head of the Directory of the Ukrainian People's Republic

Volodymyr Vynnychenko (1880–1951), best-selling writer and head of Ukrainian governments from 1917 to 1919

Nestor Makhno (1888–1934), anarchist revolutionary and commander of a peasant army in southern Ukraine (1918–1921)

Isaac Babel (1894–1940), journalist, writer, and author of *Red Cavalry* (1926)

Yurii Kotsiubynsky (1896–1937), son of the Ukrainian writer Mykhailo Kotsiubynsky, Bolshevik, and commander of the Red Army in Ukraine in 1918

Figures of the Cultural Renaissance (1921–1933)

Mykola Skrypnyk (1872–1933), communist official and promoter of Ukrainization who committed suicide in the wake of the Great Famine

Pavlo Tychyna (1891–1967), leading poet whose work evolved from symbolism to socialist realism

Mykola Khvyliovy (Nikolai Fitilev) (1893–1933), leading communist writer and founder of Ukrainian proletarian literature who committed suicide in the wake of the Great Famine

Oleksandr Dovzhenko (1894–1956), screenwriter, director, and pioneer of Soviet film montage

Dziga Vertov (David Kaufman) (1896–1954), pioneer documentary filmmaker whose best works, including *The Man with a Movie Camera* (1929), were produced in Ukraine

World War II Heroes and Villains (1939–1945)

Metropolitan Andrei Sheptytsky (Roman Aleksander Maria Szeptycki) (1865–1944), head of the Ukrainian Greek Catholic Church (1901–1944) and leading figure in Galician society

Sydir Kovpak (1887–1967), Soviet partisan commander

Mykhailo Kyrponos (1892–1941), Red Army general and commander of the defense of Kyiv in 1941

Erich Koch (1896–1986), Nazi *Gauleiter* of East Prussia (1928–1945) and *Reichskommissar* of Ukraine (1941–1943)

Nikolai Vatutin (1901–1944), general and commander of the Red Army's First Ukrainian Front

Otto von Wächter (1901–1949), Nazi governor of the District of Galicia

Roman Shukhevych (1907–1950), a leader of the Organization of Ukrainian Nationalists and commander in chief of the Ukrainian Insurgent Army (1943–1950)

Stepan Bandera (1909–1959), leader of the Organization of Ukrainian Nationalists and its chapters in western Europe and North America (1933–1959)

Communist Leaders of Ukraine (1938–1990)

Nikita Khrushchev (1938–1949)
Lazar Kaganovich (1925–1928, 1947)
Leonid Melnikov (1949–1953)
Oleksii Kyrychenko (1953–1957)
Mykola Pidhorny (1957–1963)

Petro Shelest (1963–1972)
Volodymyr Shcherbytsky (1972–1989)
Volodymyr Ivashko (1989–1990)

Leaders of the Dissident Movement (1960s–1980s)

Levko Lukianenko (b. 1927), lawyer and political activist who spent more than twenty-five years in prison and internal exile, author of the Declaration of Ukrainian Independence (1991)

Georgii Vins (1928–1998), Baptist pastor and religious activist twice arrested and sentenced by Soviet courts before being expelled from the USSR in 1979

Viacheslav Chornovil (1937–1999), journalist, chronicler of Ukrainian dissent in the 1960s, and inmate of Soviet prisons and concentration camps

Mustafa Dzhemilev (b. 1943), leader of the Crimean Tatar national movement who was arrested six times and spent years in Soviet labor camps and internal exile

Semen Gluzman (b. 1946), psychiatrist and human rights activist sentenced to seven years' imprisonment for exposing Soviet use of psychiatry against political dissidents

Presidents of Ukraine (1991–2015)

Leonid Kravchuk (1991–1994)
Leonid Kuchma (1994–2005)
Viktor Yushchenko (2005–2010)
Viktor Yanukovych (2010–2014)
Petro Poroshenko (2014–2019)
Volodymyr Zelensky (2019–)

GLOSSARY

Central Rada—Central Council; Ukrainian revolutionary parliament in 1917 and 1918

chaiky—Cossack longboats

Directory—revolutionary government of Ukraine in 1919 and 1920

dumas—Ukrainian folk songs

Gubernia—province of the Russian Empire

Haidamaky—brigands; participants in popular uprisings in eighteenth-century Right-Bank Ukraine

hetman—Cossack commander (from the German *Hauptmann*)

Hetmanate—Cossack state from 1649 to 1764 and again in 1918

kurhany—burial mounds

Kurkul' (**Russian:** *kulak*)—elastic Soviet term for a well-to-do peasant in the 1920s and 1930s

Maidan—square or plaza; shorthand for Independence Square in downtown Kyiv and the revolutionary events there in 2004 and in 2013 and 2014

oblast—province of Soviet or post-Soviet Ukraine

otaman—Cossack official

Raskol'niki—members of the Old Belief church

Samvydav—self-published dissident literature in Soviet Ukraine

voevoda—Rus' and Muscovite military commander

yarlyk—permit for conditional right to rule a principality, issued by Mongol khans

Zaporozhians—Cossacks who established their headquarters beyond the Dnieper rapids in the sixteenth century

FURTHER READING

Introduction: General Histories of Ukraine

Dmytro Doroshenko, *A Survey of Ukrainian History*, with introduction by O. Gerus, upd. ed. (Winnipeg, 1975); Mykhailo Hrushevsky, *A History of the Ukraine* (New Haven, CT, 1940; Hamden, CT, 1970); idem, *History of Ukraine-Rus'*, vols. 1, 6–10 (Edmonton and Toronto, 1997–2014); Ivan Katchanovski et al., *Historical Dictionary of Ukraine*, 2nd ed. (Lanham, MD, 2013); Paul Kubicek, *The History of Ukraine* (Westport, CT, 2008); Paul Robert Magocsi, *A History of Ukraine*, 2nd ed. (Toronto, 2010); idem, *Ukraine: An Illustrated History* (Toronto, 2007); Anna Reid, *Borderland: A Journey Through the History of Ukraine* (London, 1997); Orest Subtelny, *Ukraine: A History*, 4th ed. (Toronto, 2009); Roman Szporluk, *Ukraine: A Brief History*, 2nd ed. (Detroit, MI, 1982); Andrew Wilson, *The Ukrainians: Unexpected Nation*, 3rd ed. (New Haven, CT, 2009); Serhy Yekelchyk, *Ukraine: Birth of a Modern Nation* (New York, 2007).

I. On the Pontic Frontier

Paul M. Barford, *The Early Slavs: Culture and Society in Early Medieval Eastern Europe* (Ithaca, NY, 2001); David Braund, ed., *Scythians and Greeks: Cultural Interactions in Scythia, Athens and the Early Roman Empire* (Exeter, UK, 2005); Martin Dimnik, *Mikhail, Prince of Chernigov and Grand Prince of Kiev, 1224–1246* (Toronto, 1981); idem, *The Dynasty of Chernigov, 1146–1246* (Cambridge, 2003); Simon Franklin and Jonathan Shepard, *The Emergence of Rus', 750–1200* (London, 1996); Edward L. Keenan, *Josef Dobrovský and the Origins of the Igor' Tale* (Cambridge, MA, 2003); Jukka Korpela, *Prince, Saint and*

Apostle: Prince Vladimir Svjatoslavic of Kiev (Wiesbaden, 2001); Omeljan Pritsak, *The Origin of Rus'*, vol. 1 (Cambridge, MA, 1981); Christian Raffensperger, *Reimagining Europe: Kievan Rus' in the Medieval World* (Cambridge, MA, 2012); Renate Rolle, *The World of the Scythians* (London, 1989).

II. East Meets West

Ludmilla Charipova, *Latin Books and the Eastern Orthodox Clerical Elite in Kiev, 1632–1780* (Manchester, UK, 2006); Brian L. Davies, *Warfare, State and Society on the Black Sea Steppe, 1500–1700* (London and New York, 2007); Linda Gordon, *Cossack Rebellions: Social Turmoil in the Sixteenth-Century Ukraine* (Albany, NY, 1983); Borys A. Gudziak, *Crisis and Reform: The Kyivan Metropolitanate, the Patriarch of Constantinople, and the Genesis of the Union of Brest* (Cambridge, MA, 1998); David A. Frick, *Meletij Smotryc'kyj* (Cambridge, MA, 1995); Iaroslav Isaievych, *Voluntary Brotherhood: Confraternities of Laymen in Early Modern Ukraine* (Edmonton and Toronto, 2006); *The Kiev Mohyla Academy*. Special issue of *Harvard Ukrainian Studies*, 8, no. 1–2 (June 1984); Paulina Lewin, *Ukrainian Drama and Theater in the Seventeenth and Eighteenth Centuries* (Edmonton, 2008); Jaroslaw Pelenski, *The Contest for the Legacy of Kievan Rus'* (Boulder, CO, and New York, 1998); Serhii Plokhy, *The Cossacks and Religion in Early Modern Ukraine* (Oxford, 2001); idem, *The Origins of the Slavic Nations: Premodern Identities in Russia, Ukraine and Belarus* (Cambridge, UK, 2006); Ihor Ševčenko, *Ukraine Between East and West: Essays on Cultural History to the Early Eighteenth Century*, 2nd ed. (Edmonton and Toronto, 2009); Frank E. Sysyn, *Between Poland and the Ukraine: The Dilemma of Adam Kysil, 1600–1653* (Cambridge, MA, 1985).

III. Between the Empires

Daniel Beauvois, *The Noble, the Serf, and the Revizor: The Polish Nobility Between Tsarist Imperialism and the Ukrainian Masses, 1831–1863* (New York, 1992); Serhiy Bilenky, *Romantic Nationalism in Eastern Europe: Russian, Polish, and Ukrainian Political Imaginations* (Stanford, CA, 2012); idem, ed., *Fashioning Modern Ukraine: Selected Writings of Mykola Kostomarov, Volodymyr Antonovych, and Mykhailo Drahomanov* (Edmonton and Toronto, 2014); Martha Bohachevsky-Chomiak, *Feminists Despite Themselves: Women in Ukrainian Community Life, 1894–1939* (Edmonton, 1988); Alan W. Fisher, *The Russian Annexation of the Crimea, 1772–1783* (Cambridge, UK, 1970); Alison Frank, *Oil Empire: Visions of Prosperity in Austrian Galicia* (Cambridge, MA, 2005); Leonard G. Friesen, *Rural Revolutions in Southern Ukraine: Peasants, Nobles, and Colonists, 1774–1905* (Cambridge, MA, 2008); George G. Grabowicz, *The Poet as Mythmaker: A Study of Symbolic Meaning in Taras Ševčenko* (Cambridge, MA,

1982); Patricia Herlihy, *Odesa: A History, 1794–1914* (Cambridge, MA, 1986); Faith Hillis, *Children of Rus': Right-Bank Ukraine and the Invention of a Russian Nation* (Ithaca, NY, and London, 2013); John-Paul Himka, *Socialism in Galicia: The Emergence of Polish Social Democracy and Ukrainian Radicalism, 1860–1890* (Cambridge, MA, 1983); idem, *Galician Villagers and the Ukrainian National Movement in the Nineteenth Century* (New York, 1988); idem, *Religion and Nationality in Western Ukraine: The Greek Catholic Church and the Ruthenian National Movement in Galicia, 1867–1900* (Montreal and Kingston, ON, 1999); Zenon E. Kohut, *Russian Centralism and Ukrainian Autonomy: Imperial Absorption of the Hetmanate, 1760s–1830s* (Cambridge, MA, 1988); idem, *Making Ukraine* (Edmonton and Toronto, 2011); Natan M. Meir, *Kiev, Jewish Metropolis: A History, 1859–1914* (Bloomington, IN, 2010); Alexei Miller, *The Ukrainian Question: Russian Nationalism in the Nineteenth Century* (Budapest and New York, 2003); Serhii Plokhy, *Tsars and Cossacks: A Study in Historiography* (Cambridge, MA, 2003); idem, *The Cossack Myth: History and Nationhood in the Age of Empires* (Cambridge, 2012); Thomas Prymak, *Mykola Kostomarov: A Biography* (Toronto, 1996); Ivan L. Rudnytsky, *Essays in Modern Ukrainian History* (Edmonton, 1987); David Saunders, *The Ukrainian Impact on Russian Culture, 1750–1850* (Edmonton, 1985); Orest Subtelny, *The Mazepists: Ukrainian Separatism in the Early Eighteenth Century* (Boulder, CO, and New York, 1981); Willard Sunderland, *Taming the Wild Field: Colonization and Empire on the Russian Steppe* (Ithaca, NY, and London, 2004); Stephen Velychenko, *National History as Cultural Process: A Survey of the Interpretations of Ukraine's Past in Polish, Russian, and Ukrainian Historical Writing from the Earliest Times to 1914* (Edmonton, 1992); Larry Wolff, *The Idea of Galicia: History and Fantasy in Habsburg Political Culture* (Stanford, CA, 2010); Charters Wynn, *Workers, Strikes, and Pogroms: The Donbass-Dnepr Bend in Late Imperial Russia, 1870–1905* (Princeton, NJ, 1992); Andriy Zayarnyuk, *Framing the Ukrainian Peasantry in Habsburg Galicia, 1846–1914* (Edmonton, 2013); Sergei I. Zhuk, *Russia's Lost Reformation: Peasants, Millennialism, and Radical Sects in Southern Russia and Ukraine, 1830–1917* (Washington, DC, Baltimore, and London, 2004); Steven J. Zipperstein, *The Jews of Odessa: A Cultural History, 1794–1881* (Stanford, CA, 1985).

IV. The Wars of the World

Henry Abramson, *A Prayer for the Government: Ukrainians and Jews in Revolutionary Times, 1917–1920* (Cambridge, MA, 1999); John A. Armstrong, *Ukrainian Nationalism*, 3rd ed. (Englewood, CO, 1990); Karel C. Berkhoff, *Harvest of Despair: Life and Death in Ukraine Under Nazi Rule* (Cambridge, MA, 2004); Bohdan Bociurkiw, *The Ukrainian Greek Catholic Church and the Soviet State, 1939–1950* (Edmonton, 1996); Kate Brown, *A Biography of No*

Place: From Ethnic Borderland to Soviet Heartland (Cambridge, MA, and London, 2004); Robert Conquest, *The Harvest of Sorrow: Soviet Collectivization and the Terror-Famine* (New York, 1987); Theodore H. Friedgut, *Yuzovka and Revolution: Life and Work: Politics and Revolution in Russia's Donbass, 1869–1924*, 2 vols. (Princeton, NJ, 1989–1994); Andrea Graziosi, *The Great Soviet Peasant War: Bolsheviks and Peasants, 1917–1933* (Cambridge, MA, 1996); Jan T. Gross, *Revolution from Abroad: The Soviet Conquest of Poland's Western Ukraine and Western Belorussia*, exp. ed. (Princeton, NJ, 2002); Mark von Hagen, *War in a European Borderland: Occupations and Occupation Plans in Galicia and Ukraine, 1914–1918* (Seattle, WA, 2007); Halyna Hryn, ed., *Hunger by Design: The Great Ukrainian Famine and Its Soviet Context* (Cambridge, MA, 2008); Bohdan Klid and Alexander J. Motyl, eds., *The Holodomor Reader: A Sourcebook on the Famine of 1932–1933 in Ukraine* (Edmonton, 2012); Bohdan Krawchenko, *Social Change and National Consciousness in Twentieth-Century Ukraine* (London, 1985); Andrii Krawchuk, *Christian Social Ethics in Ukraine: The Legacy of Andrei Sheptytsky* (Edmonton, 1997); Hiroaki Kuromiya, *Freedom and Terror in the Donbas: A Ukrainian-Russian Borderland, 1870s–1990s* (Cambridge, 1998); idem, *Conscience on Trial: The Fate of Fourteen Pacifists in Stalin's Ukraine, 1952–1953* (Toronto, 2012); George Liber, *Alexander Dovzhenko: A Life in Soviet Film* (London, 2002); Wendy Lower, *Nazi Empire-Building and the Holocaust in Ukraine* (Chapel Hill, NC, 2005); James E. Mace, *Communism and the Dilemmas of National Liberation: National Communism in Soviet Ukraine, 1918–1933* (Cambridge, MA, 1983); Paul Robert Magocsi, *The Shaping of a National Identity: Subcarpathian Rus', 1848–1948* (Cambridge, MA, 1978); Terry Martin, *The Affirmative Action Empire: Nations and Nationalism in the Soviet Union, 1923–1939* (Ithaca, NY, and London, 2001); Alexander J. Motyl, *The Turn to the Right: The Ideological Origins and Development of Ukrainian Nationalism, 1919–1929* (Boulder, CO, and New York, 1980); Yohanan Petrovsky-Shtern, *The Anti-Imperial Choice: The Making of the Ukrainian Jew* (New Haven, CT, 2009); idem, *The Golden Age Shtetl: A New History of Jewish Life in East Europe* (Princeton, NJ, 2014); Serhii Plokhy, *Unmaking Imperial Russia: Mykhailo Hrushevsky and the Writing of Ukrainian History* (Toronto, 2005); idem, *Yalta: The Price of Peace* (New York, 2010); Anna Procyk, *Russian Nationalism and Ukraine: The Nationality Policy of the Volunteer Army During the Civil War* (Edmonton, 1995); Thomas Prymak, *Mykhailo Hrushevsky: The Politics of National Culture* (Toronto, 1987); George Y. Shevelov, *The Ukrainian Language in the First Half of the Twentieth Century, 1900–1941: Its State and Status* (Cambridge, MA, 1989); Timothy Snyder, *The Reconstruction of Nations: Poland, Ukraine, Lithuania, Belarus, 1569–1999* (New Haven, CT, 2003); idem, *Bloodlands: Europe Between Hitler and Stalin* (New York, 2010); Stephen Velychenko, *State Building in Revolutionary Ukraine: A Comparative Study of Governments and Bureaucrats, 1917–1922* (Toronto, 2011); Serhy

Yekelchyk, *Stalin's Empire of Memory: Russian-Ukrainian Relations in the Soviet Historical Imagination* (Toronto, 2004); idem, *Stalin's Citizens: Everyday Politics in the Wake of Total War* (New York, 2014).

V. The Road to Independence

Anne Applebaum, *Between East and West: Across the Borderlands of Europe* (New York, 1994); Timothy Ash, Janet Gunn, John Lough, Orysia Lutsevych, James Nixey, James Sherr, and Kataryna Wolczuk, *The Struggle for Ukraine* (London: Chatham House, 2017); Omer Bartov, *Erased: Vanishing Traces of Jewish Galicia in Present-Day Ukraine* (Princeton, NJ, 2007); Yaroslav Bilinsky, *The Second Soviet Republic: The Ukraine After World War II* (New Brunswick, NJ, 1964); Marek Dabrowski, Marta Domínguez-Jiménez, and Georg Zachmann, "Six Years after Ukraine's Euromaidan: Reforms and Challenges Ahead," Policy Contribution 2020/14 (2020), Bruegel; Marta Dyczok, *The Grand Alliance and Ukrainian Refugees* (New York, 2000); idem, *Ukraine: Movement Without Change, Change Without Movement* (New York, 2000); Valeria Gontareva and Yevhen Stepaniuk, *Mission Possible: The True Story of Ukraine's Comprehensive Banking Reform and Practical Manual for Other Nations* (London: LSE Institute of Global Affairs, 2020); Andrea Graziosi, Lubomyr A. Hajda, and Halyna Hryn, eds., *After the Holodomor: The Enduring Impact of the Great Famine on Ukraine* (Cambridge, MA, 2013); Bohdan Harasymiw, *Post-Communist Ukraine* (Edmonton and Toronto, 2002); Askold Krushelnycky, *An Orange Revolution: A Personal Journey Through Ukrainian History* (London, 2006); Taras Kuzio, *Ukraine: State and Nation Building* (London and New York, 1998); Borys Lewytzkyj, *Politics and Society in Soviet Ukraine, 1953–1980* (Edmonton, 1984); Paul Robert Magocsi, *This Blessed Land: Crimea and the Crimean Tatars* (Toronto, 2014); David Marples, *The Social Impact of the Chernobyl Disaster* (New York, 1988); idem, *Ukraine Under Perestroika* (Edmonton, 1991); idem, *Stalinism in Ukraine in the 1940s* (Edmonton, 1992); idem, *Heroes and Villains: Creating National History in Contemporary Ukraine* (Budapest, 2007); Ivan Miklos and Pavlo Kukhta, eds., *Reforms in Ukraine after Revolution of Dignity: What Was Done, Why Not More and What to Do Next* (n.p., 2019); Kostiantyn P. Morozov, *Above and Beyond: From Soviet General to Ukrainian State Builder* (Cambridge, MA, 2001); Alexander J. Motyl, *Dilemmas of Independence: Ukraine After Totalitarianism* (New York, 1993); Olga Onuch, *Mapping Mass Mobilization: Understanding Revolutionary Moments in Argentina and Ukraine* (New York, 2014); Serhii Plokhy, *The Last Empire: The Final Days of the Soviet Union* (New York, 2014); Serhii Plokhy and M. E. Sarotte, "The Sholas of Ukraine: Where American Illusions and Great-Power Politics Collide," *Foreign Affairs* (January/February 2020): 81–92; William J. Risch, *The Ukrainian West: Culture and the Fate of Empire in Soviet Lviv* (Cambridge, MA, 2011); Gwendolyn Sasse, *The Crimea Question: Identity, Transition, and Conflict* (Cambridge, MA, 2014); Roman Szporluk, *Russia, Ukraine, and the Breakup of the Soviet Union* (Stanford, CA, 2000); Alberto Veira-Ramos, Tatiana Liubyva, and Ievhenii Golovakha, eds., *Ukraine in Transformation: From Soviet Republic to European Society* (London, 2020); Yuriy Vitrenko, *National Joint Stock Company Naftogaz of Ukraine vs Gazprom: An internal perspective on the largest commercial arbitration in world history with an amount of claims against both parties higher than the national economy of Ukraine* (Stockholm, 2020); Catherine Wanner, *Burden of Dreams: History and Identity in Post-Soviet Ukraine* (University Park, PA, 1998); idem, *Communities of the Converted: Ukrainians and Global Evangelism* (Ithaca, NY, and London, 2007); Amir Weiner, *Making Sense of War: The Second World War and the Fate of the Bolshevik Revolution* (Princeton, NJ, 2001); Andrew Wilson, *Ukrainian Nationalism in the 1990s: A Minority Faith* (Cambridge, 1997); idem, *Ukraine's Orange Revolution* (New Haven, CT, and London, 2005); Kataryna Wolczuk, *The Moulding of Ukraine: The Constitutional Politics of State Formation* (Budapest, 2001); Sergei Zhuk, *Rock and Roll in the Rocket City: The West, Identity, and Ideology in Soviet Dniepropetrovsk, 1960–1985* (Washington, DC, Baltimore, and London, 2010).

Epilogue: The Meanings of History

John-Paul Himka, "The History Behind the Regional Conflict in Ukraine," *Kritika* 16, no. 1 (2015): 129–136; Volodymyr Kulyk, "Ukrainian Nationalism Since the Outbreak of EuroMaidan," *Ab Imperio*, no. 3 (2014): 94–122; Edward Lucas, *The New Cold War: Putin's Russia and the Threat to the West* (New York, 2014); Alexander J. Motyl, *Imperial Ends: The Decay, Collapse, and Revival of Empires* (New York, 2001); Richard Sakwa, *Frontline Ukraine: Crisis in the Borderlands* (London, 2014); Andrew Wilson, *Ukraine Crisis: What It Means for the West* (New Haven, CT, and London, 2014).

INDEX

SUSAN WILSON

Serhii Plokhy is the Mykhailo Hrushevsky Professor of Ukrainian History at Harvard and the director of the university's Ukrainian Research Institute. The author of numerous books, including the award-winning *The Last Empire: The Final Days of the Soviet Union, Chernobyl: A History of the Nuclear Catastrophe,* and most recently, *Nuclear Folly: A History of the Cuban Missile Crisis,* Plokhy lives in Burlington, Massachusetts.